Malcolm C. Searles

A POST HILL PRESS BOOK
ISBN: 978-1-64293-324-6
ISBN (eBook): 978-1-64293-325-3

Bread: A Sweet Surrender
The Musical Journey of David Gates, James Griffin & Co.

Published by arrangement with Helter Skelter Publishing, Ltd.

Post Hill Press
New York • Nashville
posthillpress.com

Published in the United States of America

This book is dedicated to my wonderful wife Louise and our two boys, Sam and Matt. Thank you for being so patient.
xxx

And for Mike Foster. YNWA.

Contents

Photo by Lorrie Sullivan

Preface

The two musicians stood in the wings during a break in the performance, watching as their two colleagues, still on stage, mesmerized their audience with a scintillating two-song medley that had won them both prestigious awards earlier in their career. Then, as the keyboard melody took a slight twist, a gentle diversion of notes, an added flourish, the elder of the two standing in the wings muttered to himself, barely audibly but enough so that the other could hear...

"Goddamn him! Can't he just play it for one night like the record..."

Welcome to their world. A collection of musicians, a collection of diametrically opposing talents, and a sound that gelled. The Sound Of Bread.

Introduction

Just five men... but a wealth of recorded material and compositions that few who listen to popular music could have missed. Adult soft rock, country, '60s beat, rock'n'roll, blues, jazz, soul, reggae, showtunes, film scores... these five musicians have just about covered the entire spectrum of popular music since the birth of rock'n'roll – and perhaps without even knowing it, the listening audience has almost certainly had the musical talents or compositions of one of these five drifting over the family airwaves or music systems.

If anyone were to play "Everything I Own," "If," or "Make It With You" on the record player, or more than likely these days on either the CD player or iPod, then it would almost go without saying that someone, somewhere, perhaps even subconsciously, would start silently humming the unforgettable melody under their breath, or maybe start singing along out loud. But when one considers that the provider of such a musical performance could just have easily played Simon & Garfunkel's timeless "Bridge Over Troubled Water," the Carpenters' chart-smash "For All We Know," the Beach Boys' heart-rending "Pet Sounds," Linda Ronstadt's driving country rock, or many of Phil Spector's unforgettable "Wall of Sound" anthems, then you begin to realize how deeply ingrained into the history of modern music these musicians are.

Numerous million-selling releases, Academy Awards, a Grammy Award, studio sessions numbering into the hundreds, sold out concerts worldwide, and cover versions courtesy of artists as diverse as Frank Sinatra, Ken Boothe, The Monkees, Hank Marvin, Earth Wind & Fire, Aretha Franklin, Perry Como, Isaac Hayes, Dusty Springfield... and even The Brady Bunch (along with so many more), should make these individuals household names. There were probably in excess of 250 compositions recorded between 1958 and 1969 that these individuals were responsible for writing, arranging, or producing... but today they remain almost as unknown as the faceless wonders they were when they first combined forces back in the long-gone summer of love or when, as individuals, they first appeared on the music scene, back in the halcyon days of the post-rock'n'roll boom. Maybe this is partly by choice, partly because the music they conspired to make together fit into a mold that never really comfortably accepted a position in the media limelight, and partly because they achieved a significant amount of success at the same time as the "glam-era" Osmond and Cassidy-mania. Or that they were surrounded by musical heavyweights such as Led Zeppelin, Creedence Clearwater Revival, The Moody Blues, Three Dog Night... and the beginning of four individual solo careers from a former beat group hailing from the riverside port of Liverpool, England. Yeah, yeah, yeah. The music press and establishment at the time had enough "personality" under their watchful gaze without having to worry about these five musicians and their subsequent recorded output, releases that fit nicely into the safe "soft rock" genre – despite the unquestionable pedigree of their creators.

Time has maybe been kinder to one of the chosen five, now retired and financially secure, and it became a source of anger and frustration to some of his colleagues that gradually, as commercial success beckoned, his name was thrust further into the spotlight, clearly to the detriment of the collective unit, due to his knack and ability of composing a succession of amazingly beautiful love songs that appealed to the softer side of their audience. So much so that it eventually broke the back of the group, with the nucleus of the writing partnership splitting apart, a wedge being driven between the once healthy pairing that subsequently endured through many years of lawsuits and court battles. The edgy "rock-orientated" recordings that the band committed to tape were often overlooked, smothered by the overwhelming success of the ballads and, almost unbelievably, the group name itself even began to be relegated to the sidelines… an "AND" factor, following on after the name of the successful balladeer. How that must have dug deep into the souls of the seasoned session musicians and writers, award winners included, finally reaping the rewards of success in their own right...

While researching this story, initially from a musical viewpoint, I began to realize exactly how much talent, frustration, egotism, hard work, love, bitterness, disappointment, deceit, and heaven knows what else ran through the veins of this band. It wasn't all sweetness and light as the regularly released "Greatest Hits" collections would have us believe. Sure, there was a bond there that only this band of players could have achieved. Drop one out of the equation and something wasn't quite right. But in order to achieve this united bond, then some bad had to come with the good. And I found that sad. Thankfully, many people were prepared to talk freely with me, reminiscing through the mists of time, albeit occasionally somewhat hazily, while others preferred to decline politely, possibly reluctant to rekindle all of those instances and incidents that they prefer laid to rest. For some, clearly, the hurt is still there. Others still had their own agenda for not wishing to contribute, and I respect that, but hey...

One of the many contacts I interviewed for this project summed it up nicely: "Bread was a band that continually killed the Golden Goose." That goose has laid a number of eggs before and since, but none of them was quite as golden as the original.

To the memory of James, Michael, and Larry – God bless you, may your music live on. To David and to Robb – thank you.

Chapter One

Welcome To The Music

July 1962, and with the sound of the recent Johnny Burnette single, "Fool Of The Year," composed by a new songwriter hailing from Tulsa, Oklahoma, ringing in his ears, and Dorsey Burnette's address safely stored in his pocket, the young musician headed out across the country towards the Golden State of California. Go west young man.

James Arthur Griffin was born in Cincinnati, Ohio, on August 10th, 1943, two years after the United States had entered the Second World War. His father Marvin was currently to be found serving his country abroad, fighting against the Japanese army in the Philippines, and the young family – comprising of James's mother Neva, and his elder sister Carol Ann – had relocated to Ohio from their home state of Tennessee to live with Neva's mother, Minnie, and her second husband, Les, while Marvin was away on duty.

Neva Greenroos had been born on May 13th, 1921, to David Greenroos and Minnie Lutts, residents of Shelby County in Tennessee, and she married Marvin Hayden Griffin during the early winter of 1943. Marvin himself was one year older than his wife, having been born on May 18th, 1920, and he had grown up in Kentucky before venturing south across the state border. Marvin and Neva's first child, a daughter named Carol Ann, had been born out of wedlock on March 22nd, 1938, when Neva was barely sixteen years of age and still living in her home city of Memphis, and a second child followed in similar circumstances five years later, although by this stage, with the war taking away thousands of young American men from their homesteads, the family had moved the 500 miles north to Ohio. Along with Minnie and Les, they lived on Warsaw Avenue, situated to the northwest of the city, in a commercial yet predominantly German neighborhood on the northern shore of the Ohio River. Among their neighbors on the street was a family of German descent, the Von Kappelhoff family, who had a teenage daughter named Doris. This young girl would later find fame under the stage name of Doris Day.

During this tough period, Neva had found work making spare parts for airplanes, assisting with the war effort, and Minnie, as the family matriarch, would often take care of the young children herself. For much of his very early life Jimmy was not a well child and it was the constant love and care of his maternal grandmother that was to often pull him through these notably barren times. Indeed, research now tells us that this period was infamous for one particularly severe health epidemic sweeping through the city streets, claiming the lives of many young children, and yet, despite these early setbacks, Jimmy's positive love of life and fun was clearly apparent, as his elder sister would later recall:

"He had such a sense of humor. Even as a little tiny baby. He was always laughing and doing things to make us laugh. I remember him in his crib, jumping up and down and making all kinds of sounds, laughing, and being the most joyous soul you can imagine."

Minnie was a great lover of music, as well as being a keen songwriter, and she played guitar and encouraged all those around her to join in and develop their own passion. Still only a child herself, Carol Ann would often perform on local Cincinnati radio, standing on a box in order to reach up to the microphone, and she took up piano lessons at the age of nine, whereupon she would sit her younger brother alongside her and teach him the rudiments of the keyboard. They would often accompany each other's playing by singing and harmonizing together with, once again, Carol Ann offering instructions to her young sibling.

By 1945, following on from the allied victory across the seas, Neva moved the family back to their home city of Memphis, Tennessee, where they briefly lived with her husband Marvin's sister and her family, while Marvin himself made the long journey back home to America. Shortly afterwards, following a number of temporary accommodations, they settled into a new family dwelling on Manhattan Street.

It was in the great city, bordered by the swirling currents of the Mississippi, that the young James was to grow up and where he truly began developing his first musical aspirations. At the tender age of seven his parents signed him up for accordion classes at the Central Academy of Music in the city, where he was considered by many to be a child prodigy, reportedly capable of playing by ear as opposed to reading notation. His first recording, an accordion variation of "Lady Of Spain," was taped during one of his early concert recitals, albeit accompanied by the family pet dog, a black and white Spitz named Poochie Pie, whining alongside. However, no doubt further and more serious encouragement came along in the form of the Burnette family who, having previously lived in the Lauderdale Courts area of Memphis, moved into residence opposite the Griffin family home. (This street was also home to Delta bluesman Charlie Musselwhite.) The new family included two teenage sons, Dorsey and his younger sibling Johnny, and although the latter was still attending high school both were burgeoning musicians on the local nightclub scene, and destined for greater things in their own right, and they soon befriended the keen young musician living opposite. Seeing the example his neighbors were setting, and being surrounded by the increasing influence of rock'n'roll, "rockabilly," gospel, and the early blues music his home city had to offer, this must have been a major encouragement for Jimmy, or Jimbo, as he was often referred to, and one of the reasons why, at the age of twelve, he picked up the guitar for the first time, reportedly with the encouragement of his grandmother Minnie, and began his first attempts at songwriting.

"My room was next to his," Carol Ann continued to recollect, "and I was privy to listen to him sing and write songs through the wall! Jimmy and Johnny Burnette would also play together. Johnny could play bass really good, he had one of those standup bass guitars, and of course he could play guitar too, and Jimmy would take his accordion and they would play. So there's this senior in high school and this seven-year-old kid, and they really enjoyed each other's company. Johnny taught Jimmy a lot about what he knew about music and writing, and at one point they wrote a song together which got published but I don't remember the name. Jimmy got a credit."

It is worth noting at this point that during the early rise to success of the Burnette brothers, their band at the time, The Rock & Roll Trio, featuring both Dorsey and Johnny alongside Paul Burlison on lead guitar, was often pushed by the manager to appear under the name of "Johnny Burnette and The Rock & Roll Trio." This was presumably because younger sibling Johnny, who provided the majority of the vocals for the trio, was deemed by many as the main focal point for the band, while another factor was that for regular touring requirements the "trio" had also recently added a drummer to the line-up, thus officially making them a quartet. Nevertheless, this "re-labeling" for whatever reason, caused a major rift between the performing brothers as Dorsey, the band's bassist, had also been a major songwriting contributor to the act and thus, in his eyes, deserved equal billing. The result was that, after a number of significant disagreements between the two, older brother Dorsey quit the band, clearly unhappy that both he and Burlison were being relegated in the eyes of the media to supporting sidemen. Both brothers eventually found their way out to California where, by the turn of the decade, reunited, they were finding success once more as songwriters, working for Ricky Nelson among others. And yet, whether that early setback, and the unhappy feuding over the band's unbalanced billing, was to play on the mind of the young James Griffin in his future band, remains undocumented.

Throughout his teenage years, life for Jimmy was, as one would expect for someone his age, school, homework, cars, and girls. He dated one particular girl, Kathy, throughout most of his time at Kingsbury High School, spending their non-school periods either at the drive-in or wherever the action was to be found. A typical teenage lifestyle. As for school itself, he was particularly keen on history during lesson periods, and had plans for going to college to study engineering, having taken on a summer job as an engineer's assistant. And then rock'n'roll hit.

"Jimmy loved rock'n'roll," says Carol Ann. "I don't think there was any genre of music he didn't love. It was just a part of him. I would listen to the black radio stations, and that's where we would hear Jerry Lee Lewis and Elvis. We had been exposed to bluegrass from my grandmother, and the blues from my mom, my aunt and my dad, and the '40s and '50s World War II music – we had had a vast variety from various generations. But gospel was a big part of the music here in Memphis and Jimmy also loved it.

"As life went on I would continue to sing in the choirs, and Jimmy was always real interested in what I had learned. At school I had sung in the choruses and we had won some kind of award and they made a vinyl record of our choir singing. There was a negro spiritual on it called 'Soon I Will Be Coming' and Jimmy loved this song because of all the intricate harmonies we did. He would sing all of the different parts... the bass, the tenor, whatever was needed. He actually stole the record and played it until all the vinyl was worn off!"

Despite his overall shy persona, his underlying love of music continued to shine to the fore as his own ability developed. He even began to undertake a few small club dates as his confidence began to grow, standing up before an audience for the first time. Carol Ann remembers him performing the 1940s standard, "You're Nobody 'Til Somebody Loves You," later a big hit for Dean Martin, one of their father's favorite tunes.

"He had a real killer rendition of it," she laughs.

With his own musical standing beginning to take off, he was also all too aware of the growing reputation that his neighbors were achieving in the industry, and during the successful early years of the Burnettes' career the younger of the two brothers, Johnny, often stayed in touch with his friends at home in Memphis, inviting them to come and see him play whenever he performed locally. On one particular return visit, around the turn of the decade, Johnny contacted Carol Ann asking her to come and attend a record company promotional party at the historic Peabody Hotel to celebrate the success of his recent solo single releases. As a new mother herself by this stage, Carol Ann had to arrange to have her three young children looked after at short notice, but, having found a suitable babysitter, she asked Burnette if she could bring Jimmy, by now a growing teenager, along to the party as well. Johnny agreed and much to their excitement the two siblings soon found themselves in a luxury hotel suite, surrounded by Johnny's "people," all drinking cocktails while Jimmy sipped from a coke bottle and Carol Ann drank tea.

"Somebody asked Johnny to perform, so he got up and did some of his songs which was just so exciting," Carol Ann continued. "Then after we got to talking I said 'Johnny, Jimmy's been writing and he's got a couple of really neat songs,' and Jimmy's looking at me like 'don't you do this!' Jimmy was very, very shy, but Johnny handed him his guitar and Jimmy got up and performed two or three original songs, and he acted just like a professional. I nearly fell off the sofa. He's eighteen years old now, a good-looking kid, and he's singing like a professional and he just knocked the socks off of everybody."

Also in attendance at the party was Frank Thorne, a music agent and an associate of the brothers, who was suitably impressed by the young teenager's unrehearsed performance. He approached Carol Ann and asked if their parents would consent to meeting with him because he could see the potential this young man had to offer. He wanted to take Jimmy out to the West Coast where opportunity was rife, where the Burnette brothers were reaping the rewards, and where Jimmy could develop that potential that he had so professionally displayed. The following day, having met Marvin and Neva, arrangements were made for Jimmy to move out of the family home, to head west, and build a potential career in the music industry. It was as instant as that. Jimmy had already made various demo recordings while still in Memphis, honing his young talent, and now, at the tender age of eighteen, the handsome youngster had the opportunity handed straight to him. The decision was easy. It was the summer of '62 and, upon finishing his education at Kingsbury, James Arthur Griffin packed his bags, jumped into his prized red-and-white Ford convertible, and headed out towards Los Angeles presumably joining, at one stage, the fabled Route 66. Get your kicks.

Immediately upon his arrival in the City of Angels, Jimmy looked up his Memphis friend and musical peer Dorsey Burnette, the elder of the two brothers, who had supplied him with his address should he ever visit the West Coast. Jimmy played him a number of the compositions and songs he had been working on back home and, suitably impressed, Dorsey and Frank Thorne arranged a meeting with Reprise Records, the fledgling label formed by Frank Sinatra two years previously. As James himself was later to recall:

"Dorsey was recording for Reprise Records at this time and was impressed with my songs enough to take me to meet his producer Steve Venet, and I played some songs for him that I had recorded demos of in Memphis. I also sang two or three songs live. This was in August and I had a deal by September. He (Steve) was a very talented producer. His brother, Nik Venet, produced many Capitol Records acts, including Bobby Darin."[1]

Within weeks of arriving in Los Angeles not only had the Memphis youngster secured himself a recording deal, but he also signed up to attend the Los Angeles City College where he undertook music classes taught by the pianist Natalie Limonick. "He was very curious," recalls sister Carol Ann. "He was a student of life. He loved learning."

With music his principal focus, he immediately went into the studios to tape some tracks that would soon appear as his debut single on the label, "Girls Grow Up Faster Than Boys" backed with (b/w) "It's A Free Country" (Reprise 20114). The A-side, composed by the songwriting partnership of Paul ("Roses Are Red") Evans and Fred Tobias, offered up a distinctly mellow-country affair, sadly spoiled with the unnecessary female vocal introduction and a cloyingly annoying acoustic guitar riff. Nevertheless, for a debut release, Jimmy supplied a surprisingly mature vocal performance, with acute phrasing, and it clearly suggested the vocal range he had at his disposal.

Griffin: "It didn't get much airplay, except in certain cities. I kept up in different markets. I went to San Francisco, where I was having a lot of airplay on the radio, and I did my first live show at the Cow Palace, which was *the* venue at the time. On the show was Tony Bennett, Donna Loren, The Angels, and Annette Funicello."[1]

However, undaunted by the relative lack of success for his debut release, Reprise took the youngster back into the studios. Venet had left the label by this stage, following Sinatra's sell-out to the larger Warner Brothers stable, and so upcoming producer and arranger Jimmy Bowen now took over the reins. Bowen began his tenure at Reprise by dropping a large proportion of the acts that Venet had signed and began focusing on the youth market. Fortunately for Griffin, he kept the Memphis boy on the books and took him back into the studios to record what would eventually become Jimmy Griffin's first album release. What made Bowen retain the services of this untried newcomer? Possibly he saw that the youthful good looks of Griffin, and his undeniable raw talent, could compete favorably with the popular "teen-artists" of the day, especially in light of the label's new youth policy. A later 1964 issue of the US trade magazine *Billboard* confirmed Reprise's commitment to their favored teen-artists, including Dick and DeeDee, The Routers, The Mar-Kets, Tina Turner, and Jimmy Griffin among the names featured, and it was certainly a key market at that time with the likes of Frankie Avalon, Fabian, Bobby Vee having been very much the poster boys of '62-'63.

Choosing not to include any of his own original compositions, Griffin and Bowen taped a series of cover versions, with arrangements by Jack Nitzsche, and the session skills of some of the top studio musicians of the time. Russell Bridges played piano, Arkansas-born Glen Campbell performed guitar duties, the legendary Hal Blaine occupied the drum stool while, reportedly, a young musician/arranger hailing from the state of Oklahoma, David Gates, assisted on bass guitar duties. Griffin, for his part, provided vocals only.

Griffin: "As I recall, we had three sessions in which we recorded four songs per session with a 28-piece orchestra. We did the whole album in three days. Reprise Records was new at the time and they did a pretty good job on promotion. There was a rumor in town at the time, I recall, that Reprise Records was a tax write-off for Sinatra and they weren't really looking to get hits."[1]

Starting with the title track, the album (issued as *Summer Holiday* by Reprise the following year as R6091) contained twelve relatively lightweight songs, all heavily orchestrated, and all tending to play it safe and remain solidly within the territory that Bobby Vee and Paul Anka held in favor. "Summer Holiday" had been a huge hit in England during March of 1963 for Cliff Richard, topping the charts for three weeks, although the original arrangement relied heavily on the nimble fretwork of Hank Marvin, the lead guitarist in Cliff's backing band, The Shadows. Jimmy's new take on the song unfortunately lacked this factor, although the melody (co-written by Bruce Welch and Brian Bennett, rhythm guitarist and drummer for The "Shads") remained so infectious that it carried the overly-heavy string arrangement, as conducted by Jack Nitzsche himself, successfully. Issued as the second single from the album (b/w "Love Letters In The Sand") it once again failed to give Griffin that elusive hit release. Other cover versions of well-known compositions on the album included an upbeat take on "Too Young" (Nat King Cole, 1951) that Jimmy used to perform solo on guitar around Memphis, "Summertime Blues" (Eddie Cochran, 1958) featuring some nice drum fills from Blaine, "Love Letters In The Sand" (Pat Boone, 1957), and Brian Hyland's 1962 hit "Sealed With A Kiss," all recorded in a slick, polished fashion, as were the remaining seven cuts. The lovely ballad "She Used To Be Mine" was one of a number of songs submitted at the request of Bowen for the project, as were two offerings by Glen Campbell – a burgeoning songwriter himself, and one who was starting an established run as one of the more in-demand session guitarists around Los Angeles. Campbell's two compositions were "What Kind Of Girl Are You," co-written with Jerry Capehart, issued as the first single from the sessions, and "My Baby Made Me Cry." Certainly these recordings were two of the strongest cuts on *Summer Holiday* and it must have been a considerable blow to Reprise that the single (b/w "A Little Like Lovin' You") failed to make an impact, either nationally or locally.

To market the release, Reprise chose to package the record in a bright, colorful sleeve with a distinctive nautical flavor. A summertime image of Jimmy, set against the deep blue sky, aboard a boat moored in the Marina Del Ray with two attractive models alongside, appeared prominently on the front cover. One of the models, a young actress hailing from Spokane, Washington, Mikki Jamison (a former Warner Brothers' Deb Of The Year), ended up becoming Mrs. James Griffin for a period of time shortly afterwards (the marriage taking place on September 13, 1963, in Jamison's hometown Episcopal Cathedral). But, like Jimmy's short romance with Reprise Records, the liaison wasn't to last, and after a brief flirtation in the Hollywood TV and movie industry, including appearances in *77 Sunset Strip* (1962), *The Adventures of Ozzie & Harriet* (1963), *Beach Ball* (1965), and later *Adam 12* (1969), Jamison remarried and disappeared from the limelight, returning to upstate Washington where she lived for the remainder of her life, before sadly dying in an automobile accident during the early summer of 2013.

To promote the album, Jimmy undertook a series of publicity events and appearances, including a number of brief television guest spots and concert dates. In the meantime, despite the relative lack of success for the album (it should be noted here that it was mainly a singles market for the American teen-stars of the day, with Bobby Vee only reaching the Top 30 albums with a Greatest Hits collection. None of Vee's other post-1960 albums were huge sellers), Reprise continued to market their young prodigy, with his name regularly featuring in the music trade press as they attempted to bring him into the wider media spotlight. 1963 saw one more release in the homeland, a single containing two songs that had not appeared on the *Summer Holiday* album, and while "Little Miss Cool" b/w "Marie Is Moving" (Reprise 20221) suffered a similar fate to its predecessors, the A-side is certainly one of the standout tracks from Jimmy's early era, building up nicely as it progresses through its two minute length. However, Reprise clearly saw a potential new audience for their faithful youngster, with an attempt to exploit the European market commencing towards the end of the year. "Marie Is Moving" was re-recorded, utilizing the same backing track, but with Jimmy singing the lyrics phonetically in Italian. Released as "Nei Baci Di Un Altro" (translated as "In Kisses Of Another") it failed to make a dent abroad, as did a French 4-track EP featuring songs taken from the debut album.

Despite the relative setbacks of these releases, Jimmy was still popular enough among the teenage audiences that a fan club was created in his name, with his approval, offering subscribers, at $1 a membership, up-to-date information on their favorite star. The popular *Teen Screen* magazine even ran an advertisement publicizing the club, and president, Judy Donofrio, today recalls that it managed to maintain a significant following for a couple of years.

1964 saw Jimmy's final period with Reprise Records, with three more single releases issued throughout the year. The first, "My Baby Made Me Cry," the second of the two Glen Campbell songs featured on the album, was a final promotional plug for the LP, and even with a new flip-side, it saw little activity. And yet, that newly recorded flip-side was significant in more ways than one in that it was a cover version of the Beatles' recent release, "All My Loving." February 1964 had seen the acceptance of the fab four in the United States in such a way that could not have been anticipated. Their U.S. debut album, *Meet The Beatles*, was commencing a reign that was to run supreme in the *Billboard* charts for almost three months (only to be succeeded by *The Beatles' Second Album*) and the phenomenon was washing across the country with such abundance that had not been seen since the inception of rock'n'roll eight years previous. Everybody in the music business was affected in one way or another, whether they liked the new "beat" music or not. Artists raced to jump on the Beatle-bandwagon, fringes a-flailing, beatle-boots a-tappin', and although some of the more established American acts such as The Beach Boys and The Four Seasons struggled to hold their own in the wake of the invasion, other artists, some not so successful, simply recorded covers and tributes to John, Paul, George, and Ringo and waited for the attention to come beatling in. For some it worked, for others it didn't, and with Jimmy's version of the 1963 Lennon-McCartney composition, placed alongside a syrupy, yet thoroughly enjoyable ballad, the release had a real chance of picking up Jimmy's stalling career.

It simply cannot be overstated how *much* of an impact the four Liverpudlians had made in the U.S. during that heady period of early 1964 and, in fact, Jimmy's was not the only cover version of this composition taped. During the initial impact of Beatlemania, following the aftermath of the group's touchdown at New York's newly renamed John F. Kennedy airport on February 7th that year, both Annette Funicello *and* the Hollyridge Strings issued versions of the song, while the Beatles' original recording, although not officially released as a U.S. single, still managed to hit the middle reaches of the *Billboard* chart courtesy of a Canadian import on the Capitol label and as part of a *Four By The Beatles* EP. The competition was hot. The Jimmy Griffin version of "All My Loving," still under the production auspices of Jimmy Bowen, remains vocally faithful to the Beatles take, complete with Beatle-wigged, fringe-shakin' *woooh's* during the fade, accompanied by a driving Ringo-styled drumbeat, although Bowen's overall arrangements once again took it back into the mainstream of the early '60s teen-pop era. Sadly misplaced female backing vocals and unnecessary horn arrangements place it firmly in the pre-Beatles mold. The times they were a-changin' but unfortunately, for Jimmy, Reprise wasn't quite ready to take him in that direction yet.

During July he undertook a series of concert performances that, potentially, were the most prestigious on his record to date. Friday, July 3rd and Saturday, July 4th saw him perform at the Honolulu International Center in Hawaii as a part of the "Million Dollar Party" concert, sponsored by the K-Poi radio station, and billed as "the biggest show ever to play Hawaii." Although fairly low on the bill he found himself sharing the stage with headliners The Beach Boys, along with Jan & Dean, Jimmy Clanton, Ray Peterson, The Kingsmen, The Rivingtons, Jody Miller, Bruce & Terry, Peter & Gordon, Mary Saenz, and the K-Poi All-Star Band (featuring friends and sessioneers Hal Blaine and Glen Campbell). Sunday the 5th saw a further two shows in Honolulu, before The Beach Boys headed out on their 36-date "Summer Safari Tour," taking both The Kingsmen *and* Jimmy (in addition to Freddie Cannon and Lynne Easton) along as support for a number of shows. Accepted, Jimmy would have only had the opportunity to perform a handful of songs, or possibly only his current single, but The Beach Boys were at the pinnacle of their early career at this point with the Brian Wilson-Mike Love composition, "I Get Around," reaching the #1 position on the *Billboard* charts while the performers were all still in Hawaii, and he would often have found himself performing for audiences in excess of 10,000. Certainly, this was a *major* publicity tour for a performer struggling to find that elusive hit record and, in fact, this so nearly led onto far greater things for Jimmy, far sooner than the eventual course of fate would eventually turn.

During December 1964, mid-way through a flight to Texas for a Beach Boys performance in Dallas, the band's leader and principal songwriter, Brian Wilson, suffered a well-publicized breakdown en route, resulting in his eventual withdrawal from the touring responsibilities of the band. Naturally, a swift replacement had to be found and studio guitarist Glen Campbell briefly stepped into the role for the next couple of months. However, Campbell's position was deemed only temporary and shortly afterwards the call went out for a more permanent replacement to fill Brian's touring boots. The initial responsibility for finding a suitable face to fill the void went to songwriter, producer, and performer (and band friend) Bruce Johnston, who eventually took the role himself.

Bruce recalled: "I contacted Jerry Cole and Eddie Carter for Glen's replacement but they were not available. Jimmy Griffin was also a consideration of the band's and would have been a great choice." As to whether Jimmy ever got to hear of the band's interest at that point is unclear, as the call may never have been made, but Bruce continued, "He was a very nice guy and I knew him well when he was a staff songwriter for Metric Music."[2]

Nevertheless, the life of a Beach Boy was not to be, and it was indeed hit singles and record sales that would keep the name of Jimmy Griffin in the spotlight, even more so than a supporting slot on one of the hottest summer tours, so it was no surprise that Reprise continued to push their investment with two further releases – although possibly the last push unless a hit record prevailed.

In order to develop his potential career yet further still, he had also recently taken up acting studies, undertaking an "artist in development" role at the MGM studios. The next twelve months subsequently saw Jimmy take in this new medium with two big-screen appearances, although neither of the roles he took were significantly major parts, and the first was even uncredited. The producers of both films must have seen something in the handsome youngster though, the same things that the teen-idols of the previous years – Fabian, Bobby Darin, John Leyton, Cliff Richard – had to offer during their transition from recording studio to movie set. However, his sister feels that this medium was something that he was never really at home with:

"He was a little ambivalent to it all, because he was a little shy. He never wanted to be out front. Being in front of the camera, and being singled out, he never seemed to be really comfortable with it."

For Those Who Think Young, the first of Griffin's two films, was released by United Artists during 1964. Essentially, an extension of the popular "beach" genre of movies at the time, it was really a vehicle for James Darren to take on the good-looking surfer-boy image previously portrayed so successfully by Frankie Avalon in the official Beach Party series with, in this instance, Nancy Sinatra, Tina Louise, and Pamela Tiffin taking the lead female roles. Decked out in a smart blue suit and tie, no cut-offs or huarache sandals in sight, and with his hair coiffured to perfection, Jimmy pouts and shimmies, occasionally flashing his gleaming smile, and singing his own composition "(I'm Gonna Walk) All Over This Land," a rockabilly-pop number co-written with screen-composer Jerry Fielding, while various excerpts of plot dialogue talk over the instrumental break. Backed by an established crew of "surf musicians" (including "Challengers" Richard Delvy and Glen Grey, along with guitar virtuoso Paul Johnson) Jimmy performs "live" to a gathered crowd during a club scene, but other than that he has no spoken lines or indeed relevance to the film. Short but sweet. However, he also receives no credit on film for either the appearance or the song – even though the melody *was* additionally used as theme music on one occasion.

The second of the 1964 singles was led by a Mark Anthony composition entitled "Running To You," coupled by "Gotta Lotta Love (Ciribiribin)," an old 1930s standard written by Jack Lawrence and Harry James, which itself was based on an even earlier composition of Italian origin, dating back to 1898, by Alberto Pestalozza and Carolo Tiochet. Both sides were strong enough compositions but suffered from the same fate as the previous release: it was clearly aimed at the wrong market. One only has to look at the top-selling records of '64, even taking the Beatles out of the equation, to see that a shift in the dynamics had occurred. Only one solo artist of note from the "teen-era," Bobby Vinton, maintained a successful presence in the *Billboard* Top 10 lists of that year, with the remainder of the positions being held down by artists in the caliber of The Four Seasons, The Beach Boys, The Supremes, Peter & Gordon… and as the year progressed The Animals and Manfred Mann made their impact. Legendary balladeer Roy Orbison also struck gold that year with "Oh, Pretty Women" but it was noticeably his last Top 20 hit of the decade, and he could hardly be deemed as representational of the "teen-era" with his dark, moody image, and sunglasses. No, sir...

"Gotta Lotta Love," even in its updated form, certainly maintained a sufficient amount of "rhythm'n'beat" throughout and, had the current influences of the then-new guitar bands been utilized, it may well have achieved a modicum of success, appealing to the newly aware and revitalized teenage market, but the intruding Jimmy Bowen Latino-horn arrangements that were still being pushed into the mix were far more detrimental than enhancing. The same can also be said for Jimmy's final release on the label: "Try," a lively number composed by the relatively unknown partnership of Hill and Lanier, along with a version of the more widely recognizable ballad "You're Nobody Till Somebody Loves You" written by Russ Morgan, Larry Stock, and James Cavanaugh. This standard had already seen significant success courtesy of recordings by Frank Sinatra, Nat King Cole, Dinah Washington, Peggy Lee, and Connie Francis, which perfectly summed up the confusing Reprise attitude towards the young Jimmy Griffin. He was clearly not an artist that would appeal and sell in vast quantities to the audiences of these great acts. He was youthful, clean-cut, handsome – ideal teenage fodder in the eyes of the media – and putting him on a recent tour accompanied by current top pop artists such as The Beach Boys and The Kingsmen ("Louie Louie") would only mislead the audiences who purchased his misguided Reprise singles. "All My Loving," for all its production faults, was a step forward in the right direction for an artist clearly intent on success in the youth market, but the two subsequent releases were firmly planting the feet in a backwards motion. Reprise may well have been proven correct in their song selection, with Rat Pack crooner Dean Martin giving the label a #25 position the following year with the Morgan-Stock-Cavanaugh tune (even achieving the #1 position on the "Easy Listening" lists), and Jimmy's powerful bluesy rendition is a very mature performance from the 21-year-old, offering up comparisons in vocal approach to that of Elvis Presley at times, but it was a mismatch that could not work. A mismatch proven so when, two years later, The Four Seasons attempted another version under the guise of The Wonder Who? With numerous hits already under their belts they barely scraped the Hot 100. It was time to move on…

August 1964 saw Jimmy back out on the promotional circuit, performing "Try" on the nationally televised *Steve Allen Show*, the hugely popular NBC series broadcast from an old vaudeville theater on North Vine St. in Hollywood. However, despite his continuing efforts to seek success, during the latter half of the year Jimmy Griffin and Reprise Records parted company. Reprise, along with most labels, finally saw the writing on the wall for the individual teen-star in the wake of the British invasion. The "beat" groups were now the order of the day and the more they could find the better. Gerry & The Pacemakers, The Dave Clark Five, The Animals, The Rolling Stones… and for Reprise it was to be The Kinks. Within the space of eight weeks over the summer and fall of 1964 this British band hailing from the suburbs of North London gave Reprise exactly what it wanted, two Top 10 hits. But for Jimmy Griffin pastures new were waiting and Liberty Records was the first point of call.

Following his signing with Liberty Records during late 1964-early 1965, Jimmy also entered into a deal with Metric Music to handle his songwriting affairs. He was rapidly developing his own songwriting skills and Metric was Liberty Records' own publishing company based in the label's headquarters in Los Angeles and run by Lenny Waronker, son of Liberty's founder Si Waronker. In the early 1960s the company also handled up and coming staff writers such as Randy Newman, Sharon Sheeley, Jackie DeShannon, P.J. Proby, David Gates, and Michael Gordon. The latter had been the principle member and songwriter for two L.A.-based surf bands, The Mar-kets (later the Marketts) and The Routers, and he had hit big with such releases as "Surfer's Stomp," "Balboa Blue," "Out Of Limits," and "Let's Go!" However, tired of both bands' touring duties, Gordon had returned to Los Angeles to concentrate on his songwriting. He would shortly link up with Liberty Records/Metric Music's newest songwriting talent and together they would form a formidable partnership.

Although his liaison with Reprise Records had now ended, Jimmy's involvement with the label's parent company, Warner Brothers, was to continue on into the new year. The cinema release of the film *None But The Brave*, issued by the Warner studios in February 1965, was to be Jimmy's second big-screen appearance and this particular film was given additional interest due to it also being the directorial debut of its star, the founder of Reprise Records, and subsequently part owner of Warner Brothers Records, Mr. Sinatra himself, undertaking a bit of multi-tasking on the project. A WWII movie, detailing the relationship between groups of U.S. and Japanese soldiers marooned on a small Pacific island, the movie starred Sinatra, alongside Clint Walker, Brad Dexter, and former teen-idol Tommy Sands. Griffin, starring as Private Dexter, took on a far bigger role for his second movie, and although his character only lasted 30 minutes into the film before succumbing to a Japanese sniper bullet he did manage three spoken lines, and all in a scene with the great man sitting nearby – plus he managed to get his name in the closing credits this time.

Movie commitments completed, Jimmy Griffin made his debut for his new recording label in more ways than one. Not only did he release his first single with them, a cover of the 1960 Fats Domino hit recording "Walking To New Orleans," but he also composed the flip-side himself, marking the first time that the name of J. Griffin appeared as a songwriting credit on vinyl. "Walking To New Orleans" stands out as the first time Jimmy really got a grip with the "feel" of a song. His gritty vocal stands out as the focal point, bereft of Reprise's overly-used horn section. The swirling organ and keyboards that dominate the track counterbalance his voice and while the composition itself is void of any true hook or catchy melody, the "mood" of the composition is sound, with a raw dirty-blues overtone. Jimmy's own composition, "These Are The Times," was equally interesting, having been given the artistic freedom to develop the soulful side of his raw talents and, no longer held back by the restraints of his previous employers, he delivered. Issued as Liberty Records 66108 this wonderful release went... nowhere.

It would be another year before a second release would appear on the Liberty Records label and when the follow-up did arrive, during 1966, Jimmy was to be found moving further into a "soul" sound, covering the Jerry Butler-Curtis Mayfield-Calvin Carter horn-driven "He Will Break Your Heart" (a solo hit for Butler back in 1960 and later a #1 for Tony Orlando). With a different producer on board, this track was notable for the first airing of what would become the trademark Griffin high-harmony, a vocal reach that would become a familiar sound for followers of Bread in later years. Paired with "Hard Row To Hoe" the failure of this track would signal another fork in the road for Jimmy. Now approaching his mid-twenties, and after four years of unsuccessful record releases on two differing labels, luck was finally to be on his side following a fortuitous meeting with the former Mar-ket and Router Michael Zane Gordon. For the time being, songwriting was to become the main focus for Jimmy, although a further number of recordings featuring his distinctive vocal abilities were to appear before the decade was out.

Gordon recalled: "I first met Jimmy when I was writing songs for Imperial Records. Their publishing firm was Metric Music which was being run by Lenny Waronker and Lenny was so impressed by the two of us that he made a deal with producer Snuffy Garrett to start a new publishing company and sign us as a team under Snuffy's own Viva Records label (formed with Ed Silvers). We worked with Lenny for a while and then he left and went on to become the head of Warner Brothers Records."[3]

Garrett already had a considerable track record in the industry, having played a major role in the achievements of Bobby Vee, Gary Lewis, and Johnny Burnette. Following their move from Liberty Records to Garrett's own Viva label, the new partnership of Griffin and Gordon was to achieve a significant amount of success, and was to prove particularly fruitful in developing Jimmy's writing and arranging abilities. The new publishing company was labeled Stone Canyon Music.

Gordon: "I wrote the music on many of the songs and most of the lyrics but Jimmy put it all together in the studio when we made the demos. He played all the parts and sang all the vocals. His arrangements on our demos were so good that most of the artists actually used the exact arrangement that was on the demo when they cut the master. Jimmy made the magic happen in the studio. So you see, we had a different kind of writing partnership."[3]

Over the course of the next two years, from the first meeting between Jimmy and Michael Gordon during 1966, the pair composed in excess of 60 songs, with over one hundred recordings being made from a wide selection of artists (BMI, one of the three US Performing Rights societies, currently has 62 compositions registered by the duo). Some were fairly reasonable hits, achieving higher chart positions than any of Jimmy's solo releases from the previous four years, while others remained unrecorded, although Gordon is certain that all reached the demo stage:

"All of the songs were committed to tape in demo form, but as to whether the tapes still exist… I tried to get Warner Music to answer that same question (in recent years) but I just got the run-around. I finally sued them and got some money but the most important thing was that I got my songs back. One that stayed unreleased was 'Take Away' which was recorded by Bobby Vee but it never was issued… good song. I think the first one we wrote was called 'Back To The Drawing Board' but I'm not certain."[3]

Among the many recorded compositions created by the duo that were released to a listening world, mainly between the years 1967 and 1969, were "Main Street" (recorded and released by The Cascades), "(Who Likes) Good Pop Music" (Rudy Vallee), "Hotel Indiscreet" (Sagittarius), "Jessie" (issued as an album track by Harpers Bizarre), "Brink Of Disaster" (Lesley Gore), "Get The Message" (Bobby Vee, Brian Hyland, The Young Men, *and* Sagittarius), "Save A Love" (Bobby Vee, reportedly with Jimmy singing harmonies), "Love Machine" (The Roosters, Pastoral Symphony, Harper & Rowe), and perhaps, most notably, "Apologize," recorded with varying arrangements by Ed Ames, Gary Lewis, and Brian Hyland.

"Hyland did the better version of 'Apologize' but Ames got his out first," recalled Gordon, "but we also had songs recorded by Gary Lewis, Annette, The Second Helping, The Standells, Michael J. James, The Roosters, Freddy Cannon, Marc Cavell, Tommy Sands, The Doodletown Pipers, Jessie Lopez, Pastoral Symphony, The Astronauts, Bobby Vee, and Bill Buchanan to name a few that I can think of."3

"Apologize" not only reached the US Top 10 in the Adult Contemporary charts for Ames, but also earned the songwriting duo a BMI Award, and both "Get The Message" and "Brink Of Disaster" reached the Hot 100 on the *Billboard* charts for Brian Hyland and Lesley Gore respectively. "Love Machine," when issued by The Pastoral Symphony in Australia, also achieved Top 10 status. One can only wonder as to the fortunes of the writers had "Hokie Pokie Girl," "In My Hair," "That Old Cathedral," or "Up Popped Cupid" received greater attention…

"I totally do not remember 'Up Popped Cupid' or 'In My Hair'..." laughs Gordon, forty years on.

The dominant influence of country music that permeates throughout "Apologize," reminiscent of the melodies that ran through many of Jimmy Webb's compositions, clearly shows the route that lay ahead for Jimmy, and while Ames' clinical pronunciation is often at odds with the laid-back approach of the track itself, the instant appeal of the melody is what makes the recording so successful. Equally satisfying, but a distance apart in both style and feel, is the Lesley Gore rendition of "Brink Of Disaster," a #82 hit on *Billboard* for Griffin and Gordon during 1967. Pure pop in sound, with a hint of the Summer of Love creeping through the harpsichord arrangement and harmony drenched vocals, it stands out as a truly well-crafted composition, lyrically and musically, but even that pales into psycho-insignificance when compared with the strange vocals and arrangements of "Hotel Indiscreet" by the studio-based band Sagittarius. A creation of producer Gary Usher, and masterminded by the inventive imagination of Curt Boetcher, this was another arrangement dominated by alternating harpsichord patterns and time shifts, with the melody bubbling along in a dreamy haze of harmonies. This band also cut a version of "Get The Message," albeit in a less "enlightened" arrangement, although the definitive version of this particular tune is without doubt courtesy of hit maker Brian Hyland ("Sealed With A Kiss"), a #91 hit in 1967. This shows the true commercial potential that Jimmy had at his disposal, and it remains a mystery as to why it stalled in the lower reaches of the charts. A wonderful hook line, a great arrangement and some pure West Coast harmonies should have sent this one soaring, but alas, the *big* breakthrough in commercial terms was still a way off for Jimmy.

One other notable tune recorded during 1967 was a version of the Griffin-Gordon composition "The Other Me," a sunshine pop offering that was credited to The Surprise Package, a quartet hailing from Seattle that produced a series of releases during this period. This was pure pop at its 1960s best and shows that the songwriting partnership really could supply commerciality, and had they chosen that route intentionally could well have notched up a number of chart successes. However, the gains that such a direction would have taken them was something they would not consider.

"We never wrote to a certain 'style,' we just wrote whatever came to mind," confirms Michael.

Jimmy also took to producing a number of artists during his stint working and writing with the Viva label, having signed an exclusive producer's contract with Ed Silvers, Snuff Garrett's business partner, during the spring of 1967. His initial productions included bands such as The Roosters, The Beethoven Soul, and The Travel Agency but, as with his own releases, none of his work achieved any significant success, although some of the product certainly warrants further scrutiny. The Beethoven Soul, a six-piece psychedelic pop band fronted by a glamorous violin player named Andrea Kouratou, was signed to Dot Records, and they released one album during 1967, with production credits afforded to James Arthur Griffin. In a bold move, the unsuccessful recording career of Jimmy Griffin was finally laid to rest and James Arthur Griffin, now on a new record label, stepped forward. The production and arrangements on the eleven-track release are now regarded as standard for the times – typical harpsichord and interchanging baroque time patterns – and with two of the songs composed by the Gordon-Griffin partnership ("Dreams" and "Beggin' Your Pardon M'Lady"), and a third by Griffin and a new writing partner, it stands as a pleasant "timepiece," reminiscent of the blend that Harpers Bizarre so successfully achieved. Although out of context, as with a great number of so-called "psychedelic productions" from this era, it has not aged well. The 1968 release by The Travel Agency is far more interesting, containing twelve songs played in a notably more rock vein, reliant on fuzz guitars and harmony, a vein that James would explore more and more in the near future. Production was again credited to J.A. Griffin, and, although all compositions were by the three-piece band themselves, some of the rhythm guitar arrangements, such as on the closing "Old Man," can easily be comparable to later recordings by James. Nevertheless, despite the important developments and experiences these productions had to offer, it was via his partnership with Gordon that the hard work finally began to reap recognition and reward.

"The Miracle Worker," a 1967 release on Viva, coupled with "Lookin' So Much Better," were two more compositions from the now successful working partnership of Griffin and Gordon. These two songs were the first solo releases for James under his new contract with Snuff Garrett, and both were by far and away the most adventurous recordings from him to date. "'The Miracle Worker' deserved far greater attention," recalled Michael Gordon. "One of my all-time favorites. Jimmy recorded that and it was pick of the week in *Cash Box* but nothing happened…"[3]

However, the summer of love was now here. Attitudes were changing. Recording sessions were becoming more adventurous. The Beach Boys' smash "Good Vibrations" had started the move away from the two-minute pop song, and then "Strawberry Fields Forever" had raised the benchmark. The doors were open. Love. Strawberry Alarm Clock. Flowers in your hair. James, meanwhile, had been introduced to another young songwriter, one who was equally in tune with him (and with whom he crafted the song "A Violent Crime" for the *Beethoven Soul* release), and like his current partner Michael Gordon, this new acquaintance was also locally born in the urban metropolis of Los Angeles.

Chapter Two

I Want You With Me

Robert Wilson Royer was born in the City of Angels on December 6th, 1942. By far the most elusive, and often overlooked member of his former band, his importance in the development of what would become the success story that is / was Bread cannot be underestimated. Even after his departure from the official ranks of the line-up during the spring of 1971, his influence was maintained via the ongoing songwriting partnership with James Griffin, and despite David Gates' increasing stature as the figurehead of the group in the latter years, it was more often than not the strength of the Griffin-Royer partnership that maintained an even keel in the band's creativity and credibility.

Neither of Robert's parents was particularly musical, with his father preferring the challenge of economy, history, and politics to an entertainment lifestyle, although his mother, as he was later to recall in conversation with the author, "did sing a little and danced quite well." Nevertheless, even during his formative years at junior high, music was beginning to play an important part in his life, with memorable moments such as The Four Lads' "Istanbul (Not Constantinople)," a *Billboard* Top 10 hit for the Canadian quartet during 1953, along with the early recordings of Bo Diddley, finding favor in the mind of the pre-teen youngster. However, it wasn't just the popular hits of the day that were to remain with him over the years that were to follow:

"I am, and always have been insanely into classical music," he recalls. "Some salesman sold my parents about forty 78s of classical themes, I probably wore them out. When I was a teenager I discovered Beethoven, and eventually I went off into the Russians... Borodin, Rimsky-Korsakov, and went insane about them. Amazing..."

During the mid-1950s the family relocated away from the vastness of the city, choosing to settle into a more relaxed lifestyle, and based themselves near the beautiful Bass Lake reservoir in Madera County, central California. It was in this idyllic setting that the true character of the young teenager was to form while attending the nearby Sierra High School. Not being yet able to drive, Robert, or Robb as he preferred to be known, was often to be found on the lake, racing in his father's speedboat or skiing along behind it. "I was almost thinking about water skiing seriously when I (later) hit L.A. Not as a profession, but to make money while I was at college."

Following this period of idyllic existence Robb indeed moved back to Los Angeles during 1960 to attend San Fernando Valley State College in Northridge and, despite his academic intentions of a career in law, once he picked up a guitar, in his own words: "It was over, forget it. Everybody had to have a Goya gutstring." It was here at Valley State that, alongside fellow student Timothy Hallinan, another local Los Angelino with whom he was soon to share a typical bachelor condo, he was often to be found either engrossing himself in the burgeoning folk music scene, developing his songwriting skills, or entering into some other form of writing. Folk music was bursting onto the scene around the campuses of 1960s America and the poetry and melodies of the more popular performers such as Dylan, Phil Ochs, and Joan Baez were ingrained into much of the student population but, alongside Hallinan, and fellow students David Kaufman and Michael Levesque, Robb found the influence of his peers taking in a far broader perspective.

"He (Tim) was much more intellectually developed than the rest of us. I had a certain artistic vision that he signed in with, but he had a philosophy and a way of expressing things and a sense of humor and all this stuff going on, and I just went 'Wow!' We ended up as roommates and we wrote a musical together for the college, which unfortunately came about a year late. Tim wrote the lyrics, I did the music, David Kaufman wrote the book, and another guy, Richard Blakeslee, worked on the lyrics too."

That project, initially entitled *The Plastic Sibling*, was to undergo various changes through the years, later bringing in one of Robb's future songwriting partners to co-write and develop the lyrical aspect.

Another student attending California State at that period was classical guitarist Stephen Cohn. "Robb and Tim had formed a singing group to perform the songs that they were writing, occasionally performing as a duo at The Troubadour Club under the auspices of club owner Doug Weston. They then added Michele Cochrane, who was a theater major at the same University (initially calling themselves We Three). She had also done some musical comedy work and some professional acting. I had just given my senior recital on classical guitar at CSUN and Robb wanted a classical guitarist and a jazz guitarist to accompany the group. He first found the jazz guitarist, Mike Petruso, and then asked me to join. We played a few gigs in this format but then Mike decided to leave. The singers found that I could do vocal arrangements and asked me to do some for the group. Then, almost by accident, I started writing songs – three of which got recorded immediately. As a result, Robb and Tim asked me to write with them and sing with them and this became our standard for songwriting and performing. My classical guitar style of playing and voicing chords was a major influence on the group's songwriting and our sound."[5]

"I would write music based on my early guitar abilities, whatever they were," adds Robb, "and when the group expanded Tim, Steve, and I started writing together, but Tim became very busy and didn't want the exhaustive day-to-day thing that went with it, so Steve and I would get together and write, and it was a very structured period for me. I knew what I liked about it and I knew what I didn't like about it, and I knew what I wanted to do next. To me, what I did with Steve was too mannered, too classical. The vocal arrangements were something that the four of us worked up together, and I would give everyone credit on that, Tim, Steve, Michele, and me, we just worked up the vocal parts. All we had were two acoustic guitars. That was the great hunger I had..."

The fledgling group soon picked up a manager, Arnie Mills, who also looked after the phenomenal successes of the Texas-born vocalist Vicki Carr at the time, and they immediately found themselves, billed as The Rainy Day People, or occasionally The Inn Group, doing the rounds amongst the various agents.

From her home in Los Angeles, Michele Cochrane (now Michele Shaw) recalls today: "I wasn't into the business side. Robb was the business guy, I was just the pretty blonde singer. I have a pretty good voice. But we signed up with Arnie and he took us around all of these big agencies... William Morris, G.A.C. I remember we played at The Troubadour this one time. G.A.C., this agency, had set us up there and we were up on stage, and I was so shy back then and I did the introduction and I forgot to introduce myself! Oh God, it was so painful!" she adds with a laugh.

Mills also scheduled the group to work alongside producer Snuff Garrett, although by this stage, Garrett had consolidated his reputation enough around the industry that he had a regular team of musicians and assistants on hand to virtually run the various sessions without him. One of this team was a multi-talented musician from Oklahoma named Claude Russell Bridges.

Born in 1942, Bridges had grown up in Tulsa, Oklahoma, but had relocated to Los Angeles in his late teens, swiftly becoming a regular at recording sessions overseen by Phil Spector. Working under the professional name of Leon Russell the youngster performed on many hits of the era, including releases by Gary Lewis, The Byrds, The Beach Boys, and Herb Alpert. Success proved swift and by the middle of the decade Russell was to be found living in a large house on Skyhill Drive, up in the Hollywood Hills, often frequented by musical friends that had followed his route west from Oklahoma, among whom was singer, songwriter, and guitarist JJ Cale. In return for accommodation, sleeping on the floor being one option, Russell would often utilize his friends in the studio that he had installed into the house, at accommodating rates for producers who needed "all-in" sessions. Snuff Garrett reportedly used this obliging scenario himself, using both the studio and the team of musicians that came with it for his own sessions, although in some instances the mix of Oklahomans and Los Angelinos was an uneasy blend:

Cohn: "The guys from Oklahoma brought their culture with them and the interface between us hippies and the beer-drinking Oklahomans was sometimes comical, sometimes a bit dangerous. I remember Michele being hit on by a semi-drunk musician and her response was to humiliate him. Some of the guys had live-in girlfriends and we were all fairly naive and sheltered at that point so this culture we walked into was at the same time funny, shocking, scary, and educational.

"The two recordings (we did) ended up on the Hanna-Barbera label, but we were not enthusiastic about the quality of production that resulted. I had visions of pushing the group in the direction of pop with classical underpinnings. The musicians at Leon's were about as far from this vision as one could get."[5]

The Hanna-Barbera record label, distributed via Columbia Records, was a spin-off for the company universally famous for the popular animation films seen around the globe. Headed by a young upcoming songwriter, and a man with his finger on the pulse, Danny Hutton (later of Three Dog Night), the short-lived enterprise issued recordings by an array of performers, reflecting the rich musical variety of the day. Artists as diverse as Louis Prima, The 13th Floor Elevators, Les Baxter, Squiddly Diddly, and the Five Americans all saw HB releases, as did The Rainy Day People, who, in 1966, saw their single "Junior Executive" b/w "I'm Telling It To You," both co-written by the trio of Stephen Cohn, Robb Royer, and Tim Hallinan, issued as HBR512.

"Junior Executive," a song with its roots based deeply within the folk genre, both vocally and structurally, but with a groove daring to break out into a more rhythm'n'blues vein (Robb later commented that it was their attempt to write in a Ray Davies/Kinks style) is an impressive composition, but despite the inventive vocal arrangements and clever lyrical content, the noticeably flat production utilized for the finished track, courtesy of the Leon Russell "team," leaves it clearly wanting. One cannot fault the musical contribution of the Oklahoma studio crew, with both the organ and guitars contributing nice patterns, but the combined mix just sounds resolutely dull as a finished product. The accompanying side, however, features a far harsher edge, with fuzz guitar and a vocal arrangement comparable to the earlier work of The Association, another recently formed folk-rock act, but one that was destined to hit the top end of the *Billboard* charts before the year was out. The up-tempo "I'm Telling It To You" also features a lot more refined harmonies than its flip, with the four vocalists blending into a fine array of backing vocals and showing the true potential of the band. This track alone, regardless of the disillusion of Cohn's comments, must have given the band hope for the future and, despite the unsuccessful launch of this first offering, the follow-up was swift.

However, around the same time that The Rainy Day People were taking their initial tentative steps in the studio, Robb had first been introduced to another songwriter trying to further develop his stuttering career in the industry. Recollections are vague from those concerned as to specifics, but Royer believes that it may have been during the actual sessions at Russell's house in the Hollywood Hills that he first came across the Cincinnati-born James Griffin. Although his first formal introduction to the former teen-star came a short while later courtesy of a friend, the former girlfriend of Tim Hallinan, a Mexican Valley State student named Maria Aguayo, who was now dating Griffin himself and would later go on to become his second wife.

"She was a beautiful, slender Mexican girl and she said, 'You have to meet my boyfriend, he's in music too.' So she arranged one evening for me to come down to West Hollywood where they were living. She said he'd probably be home around eight-thirty so I came around that time. She was there but he wasn't, so we opened a bottle of red wine and we drank that, and then we decided to have another one, so when Jimmy finally strolled in about eleven at night I was sitting there potted out of my mind with his girlfriend!" Robb remembers with amusement. "I figured, boy, this could be a bad situation and she said, 'Jimmy, this is Robb – Robb, this is Jimmy,' and so we thought for a few minutes and finally Jimmy says, 'Hey man, do you do horn parts?' and I said, 'Yeah, I can write a horn part,' and he said he was taking a scholarship at L.A. City College and needed horn parts by tomorrow, and from that moment on... It took maybe a little while."

So, with a number of successful compositions for other artists, but sadly none of his own to date, the talented James Griffin entered Royer's immediate circle of acquaintances, and as both were keen to develop their songwriting they began to explore the possibilities of working together. It was a creative time for all, as Robb was later to comment: "The Beatles were king, the business had structure, and optimism was rampant."[7]

And while none of the early collaborations between the two were to appear on any of Robb's current group recordings, the new partnership was enough to drive a wedge between Griffin and his former partner, Michael Gordon.

"I wrote three songs with Jimmy for his (Viva) singles deal," says Robb today, "(and) the relationship was not great between Michael and me at that time. I worked with Jimmy, and he did too, and Jimmy was definitely choosing to go with me."

"Unfortunately, drugs seemed to be the impetus for our final split. We just sort of drifted apart," reflects Michael today, with a sense of sadness. "Jimmy started hanging around with a new crowd, and I was never into drugs of any kind which I'm thankful for to this day."[3]

The career of Gordon was certainly to achieve new heights over the subsequent years, following on from the split of his songwriting partnership with James. Over a 30-year period he was to go on to develop an extremely successful position for himself within the Hollywood industry, making significant contributions to hit films such as *Pulp Fiction*, *Narc,* and the award-winning *Mafioso: The Father, The Son*, although he does look back at their time together with affection:

"Jimmy was a great guy. The best. He was one of the most talented artists I have ever met, and we never had an argument and never had any bad feeling toward each other."[3]

Following on from the disappointment of The Rainy Day People release, and while the new friendship of Griffin and Royer was still in its infancy, the four-piece line-up returned to the studios with new songs – and a new name.

Cohn: "Nothing much happened with that first release so we were released from our contract. Uni Records was a new label at that point and the first president was Dave Pell, who had previously been at Liberty. Our manager Arnie and Dave were friends, so after an audition we were signed to do an album with Uni. We also did a few performances in L.A. and San Diego (The Troubadour and The Icehouse) but by the time we changed our name and became The Pleasure Fair we were primarily a studio band..." Forty years later, with some of the memories now a distant haze, Cohn continued, "Why Pleasure Fair? My memory on this is now somewhat vague, but I think we felt we needed a new name and we just kicked around ideas. We landed on The Pleasure Fair as it had a familiar ring and because it seemed to say something about our musical intentions. The (Renaissance) Pleasure Fair is a yearly gathering here in California which re-enacts the period of sixteenth century England."[5]

Adds Royer: "We knew Barry DeVorzon, who had Valiant Records, which owned The Association, and Barry had made himself a big deal by having The Association and selling it all to Warners, and he offered us a deal at the same time Uni Records offered us a deal. He commented (about the debut single) the song sucked but the sound was great, so we went with Uni! Arnie Mills was also adamant we sign."

Tim Hallinan, with much humor, also has his recollections about some of the shows they played during this period. "We wrote songs together, went on the road together, and played some of the worst nightclubs in the world together. We were attacked by a wrench-wielding motorcyclist in San Diego, and for two memorable nights we shared a camper shell in a garage with half a dozen dogs that devoted their lives, day and night, to pooping. The owner of the club we were playing had promised us accommodation, and this was it. The stench in the garage was so bad we could smell it from the street. With the garage door closed!"

Michele picks up the story: "I stayed with my grandmother in Laguna while they were in that garage. My father said 'What! You're not going there and staying with the guys.' So I drove from San Diego to Laguna at three o'clock in the morning, and I think it was the second night and a policeman pulled me up as I was veering across the street. I must have been falling asleep!"

With a new name and record label, the group continued to hone their act and vocal abilities while the three writers developed their songwriting partnership.

"I think our strengths were Michele's vocals, along with the writing abilities of Robb, Tim, and myself,"[5] Cohn was later to comment, "and also my vocal arrangements and the unique classical guitar voicing I brought to the group. But I was never really comfortable as a performer, I don't have a performer's temperament. I have a lot more to offer as a composer."[6]

Indeed, many years after the dissolution of the group, and with the late 1960s recording era but a distant memory, Stephen Cohn went on to achieve significant worldwide acceptance and critical acclaim as a composer of major orchestral works and soundtracks, along with a brief flirtation as a solo recording artist with Motown during the early 1970s. That too had a further connection of interest, but more on that later...

Adorned with a photograph strikingly similar to that which graced the front of The Beatles' *Rubber Soul* album from two years previous, the debut recordings by The Pleasure Fair made their appearance on a self-titled album issued by Uni Records during 1967. With seven of the twelve featured songs composed by the group's songwriting trio, and the remainder made up with compositions from established tunesmiths such as Van Dyke Parks, Neal Hefti, Lennon & McCartney, and Graham Gouldman, the release offers up a nice melodic affair with clear comparisons coming in the shape of groups such as the aforementioned Association, who by this time had notched up two Top 10 smash hits with "Along Comes Mary" and the chart-topping "Cherish," and the overwhelming folk-rock orientated success story that was The Mamas & The Papas.

"We talked about The Association a lot. Their harmonies…" remembers Michele. "We were influenced by them, but this was before The Mamas & The Papas."

While they perhaps lacked the visual impact, or vocal prowess, of John and Michelle Phillips, Cass Elliott, and Denny Doherty that was subsequently to follow to much acclaim, and one may also argue the commercial composing skills to match, the intricate arrangements and intertwining of their vocals certainly gave The Pleasure Fair good stead in their quest for success. Michele Cochrane may not have had a second female voice alongside to counterbalance, as per the Elliott/Phillips combination, but nevertheless the blend they produced was a satisfying mix of delicacy and strength. Sadly, however, the success story wasn't to be, and the finished product didn't actually meet with complete approval from the band themselves either…

"I wasn't pleased with the mix on *The Pleasure Fair*. I just thought the voices needed to be shown more," continues Michele, a fact that Stephen Cohn concurs with. "The making of the album lacked the kind of in-studio creativity that was beginning to emerge at the time," he adds. "I think we were all disappointed in the blandness of the arrangements and the lack of using multi-track recording in an edgy, creative way. We had a skillful producer and arranger but it was rather conservative for our taste. We did our own vocal arrangements, which he didn't alter, but he did the instrumental arrangements, which we were not invited to participate in. We never felt that our vocal sound was well represented on the album."[5]

In recalling how the choice of producer came about Robb says: "We thought we were going to sign with Valiant for a while, they were serious and we were serious, but Arnie said 'No, no, no, my friend Dave Pell has formed a label with Universal,' so we sat down with Dave and Russ Regan and they said who do you want to produce you? And we really liked Leon (Russell) and JJ (Cale) but Dave Pell said 'I think I've got somebody even better than that for you.' We had to make a choice and we met David Gates and we liked him and he showed a lot of interest in our music, so we went with David."

This young man, who was credited with taking charge on *The Pleasure Fair* album was a musician himself, and another who hailed from the creative state of Oklahoma and, as had many of the budding L.A. musicians at the time, made his way west in order to develop his musical career. Despite his youth, Dave Gates (as he was listed on the album sleeve) was, by this stage, experienced in both song-writing, performing, and studio production, with a number of "hit" compositions under his belt, and he was deemed as the ideal choice by the company to take this fledgling folk group into the studio and build on their new sound. Indeed, there are a number of cuts that remain impressive to the ear four decades on, despite the initial negativity that seemingly emerged from the group themselves, and Gates' instrumental arrangements play heavily in the album's overall construction and sound, utilizing the talents of seasoned session players such as guitarists Larry Carlton and Glen Campbell, bass player Carol Kaye, along with drummers Hal Blaine and Jim Gordon, to the best of his ability.

Opening up with two of the finest collaborations between Royer, Hallinan, and Cohn the album initially suggests a very powerful combination of folk meets '60s pop, with both "Stay Around For The Good Times" and "Turnaway" highlighting the clever vocal patterns that were clearly the quartet's forte. However, what follows is such a diverse collection of songs, performances, and arrangements that the album never really gels cohesively. From a disappointing cover of Van Dyke Parks' joyful "Come To The Sunshine" (a Top 40 hit for Harpers Bizarre that same year) and another self-composed number, "Nursery Rhyme," neither of which manage to maintain the initial impact, through to the closing refrains of the two final group originals, the Stephen Cohn offering "Talk" and the Royer, Cohn, and Hallinan tune "Put It Out Of Your Mind," the album sits uncomfortably, caught in between the varying influences and genres it attempts to envelop. Although, it remains open to debate as to whether the album truly was a mismatch of producer and artist, or simply a misguided concern. The Mamas & The Papas took their East Coast origins and four-part harmonies and California-ized them while The Pleasure Fair chose to stick to the vocal harmonies and clever arrangements of the more traditional folk sound, initially made popular by the likes of Peter, Paul & Mary and The Seekers. The Mamas & The Papas tuned in and sounded "hip" and adventurous; The Pleasure Fair sounded safe and unthreatening, and maybe that was their downfall. Los Angeles in 1967 no longer needed a clean cut, wholesome folk group, regardless of how strong the arrangements really were underneath the rather understated sound.

At some stage during the 1967 recording sessions, or during the subsequent post-release period, and as a clever piece of inner-Universal group marketing, the four-piece made a brief appearance on primetime U.S. TV during an episode of the popular detective series *Ironside*, airing on October 26th. Appearing alongside Don Galloway as Detective Sergeant Ed Brown (the star of the series, Raymond Burr, was not present in this particular scene, nor was the guest appearance from martial arts expert Bruce Lee), the group is filmed through the glass of a recording studio control room, listening to the playback of "Turnaway," nodding heads and swaying along approvingly, with Robb resplendent in dark shades. It was clearly a way of getting the group name into the minds of the watching public, a Universal recording act on a Universal show, and, as if to emphasize a point, the bass drum in the studio, prominently featured, has the name "Pleasure Fair" in bold, bright letters right across it. If anything, the image is actually over-emphasized, and totally unnecessary to the plot, as the group has actually nothing to do with the script whatsoever. Likewise, a freeze frame on the sheet music for the song, with "Turnaway" written clearly along the header, seems a strange and almost superfluous addition to the scene, especially as the track itself was only available on the group's album, and was never in the stores as a single release. Instead, that honor fell to the opening tracks on side two of the album, "Morning Glory Days" b/w "Fade In, Fade Out," although neither was strong enough to achieve radio play, and subsequent success, despite a televised promotional appearance on the series *Pat Boone In Hollywood* to promote the single (resplendent in glorious Technicolor). Nevertheless, with 1967 now drawing to a close, the picture was beginning to form. Robb was becoming increasingly frustrated in his role within The Pleasure Fair.

"Around that time we went over to Levesque's house looking for some grass and he said, 'Well, I don't have any of that but I have this Owsley acid!' Uh-oh," he laughs, "and he gave us some and we hung around, and I saw everything with this incredible clarity. I saw the whole thing. I just went… OK, I hate The Pleasure Fair and I've been afraid to quit that band because of all the time I had invested. Nobody likes me because I'm really angry about being there, and I don't have to be there, because time wasted in the past does not mean time wasted in the future, and my future lies with Jimmy. That's obvious."

The following year was to see the first fruits appear from the new Griffin-Royer songwriting team. In May 1968, Robb signed up alongside James as a part of Snuff Garrett's publishing house, with one of their early collaborations being a song entitled "Together" and, true to the title, this new partnership would together lay the foundation stone towards the formation of a new group – a group for whom the quality of the songwriting was paramount.

And yet 1968 was not without other major notable moments in musical history. The Beatles launched Apple Corps. Jimi Hendrix released his *Electric Ladyland* album. The Beatles, along with Mia Farrow, Mike Love, Donovan, and other friends, traveled to Rishikesh in India to study meditation under the roving eye of Maharishi Mahesh Yogi. David Gilmour joined Pink Floyd. Graham Nash first harmonized with David Crosby and Stephen Stills. Led Zeppelin performed together for the first time, under the name of The New Yardbirds. Creedence Clearwater Revival released their debut album. Elvis Presley performed his Comeback Special for NBC TV. And the best-selling singles releases for that year included such timeless classics as "Hey Jude," "(Sittin' On) The Dock Of The Bay," "Jumping Jack Flash," "(What A) Wonderful World," "Born To Be Wild," and "Mrs. Robinson." It was no longer an era for the lightweight "pop" that had graced the charts over the previous decade. Rock'n'roll music was now getting serious, and progressively heavier. "Rock Music" was the new music... although there was still room for a little bit of sentimentality and cleverly constructed three-minute compositions. It just needed the right composers.

Despite the recent successes that his partnership with Michael Gordon had achieved, James Griffin still harbored ambitions for his own career. As he was later to say: "I was so tired of getting my songs recorded by other people who would miss the point or change the hooks or tempo."[8]

And with his contract with Viva Records still very much alive he took the opportunity to record and release one final single under his own name: the first release to bear the songwriting legend of the James A Griffin-R Wilson Royer combination on the label. "Thank You Love," coupled with "The Light Of Your Mind," appeared as 1968 Viva release V-627, with production credit afforded to James himself, and this release effectively brought the 1960s solo career of James Griffin to an ending. Although Robb Royer seemingly had no involvement with the actual recording of this single, restricting himself to the co-composing credit, this was the last time James would undertake the "solo" role for a number of years.

"Thank You Love," pushed as the lead side of the release, is a fine composition. Very simple in construction, with a bare piano riff as the introduction, it places the lone vocal track prominently to the fore as it gradually builds up the instrumentation, before climaxing with a glorious Beach Boy-esque harmony bridge, and a lovely muted trumpet on the fade. Mature and very well constructed. The same could also be said for the flip side, "The Light Of Your Mind," although the arrangement and production is at the complete opposite end of the scale this time around. Commencing with a brief classical violin introduction, arranged by Al Capps, clearly inspired by the works of Austrian composer Anton Bruckner, James's vocals sit on top of a very sophisticated string arrangement, and the melody twists and turns as it builds up over the accompanying strings and horns. Yet one can now clearly hear the ripeness of the Griffin vocal chords, soon to be adorning familiar melodies the world over, as the rich baritone interchanges with the higher register requirements of this particular composition. It certainly shows off the ambitious nature of the new songwriting partnership, free from commercial restraints, and it laid out the potential boundaries within which they were to develop. And although none of their future works were, perhaps, to be presented in quite such an avant-garde style, it showed that both composers were prepared to take risks, liberated from any traditional songwriting restrictions. If the work doesn't need a bridge or a middle eight, then don't use one.

However, regardless of Robb Royer's feelings towards his current band, and his developing passion for his partnership with James, The Pleasure Fair were still an ongoing concern and, following on from the lack of commercial success the debut *Pleasure Fair* album achieved, the group was keen to issue a new single, featuring two brand new recordings, once again arranged and produced by David Gates.

"We didn't get much reception (with the album), we figured we were too white, so we thought we could fix that by firing Michele and bringing in a black girl singer," says Robb. "We thought she could somehow pour some soul off into us. Michele was about ready to leave anyway so we eased out of that, and I was about ready to ease out of the whole thing but we decided to do just one more.

"We went in (with a new singer) and I was talking with David, I didn't like his process of arranging everything for a sixteen-piece orchestra and putting that on two tracks, and then you're stuck with that. I said, 'David, if we're going to cut this time let's go in and cut like you cut a rock'n'roll record, we have eight-track now.' When we cut the *Pleasure Fair* album it was on four-track, so we had two tracks for the band and then had to bounce a couple of tracks around like they did on *Sergeant Pepper* in order to get enough vocals on that. We pretty much sang that live. I remember there was one part we couldn't get so David came out and sang it; we played with the tracks a little bit but it was mostly two tracks instrumental and two tracks of vocals. But I said I didn't want to do it like that anymore, I said we need to do it like a rock'n'roll record so let's get the drums on a track, put the bass on a track, put two guitars down, and then we'll do the rest of them with vocals and sweetening. We did a song called "(I'm Gonna Have To) Let You Go." Great chords in it, and some of Stephen's best writing. Stephen had started it and brought it to us and Tim and I had finished it up. At that point they put it out and it didn't do very well, and so we were all on our own."

"(I'm Gonna Have To) Let You Go," coupled with "Today," an outing for the Royer-Cohn pairing, saw the new line-up adopt that more soulful vein. Essentially it was an opportunity for Michele's replacement, a talented vocalist also named Michelle (but known as Shelly), to display her talents and integrate into the band, and it was certainly a strong ballad, beautifully performed, with a subtle backing and delicate structure. But perhaps it was not quite strong *enough* to garner the acceptance the band was now surely due. The more familiar sounding flip-side, "Today," maintained a certain ethnic simplicity, although it retained many of the qualities so resplendent on the album, and it saw the group on more comfortable territory. A swirling organ sound, a heavier drumbeat, a simple arrangement, and the familiar vocal blend, but it sadly never really goes anywhere. Which was ultimately the final destination for the group. Nowhere. Despite the revised personnel, and after a two-year lifespan, The Pleasure Fair had run its course. A lack of chart success and a feeling that, despite the more adventurous approach on "(I'm Gonna Have To) Let You Go," they were stuck in a groove that had seen its moment in time, the band parted company. Robb Royer, in particular, had new musical areas to explore and while he retained his connections with Timothy Hallinan, Stephen Cohn relocated to the Venice Beach community and blended into the haze of '68. He would later reappear, as previously noted, to considerable acclaim and success (as would Hallinan as a successful novelist) but their original partner, Michele Cochrane, would simply disappear from view, forging her own path through life – via happiness, tragedy, and contentment – before rediscovering her bandmates over 40 years later, courtesy of the author, during research on this book. Nothing else is known, or remembered, of her brief replacement.

"They were very good to me, but I didn't really open up to them," Michele summarizes on her time with the group. "But at that time I was 23 and I really wanted to pursue musical theater. I remember we were at a rehearsal at Steve's house (at the end) and I think I was just ready to move on. At that time everybody was a writer and I felt that if you were not a writer, just an interpreter, you were looked down on, and I didn't write. I could just sing. But to me, listening to The Pleasure Fair, my voice just wasn't a rock'n'roll voice. I tried so hard to sound like Grace Slick, and Dave Pell at Uni Records was talking to me about maybe starting to smoke so I could get more of a Dionne Warwick sound. But I wanted to have a family and all those normal things. Within six months I was off touring the country in a musical…"

"I only saw her once again," recalled Robb in later years, "that was when Bread was playing at the Whisky-A-Go-Go over Christmas of 1969. She came by with her husband, Murray Roman, who was a comedian. We hadn't hit yet and we were playing the Whisky to a bunch of coke freaks. She was happy then but Murray died a few years after that. We never saw her again..."

"That's not the way I remember it!" laughs Michele today. "I don't even remember Bread being at the Whisky. However, I recall thinking it was so nice that Robb and his wife Anabel came to the Whisky to see Murray perform there! I never saw Bread perform, but I do remember that within a year they had their first golden album and I said 'Gee, all I had to do all those years ago was leave!'"

"I was finally free of The Pleasure Fair," Robb continues, "and that's when David and I started sailing. We would sail a couple of times a week, and the rest of the time I was with Jimmy. And then I took Jimmy over to David's house."

What followed next was a period of musical development for the new partnership of James Griffin and Robb Royer. They continued to write a number of compositions for Viva Records, including one new song that was unsuccessfully pitched as the title track for a forthcoming film, the Ringo Starr vehicle *Candy*, and they continued to develop the mini-rock musical, *The Plastic Sibling*, that had been conceived by Robb and his college friends in Northridge. They would also cross paths on a more frequent basis with David Gates, and gradually develop a formula that would take them beyond working as a duo, taking them into a more marketable area. Yet, before that moment was to arrive, before their acceptance into the commercial market, two more record releases would appear that would explore further areas of their new partnership, pushing the boundaries once more. Both could have come from nowhere else in the musical sphere other than the late 1960s. Both are essential by-products of the era and, due to their lack of success, both would retain the aura and obscurity of the period, and ultimately the valuable rarity status that comes with it.

The first such release is truly notable in that the record label itself, bearing the Dot Records logo, is the very first one to include the three names of Griffin, Royer, and Gates together, albeit with differing credits of producer, arranger, and songwriter. Issued as catalogue number Dot 45-17093, and sandwiched between the equally obscure releases by Nikki Britton ("Live Again," 45-17092) and Jean and Joe ("Don't Shoot Me Down," 45-17094), this valuable item appeared under the collective name of The Curtain Calls, with the two songs shown as "Sock It To Me Sunshine" and "Say What You See." This was the result of a number of projects that James was handling for Snuff Garrett, and he subsequently brought in his new partner Robb, and then David, to assist on this particular one.

"I was obviously the tie between Jimmy and David," claims Royer today. "On The Curtain Calls I got Jimmy to hire David on that."

Listening to the two songs now, it is clearly apparent that neither Griffin, Royer, or Gates offer any significant vocal contributions to these recordings, and were more than likely never in the studio all at the same time. The names of Stan Jay, Merryl Joy, and Garry Lynn are listed as the three Curtain Calls "group" members (Lynn is mistakenly listed as both Carry and Garry on alternate sides), although the obvious novelty approach to the recordings, specifically with the A-side, "Sock It To Me Sunshine," clearly link them with the 1960s American comedy shows, *Laugh-In* and *The Beautiful Phyllis Diller Show*, from where these three singer/actor/comedians made their collective name. With James A. Griffin taking the production credit and David Gates listed as arranger, this single was presumably released as a gimmick for the novelty act, probably intended to gain popularity among the notably high viewing figures that the former show attracted, and from where the "sock it to me" phrase originated (although that, in itself, came courtesy of the Aretha Franklin hit "Respect"). The trio had initially appeared during the first season of *Laugh-In* (aired on April 15th, 1968), dressed as flowers, and were subsequently renamed by the TV series as The Morning Glories (a subtle link between the flower of the same name, and hallucinogenic favorite of many of the "in-crowd"). They followed this, still using the "Curtain Calls" name, with a stint on the short-lived series (running for just 12 episodes during the fall/winter of 1968) featuring Phyllis Diller, herself an American comedic institution during this period. Unfortunately, like its predecessor, *The Phyllis Diller Show* (not quite so "beautiful"), this particular series failed to catch on with the *Laugh-In* crowd it was so clearly intended for, and The Curtain Calls, as a television act, ended there.

"Sock It To Me Sunshine," composed by Mac Davis, Bob Lind, and Freddy Weller, is a catchy little number, complete with comedic falsetto-styled vocals (not dissimilar to the somewhat surprisingly successful approach of Tiny Tim), performed over the top of a music-hall, banjo-themed backing track, topped off with various whistles and cymbals, and totally unlike any other production that Griffin or Gates had attempted before. However, from a Bread-perspective, it is side two of the single that deserves the greater attention, coming as it does with the added bonus of the songwriting credits afforded to Robb Royer and Tim "Speed" Hallinan. "Say What You See" could so easily have come from the earlier Pleasure Fair songwriting sessions, as the melody retains the same balance and structure that made Robb and Tim's former band so distinctive. However, according to Royer:

"Tim and I had written that song because we had a writing deal with the Charlie Koppleman and Don Rubin publishing team, and we had gotten these few cuts, but no hits as Koppleman-Rubin writers. Tim was never actually at the Curtain Calls sessions, but it was a song we had written and Jimmy liked, so we cut it. Jimmy brought me in and I helped him with the arrangement on the session a little bit. I was sort of a cheerleader and provided the song for him."

Unfortunately, the vocal abilities of Merryl Joy, and the accompanying harmonies of Jay and Lynn, are by no means comparable with the smooth feel of Michele Cochrane's delicate tone and pitch, and despite the performance, production, and arrangement being near faultless, the attempt at a serious vocal approach on this track leaves the overall sound floundering. It is a lovely song, and as a relevant artifact in the pre-Bread story this is as important as it can get, but on a purely musical level it is sadly not on a par with the later combined works of Griffin, Royer, and Gates.

The second single to appear that year, with equal claim to be one of the rarest releases in the Bread catalog, appeared on the Warner Brothers label and was actually credited to The Morning Glories. This reportedly featured the same trio of Joy, Jay, and Lynn that had featured on the previous single, albeit this time utilizing the secondary name afforded to them by the television executives at NBC. The two featured songs on this release were titled "Love-In" and "You're So Young," and both were real period pieces; the hands of time stuck in the groove of a 1968 Californian summer. Flowers, beads, love, and hallucinogenics...

"Love-In" was composed by James Griffin, along with two previously unheard of songwriters by the names of TX Farthingsworth XIV and Eddie LeBlanc. However, in a bizarre twist, James had not really found himself another series of new songwriting partners, for in reality these were none other than Robb Royer and Tim Hallinan, working under pseudonyms.

Robb: "Believe it or not, you couldn't be a BMI writer and write with an ASCAP writer. That was just Tim's joke name for himself and mine to allow us all to work together."

This wasn't actually the first time that the name of TX Farthingsworth XIV had appeared, as June of the previous year had seen the registration of one of the earliest Griffin-Royer compositions, "A Violent Crime," as featured on the *Beethoven Soul* album, with the credits once again listed to James A. Griffin and TX Farthingsworth XIV. However, "Love-In" was to be the first single outing for the pseudonym.

The song is a fantastic slice of psychedelic pop, yet one destined to join the hundreds of other recordings from the genre, lost in the mists of a post-flower power generation. Had this appeared during the summer of love, one year before, as had benefited such anthemic compositions as Scott McKenzie's "San Francisco (Be Sure To Wear Flowers In Your Hair)" or the Flowerpot Men's "(Let's Go To) San Francisco," then we could so easily have been talking "hit single," such was the successful way that this song brings the images and sounds of the period to light. From the brass instrumental introduction, through the "groovy" references to Piccadilly Square, paisley fantasies, weaving braids, and painting flowers, it's all captured within the two-minutes forty-second timeframe. It really does do as it promises: it takes you directly to the love-in. But sadly, by 1968, much of the original "love" crowd were too far gone to notice this slice of near-pop perfection. They were far too busy being busy, and it just wasn't the right time anymore; which is sad, for, in comparison with their previous vocal efforts, the singing trio, if indeed it was them on this track, turns in a fine performance. But was it *really* them? It could so easily be James himself.

"You're So Young," featuring on the flip side of the single, was a far darker recording. Moody, bluesy, and with a slightly disturbing lyrical content: waiting for the "little girl" to grow up while "he" waits for her ("so while you play with teddy darlin', I'll be here and ready…"), and with a slightly confusing history to go alongside. James clearly provided the lead vocals on the track, with no evidence to suggest any involvement at all from the Curtain Calls/Morning Glories threesome, and the songwriting credits were shared among James, his former writing partner Michael Gordon, and one of the Oklahoma musicians that had arrived on the scene courtesy of Leon Russell's Hollywood house parties.

John Weldon Cale, known as JJ, had ventured west to the golden coastline along with a number of fellow musicians from his hometown of Tulsa. Having hitched up with fellow Okie Leon Russell, Cale had slowly begun to make his own mark on the L.A. recording scene, and his recognizable fretwork was featured on a number of sessions and releases from the period. One of these sessions had resulted in an album credited to The Leathercoated Minds, a mind-blowing moniker if ever there was one, although there was no actual group performing, or even existing, under this inspiring name. Producer Snuff Garrett reportedly put together this album, *A Trip Down The Sunset Strip*, a true concept release, supposedly giving the clueless wannabe a musical idea as to what Hollywood's infamous strip was like on a typical L.A. night. The sounds, the music, the "vibe."

However, in reality, the music featured was simply a number of reasonable rehashes of some of the drug-culture hits of the day, notably "Eight Miles High," "Kicks," "Along Comes Mary," and "Psychotic Reaction," performed mostly by the established Oklahoma crew, including vocalist Roger Tillison, Leon Russell, and drummer Jimmy Karstein. These were then overdubbed with some of Cale's guitar picking, and topped off with a tab of psychedelia randomly layered on the surface. Garrett and Cale also added a few instrumental recordings into the mix, including a bizarre take/toke on "Puff (The Magic Dragon)," and hey, there you go, the trip is complete. However, when you realize that Garrett had actually chosen the photograph that adorned the front sleeve *before* the music was recorded, you surely must wonder as to his priorities. We've got a great picture, now just get some music to match!

One of those instrumental tracks, featuring a lone composing credit to Cale himself, was a number entitled "Sunset And Clark," a track dominated by some fine interweaving guitar work. Yet, this is where the Morning Glories release comes into play, for James Griffin seemingly took the instrumental track directly from the Garrett sessions, with no additional work, and overdubbed a vocal, "You're So Young," over the top of the existing take. Assuming Cale had approval of the move, then one has to assume that the Cale/Garrett axis also played some role in the release but, to confuse the situation further, James's former partner, Michael Gordon, reveals:

"'You're So Young' was a song that Jimmy and I composed when we were writing together. I wasn't aware of the other JJ composition until now so I suppose he just put his name on it. That was very common in those days."[10] Thus confirming that it was, in fact, originally a Griffin-Gordon composition and Cale was clearly taking some additional liberties by way of adding his name to the composing credits, or even more blatantly by taking full credit on the Leathercoated Minds' version. It may well have been due to the necessary musical arrangements Cale may have made for inclusion on the album, but Robb Royer elucidates further over the situation with Garrett:

"I remember the song 'You're So Young,' and my version was that it was a Griffin-Gordon song, and what I think happened there was that Snuff had some sort of deal with JJ, like he had a deal with Leon. I think they were all contractually together, and JJ was probably instructed to cut it, the Griffin-Gordon song, because Snuff had the publishing on it, to push the duo."

Whatever the facts may be, so obscure is the original vinyl version of "Love-In" today, with surviving copies so few and far between, that this now stands as one of the primo nuggets in the Bread collectors' circle.

Nevertheless, by this stage, strong bonds were forming in the relationships of this ever-changing circle of musicians. Three people in particular were now very keen to commence working together, perhaps sensing that the united strength of the trio would be beneficial to their developing careers, perhaps sensing, as they combined their acoustic guitars and their harmonies, that this was truly something special. All three had proven their worth in the studios and with their songwriting skills to date, but the more they began spending time in each others' company the stronger the sense came that, as a trio, the potential for greater things was just waiting to happen...

Chapter Three

Tryin' To Be Someone

David Ashworth Gates arrived in the world on December 11th, 1940. Born in the city of Tulsa, home to the second largest population in the state of Oklahoma, David's parents were both musically inclined and right from his early years the youngster was exposed to the musical surroundings in the family home. His father, Clarence Gates, was a band and orchestra director of public schools, and his mother a piano teacher. Both were encouraging of their son's abilities, and of those of his two older brothers and one sister, so much so that by the age of five the young David and his siblings were all indulging in one musical form or another. His father was also responsible for writing out charts and transposing work in his role as schools director, as well as writing for himself, and his young son often used to lean over his shoulder, watching and learning, as he scribbled out the notes on the sheets before him. His mother would later recall him sitting in front of the family phonograph, as close to the speaker as he could get, playing classical records over and over. "He played Ravel's 'Bolero' so many times I thought I would go crazy!" she would say. "But I should have known he was going somewhere in music when I put him in his first recital. David was only two and a half years old, but he stood on stage and sang without accompaniment, without ever straying from pitch."

David was soon studying violin from the concert master of the Tulsa Philharmonic, and before long he was equally proficient on both piano and guitar, although initially his father had introduced him to the ukulele, seeing that his hands were too small to grip the neck of the guitar. Within a matter of weeks he was entertaining anybody who would listen.

"I grew up listening to classical music," he recalled in conversation with *Record Collector* magazine during 1997, "like Ravel, Debussy, and Beethoven, but in my teens I discovered rock'n'roll. I always loved Chuck Berry because he wrote great lyrics which were so well crafted."

For the next few years his interest never waned and by the time he enrolled in Tulsa's Will Rogers High School the initial rock'n'roll boom was in full swing. Despite his involvement at the school as choir president, orchestra officer, varsity cheerleader, and guitarist for the school dance band (The Metronomes), the new music of Berry, Buddy Holly, and Little Richard had fully turned the ears of the musical protégé. Furthermore, individual songs by artists in the mold of The Penguins and The Crew-Cuts encouraged David and his friends that, just maybe, they could form a band themselves and recreate much of the music they were hearing on the radio. One other musician in particular that caught the attention of David was guitarist James Burton, as David was later to remember:

"We all loved James Burton. He played on Ricky Nelson's songs. We would wait for the next Ricky Nelson album so we could hear James's solo. He was probably more idolized than Chuck Berry and his licks, but I decided early on that I'd rather write songs than spend time practicing the guitar. I never was that good at lead guitar!"[9]

Sure enough, David and his classmates began hanging out together after school, and before long they had formed a band and were playing at various local hops and high school dances, the highlight of which was during 1957 when legendary rock'n'rollers Chuck Berry, already the possessor of numerous Hot 100 and R&B Top 10 smashes, Carl Perkins, Gene Vincent, and Johnny Burnette came to Tulsa at various stages to perform. David and his bandmates, with interchanging line-ups, received the prestigious honor of supplying backup to these great musicians and vocalists, the first taste that David had of a real rock'n'roll lifestyle.

"That made a long-lasting impression," he was to remember. "There were about six or seven pretty good musicians floating around town. We got the job of playing behind Chuck Berry. We were all nervous as hell when we met him. He wanted to hear us, so we played a few of our own songs, but he said he wanted us to play his things, so I sang 'Maybellene,' 'Roll Over Beethoven,' and 'Too Much Monkey Business.' On the third one he joined in, and afterwards he reckoned that we'd sung a verse to 'Roll Over Beethoven' that he'd forgotten. We were note perfect on all of his songs, but when it came to the show he didn't want our lead guitarist to play. I suppose he didn't want the competition."[11 13 25]

This group of youngsters, a number of whom were now calling themselves The Accents, played mostly cover material but two compositions that David had written himself were beginning to get a good response during a number of the local shows, and so the band went into hock, taped the songs at a local recording studio, and had 500 copies pressed up. Issued on Perspective Sound Records, a small independent Tulsa-based label owned by a Sonny Gray, catalogue number 121057500 (it has been suggested this may refer to the actual recording date), the two songs in question were "Jo-Baby," written for a young lady at school who was the focus of David's attention, and "Lovin' At Night." The single achieved some local airplay and sold so well that they pressed 500 more, and then ordered a third batch.

"We stopped there. We had sold 1500 copies and had made fifteen bucks apiece (but) it really worked out great," he later said in an interview. "It became an overnight local hit and, of course, everyone in school knew who it (the A-side) was written for. The final straw came when she was at a dance with her old boyfriend and someone put on 'Jo-Baby.' What a moment… he soon gave up."

Early Accents line-up, with David, Don Kimmel, Gerald Goodwin, and Russell Bridges

The label lists the artists solely as The Accents, although the line "vocals by David Gates" appears in smaller print underneath, clearly suggesting who was the principal member of this core of musicians. One other musician on the session, albeit without credit, was fellow Tulsa resident and piano player Russell Bridges, himself a Will Rogers student, although one year younger than David. This release was the second of three records issued on the Perspective Sound label during this period, and although no information is forthcoming as to the full details of the first of the releases ("Cherry Pie" b/w "Always Be True," credited to the Tri-Lads and also issued during 1957), David himself would be responsible for the third and final offering the following year.

"Jo-Baby" starts with a simple piano progression, chords that would grace a dozen or so similar doo-wop recordings over the next year or so, but once David's lead vocals commence the song takes on a whole new light. For someone so young – this was recorded the day before his seventeenth birthday if the catalog reference number is to be believed – this is an extremely mature performance, with the distinctive soft quality of his voice and the lyrical phrasing gliding effortlessly across the composition. The instrumental track itself remains basic throughout, bar the tinkling flourish of Bridges' piano at the end, and yet it stands as a typical example of the early doo-wop era, but what is important to note is that it precedes the monumental successes that were to follow for The Teddy Bears' "To Know Him Is To Love Him," The Skyliners' "If I Can't Have You," and The Flamingos' recording of "I Only Have Eyes For You." It never achieved much recognition at the time, restricted to the limited pressing of such a small label, but fifty years on and one can clearly see how influential it could have been.

By comparison, "Lovin' At Night" is a more upbeat, raw rockabilly number with a touch of Buddy Holly running throughout, but such is the poor quality of the recording that it loses any true appeal in the process. Nevertheless, the release would surely have offered encouragement to the musicians, Gates and Bridges in particular, and this was only the beginning.

The following year David enrolled at the University of Oklahoma, majoring in English and becoming a member of the Delta Tau Delta fraternity and the Vikings social club, although he later intended to transfer to the nearer University of Tulsa, situated just a short drive from the family home at 1202 South Delaware Place. He also married his sweetheart Jo Rita Miller, a graduate of Tulsa's Central High School, on June 12th that year, exchanging vows in Coweta, a short distance beyond the city limits. Over the next two years he was to gain considerable experience performing around the nightclubs and fraternity parties of Tulsa and the surrounding regions, while also building on his songwriting and recording catalog. Five more singles were to appear between 1958 and 1961, all released on a variety of labels, all destined for relative obscurity outside the confines of his home city, and yet experience counts for a great deal and the lack of success only spurred the talented musician further towards his goal. His nightclub work also brought home a meager wage, but every cent brought home was a help to his family as not only was his wife now living under the Gates' family roof, but the addition of two small children, Ricky and Angelyn, over that period also added to the pressure to succeed.

The second single release, "Pretty Baby (I Saw You Last Night)" b/w "Crying For You," again appearing on the Perspective Sound label, was issued in May of 1958, although this time around neither song was composed by David nor, in fact, did his name appear anywhere on the label. Credited to The Vibes, featuring vocals by Ronnie Franklin, these two compositions were both written by Hugh Whitlow, founder of Wheel Records (another Oklahoma independent label). Whitlow was slightly older than his fellow Tulsa musicians, who viewed the songwriter as an influential figure among them, and several were often to be found around his house, soaking up the atmosphere. This particular group of young musicians, Gates and Bridges included, were the basis of what was later to become known as "The Tulsa Sound": essentially a combination of the various influences around at the time – rockabilly, blues, and raw rock'n'roll – and it was taken to heart by the many local musicians and singers and developed into their own style of performing. Vocalists such as Jack Dunham, Bobby Taylor, Jack Thurmon, Jimmy Markham, Roger Tillison, and Flash Terry were the heart of the sound, but the true "soul" came from a conglomeration of various musicians also added to the mix. Fellow Accents such as Tommy Crook, Jimmy Karstein, Carl Radle, and Russell Bridges, along with George Metzel, Chuck Blackwell, Johnny Williams, Buddy Jones, Bill Boatman,

JJ Cale, Rocky "Curtis" Frisco, and Doug Cunningham were all essential figures in the overall sound of late '50s Tulsa, as was the dual role that vocalist and musician David Gates added.

"Pretty Baby (I Saw You Last Night)," as composed by Whitlow, was a real rockabilly number, shallow in production but high on enthusiasm, complete with guttural scream during the guitar break, and despite the vocals credits being afforded to Ronnie Franklin, this was clearly none other than David Gates singing under a pseudonym. In comparison to the great many other rock'n'roll compositions being recorded during this productive period, it never really stood a chance of getting airplay among the masses, the limited distribution of Perspective Sound also hindering the quest, but as a stepping stone it certainly showed that these Tulsa youngsters could rock.

As a contrast, "Crying For You" is but a tepid, repetitious ballad, and is no more than a throwaway in commercial terms, which is ultimately perhaps what David Gates himself was thinking at the time, as shortly afterwards, on July 14th, 1958, "Jo-Baby" and the accompanying "Lovin' At Night" were picked up again and re-issued via a bigger label with more widespread distribution. Robbins Records, based in Nashville, Tennessee, and founded by legendary country artist Marty Robbins, issued The Accents' recordings, this time credited to Dave Gates and the Accents. Notably, the matrix numbers of the disc labels suggest that "Lovin' At Night," perhaps more in line with the country-feel of Robbins Records' homeland, was being pushed as the lead-side but, sadly, it still went largely nowhere.

David's final single of the 1950s arrived on February 9th, 1959, and for the third time it appeared on a new independent label, this time on East-West Records based in New York City. As to who provided the backing remains unclear, and there are certainly no indications that any of his former band The Accents make an appearance, although one has to assume that he was still socializing within the same circles, and one didn't dismiss easily the talented crew that David had been working with to date. Issued as 45-EW123, this featured the first credit to David Gates as the solo performer, and both sides of the release featured self-composed tracks. The lead side was "Swingin' Baby Doll," while the flip went under the title of "Walkin' And Talkin'," and the February 9th, 1959, edition of *Billboard* magazine even gave space to the single, giving both sides a credible three-star review and adding that it was an "exuberant rockabilly" recording and that the "lad has a sound and merits exposure..."

"It never did anything," David later recalled during an interview with *Discoveries* magazine. "It was kind of an early stab at rock'n'roll. It's kind of fun, but it's not great!"[11]

"Swingin' Baby Doll" establishes a real Buddy Holly rhythm throughout, and even David's vocals maintain a hint of Buddy in the delivery, while the accompanying tune combines the drive of Jerry Lee Lewis with the solid foundation of Fats Domino. It seems apparent that David was absorbing all of the influences that came his way during that heady period and 1959 was certainly not short of inspirational offerings: "Stagger Lee," "La Bamba," "Raining In My Heart," "Mack The Knife," "Poison Ivy," "Sea Cruise."

With the start of the new decade, the 1960s, a new spirit of optimism began spreading across the United States of America. John F. Kennedy declared his intentions to run for the Oval Office, Japan and the U.S. signed the treaty of mutual cooperation, Cassius Clay won the gold medal at the summer Olympics, President Dwight Eisenhower signed the Civil Rights Act, and the king of rock'n'roll, Elvis Aaron Presley, returned home to U.S. soil after a two-year stint serving his country in the army.

1960 also saw the first of the "Tulsa Sound" musicians spreading their wings. Popular vocalist Jumpin' Jack Dunham was the first to begin the migration west to Los Angeles, keen to break away from the restrictions of home, to visit the land of opportunism, and within a few short months others were to follow. The voyage was underway. It would take another year before the young David Gates would make his move west, time enough to sign up with yet another recording label, the newly formed Mala Records, a subsidiary of the larger Bell Records, and time enough for three more single releases.

Mala 413 was David's first offering of the year, featuring the song "What's This I Hear," coupled with "You'll Be My Baby," both Gates originals. This was followed shortly afterwards by "The Happiest Man Alive," penned by Bobby Stevenson, with "The Road That Leads To Love," written by influential rhythm and blues collaborators Billy Dawn Smith and Bert Keyes, on the reverse (Mala 418). Keyes himself was a successful producer and arranger, assisting David with the arrangements on the latter release, and was later to play a significant factor in the development and success of the New York music scene. Both of these early releases on Mala featured David offering up a variety of styles, with "You'll Be My Baby" being another polished piece of rockin' Buddy Holly interpretation, all pounding keys and driving bass, while the gospel influenced "What's This I Hear" bears a distinct similarity to the doo-wop simplicity of "Jo-Baby" from three years previous.

By contrast "The Happiest Man Alive" is the first indication that David was prepared to take any route to success, jumping aboard the increasingly popular Neil Sedaka bandwagon, who was himself experiencing the delights of a newly found popularity within the industry. The sheer exuberance of the bouncy, middle-of-the-road Bert Keyes arrangement, complete with female bops and shoo-wops chiming along in the background, is one that David sounds notably comfortable with, and over the next few years, further examples of this easy listening, orchestrated sound would permeate through both his own works and of those whom he worked alongside. "The Road That Leads To Love" also maintains a similar approach in the arrangement, although the song itself, a ballad featuring David doubling up on some wonderful Everly Brothers-styled harmonies, keeps him in more familiar territory. Yet, it is apparent in this release alone, how the influential sounds of the early rock'n'roll recordings in his music were on the wane, and it all too clearly indicates the direction and easy listening audience that the young performer was now attempting to reach out to, an audience for whom at present he was an unknown quantity, but one that would ultimately be matched to perfection.

However, David wasn't yet quite prepared to leave his early leanings behind, for his third and final release on the label saw him revisit and subsequently re-record his very first single, the gentle lilting doo-wop anthem dedicated to his now-wife, Jo Rita Gates, this time backed with a brand new composition, "Teardrops In My Heart," both produced by Buddy Smith. With a slicker production, and a suitable string accompaniment, David once again whimsically extols the virtue of his childhood sweetheart, and yet it was almost too late to reconsider the true credentials of the composition. The previous release, "The Happiest Man Alive" had shown where the current music scene was going, for better or for worse, delving into a brighter, poppier world where vocals and strings would softly collide in a Frankie Avalon-driven fantasyland of candy floss and bobby sox. By 1961, doo-wop was definitely out. The accompanying side is a first for David, venturing nicely into a soulful jazz theme, and is a further example of the many styles that he was absorbing into his accumulating repertoire. Needless to say, despite the promise all these recordings had to offer, and the adventurous diversion of styles, none of these releases on Mala achieved any notable success and with bills to pay, mouths to feed, new areas of exploration had to be found, and the road out of Oklahoma – Route 66 – was beckoning.

At the climax of the junior year of college, with the summer vacation looming, David made the decision to expand his musical horizons. His grades were slipping, and he was fast losing interest in continuing his studies. The music bug had bitten deep. With his parents' reluctant blessing – two years to give it a shot or back to college – he planned his future out before them. In July of 1961 David made a trip out to California on his own and lined up some work. Then, upon returning to Tulsa, he loaded his young family into an old Cadillac he'd bought off an associate of his father, and with $200 in his pocket, he drove across the borderline once more, westward-bound.

"The reason I moved to Los Angeles from Oklahoma... I'd gone about as far in music as you can go in Tulsa. There's not much to do there, you know. You work clubs and play dances and fraternity parties and so forth, and I wanted to go to Los Angeles where all the action was and try my hand as a musician and songwriter. My main focus was really to become involved right in the middle of the music scene if I could possibly write songs. You know, the movie and television industry were there, Las Vegas was close and Reno, Tahoe, that whole circuit. So I had eyes to play some live performances, to get into the clubs, to write, produce, anything

I could. I just loved music and I could read and write music which gave me a bit of a leg up on a lot of the guys who were there that were good players but they couldn't read or write.

"I had a nightclub job waiting because of some friends who had already made the trip from Oklahoma before me. I go out there, and on my third night in the club we got fired and the $200 is gone. The first month's rent, gas deposit, phone deposit, groceries, and nobody around to help me except my uncle who lived in Whittier. He couldn't give me any money, but he brought me food. We drove from club to club, three a night, auditioned for everybody until we finally got a job and got rolling again."[9]

A tough introduction to life in the golden state, but he wasn't the only one with the vision of stardom in his eyes, and a succession of fellow-minded Oklahomans followed suit over the coming months (the "Oklahoma Mafia" as they were to be called by local Los Angeles musicians). Former member of The Accents, Russell Bridges (soon to adopt the stage name of Leon Russell), also made the 1,400-mile journey, initially to pursue a career in advertising but the music soon followed, as did drummer Chuck Blackwell, guitarist JJ Cale, and bassist Carl Radle. The road was paved with opportunity, or so they were led to believe.

On Saturday nights, after the clubs had shut, young musicians from all over the vast city would meet at a place called the Crossbow, situated in the San Fernando Valley, and it was here that David first met aspiring and equally talented musicians such as saxophonist and arranger Steve Douglas, and guitarists Glen Campbell, James Burton, and Jerry Cole. He also found himself once again meeting up with new arrivals in town such as Russell and Blackwell. Slowly, this band of like-minded brothers began getting themselves into the potentially lucrative Los Angeles recording industry, mostly via demo sessions, but also, if they were fortunate, some union jobs. By hanging out and jamming with these people, David soon found himself getting more work.

"I ran into some good people pretty quick and got to work on recordings doing some arrangements, writing a few songs, playing piano, and so on. I could do a lot of different things to make a living! My father always said, 'You can do music as a hobby, but it is hard to make a living at it.'"[9]

Certainly, his ability to score sheets was a bonus in the city, where up-and-coming songwriters were aplenty, but true musical capability was limited. "A lot of songwriters could not put down on paper the songs they had written, and they couldn't copyright them unless they did. So I would take their songs, and their tapes, and go home and write out a lead sheet that they could then copyright. And I also did some early arranging, you know, for brass and strings and stuff, which enabled me to have enough income. There was nobody in L.A. at that time, really, that had a feel for country and rock'n'roll, who could read and write music. So I had this little niche of my own."[11] The recently arrived talents of both Gates and Russell were also noticed by session vocalist Ron Hicklin, as he recalled in a 1992 interview with Australian researcher Stephen J. McParland: "Leon had come into town with David Gates. They were partners but completely different people. David is a buttoned-up writer who scores everything and Leon is a God-given church organ player. For him it's all feel. I did vocal work for both of them. So many people had come from every place to try to get something going."

One of the first projects that David found himself involved with after arriving in L.A., alongside both Glen Campbell and Leon Russell, was recording a series of studio demos for songwriter Sharon Sheeley. A successful composer in her own right, Sheeley had achieved considerable success during the previous decade, following up her #1 *Billboard* chart-topper "Poor Little Fool" (recorded by Ricky Nelson) with the unforgettable Eddie Cochran anthem, "Somethin' Else," co-composed with Cochran's elder brother Tom. By the time the decade had turned, Eddie and Sharon had started a relationship together, and were reportedly due to announce their forthcoming engagement when, during a tour of the U.K. in April 1960, they were involved in a tragic automobile accident, that claimed the life of the young rock'n'roll star. Once she had recovered from her own potentially life-threatening injuries, Sheeley returned to Los Angeles to resume her interrupted career, and these sessions, featuring David on bass guitar, were the results of her liaison with Metric Music, the publishing company representing her work, who were keen to shop the new compositions around. Listening to these demos today, almost half a century later, it's immediately apparent how "complete" a number of them sound. Quality productions, with polished harmonies and instrumental backing intact, they could almost be deemed as studio masters themselves, and with vocalists James Marcus Smith and Glen Campbell included, the latter providing some of his earliest studio vocal work, these remain prized additions to the Gates catalog, although David's own contributions are noticeably minimal to the overall sound.

However, these sessions would ultimately lead to further studio work, proof that word of mouth did circulate around the industry and benefit many, notably so when Liberty Records ultimately released the first single by session vocalist James Marcus Smith, who had recently rechristened himself P. J. Proby, at the suggestion of Sheeley herself. The songs featured on this release (Liberty 55367) were "Try To Forget Her" and "There Stands The One." As accompaniment on the recordings Proby was supported by a number of the upcoming "Crossbow" crowd, including colleagues from the earlier demo tracks, with Glen Campbell providing guitar, Leon Russell on keyboards (still listed with his given surname on AFM sheets and label credits during this period), and David Gates on bass. Established performers such as drummer Hal Blaine and the Johnny Mann Singers filled out the sound, and although the record failed to break nationally, supposedly due to a lack of promotional support, it kept the ball rolling, and the demand for the obvious talents of these young musicians increased.

Reportedly, at this early stage of their Californian adventure, both Gates and Russell were living in the same property, a large house on Canyon Drive situated to the north of Sunset Boulevard. Yet, with David's young family in tow, it seemed unlikely that this arrangement would last long, although their musical partnership was to continue for a further year or so. The primary focus for David during these years was his ability in providing arrangements and lead sheets for studio sessions and, although musical session work, particularly at union scale, would assist with the rent and bills, it was his talents behind the scenes that were to build up his initial reputation as a gun for hire. His proven ability as a songwriter however, would also prove beneficial to his standing in the community. He would later recall:

"I started playing on some demos for Screen Gems, for Jackie DeShannon and Randy Newman. They were writing for Screen Gems and Aldon Music, and I was doing some lead sheets, as well as playing guitar on their demos, and I began to see how the process worked. I needed a little supplementary income, so I went to them and said, 'I'd like to be a staff writer for you guys.' They knew me anyway, I was playing demos for them, and I could live on that hundred dollars a week that I got in those days. It was just a natural progression.[11]

"As for arranging and production techniques, I learned from Ken Nelson, who was a country producer of Buck Owens and Merle Haggard, to keep it simple. He believed very strongly in that. Don't cover up your really good song, keep your background simple, don't distract the listener from what you want them to hear – the music and the lyrics, or a particularly good vocal performance. If you've got a good, beautiful song, just kind of stay out of the way. Some of the artists I worked with were really outstanding singers and musicians, but I never wrote with any of them. I'd learn little things from them as they were working in the studio."[9]

The following year would start to see a flow of regular studio work coming in, and the Oklahoma crew would also find a firm residency in one of the city's principal clubs of the area. Situated at 8118 Sunset Boulevard, on the intersection of Crescent Heights and Sunset, the relatively small Pandora's Box was at the gateway to the Sunset Strip night life, and while, according to music author and sixties historian Dominic Priore in his wonderfully detailed and informative *Riot On Sunset Strip* (Jawbone Press 2007), it held no comparable claim to fame like the neighboring Whisky-A-Go-Go, Ciro's, or the Hullabaloo, its prominent location made it the first notable landmark that came into view as you headed onto the strip from downtown Hollywood. To some it wasn't a particularly prestigious place to play – it was in a weird location, situated in the middle of the intersection on a small traffic island, and it seemingly had no age restriction policy – and to these select few it wasn't seen as a "hip" place to be, but to countless others, this bright purple and orange building, initially launched as a jazz joint back in 1954, was deemed as a home where dreams could be fulfilled, and where nobody was excluded. A local KRLA disc jockey named Jimmy O'Neill had purchased the club at the start of 1962, and had turned it into a thriving teen bar. Perhaps its most notable moment, certainly the one that has held the legend of the club alive for such a lengthy period of history, came in late October that year when The Beach Boys, hot on the success of their "Surfin' Safari" *Billboard* success, held down a brief residency on the tiny stage, and leader Brian Wilson managed to spill a hot chocolate down the blouse of a young 14-year-old girl in the audience, who would ultimately go on to become his first wife.

Appearing under the collective name of The Fencemen, David Gates, Leon Russell, and Chuck Blackwell held down their placement as the house band at Pandora's Box during the same period that The Beach Boys appeared there, maintaining the booking for virtually a full twelve month period. Although the complete details of how the residency was agreed upon remain undocumented, suggestions would indicate that connections with O'Neill's new girlfriend, and soon-to-be wife, songwriter Sharon Sheeley, would certainly have assisted. Alternating their daily session work with the evening club residency undoubtedly honed their chops for both studio work and paying gigs, and while other musicians have been listed as appearing as a part of this loose aggregation of performers, the core of the band were these three seasoned Oklahoma natives. Reportedly, they often brought along "guest" singers and musicians with whom they had been working during the daily studio hours, and the intimate setting would occasionally play host to the more established names such as Jan and Dean, Jackie DeShannon, or Lou Rawls. The success of their position, and the new friendship with club owner O'Neill, was once again to lead them on to pastures new, and shortly before the end of the year they found themselves in a large TV studio rented from CBS, supplying arrangements and accompaniment on a new television pilot for NBC, produced by legendary U.K. promoter Jack "Oh Boy" Good. Good himself had heard of David's emerging talent, and had asked specifically for him to assist with the arrangements on the show which, initially titled *Young America Swings The World*, featured a host of young singers and performers, including P. J. Proby, Jackie DeShannon, The Blossoms, James Burton, Bobby Sherman, and Donna Loren. In addition to David's arranging responsibilities, The Fencemen appeared in a similar role to that which they populated nightly at Pandora's Box – the house band. It would take almost two years before the pilot show was developed into a fully-fledged national phenomenon, but when it did take off, with Jimmy O'Neill acting as MC, it would take some members of The Fencemen along for the ride. The finished article? *Shindig!* Alas, David would find himself occupied elsewhere by the time the show finally did arrive on national television, and he was not destined to be a part of this moment in TV history...

However, as of 1962, this was all still a long way off, and with the growing demand for his services, David Gates was to find himself entering an impressively productive period of his life. Not only was he busy with supplying sheets and arrangements for other artists in the recording studio, along with offering his services as multi-instrumentalist for hire, he was also starting to see his own compositions being taken up around the city, as well as maintaining his own desire for personal recording success. One of the first artists to benefit from a David Gates composition was former Memphis resident and rockabilly pioneer Johnny Burnette.

Burnette was now pursuing a relatively successful solo career, having parted company for a second time with his brother Dorsey, but by 1962 the brief run of hits he had achieved had started to show signs of drying up. "The Fool Of The Year," as composed by David Gates in partnership with session player Jo Osborn and the singer himself, was to be one of the last releases Burnette made with Liberty Records before he changed labels and attempted to resurrect his ailing career.

"He was the first major artist to record one of my songs after I got to L.A.," David would remember in his interview with *Discoveries* magazine. "It didn't hit, you know, but it was a nice record. He did a good job. Of course, I happened to be pretty excited."[11]

The song was recorded at a session held at United Recordings along Sunset Boulevard on March 26th, 1962, and is another prime example of the heavily orchestrated pop single so prominent of the time. David doesn't appear to have been involved in the actual session itself, nor a subsequent session three months later when Burnette attempted another Gates original, "I Just Called Up To Say Goodbye," and sadly neither recording was to push Burnette back into the charts. Indeed, despite a third attempt at working with David Gates two years later, this final time with David leading the arrangements in the studio during a March 1964 session held at Capitol, his subsequent career was never to recover, and he was never to reclaim his place in the spotlight – until his death, in the summer of 1964, in a tragic boating accident, made headline news. Also of interest is the fact that Johnny's estranged brother, Dorsey, also made a recording of one of David Gates' compositions, taping a rendition of "Pebbles" during April of the following year (1963).

The unsuccessful 1962 recording by Johnny Burnette was followed shortly afterwards by other tapings of Gates originals. These included The Fleetwoods performing the enchanting ballad "My Special Lover," Johnny Crawford's "No-One Really Loves A Clown" (the flip-side of his November 1962 Top 20 hit "Rumors"), and "Ya Ya Wobble," the latter being recorded as an album track by instrumental virtuosos The Ventures, co-written with arranger/guitarist Billy Strange, along with Bob Bogle and Mel Taylor. As for his own recording career, David was also still very much active in the studio, although his various 1962 releases were to be with differing combinations of the Oklahoma mafia. The Fencemen line-up of David, Leon Russell, and Chuck Blackwell, assisted in the studio by local-born guitarist Billy Strange, put out two singles that year: "Swingin' Gates," composed by David and Cliff Crofford, was backed with Leon Russell's "Bach'n'Roll" (Liberty 55509) while "Sunday Stranger," a Billy Strange original, was paired with "Sour Grapes," another Gates solo offering (Liberty 55535). All four recordings were instrumentals, produced by Dick Glasser, and all contained a hint of rhythm and blues meets

The Fencemen, 1961

pop, with Russell's bluesy organ feel on "Swingin' Gates" sounding remarkably akin to the summer of 1962 smash "Green Onions," by Booker T & The MGs. With David providing bass guitar on all four of the recordings, these are exceptionally fine examples of the style of music that would have been pounding out from the small stage at Pandora's Box during the band's lengthy residency at the L.A. night-spot. And who said it wasn't "hip"?

Towards the end of 1962, a further series of sessions were undertaken by the Gates and Russell partnership, with two more releases subsequently appearing on vinyl. The duo were still working prolifically together during this stage, co-composing a number of new songs such as "River Of Tears," "Boys Aren't Supposed To Cry," and "Haven Of Love," although "The Girl I Lost In The Rain" b/w "The One That Got Away," appearing as a single on the Mercury label, was credited solely to "CJ" Russell and featured David as the lone composer on both songs. Then, on October 13, 1962, one further session resulted in an issue under the combined names of "David & Lee." Surprisingly however, the lead side of the new single wasn't one of their own tunes. That release, "Sad September" b/w "Tryin' To Be Someone," appeared on Garpax, a new label that had just been founded by singer, songwriter, and producer Gary S. Paxton, himself a million-selling performer courtesy of the 1959 hit "It Was I." Leon had already assisted Paxton once in the studio, a session that had culminated in the label's debut release during the summer of '62, "Monster Mash," a *Billboard* chart topper credited to Bobby "Boris" Pickett and The Crypt-Kickers and, although David had not been directly involved with that smash hit, his partnership with Russell was to see "Sad September" released as Garpax 1001. Both songs were published by Garpax Music, with the A-side being a Paxton composition, co-written with fellow "Monster Mash" musician and vocalist Johnny McCrae, while "Tryin' To Be Someone" was yet another David Gates solo number. "Sad September" is a gorgeous harmony-influenced ballad, prominently featuring David in front of the microphone, and combining the vocal arrangements of the Everly Brothers' distinctive influence with Paxton's own "It Was I." By contrast, "Tryin' To Be Someone" was a real hokey upbeat country tune, full of nasal twang, guitar pickin' – and a good three or four years before Gram Parsons plied the same approach to the hip L.A. crowd. With the two vocalists singing along in unison, the theme of an individual who harbors dreams of stardom – "he used to be no one, but now he's someone" – could almost have been written with their own stories in mind. Certainly, for two young Oklahoma musicians who started in the backwoods of Tulsa they were now starting to see the hard work and long hours beginning to bear fruit. Both were now indeed *someone*...

Chapter Four

The Okie Surfer

1963 in Southern California was a good place to be. If the words of the hit songs of the day were to be believed, the sun was always shining, the surf was always up and there were, in the immortal words of Jan Berry and Brian Wilson, "two girls for every boy..."

By now the Oklahoma mafia had a good footing in the Los Angeles music industry. As time rolled by, this group became more focused on the central figure of Leon Russell, and the up-and-coming musicians of the city began to draw in around him like a magnet. But David Gates was also beginning to strike his own stake into the community, and this year in particular saw his contribution increase further still, marking his independence from his former home state compatriots. The craze for surf music was still washing over the shoreline of the city and since its initial inception, following the arrival of guitar virtuoso Dick Dale and a host of surf-orientated bands such as The Belairs, The Lively Ones, and The Surfaris, the focus had turned to a more vocal approach and artists in the caliber of The Beach Boys, Jan & Dean, PF Sloan, Terry Melcher, and Gary Usher had swiftly come to prominence. David's sessions for this year, particularly in the latter part, were to encompass the entire spectrum that "surf music" had built up and developed into – surfing, hot-roddin', skiing – along with the full-on production that came with the wall-of-sound girl-group phenomenon. Legendary producers Phil Spector, Brian Wilson, Bob Keene, and Kim Fowley would all cross his path and to top the year off – there could be no better festive gift than a Top 3 placing on the *Billboard* charts! This Okie surfer was riding high on the crest of a new wave, but the wave ultimately has a habit of crashing down.

The early part of the year saw David's name linked with a number of established artists, one of the first being Dorsey Burnette. Having worked the previous year with his younger brother Johnny, David was now provider of a song to the senior brother, and the song in question, "Pebbles," was a remarkably serious composition, full of lyrical vision and sweeping statements:

Have you ever watched a small boy
Just walking down the street
He don't seem to know what he's doing

He don't even care where he's going
Just keeps kicking pebbles with his feet

"Pebbles" (Composed by David Gates)

Recorded during April of 1963, and appearing the following month as the flip-side to the single "Invisible Chains" (Reprise 20177), it was unfortunately yet another sign of the flailing fortunes for the once rockabilly kings, and, like Johnny's recording of "The Fool Of The Year," the Burnette-Gates partnership once more failed to set the chart listings alight.

The same month David also joined another former rock'n'roll legend in the studio, offering up assistance to a Duane Eddy session on April 19th. As both writer and arranger on the song "Blowin' Up A Storm," a track featured on the Gates-arranged *Twangin' Up A Storm* album, David was assisted in the studio by a number of seasoned L.A. session musicians, under the production guidance of Lee Hazelwood. They included one native Los Angeles-born performer, an extremely versatile musician, at home on both keyboards and bass guitar, and one who would be the backbone of literally dozens, maybe hundreds, of hit recordings during the halcyon days of 1960s pop, Larry Knechtel. This session for Eddy may well have been one of the first times the duo worked together within a recording studio, although they had reportedly first met while hanging out at the Saturday night "jam-sessions" at the Crossbow. Nevertheless, this studio date would certainly not be the last such occasion.

Yet, it was not always the more established artists who were to benefit from the inspiration that came out of the Gates' songwriting pen, or from his prevailing studio talents. At one point during this busy year an obscure single release appeared on the Charter Records label, catalog number CR14. This rarity was credited to a previously unknown vocal duo named Dotty and Kathy and both sides of the single were brand new David Gates compositions. Although no producer names were to feature on the record label, a credit to "Ravenswood Production" suggests it was David holding the reins, seeing that this company name would regularly appear on many further Gates' productions, and both songs were also listed as being published by Dragonwyck Music, David's newly established publishing company. This particular record was a fine model of the sudden rise to success for the 1960s "girl group" genre and, despite the obscurity value the release now possesses, this was a clear example of how David would board a current fad and mimic the originating sound to perfection. In this case, it was the rise to stardom of producer Phil Spector, and his girl-group "wall of sound" would define a number of the following Gates' productions.

Spector himself had come to prominence during the same period that Gates was creating his own niche in the Tulsa recording industry. As writer and performer on the 1958 hit "To Know Him Is To Love Him," credited to the Teddy Bears, he had shown at an early age his uncanny knack and ability for defining a good melody within a two-minute time frame. Originally hailing from the Bronx in New York, Spector had relocated to the West Coast as a young teenager, but by the arrival of the 1960s, having made his first forays into the industry, he had moved back to the East Coast to work alongside legendary tunesmiths Jerry Leiber and Mike Stoller, songwriters to many of the early rock'n'roll greats. A succession of hits followed and, after once again returning to Los Angeles, he started his own record company, Philles Records, after which he began to churn out a series of phenomenal hit singles, all released under his production and guidance, and often his own songwriting, for a series of artists such as The Crystals, Bobb B Soxx, and The Ronettes.

His trademark during this era was the so-called "Wall of Sound," a production technique utilizing a multi-layered effect of numerous instruments, all playing in unison, and mixed down to monophonic sound for a fuller "feel." Spector himself termed the technique: "A Wagnerian approach to rock'n'roll, little symphonies for the kids." It appeared to work. By adding the glorious vocals of singers such as Darlene Love and Ronnie Bennett, and by using the same series of musicians, the central core to his work, who knew his approach and what he expected, Spector managed to pull off the "sound" time and time again. These musicians, referred to these days as the "Wrecking Crew," comprised many of the top studio cats of the day, along with a number of new, raw talents that blended into the sound. Drummer Hal Blaine often headed the troupe, accompanied by a vast array of like-minded performers such as guitarists Billy Strange, Glen Campbell, Tommy Tedesco, and Barney Kessell, bassists Carol Kaye, Joe Osborn, Max Bennett, Larry Knechtel, and Ray Pohlman, keyboard wizards Leon Russell, Don Randi, and Knechtel again, along with numerous saxophonists, percussion players, brass, and woodwind virtuosos. It was a hardcore team – but they got results, and a particular side of their amazing success was down to the use of female vocalists on a number of hits. Thus, courtesy of releases by the aforementioned Crystals and Ronettes, was born the "girl group" sound. David even had one opportunity to work on a Spector session himself, subbing for one of the regular bass players at Gold Star studios.

"I came in and played on one or two as a replacement…" he would later recall. "I actually didn't like the 'harder' sound at Gold Star that Phil Spector was getting out of it. You have to like that kind of music. I was looking for a little more delicate thing. So I'd record usually at United or Western (Recorders) on Sunset. I had a lot of respect for Gold Star and I worked in the same room, and with the same engineers. But I could see what they were after."[11]

The lead side for the Dotty and Kathy single was "The Prince Of My Dreams," a rather dramatic number, accompanied by a wonderfully over-orchestrated production, complete with marching rhythms, bells, and trumpets, and topped off with some typical girl-group harmonies. And, while the accompanying "Little Heart," also featuring a nice arrangement, is perhaps more reminiscent of late 1950s Patti Page or Doris Day, it again demonstrated the arranging abilities and studio techniques that David was absorbing from his surrounding peer group.

Nevertheless, despite the somewhat backwards step approach of this offering, David's second entry into the "girl group" stakes took the genre by the horns and damn-near turned it upside down. Kicking off with a rattling drum break that shook the eardrums to the maximum, and a dazzlingly supportive instrumental blast straight from The Crystals' current smash "Da Doo Ron Ron," The Girlfriends' 1963 release, the Gates composition "My One And Only Jimmy Boy" (Colpix CP712), was the sure-fire hit that never was. Or not quite. This trio of vocalists was comprised of Gloria Jones and Nanette Williams, one half of the original line-up of The Blossoms, who were one of Spector's favored backing troupes, along with Carolyn Willis, and it was pure Spector wall-of-sound from start to finish. Brash, big, and bold, and worthy of its #49 position on the charts and, coupled with the ballad "For My Sake," it certainly deserved a far higher placing.

One other related single of note that appeared during this period was issued by RCA Records (47-8343) and featured Reno nightclub singer Frankie Fanelli performing a heavily orchestrated rendition of "The Questions," an anglicized Italian operatic ballad. This little known number, paired with the highly enjoyable David Gates composition, "Tears, Rain," was produced by legendary RCA producer Al Schmidt, and also featured "Dave" Gates as arranger and conductor. If anything, despite its relative lack of success, random sessions like this were confirmation that if there was a paying gig around the city, and strings were needed, then the man to call was David Gates.

"I went through just about the entire roster at RCA Records and Capitol Records as an arranger," he was later to recall in an interview with Bill Kornman in 1994. "I've pushed strings on everybody. They add a quality of warmth. A bowed instrument does something and when four bowed instruments all play the same note it creates a warmth within the note. Nothing else can do it."

The year 1963 saw David's own performing career put on to a backburner while all of this session activity kept rolling in. Only one release appeared under his own name that year and, although the issue in question featured another two of his own compositions, the lead side, "No-One Really Loves A Clown," was a strange choice to push. Indeed, it wasn't even the first time this song had been released as a single. The previous year had seen Johnny Crawford release his version of the song as the flip-side on a relatively successful 45 single, but this particular number could never really be considered as having true "hit" potential in its own right as, standing it alongside David's recent work with The Girlfriends, or earlier issues as Dave & Lee or The Fencemen, it was so apparent that this offering was simply *not where it was at*. An outdated, near novelty number, with an equally confusing choice for the flip-side. The arrangement on "You Had It Comin' To You" wasn't really sure on which side of the fence to fall. Was it intended as a Del Shannon-styled number, a falsetto break over a driving beat, or was it intended as a misguided MOR brass arrangement that just simply got carried away? Whatever the reasons or intentions, this release was not going to break David into a successful solo act, although, with hindsight, there are suggestions that possibly it was released as more of a contractual arrangement. The Johnny Crawford version of the song had been released on Del-Fi Records, a label that was conceived and owned by former dance bandleader Bob Keene, initially as a label to issue releases for local Los Angelino/Chicano acts. Success soon followed when singer/songwriter Ritchie Valens struck gold with "Donna" b/w "La Bamba" but, following Valens' untimely death in the same plane crash that also took the lives of fellow rock'n'roll artists Buddy Holly and J.P. Richardson, Keene branched out in his search for success. Crawford had been a successful child actor and an original "Mouseketeer" prior to his recording debut in 1961 and, along with the burgeoning business for bands performing the new and exciting "surf" sound, Keene was quick to capitalize on the potential popularity on offer. Subsequently, he signed up both Crawford and his composer, David Gates, among his roster of artists, clearly with the intention of utilizing this jack-of-all-trades as both songwriter and performer. Gates still had the freedom to ply his trade around town as an arranger and conductor but "No-One Really Loves A Clown" was the first in a series of releases linking him with Keene's Del-Fi label. David's brief spell as a regular in the "surf'n'drag crowd," courtesy of Del-Fi, was to follow soon after. However, before David immersed himself fully into the sounds of the beach and strip, a number of further notable moments occurred.

"Surf music was really taking off. I was on the first TV show that The Beach Boys ever did. They were singing songs about surfing and we were just cracking up, you know. Who cares about surfing? It was so funny. Sure enough, it got huge. I would never have believed it. It was a Southern California phenomenon and I thought people in Oklahoma could care less."[9]

That first TV appearance by The Beach Boys took place on March 2nd, 1963, on *The Steve Allen Show*, filmed at the KFMB Studios in San Diego, and quite what David's involvement was remains unclear (possibly once again appearing as part of the house band?), but on June 14th, David also attended a recording session at the legendary Gold Star Studios on Santa Monica Boulevard. Accompanying him that day were members of Phil Spector's regular studio "crew," including Hal Blaine on drums, Carol Kaye on guitar and bass, and saxophonists Steve Douglas and Jay Migliori. The session was booked by head Beach Boy, Brian Wilson, and the team, with David supporting Kaye on guitar and bass, committed two new Wilson compositions to tape, "Back Home" and "Black Wednesday." No other Beach Boys were in attendance, and both tracks remained unreleased, but surviving tapes from the session indicate nothing as sophisticated as Wilson was later to put down on to vinyl and, apart from a couple of flourishes courtesy of Blaine and the Douglas/Migliori team, David is restricted to simple rhythm patterns.

"He (Brian) came out and told us all what he wanted us to play," David would recall in his interview with Kornman for *NetMusic*. "The interesting thing I remember was when he went around to each musician to describe what he wanted you to play, he would take his hands and form them around the imaginary instrument. He would go up to the sax guy, he'd put his hands like he was playing the sax, then he'd sing the part. He would then go to the guitar person and he'd strum with his right hand, the piano he'd use both hands. He would physically demonstrate the instrument. We got along really good."

Yet, two months later, on August 5th, the same crew, minus Carol Kaye but with the addition of harpist Maureen Love (sister of The Beach Boys' lead vocalist), once more reconvened at Gold Star, and taped the backing tracks to three further tunes, "Witch Stand," "Hot Harp," and "Girlie." Although these particular recordings were not intended for The Beach Boys, instead they were reportedly scheduled for Brian's "splinter group," The Survivors, the sessions did produce three suitable masters, yet Capitol Records, Brian's label, unfortunately rejected the offer to release them, instead picking up the option on two further Survivors recordings taped on August 27th. It is unclear whether David participated in these final sessions as, during the same period, he was working on another "surf-related" project.

Jack Nitzsche was known as being Phil Spector's right-hand man during this period, responsible for much of the arrangements that graced the infamous "wall of sound." However, during the early summer of '63, Nitzsche had scored a surprise "solo" hit for himself, a moody orchestrated instrumental, featuring Glen Campbell and Leon Russell, entitled "The Lonely Surfer." Such was its surprise Top 40 success that Nitzsche immediately went back into the studio, more than likely Gold Star once again, and, utilizing the many talents of Tommy Tedesco and Ray Pohlman on guitar, Leon Russell on piano, Hal Blaine on drums, and David on bass, recorded an entire album's worth of instrumental tunes. Truthfully, these string-based recordings, issued as *The Lonely Surfer* LP (Reprise R/S6101) during September of that year, and ultimately topped off with liner notes by Spector himself, had little or no connection whatsoever with the new "surfin'" sound. But such was the lure of the West Coast-based sport among the youth market of America during this period that so many unrelated releases simply used the hip "surf" terminology to capitalize and gain sales. Cowabunga.

Another early venture into this territory came with the November 1963 release of "Surfer Street," a single issued by the female group The Allisons (not to be confused with the Top 10-selling UK group of the same name). Although David's actual involvement with this release remains uncredited (with the songwriting unofficially attributed to Don Harris and Dewey Terry) his own publishing company, Dragonwyck, does appear on the label, suggesting that David was somehow part of this lowly placed *Billboard* #93 hit. Yet, by the time this recording hit the charts, David was now working on a large group of sessions for Bob Keene's Del-Fi label, starting with a further writing credit for the next Johnny Crawford release. "Living In The Past" was issued as the accompanying side to "Judy Loves Me," a song that Keene hoped would further Crawford's limited success to date. Indeed, Keene had even drafted in Jan Berry, a successful writer, arranger, producer, and performer himself, as part of the chart-topping surf act Jan & Dean, to write and produce the A-side for Crawford, but the single barely scraped into the Hot 100, ending Crawford's run of hits.

By now, finding himself bonding within this close knit group of session musicians, and skirting along the outer edges of the infamous "wrecking crew" studio team, David was booked into a series of recordings that would result in three further entries into the youth orientated "hot-rod" market. Essentially, an auto-influenced spin-off of the surfing craze, cool hot-rods and drag strips were now the current fad among much of America's youth, being far more within the understanding and reach of the landlocked population, and subsequently a host of auto-themed songs followed. While this particular series of instrumental recordings would never rival the popularity achieved by the more accessible vocal "hot-rod" recordings by the likes of The Beach Boys, Jan & Dean, and friends, the essence of the hot-rod music was very much in the "feel" of the song and, more often than not, the sound of squealing tires accompanied by a frantic, staccato rhythm was far more in the groove than a soporific ballad extolling the virtues of an ol' jalopy named Betsy, or a tribute to a rockin' grandma from Pasadena. To each his own...

The Deuce Coupes' 1963 album *Hotrodders Choice*, The Defenders' 1964 album *Drag Beat*, and the March 1964 album *Hollywood Drag* by The Darts all came about as a result of these late 1963 sessions for Del-Fi, and while all 30-plus compositions sound very much alike to the uninitiated – often inspired, more often uninspired – one can quite clearly hear the effective bass runs and riffs that David contributed to the tapes. Needless to say, Del-Fi was not a label for surefire success and all these releases disappeared into the vast market of the period, lost under the far superior roddin' releases of the genre. Nevertheless, to the paid-up session musician it was often a case of finish one project, give it not a second thought, move on to the next, which is basically what David was to do so successfully during this period. Paid session work was simply that. No emotional attachment, just chart sheets.

November 1963 was also to see the influences of the original surf sound taken one step further away from the ocean, and into the snow-peaked mountains of America. Created to combine the thrills of surfboard riding with those of downhill skiing, The Avalanches' release on Warner Brothers, *Ski Surfin'*, took the exploitation to extremes, and the MOR influences that permeated from the grooves of "Avalanche," "Slalom," and the title track, coupled with bluesy-rock versions of "Winter Wonderland," "Sleigh Ride," and "Baby, It's Cold Outside" make for a slickly produced, but bizarre, listening experience. There was really no Avalanches band per se, just a manufactured group name, created to match the product, attached to the album. Masterminded at Gold Star studios by writer/producer Wayne Shanklin, with Spector's in-house engineer Stan Ross sitting alongside, and accompanied by David's dependable Fender bass duties, familiar session names, such as Tommy Tedesco, Wayne Burdick, and Billy Strange, were also on hand to provide the guitars, with Al DeLory sitting on the piano stool, and the ever-reliable Hal Blaine behind the drums. A similar line-up featuring Gates and Blaine, but this time with Glen Campbell, Bill Pittman, Leon Russell, Ray Pohlman, and Marshall Leib, also put together another "skiing" release, this time credited to The Glaciers (*From Ski To Sea*) and released on Mercury Records the following year. In fact, drummer Hal Blaine had already taken these studio sessions one step further during the winter of 1963 when he had gathered together some of his usual crew of session friends, including David and Leon Russell, and taped a series of drum-driven recordings for release in early 1964 under his own name. Credited to Hal Blaine & The Young Cougars this subsequent album, entitled *Deuces, T's, Roadsters & Drums* and released via RCA Records, featured David's talents as arranger and conductor, as well as including two of his instrumental compositions, "Mr. Eliminator" and "Gear Stripper."

Regardless of all these relentless session duties, 1963 was to end on a high for David's career, a songwriting credit on a *Billboard* Top 3 smash hit, though not before one further oddity sneaked into the Gates canon. At some stage, linking up with his former partner from Oklahoma, Leon Russell, and the Arkansas-born guitar whiz kid Glen Campbell, the trio provided a short piece of music for a television commercial, promoting Clairol Hair products. "Is it true blondes have more fun?" was the brand logo of the period, and the joyful music that accompanied the theme truly suggested they do. Or at least, that was what the 30-second commercial would have us believe...

Kim Fowley was a young record producer, trying to capitalize on the success he had achieved back in 1960 with the Hollywood Argyles' novelty number "Alley Oop." He was to recall:

"1963. I was hitch-hiking one day, and got a lift from this guy who turned out to be David Gates. He told me he was a songwriter, and I told him I was a record producer, so we went back and he played this song he'd just written, and actress Candice Bergen, who was a friend of mine, said it was a certain number one."

This new David Gates composition was subsequently taken into the recording studios by Fowley, and given to a trio of young girl singers calling themselves The Murmaids. Sisters Carol and Terry Fischer, along with neighbor and friend Sally Gordon, were looking for a suitable song to record before they headed off to college in the fall of 1963, and the Fischers' parents had taken them to see the head of the small Chatahoochee record label, where Fowley was the in-house producer. Fowley heard them in the studio working on a series of demo recordings and offered to produce a new song he had heard, "Popsicles & Icicles," for them. Issued as Chattahoochee 628 this release, coupled with a variety of B-sides (four different B-sides for the four different pressings), went on to climb the *Billboard* chart listings over the winter of 1963, finally peaking at the #3 position.

"It was one of only two songs I've ever gotten up in the middle of the night to write. I was lying there thinking about it, and I got up and wrote it. And (Kim) recorded it with this group, and played it for me, and I thought: 'Well, that's OK. It doesn't sound great, but it sounds pretty good.' It had a catchy melody and some neat words to it, and they tested it one Sunday afternoon. It was one of these things where they played five new records on KHJ or one of the other hit radio stations of the time, and the damn thing won the voting. People would call in and vote on their favorite. Then it just took off and went Top 5..."[11]

This simple song, that combines the golden doo-wop era of the late '50s with the then-current girl group sound, struck a chord with the American public, still reeling in the aftermath of the assassination of John F. Kennedy the previous month. Harking back to the innocence of five years before, it certainly offered up nothing new, and the production is noticeably shallow for the time and yet, with hindsight, it was the perfect way to close out the year. Innocent and fragile, the calm before the storm, the storm that was to sweep across from the other side of the Atlantic Ocean and turn the American music industry on its head.

Gates in conversation with *NetMusic*: "I thought (what came out of England) was very valid. Of course, The Beatles were outstanding but it was really tough on a lot of us in L.A. when that thing happened. All the radios starting playing all English groups. We starved to death from about '64 to '68. People didn't know that, but it was tough. You couldn't get a record. Anything from England or that had a British accent got played. Even the disc jockeys came across, and that's okay, but I think they overdid it."

Unfortunately, it wasn't all sweetness and light when it came to The Murmaids' seasonal offering, as it reportedly caused a breakdown in the previously close friendship between David and his former Tulsa collaborator Russell Bridges, now gaining considerable credit on the session circuit as keyboard player Leon Russell. According to David's future music partner, Robb Royer:

"The understanding that I have is that Leon thought he was supposed to be getting half of the publishing (on the song). David didn't think so, so they fell out over that." As to what input Russell had into the song remains unclear, if any, but, assuming he had some justification to his claim to share the publishing, there is certainly no acknowledged collaboration on the hit composition. And yet all of this would have been far from David's mind over the festive season, and even his recent claim to success was not the celebration he would have liked, for his father was no longer there to see it, sadly passing away before the year was out. David would later pay tribute to his guiding light in song...

Early 1964, and before the impact from the four young Liverpudlians touching down at the newly rechristened John F. Kennedy International airport was fully realized, and even during the subsequent mania that immediately followed, David participated in a further series of surf/hot rod-related projects. California still had its own identity to maintain, even if the youth that swarmed around its beaches and clubs were now wearing Beatle-wigs or combing their fringes forward. One further Brian Wilson session involving David took place on January 2nd, 1964, although once again it was a non-Beach Boys-related date.

Paul Petersen was a young TV star, courtesy of his regular appearances on the popular *Donna Reed Show*, and his subsequent fame had already brought him a series of national chart hits. However, by 1964 his popularity was seemingly on the wane and his involvement with Brian Wilson was seen as a way of redirecting his ailing career. The session held at Western Recorders in Hollywood on January 2nd was to result in the wonderfully lavish production and release of "She Rides With Me," a Brian Wilson-Roger Christian motorcycle tune (yet another spin-off from the surf/hot rod genre). According to surviving AFM contract sheets, it featured David on electric bass guitar alongside such stalwarts as Hal Blaine, Tommy Tedesco, Ray Pohlman, Jimmy Bond, Al DeLory, Plas Johnson, Jay Migliori, and Larry Knechtel, each earning in the region of $63.00 scale rate apiece. Sadly, despite the undeniable quality and sheer bravado fun that runs throughout the 1 minute 53 seconds of recorded vinyl, the single was to go nowhere on the charts, and failed to re-ignite Petersen's career. Strangely enough, shortly after the Petersen session was completed, a number of the same musicians reconvened to record both sides of a single for Shelley Fabares, wife of producer Lou Adler, titled "Football Seasons Over" b/w "He Don't Love Me." Fabares had also been an essential part of the *Donna Reed Show* and had previously hit big in the record market with the release of "Johnny Angel" during 1962 and, along with Petersen's "She Rides With Me," her new record saw a simultaneous release on the Colpix label. For the Fabares sessions, however, Brian Wilson vacated the producer's chair to make way for David Gates himself and the resulting cuts were equally fine productions, full of exquisite Blaine drum-fills and delightful backing vocals courtesy of The Honeys, a young trio of singers featuring Marilyn Rovell, the soon-to-be Mrs. Brian Wilson.

The final three contributions that David was to make to the surf-related genre were to appear shortly afterwards, although all were soon buried in the rush to market all things English, despite the undeniable quality of one of them. The first of these was essentially a David Gates solo release, self-penned (although credited to The Country Boys) and was really a tongue-in-cheek "Oklahoma" version of the surf sound. "The Okie Surfer" was full of surf terminology, the obligatory falsetto vocal, and a melody vaguely akin to The Beach Boys' own debut hit "Surfin'," and the production was fun. Sadly, the sound was weak in comparison to the genre it so heartily set out to mock. Issued as Del-Fi single 4245, and then again as 4248, and accompanied by the non-Gates instrumental "Blue Surf," it unsurprisingly went nowhere near the charts. The second release was something altogether different. "Summer Means Fun," co-written by Steve Barri and Phil "PF" Sloan, stands today as one of the definitive "summer surf" anthems, and while the songwriters were to record their own version of the song under the guise of The Fantastic Baggys, the "hit" version (a #72 placing on *Billboard*) came courtesy of producer Terry Melcher and his partner, future Beach Boy Bruce Johnston. Credited on the label as Bruce & Terry, and accompanied by musicians David Gates, Steve Douglas, Jerry Cole, Billy Strange, Hal Blaine, and Bill Pitman, along with Phil Sloan himself, during an April 1964 session, this track emphasizes what the California vocal sound of the era was all about. Put "Surfin' USA," "Surf City," and "Summer Means Fun" on any turntable and understand. Additionally, from a non-musical viewpoint, the session certainly assisted in meeting the demands of the young Gates family as well, with AFM sheets indicating over $100 paid to all participating musicians.

Unfortunately, David's final surf sessions are somewhat less than noteworthy and, unless a completist is attempting to locate anything and everything surf-related, his performing contributions to the unappealing Mr. Gasser & The Weirdos novelty release, the *Surfink* album, the third in Capitol Records' "Mr. Gasser" collection, are best avoided. He came, he provided bass duties, he left; and the surf finally went out.

The remainder of 1964 was to see David continuing to contribute to a wide range of musical activities, covering a vast spectrum of genres, as well as placing two further entries into his own recording catalog. Notable highlights include his "discovery" of the young teenage vocalist Margaret Mandolph, resulting in her first two releases on Planetary Records the following year: "If You Ever Need Me" b/w "Silly Little Girl," followed by the Russ Titelman and Cynthia Weil composition "I Wanna Make You Happy" b/w "Something Beautiful." Both releases were produced by David, and were extremely mature recordings for such a young singer, yet both stand the test of time well, featuring a very understated and slick production.

Planetary Records was a brand new label, initiated and distributed by the larger Dot Records, and created with David's own A&R involvement. Although it was to see only eight releases gracing its distinctive black and red label during 1964 and 1965, all of them featured a significant contribution from him in one form or another. The first 45 to be released, Planetary 101, produced by David, featured black soul singer Dorothy Berry performing two further Gates compositions, "Ain't That Love," a wild rhythm and blues number complete with wailing harmonica, and the mid-tempo "You Better Watch Out." Issued in October 1964, like the majority of David's releases during this period, the record fared poorly in sales and disappeared soon afterwards, as did the second Berry release on the label, another Gates original, the wonderfully named "Shindig City."

In addition to his work with Planetary, there were arranging sessions for The Rev-Lons ("It's Gonna Happen Some Day"), Duane Eddy ("Guitar Star"), and Bobby Pickett & The Filter-Tip Kickers ("Smoke, Smoke, Smoke"), plus songwriting credits on The Murmaids' unsuccessful second release entitled "Heartbreak Ahead," Gwenn Stacy's "Ain't Gonna Cry No More," Ann-Margret's "Hey Little Star," Michael Landon's "Without You," and Johnny Crawford's penultimate Del-Fi single "The Girl Next Door." Production roles included Johnny Burnette's April release of "Sweet Suzie (I Think She Knows)," The Victorians' "If I Loved You" on Liberty Records, and the July issue on the Vee-Jay label of The Honey Bees' "One Girl, One Boy." As both writer and arranger, David was also responsible for the theme tune to the 1964 feature film by Hanna-Barbera Productions, distributed via Columbia Pictures, featuring that lovable rogue from Jellystone National Park, Yogi Bear. "Hey There, It's Yogi Bear," also released as a promotional record, featured a melody that appeared to be based upon "Santa Claus Is Comin' To Town," but it seems no one ever appeared to notice or file suit, and the film went on to achieve moderate success, with one review in *Variety* magazine noting that "the songs were pleasant, if not especially distinguished..."

In a performing role, David contributed 1964 session duties to The Vanguard Voyagers' single for Reprise, "Hootenanny 1984," Carol & Cheryl's skateboarding anthem "Sammy The Sidewalk Surfer," and an obscure album release credited to The Bandits on World Pacific records. This final rarity was essentially a budget release offering guitarist Glen Campbell the opportunity to record twelve instrumental tunes highlighting his finger-pickin' abilities, ably supported by the pick of the L.A. session crew. Side one of the album featured Campbell, Leon Russell, Jerry Cole, Hal Blaine, and Larry Knechtel providing six numbers, including two Beatles cover versions and one Glen Campbell original, while the second side included an alternate backing crew – David Gates, Ray Johnson, and Thomas Gillam, alongside Campbell and Cole – covering Chuck Berry, The Everly Brothers, and a pre-Byrds Roger McGuinn-Gene Clark composition. Needless to say, despite pleasing arrangements of The Beatles' "And I Love Her" and "I Feel Fine," the obvious choices of the moment, the record, released as *The Electric 12*, went nowhere.

As well as composing "Hey Little Star" for the Swedish-born actress and singer Ann-Margret, David also participated in one further session for her, an August 1964 studio appearance for a single written and arranged by Phil Sloan, and produced by Lou Adler. The three songs taped that day, "He's My Man," "Someday Soon," and "You Sure Know How To Hurt Someone," were all accompanied by an experienced session team, including David on bass, notably high up in the mix, and Leon Russell on piano (still credited on the contract as Russell Bridges), which would suggest that the fallout over the Murmaids' publishing had not dampened the enthusiasm that Gates and Russell still had for recording together, despite any personal feelings they may have harbored. However, despite the quality of the finished products, all musicians present that day may have had difficulty focusing on the task in question, and reasonably so, for just two days earlier, on August 23rd, 1964, The Beatles had hit town, performing the first of their legendary shows at The Hollywood Bowl. The city would never be the same again.

On September 16th, another notable occurrence took place that was also to stake its claim in the annuls of American popular music. *Shindig!*, a brand new rock'n'roll television series, created and produced by British-born Jack Good, along with regular host KRLA DJ Jimmy O'Neill, premiered on the ABC network. Originating from the pilot *Young America Swings The World*, conceived two years earlier, this show would go on to revolutionize the way the American public viewed the rock'n'roll industry. Every week, beamed directly into their front rooms, artists as diverse as Del Shannon, Jerry Lee Lewis, The Beach Boys, Johnny Cash, The Temptations, The Righteous Brothers, and an ongoing list of rock'n'roll's who's who would appear on the *Shindig!* set, and it wasn't just restricted to America's finest. The subsequent British "invasion" of 1964 would see a number of the leading acts from England (The Rolling Stones, The Animals, and The Hollies) all make scheduled stopovers in Los Angeles over the coming months to appear on the show, while The Beatles even taped a series of recorded performances especially for the program. *Shindig!* also maintained an in-house band, a crew of musicians who were always on hand to supply backing to individual "solo" artists as required, and throughout its 16-month lifespan the *Shindig!* house band featured a core of performers such as Delaney Bramlett, James Burton, Joey Cooper, Russ Titelman, Jerry Cole, and two ex-members of The Fencemen, the original house band from the pilot episode. Both Leon Russell and drummer Chuck Blackwell appeared on a regular basis during the show's early run, but there was no place in the set-up for their former bass player, David Gates. He was, by now, far too much in demand to be involved. Certainly his increasing workload would have made such a weekly commitment difficult to maintain, and instead, his role on the show was often taken by the tall blond bassist who was regularly to be found gracing the studio scene of the city and with whom David was beginning to work more regularly: Larry Knechtel.

The two singles that Del Ashley was to release during 1964 and 1965 would often go unrecognized in today's collectors circles were it not for those who continue to seek out this obscure, previously unheard of artist. Followers of Ashley are keen to point out that this was merely a recording pseudonym for one of the most in-demand session players and studio arrangers of the mid-'60s era, David Gates. But as to why David chose to record and release the singles, firstly on Manchester Records and then on the small Planetary label under the pseudonym is unclear, although it is often suggested that it was merely to avoid a conflict of interest with his busy studio "day job." Nevertheless, these singles, along with three further issues on Planetary during 1965 (two credited to Grady & Brady and one more to David himself), are arguably some of the finest works he produced over this period. This particular run of his own releases began with 1964's "My Baby's Gone Away," paired with "Kiss And Tell," the only known release to appear on the tiny independent JADS label. Produced by label owner Jerry Adams, these two Gates compositions hark back to earlier days and sound far simpler in both arrangement and production than the music David was now producing for himself. This was then followed by the first of his Del Ashley singles releases, initially under the equally obscure Manchester Records umbrella. The 1965 release of "She Don't Cry" b/w "There's A Heaven," released as Manchester RW101, combined all of the influences that he had immersed himself in during his spell working within the hot-rod genre the previous year, and resulted in one of the finest examples of a mid-sixties auto-anthem. A short, lively number, with falsetto and harmonies combining with ease, this evocatively extolled the virtues of the singer's favored car, and was clearly influenced by the sessions that David had held with Terry Melcher, producer of many of the great draggin' anthems of the time ("Hey Little Cobra," "Summer Means Fun," "Three Window Coupe"). Unfortunately for David, this was twelve months too late to capitalize on the craze for four-wheeled heaven, and yet another one was to slip past the checkered flag unnoticed.

Planetary Records 103 featured the second of the Del Ashley releases and, once again, while containing clear evidence of outside influences, "Little Miss Stuck Up" simply could not compete with the other releases of this period. One only has to look at the chart-toppers of 1965 to see the shift in dynamics once again. The blue-eyed soul of the Righteous Brothers' "You've Lost That Lovin' Feelin'" battled it out with The Temptations' "My Girl," while The Beatles' dominance of "Ticket To Ride," "Eight Days A Week," and "Yesterday" fought off competition from The Rolling Stones' "Get Off Of My Cloud" and the new Californian folk-rock sounds of The Byrds' "Mr. Tambourine Man." Even The Beach Boys' lone chart-topper of the year, "Help Me Rhonda," was a world away in sound and production from the surfin' sounds of old. "Little Miss Stuck Up" would barely have stood a chance of significant radio airplay. In fact, the flip-side of the release, "The Brighter Side," containing a feel of both blues and soul, was far more in tune with the times and was notably a significant development in David's own songwriting approach. Lyrically, perhaps he even realized himself it was time to get "hip."

It seems I've spent my lifetime singing and preaching the blues
I guess it's just about time I put on my rockin' shoes

"The Brighter Side" (Composed by David Gates)

While one cannot fault the polished quality of these songs, or those of the two Planetary releases credited to Grady & Brady ("Just A Lot Of Talk" b/w "Love Or Money," and a re-recording of "Sad September" coupled with "Star Of The Show"), David's solo career would have to wait for a further few years before national acceptance was forthcoming.

The identity of the aforementioned Grady & Brady has long been discussed among collectors and fans of David Gates, and it was often assumed by many that David was actually one of the mysterious performers himself. However, surviving footage from an April, 1965, edition of *Shindig!*, along with a number of episodes from *Shivaree* (one of the subsequent music shows that arose out of the spectacle that was *Shindig!*) clearly highlight that this was not so. March, April, and June airings from the two 1965 shows confirms that the harmonically orientated Brady & Grady were actually identical twins, albeit bereft of the Everly Brothers' pure vocal abilities. Blessed with the surname of Sneed, they had previously released two unsuccessful singles during 1961 on the small Dolton Records label, and now clearly had the good fortune and benefit of working alongside David in the studio. Unfortunately, the hits still failed to materialize for the duo, and although David may well have been involved vocally in the recording of the two songs, neither Brady nor Grady was he...

By the close of this particular year, 1965, David had also issued what were to become his final "solo" releases of the decade. Although one could assume that this was not a conscious decision on his behalf, the lack of success from his own series of records, fifteen releases on ten differing labels, perhaps gave him pause for thought. His reputation was increasing as a "behind the scenes" artist, and the remaining four years of the decade were to see this reputation climb higher still. Yet it was to become a source of frustration for him as well.

"I felt like I should be doing my own stuff, just to see if I could do it better. I was frustrated with the way that songs that I had written were being recorded by others. I was feeling they were getting lost. I thought, you know, I might as well try and do these myself. Although I never really believed that I was much of a singer, I could sing well enough to bring my own tunes to life. But I certainly didn't represent myself to be some Pavarotti..."

The final two releases from this era that were to feature David's prominent lead vocals were the reflective ballad "Let You Go" (paired with the notably country-dominated "Once Upon A Time"), which became the final release on the Planetary label, and "I Don't Come From England," an anti-British-invasion beat pastiche, sung in a mocking falsetto vocal, jokingly credited to The Manchesters, that David was later to admit was essentially a steal from the hit single "Bread & Butter" by The Newbeats. Paired with another Gates tune, the instrumental "Dragonfly," this latter offering, perhaps surprisingly, failed to gain acceptance among the American youth, keen to grab a hold of anything containing a hint of "England," and although a further series of releases were to appear under The Manchesters' group name, including an album of Beatle-covers on the Diplomat label, David had no further involvement with these at all.

The years 1965 to 1968 were to see David's continuing ascendance within the industry, and a further number of notable studio activities over these years were to follow. The remaining months of 1965 saw his compositions recorded by The Astronauts ("Count Your Mistakes"), Connie Stevens ("Lost In Wonderland"), The Stairs ("Moonchild"), and Lon Chaney ("Yule-Tide Jerk"), while studio sessions saw him involved with Suzy Wallis (another young teenager for whom David arranged her debut single), Dick Kallman (star of the popular 1965 TV series *Hank*), Glenn Yarborough (former lead singer for The Limeliters), who reached the peak of his career with the 1965 release of the Grammy-nominated "Baby, The Rain Must Fall," and a young English-born singer and actor, David Jones.

David and Suzy Wallis (courtesy of Brian Gari Collection)

The success that David achieved with his arrangements for Glenn Yarborough, despite losing out at the Grammy Awards, was to continue over the next couple of years, with David contributing songwriting and arranging to a number of Yarborough's popular albums, including *It's Gonna Be Fine*, *Honey And Wine,* and *The Bitter & The Sweet*. Most notably, the lead-off track on 1965's *It's Gonna Be Fine* was a Gates' composition entitled "Never Let Her Go," a song that David would himself return to and successfully record a number of years later. Meanwhile, September 25th, 1965, saw him working with David Jones at Western Recorders on Sunset Boulevard. In attendance that day, in addition to Gates' role as session producer, were many established musicians from the circuit, including, once again, Hal Blaine, Glen Campbell, Ray Pohlman, and Larry Knechtel. Together they taped three songs for the young Englishman, although only one of which, "The Girl From Chelsea," would see an official release as Colpix single 789. Sadly, this release failed to achieve any significant success beyond Jones's young teen-orientated fan base, but would see far greater interest placed upon it when the youngster went on to star in a new television series the following year.

This show, based upon the madcap exploits of a Beatle-ish rock'n'roll quartet, would go on to levitate Jones's career into the stratosphere, outselling both the Beatles' and the Rolling Stones' *combined* record sales during 1967. Hey, hey, they were The Monkees, an act that would certainly assist David Gates once more the following year. Additionally, David also broke new ground by producing some sessions for Don Van Vliet, a wild, young performer who had recently renamed himself Captain Beefheart. Having just been signed by A&M Records, Beefheart and his group, The Magic Band, recorded a number of compositions under the guidance of Gates, including the subsequent single release "Diddy Wah Diddy," a raw, bluesy cover of an old Bo Diddley composition, and a version of David's own "Moonchild." The odd pairing of this Gates/Beefheart partnership was certainly something new to David, and was clearly an indication of his desire to explore new territories. This was a world apart from the string and horn arrangements for MOR artists such as Yarborough, Stevens, and Fabares.

"Yeah, that was really different," he was later to remember. "I did four sides, and actually wrote one, for which I still get a few royalties. But not much!"

1966 saw further involvement with Suzy Wallis and The Blossoms (writer on the wonderful "Tell Him" and "Lover Boy" respectively), along with songwriting credits for The Lively Set ("Let The Trumpets Sound"), Gary Lewis & The Playboys ("Face In The Crowd"), and Dino, Desi & Billy ("Tie Me Down"), plus further studio work with Brenda Lee, Jody Miller, and Hoyt Axton. Then, to top it off, he undertook a series of arranging sessions (which included backing vocals) for Gene Vincent, recorded for Challenge Records, that saw twelve tracks taped in an unsuccessful attempt to resurrect the career of the ailing rock'n'roll legend. However, 1966 was possibly most notable for David when the young teen star David Jones scaled new heights, and the creators of The Monkees' television series, now featuring Jones as one of the principal leads, opted to record one of Gates' compositions for the band's debut album. Screen Gems Television, a subsidiary of Columbia Pictures, was producing the series and so naturally the company insisted that all music incorporated into the show had to be Screen Gems copyrighted product. Therefore, utilizing the very best of their own in-house songwriters for the project (Neil Diamond, Goffin & King, Boyce & Hart), David Gates, in his role as Screen Gems staff writer, was also included and although this wasn't the first time that the song in question, "Saturday's Child," was recorded (local L.A. band The Palace Guard had cut a version shortly beforehand, as did Herman's Hermits shortly afterwards), The Monkees' rendition was to propel the song, and the subsequent songwriting royalties, to dizzying levels of success. The debut album went on to sell over five million copies, topping the U.S. album charts for a 13-week consecutive run before being knocked off the top spot by... *More Of The Monkees* (which itself remained atop for an amazing 18-week stretch), and, while "Saturday's Child" was never issued as a single in America, it remains one of David's most notable 1960s accomplishments, certainly from a sales perspective.

"I had known Davy Jones before The Monkees, a really nice guy. I also knew Michael Nesmith before the group, also a really good guy and a very talented musician. I was a staff writer at Screen Gems when The Monkees were being formed and 'Saturday's Child' had been under consideration for their first single, but they put out 'Last Train To Clarksville' instead. Still, it helped pay a few bills," David laughed when recollecting the song years later.

And yet, how could one beat that? Simply by playing guest in the court of the king...

Bread (courtesy of Robb Royer)

Chapter Five

Make It With You

Skip forward a full 27 months from his success with The Monkees and David Gates was to be found arranging the soundtrack sessions for the 1968 movie *Charro!*, the 29th film featuring Elvis Presley in the starring role. As the film in question was not a musical, the first of the Presley movies not to feature the star singing on screen, it was only to feature the title track performed during the credits, and sessions for this particular number, along with a further unused song ("Let's Forget About The Stars"), took place on both October 15th and November 25th to 27th, 1968, at the Samuel Goldwyn Studios in Hollywood. Working alongside fellow arranger Hugo Montenegro, along with more familiar names such as Billy Strange, Don Randi, Tommy Tedesco, and Larry Knechtel, David helped Presley complete the proposed track for the movie. Presley himself was known for working out the arrangements on the spot with his musicians. He also favored singing live with the band, as opposed to overdubbing his voice afterwards and while, according to the track session details, the heavy orchestral overdubs that featured so prominently on the song were added to the track towards the end of the November dates, possibly after Elvis had left the building, David later confirmed that he had worked on the initial arrangements, with Elvis's approval, in the studio at the same time. And who said that after achieving success in the region of five million album sales, the only way is down?

The months preceding this momentous occasion were filled with the usual rounds of studio activity for David. As well as further soundtrack work (composing the score on the 1968 movie *Journey To Shiloh* and undertaking a similar role for the surfing documentary *Follow Me*), artists such as Bobby Vee, Samantha Jones, Nino Tempo and April Stevens, The Travelers 3, Jimmy Rodgers, The Parade, and Dino, Desi & Billy (the latter with the wonderful sounding "Thru Spray Colored Glasses," a composition also featured on the *Follow Me* soundtrack) had all benefited from the multi-talents of David Gates, be it writing, arranging, or producing skills. In addition, a young folk-based group calling themselves The Pleasure Fair had also used his production abilities for their debut album and while, presumably, this was seen as no more than a routine session for the Oklahoma-born artist, it was the first step, the initial seeds, for what was ultimately to become his destiny. A friendship was to develop between David and the young songwriter and guitarist in The Pleasure Fair, and that in turn was to open up new doors, to new friendships, and new partnerships. The Travelers 3 would then get pulled into the equation. The times were indeed a-changin'...

Another song that David had composed during this period was largely ignored at the time. It was a gentle tune, "almost of Victorian gentility," author Barry Alfonso was later to note when providing sleeve notes for many of Bread's later re-issues. David had initially composed the song, a love ballad detailing the delicate findings written inside a daily journal, during 1966 while writing for the Screen Gems publishing house, and he had cut a demonstration disc of the song, utilizing just his vocals and an acoustic guitar. Byrds producer Gary Usher, himself a veteran of many a Californian musical odyssey (including an extensive period of surf and hot-rod recordings), recalled in a 1981 interview with author Stephen McParland:

"I was actually given 'Diary' (originally listed as 'I Found Her Diary Underneath The Tree' on the original demo disc) back in 1966-67 because it was one of David Gates' earlier demos. Roger Gordon from Screen Gems gave it to me and I loved it. I cut it at Together (Records), but it was never issued. In fact, David Gates even came down and played guitar and helped me sing it..."

Usher later recorded the song "Diary" during sessions with his studio band Sagittarius, intended for their second album *Blue Marble* and yet, as he himself stated, the song never saw an official release, and to this day the tapes remain, sadly unheard, in the vaults of Mike Curb, Usher's one-time business partner. A second version was also cut for Usher's Together Records label, this time by vocalist Brent Lewis, but that too failed to see the pressing factory, and David would file the song away for a further few years. Coincidentally, Gary Usher was also friends with the young songwriter from The Pleasure Fair, Robb Royer, and the two of them would often sit around together, playing chess, passing joints, listening to the impressive sounding music that Gary was now producing with fellow studio whiz-kid Curt Boettcher, most notably Boettcher's current band, The Millennium (precursor to Sagittarius). Full of hi-tech sounds, overdubbed vocals, and instrumentation, The Millennium was noteworthy for producing the most expensive, and expansive, album that Columbia Records had backed up to that point. Supposedly, it had it all.

"We really thought for three or four months there, that The Millennium was going to be the biggest thing. Forget the Beatles. And then it came out and did absolutely nothing," Robb later remembered in conversation with the author. Nevertheless, the experiences that came out of the unsuccessful Millennium project, and the reasons behind its relative failure, were to remain with Robb, and also with his future working colleagues, and help in directing their own approach, albeit in a totally opposite way.

Following the commercial failure of *The Pleasure Fair* album and that of the equally unsuccessful follow-up single, David and Robb began to spend social time in each other's company. They would sail, play ball, talk, and it was only a matter of time before David was introduced to Robb's new songwriting partner. The time-frame would date this as mid-1968.

Robb Royer: "I took Jimmy out to David's house, and we went out to the barn, and he had a bass and a little mono bass amp, and we had two acoustics and we started playing together. The minute I heard them singing together I just went 'CUT, PRINT... boys this is it! This is exactly what we want.'"

David, too, was perhaps ready to give this potential new partnership a go, seeing that the endless studio grind was beginning to take its toll on him. "I was doing something like fifty sessions a year, but I began to see that there were finite limits to it. I wanted to do something more creative." It had been two or three years since his last "solo" record had been released, and clearly it was time for a new development in his career.

"I was real focused. I didn't drink, didn't smoke, and never did any kinds of drugs, and I treated the music business as something you put up with to be able to do the music..." stated David in a later interview. "(Then I initially) began submitting songs, which got me fired up about writing because, hey, I could work at home and I didn't have to spend all nights in the clubs. It was Roger Gordon (at Screen Gems) who then suggested, 'Why don't you sing your songs? I mean, you're already singing on demos. Why don't you go for a deal on a label?' I said, 'I really don't want to go on the road. I'm happy being behind the scenes.' But I felt like I should be doing my own stuff, just to see if I could do it better than the people who were recording it. So with that motivation in mind I went to Columbia to see

1968 rehearsal (courtesy of Robb Royer)

Jack Gold. I'd done a lot of arranging for Jack's artists, so I asked him, 'Will you sign me?' He said, 'You don't want to do that. That's hard work.' He didn't take me seriously.

"In those days, there was still quite a separate group of Brill Building-type writers. I was one of them, and we used to crank out songs for singers like Dean Martin. They'd say, 'We have Bobby Vee coming up for a session. He sings between C natural and D natural. He can hold a note for three seconds and he's recording two weeks from now. Will you please go home and write him a hit?' I never wrote one in the six years I worked like that. Not one out of 100 songs, and seeing some of those nice songs go down the drain, you start to think, I ought to do them myself. Glen Campbell was probably the first guy who stepped out of the shadows, and I was somewhat influenced by him. Those of us who'd been thought of as staff writers and arrangers suddenly began to think of singing our own stuff. In a way, the real influence was the Beatles, they were the first big singer-songwriter group."

He continued the theme in another conversation: "So over one Christmas holiday, 1967-68, I told my wife that I was going to write for myself. I wrote four songs over two weeks, and one of them was 'It Don't Matter To Me.' It was a weird tune and I could never have placed it with another artist, but I could sing it. That was when I began to do my best writing, when the restrictions were lifted.[13]

"At about the same time, I had produced a small group called The Pleasure Fair. One of the guys in the group was Robb Royer, who was writing with James Griffin as a team. Robb suggested one day that I come over and meet James. And I did. He said James was a good singer and they had written some things together and maybe we'd all throw in and maybe try to have a group. At the time, groups, you know, were quite a bit more popular or becoming more popular than solo artists. Since I'd run into some resistance with my A&R friends at trying to get signed, I went over and listened to Jimmy and Robb one day. James and I harmonized well together. He was from Tennessee, I was from Oklahoma. So we kind of thought a lot alike musically. I liked some of their songs, they liked some of my stuff so we put the three of us together. The idea was that James and Robb would be one half the writing and vocal entity and I would represent the other half. And we'd have hopefully twice as much material and twice as good a chance perhaps to break through."

It sounds simple, and while the exact location of their first meeting is subject to discussion, with Robb believing he took James over to David's and David understanding that he visited with James and Robb, the fact of the matter is what came out of the initial gathering was an understanding that the sound they were creating was something worth persisting with. An immediate camaraderie was united in the music, and it was a natural progression for them all. In order to direct this development, they then began to look at what was going on around them, using external factors to influence how they were going to approach this new project.

Royer: "All three of us sat around and went 'What did The Millennium do wrong?' And we incorporated that into our formation (of Bread). We decided it was

Early songwriting sessions (courtesy of Robb Royer)

too studio, too phony, we needed to do something that we could recreate almost exactly live, and that had a big influence on us. Yet, we never performed live once before we had a deal, the whole combination worked so well. We'd spend every waking hour together. Literally morning and night. We'd go down to Music City, check out the new instruments, the new amps, then go back and write some more. We'd eat, get with the girls for a few minutes, then we'd go back and play. That was just our constant thing."

The direction was becoming clear. Country rock was notably hot and happening around Los Angeles during this heady period, with The Byrds, The Flying Burrito Brothers, The Nitty Gritty Dirt Band, The Dillards all taking the country music sound and integrating it into the rock and pop rhythms that blew freely around the beaches and palm trees of Southern California. Although David's early influences from his home state of Oklahoma would ultimately play a decisive part in building the trio's new repertoire, neither James nor Robb initially had that strong an affinity with country music. Robb was bringing in folk and rock, while James had Memphis soul, incorporating deep southern gospel and blues. Nevertheless, it was with their acoustic guitars and harmonies that this variety of influences gelled. David's high vocals blended in with James's rich lower tones, and his ability to contribute often lighter and more "pop" orientated compositions mixed well as a contrast to the heavier, moodier patterns and rhythms from the Griffin-Royer combination. David simply oozed commerciality, James and Robb counterbalanced that with a serious approach that invited the audience to listen to their compositions. Not that David's work was deemed lightweight in comparison. Far from it. One only had to listen to the music he'd written for the young Suzy Wallis, or others from that era, to appreciate what he had to offer the trio, but the division within the established songwriting structures of the new "band" was evident from the start.

"There were a few (alternate) attempts. David and I did try to write a song once, but only got about half way through," Robb says, "but Jimmy was able to write a few songs with David, I think 'I Want You With Me' was the first one."

However, despite the promise of these early gatherings, in addition to the many connections that they still held within the industry, David, James, and Robb had to try to convince others that this new concept was a valid idea, one that was worth investing in. So, in between working on the music, writing, and developing their sound, they needed an avenue with which to present their ideas.

"Maria Aguayo was still with Jimmy at this point," Robb continues, "and she was working as the A&R girl at Columbia for Gary Usher. She checks in and says 'You know, I notice whenever a manager comes in we make him sit in the lobby, but whenever a lawyer comes up he walks right in!' So we said, 'Okay, we'll get a lawyer. Who are the best lawyers we know?' We came up with Abe Sommers and Al Schlesinger. Abe had just signed as a corporate lawyer with A&M, so we went to see Al..."

Alfred Schlesinger was a renowned lawyer, specializing in the field of music and intellectual property. A graduate of the University of Minnesota, prior to becoming an attorney he had spent eight years as a music publisher and record company executive, and qualified as an early member of the National Academy of Recording Arts and Sciences as both a songwriter and record producer. During the mid-1950s, along with partner Larry Goldberg, he had set up "R And B" records in Hollywood, working with rhythm and blues acts such as The Jewels. David Gates already had connections with him, having utilized his business previously with contract negotiations, so they decided to pay a visit.

Schlesinger was later to recall: "One day (David) came into my office and introduced me to James Griffin and Robb Royer and they asked me to listen to something. They had guitars with them and they sat in the conference room I had and played some tunes and said, 'What do you think?' I told them I thought it was great, I just love what they did, and they said, 'Fine, we want you to be our manager.'"[31]

Seemingly not taken aback by the direct approach, and impressed with what he heard, Schlesinger enquired as to what their expectations were and was duly informed they simply wanted a record deal, preferably with either Elektra Records, Atlantic Records, or the Beatles' own record company, Apple. Columbia and A&M were also considerations at one point.

"Apple was a weird thing," remembers Royer. "Everybody in L.A. claimed to represent Apple, but we're not sure anybody actually did! But Jac Holzman of Elektra and Ahmet Ertegun of Atlantic both made us offers."

What potentially swayed Elektra as their favored choice was due to what was actually happening over at Atlantic at the time. In three words: Crosby, Stills,

Nash. The three members of that particular trio, formerly of The Byrds, Buffalo Springfield, and The Hollies, had recently united. If ever there was a supergroup – an amalgamation of previously successful group members – then this was it. And the sound they created together? It was the sound of 1969. Their intricate three-part harmony was almost in direct rebellion against the heavy acid rock that had been gradually permeating musical society throughout the previous 24 months. Rock'n'roll critics loved CSN at that point, with even the often-vitriolic *Rolling Stone* magazine coming out in praise of the debut album, issued in May of that year. But even before the album had hit the streets, the word had gotten around. The summer of 1968 had shown the world initial glimpses of what this power-trio had to offer when, before Nash had officially quit The Hollies, they had first performed a number of local gigs around the hippest clubs of L.A., clearly demonstrating their tight vocal prowess. So, for a new band coming together during that period, as Gates, Griffin, and Royer were, it was already apparent as to what, or whom, they would be competing against. Much of the L.A. music scene of 1968 and early 1969 was Crosby, Stills & Nash. The in-crowd of John Sebastian, Cass Elliott, and the Laurel Canyon "rock royalty" were praising and raising them, while Atlantic Records founder Ahmet Ertegun was already in favor of CSN, and it seemed to weigh against the potential that any other vocal/acoustic trio may have should they also sign with the label. Too many comparisons would be made. Hence, Elektra Records, a label formed in 1950 by Jac Holzman and Paul Rickholt, and home to successful L.A. bands such as The Doors and Love, was the initial choice for David, James, and Robb.

Fortunately for them, Schlesinger already had a foothold in the Elektra building, a state-of-the-art studio and office block located at 962 North La Cienega Boulevard. Previously, he had been acting as attorney for Arthur Lee, founder and principal member of the band Love when, still registered as a minor, Schlesinger had assisted with his Elektra contract negotiations. Schlesinger himself had been impressed with the way that label owner Jac Holzman had handled the delicate affair and had promised Jac that, should anything fall his way that may prove of interest to the label, Elektra would be his first point of call. According to Holzman himself, in his 1998 publication *Follow The Music (The Life & High Times of Elektra Records)*:

"One day I'm at my desk, 9:00 am New York time, 6:00 am L.A. time, and Al calls my private line, the red phone. He says he has a group for me. I only recognized one name, David Gates, from Captain Beefheart, but I quickly offered to have David Anderle cut a demo."[12]

Anderle was no stranger to new sounds himself, having been an essential part of the "hip" L.A. scene for a number of years, prior to joining up with Elektra in 1967. Laid-back, cool, and handsome, Anderle had previously worked alongside head Beach Boy, Brian Wilson, during his frenetic *Smile* period, heading up the initial plans for the band's own label, the ill-fated and somewhat erratic Brother

Records. An audition was set up for Gates, Griffin, and Royer, still unnamed at that point, to show Anderle what they could offer the label. With acoustic guitars in hand, they sat down in the executive's own office and performed what Royer today recalls as being early versions of two Gates compositions, "Dismal Day" and "You Can't Measure The Cost," along with one of his own co-compositions with James, that the duo had left lying around for a while, "The Last Time."

The original demo acetate (courtesy of the Malcolm C. Searles collection)

"That was my guitar riff and mostly my chord changes," Griffin would later recall to Barry Alfonso. "I wrote most of the lyric, I think. It was kind of a Neil Diamond-y thing that I thought of doing as a solo artist."

Royer continues the theme: "The song goes into a modulation at the end of a chorus, from D to E, and then out in an interesting way. It really expanded when the band worked it up."

Immediately impressed, but wary of what Jac Holzman would think seeing that, up to that point, Elektra was not really known for being a "pop" label, Anderle called up engineer Bruce Botnick, famed for his work on the first three albums by The Doors, and arranged for the demo versions to be cut that night at Elektra's own studios. At the suggestion of Robb and James, a drummer by the name of Rod Edgar was drafted in to perform percussion duties on the session. Robb was familiar with Edgar's work as he had recently played on The Millennium album, and prior to that had been a part of The Music Machine, a popular mid-'60s L.A. garage band that James had seen on a number of occasions. So, with the temporary drummer position booked, the hastily arranged session took place that evening in the Elektra studio on North La Cienega, and versions were cut of the three songs they had earlier played for Anderle, although Ron Edgar today recalls taping an early version of "It Don't Matter To Me" as well.

Edgar: "David had called and wanted me to do a couple of demos. Just take my drum kit down, do a couple of songs, and that would be it. So I got down there and David was the only one down there at the time, besides the engineer. I set my drum kit up and then David came out, he had a cast on his foot, he had broken his leg or something, and he wrote me out some charts. I believe it was 'It Don't Matter To Me,' I remember that as it went down. He was an excellent arranger, very noteworthy. We did two or three other things, 'You Can't Measure The Cost'... and after the session he said, 'That was exactly what I needed you to play, it was very good, and thank you very much for coming.'"

According to a surviving acetate featuring two of the cuts from the session, the recording took place on November 6th, 1968, and the fading label would also suggest that the still undecided band name was also at the forefront of their minds. Distinctly written on the November acetate is the handwritten name "Bread," but underneath, virtually hidden by a mass of scribbled ink, the crossed out and misspelled word "Dragonwick" is also evident. It had been during the early formation of the trio that various potential names had been discussed and Dragonwyck had been one of the first suggestions, taken from the 1940s novel and movie, and also currently used by David as the name of his own publishing company. However, having discarded this proposal, fate was then to play a decisive part. Late one night, James and Robb had been driving around the streets of L.A., searching for inspiration, when they pulled up behind a Barbara Ann Bakery delivery truck and, to Royer's apparent delight, the word "Bread" leapt out at him. They immediately called up David with the suggestion who, while not overly enthusiastic about the idea, seemingly accepted the new proposal. It would take a later meeting with Elektra, when the potential name was mentioned again, before the idea was truly accepted. Bill Harvey, the label's art director, reportedly greeted the name with a relished enthusiasm, commenting that "everybody's pretending that they're oblivious to money, so let's have a band called Bread."

Clearly the name could be taken in a number of ways, and it started with a "b" so would be found in record racks alongside The Beatles, The Beach Boys, and The Bee Gees although, as David would later recall with a smile: "One word names fascinated us a little bit, so I think we were trying to shoot for somethin' like that, but you know it took me several weeks to get used to that. I thought 'Bread,' that doesn't make any sense at all. The hardest thing was to convince people not to call us The Breads. Even on one (later) network television show,

I can't remember which one, but right there in front of several million people, 'Here they are, The Breads!'"[31]

Listening to the acetate session, over 40 years after it was recorded, one is immediately struck by how sophisticated the arrangements are, even in their original demo form, although certain parts, such as a prominent backing vocal chorus on "Dismal Day," were dropped from the eventually released versions. Robb, however, remains unconvinced on their initial studio attempts. "You listen to the demo now and it's laughable," he comments. "Some of the demos I've heard since, it's all so huge and elaborate, but we just sort of went in there and knocked something out. But (Elektra) saw something in it and so, strangely, had us redo some with them watching… just to make sure it was us!"

Holzman: "The demo was couriered to me, and I thought it was great, utterly fresh and likeable, harmonizing vocals that wove in, out, and around each other; a softer, more considerate sound than the hard rock that was now everywhere. Other labels were showing interest, especially Columbia, but (they) chose us."[12]

"Elektra was top of our list. The label and Jac had an excellent reputation of being music-orientated and worked good with artists. A nice home to be," Gates was quoted as saying in Holzman's book, although Robb Royer also remembers them having to perform before the label's head at one point, prior to signing the deal.

Within a matter of weeks after signing with Elektra, the contract dated January 1969, the trio found themselves back in the Elektra studios, working on the sessions that would ultimately become their debut album. There was seemingly no time allowed for fully honing all of the compositions prior to the recording of the album, and presumably the band, as well as the label, were keen to see product out in the market as swiftly as possible. Nevertheless, such were the obvious talents on display that many of the arrangements were made as the sessions flowed. Despite the musical dexterity of all three band members, it was apparent early on that a proficient session drummer would be needed to fill out the rhythm accompaniment. Seeing that they considered themselves solely as a studio unit at that time, with no need for a permanent fourth member, the option of bringing in a drummer to the "official ranks" was never discussed and, although having used Ron Edgar for the demo recordings, they opted to go with one of L.A.'s most experienced session players for the final product, one who had played on numerous hits over the years and who could deliver a professional studio performance at the crash of a cymbal.

James "Jim" Gordon had begun his career back in the early 1960s, supporting artists such as The Everly Brothers, and by the mid-1960s, along with Hal Blaine and Earl Palmer, he was one of the most sought after drummers for studio sessions around Los Angeles, appearing on albums by The Beach Boys, The Byrds, Mason Williams, The Monkees, and Barbra Streisand, as well as being a part-time player in Spector's established team of musicians. David Gates had become acquainted with him during the many session dates they had shared together over this period and subsequently recommended him to James and Robb as the drummer for their upcoming album. "We worked with Ron on three songs (the demos), and then brought in Jim Gordon. God, it was like floating on a cloud playing with the guy," says Robb of Jim Gordon today. "He was fantastic."

Despite David's principal focus at the time being clearly directed towards the newly christened band, a number of releases by other performers, also benefiting from his prodigious talents, continued to appear. A critically acclaimed album by Nashville artist Bergen White – *For Women Only* – arrived in stores during 1969 featuring two brand new David Gates offerings: the tender "Look At Me," a song that the newly christened Bread were also working on in the studio, and the lovely "Gone Again" (White would later cut a third Gates-penned tune, "Have You Taken A Good Look Lately," during 1975), while another new Gates arrangement, "My Imagination," appeared on a single release on the Colgems label, credited to PK Limited, a recording duo comprising of fellow Screen Gems songwriters Marty Kaniger and Dan Peyton. Former '60s teen-star Bobby Vee recorded one of David's compositions, "The Passing Of A Friend," on his 1969 *Gates, Grills and Railings* album, while he also took time out from his own sessions to assist country music star Buck Owens and his Bakersfield Brass band in the studio, offering production and arranging skills that would ultimately appear on the *Rose Garden* album the following year.

During that winter and the early spring of 1969, the recording of Bread's debut album continued, despite David being still somewhat restricted in his movements around the studio due to the cast on a broken leg, the result of a frantic basketball game with his band mates. With the production experience gained by all three individuals over the past decade, most notably David, it became an obvious decision for the group members to maintain the producer role for themselves, opting to unify the credit to a simple "produced by Bread" tag, while utilizing Elektra's own Bruce Botnick in the engineering role. There were fourteen (known) songs being considered for inclusion on the album at one point or another. The David Gates composition "You Can't Measure The Cost," one of their initial audition songs, had been copyrighted earlier in the year, as had the Griffin-Royer song "The Last Time," and both were penciled in for inclusion, and David had been holding on to "It Don't Matter To Me" for over a year now, waiting for the right moment to put a definitive version down onto tape. One further contribution that had been written and copyrighted before the sessions took place was a song that Robb Royer and James Griffin had written in partnership with Robb's former Pleasure Fair bandmate, Tim Hallinan. "Friends And Lovers," which would ultimately appear as the closing track on the album, was a glorious number that fit perfectly as the finale on the final release. James's lead vocal, set initially against a bleak backing, is neither pop nor rock, blues nor soul, it was just a perfect combination that defied categorization, and the harmony on the closing line – "did anybody touch you?" – is a wonderful example of the quality of delivery and blend that the combined voices of David and James could provide.

"That's a real interesting song," says Royer. "The whole thing was about how pieces of your life start falling away as time goes on."

All the remaining songs that finally appeared on the finished product were relatively new compositions, although there were two additional tracks attempted and ultimately abandoned when it came to the final song selection, losing out to the Royer-inspired "Family Doctor." The first of the discarded numbers, written by James and Robb, was titled "Beachwood Band," a rather pessimistic offering that the duo had composed as a tribute to their surroundings in the Los Angeles community in which they currently resided. It would remain unheard for a number of years before finally turning up in 1974 as the B-side to a James Griffin solo release. The second of the unfinished tracks was a gorgeous ballad, composed by James and Robb during the fall of 1968, which, despite the quality of the product, just didn't seem to fit comfortably into the recording process. "Look What You've Done" would be tried again during sessions for the second album. A number of further Griffin and Royer tunes, "Lucky, Look At Me," "Summer Song," "Hold On, Hold On," and "She's Everything But Mine," hailing from the same 1968 time period, didn't even reach the consideration stage.

David recalls: "We hardly ever recorded something we didn't use. If a song wasn't good enough, we wouldn't record it. We were pretty severe critics of each other. When you play something for another songwriter, you know right away, as you're playing it, whether you can hold your head up or whether you're a little ashamed. It's real quick!"[13]

Overall, the sessions were conducted in a positive light. "My main instrument was guitar, but I played a little keyboards, some bass, even some flutes and recorder. We were like the guys in The Band when they did *Music From Big Pink*. Whatever instrument was nearby we'd pick it up and play it. It was wildly instrumental and we all felt a real optimism and excitement about it all," Robb was later to tell Barry Alfonso for the CD re-issues. Indeed, another one of the featured tracks on the final release, a composition by David recalling the tale of one of London's most famous landmarks, the old bridge that spanned the River Thames, demolished and rebuilt in the Arizona desert, included one of the first occasions when a Moog synthesizer was used on a "pop" record (the first occasion is generally accepted as being on The Monkees' 1967 album *Pisces, Aquarius, Capricorn & Jones Ltd.*).

Says David, "Paul Beaver was the owner and programmer of one of them and we got Paul to come and kind of help us. I knew what I wanted to do with it musically, but I didn't know where to plug in all the cords and twist the dials."[12]

Once completed, the album was put onto Elektra's schedule for a 1969 issue, although today there remains considerable contradictions as to the actual date of release. Jac Holzman, in his book *Follow The Music*, recalls it as being two weeks before the Atlantic release of the debut CSN album, indicating late April or early May of 1969, while Robb Royer, in conversation with the author, recalls it coinciding with their first live appearance during July of that year. The 1995 CD re-issue sleeve notes suggest it first appeared in January 1969, which is highly implausible due to the contract being dated the same month, although this was amended on the 1996 notes, which correctly listed September.

Naturally, a lead-off single had to be chosen to assist with the promotion for the album, with David Anderle, upon visiting the sessions and listening to the completed tracks, initially favoring the Griffin-Royer composition "Could I."

"Robb came up with the musical idea for that one on the piano," Griffin was to tell Alfonso. "We thought that it had a real English flavor to it. Jim Gordon played drums on it. It was a real hard song for a drummer to pull off because it had a 3/4 against a 4/4 rhythm. Jim was one of the few who could've done it..."

However, the more commercial David Gates tune, "Dismal Day," was eventually picked for the first single, appearing in June of 1969, coupled with "Any Way You Want Me" (Griffin-Royer) on the reverse side. Of the flip-side, James was later to recall: "That song was the first time I had ever played electric lead guitar. I was more of a rhythm player, but as the band progressed I played more and more lead..."[14]

Unfortunately, despite the upbeat nature of the chosen track, and the faith put in it by both Elektra and the band, the release failed to gain any significant airplay or sales. Possibly the downbeat title and lyrical content harmed potential success, especially since the as yet unknown band had still to find an audience, but it is difficult to find fault with the polished harmonies and overall performance of the song. "Could I," backed with the delightful "You Can't Measure The Cost," was the next issue, following the instincts of David Anderle, and featured James providing the lead vocals. This was again released in advance of the album, and once more designed to generate interest in the forthcoming long player but, as before, while not as commercially accessible as its lively predecessor, it too failed to register with the public. This was not the scenario that the band had envisaged, particularly after the euphoria they had experienced during the early days of harmonizing together, coupled with the long hours spent in the studio crafting the songs. Nevertheless, regardless of these early setbacks, Elektra went ahead and released the band's debut album, simply titled *Bread*. Packaged in a simple sleeve design, with the three faces of the band members each framed as the centerpiece on individual cartoon-styled dollar bills, thus avoiding the obvious connotations with the band name, these were the first images that the American public had of the band.

"The only thing that didn't sit real well with me was the cover of the album, with the three dollar bills on it," said Griffin later. "We were definitely in it to make money, but we were trying to say something musically too." Holzman, however, was full of praise for the design: "I thought this cover was enormously clever..."[12]

To date there had been no pre-release shows performed, and the advance publicity had been minimal, bar the two unsuccessful singles and series of posters and advertisements placed in the press (proclaiming "you'll never outgrow your need for bread" and "the wonder of bread sliced twelve ways"), and so to drop the album into the media in such a way shows the faith that Elektra, and Jac Holzman in particular, had in the band. They were an unknown commodity. Credit for the layout of the album sleeve, and in particular for the distinctive band logo, fell into the hands of the Elektra Art Department, headed by Bill Harvey. Harvey was the man responsible for designing the familiar butterfly logo that adorned many of the Elektra Records releases, as well as the famous "Love" design that featured on all of that particular band's albums. A large part of Elektra's reputation was built around the quality of its presentation, of which the design, photography, and lettering on the album sleeves were crucial. Harvey was instrumental in achieving the high standards that Elektra set in these regards, and many of their notable releases could be identified by their lettering and logos alone. In the long run the simple, and yet effective, "Bread" logo was to become almost as famous as the faces of the individual band members.

The album eventually went on to sell in the region of 50,000 copies in their homeland, aided by a promotional 7" single (Elektra B-1), circulated around the radio stations, featuring the trio discussing how they came together, how they signed with Elektra, and how they felt about the album itself. Maybe the total sales were a disappointing figure to the band, with the album peaking at a lowly #127 in the *Billboard* Top 200 listing towards the latter end of the year and yet, critically, the release garnered a number of positive comments among media and press.

"Make no mistake, kids, this album is no synthetic bullshit," began Lester Bangs in his review of the album for *Rolling Stone*. "The three boys in the group wrote all their songs, and we're proud of them" he notes, before continuing on with further praise and encouragement to those considering the release: "You're sure to get your money's worth."

Cover versions of some of the featured songs also soon began appearing, thus acknowledging the obvious quality of the songwriting. Erstwhile Monkee, Davy Jones, chose to cover the appealing Gates ballad "Look At Me," while the album *Real Friends*, by The Friends Of Distinction, featured versions of both "It Don't Matter To Me" and "Any Way You Want Me." Yet the overall acceptance of Bread's offering among the buying public was overshadowed, pure and simple, by the earlier arrival of the debut Crosby, Stills & Nash album. Atlantic Records had scored a major victory with the immediate impact their act had achieved, and it appeared that no one was going to take away any of their success. *Bread* was simply left to bathe in the afterglow, and any possibility of significant media attention was washed away when the front pages of the world were filled with the double summer whammy of Woodstock and Tate/LaBianca. Peace, love, and destruction...

With Schlesinger now taking control of the business affairs – "Al was terrific," remembers Robb, "Five percent business, five percent legal, five percent light management" – David, James, and Robb were now able to concentrate on taking their sound out into the "live" circuit. However, despite the positive musical outlook for the band, James also had other, more personal matters to contend with.

His faltering relationship with his second wife, Maria, was not helping his state of mind. They loved each other dearly, but James simply couldn't commit in the way that his wife wished, often avoiding confrontations by walking away, despite their relationship having lasted five years. They parted soon afterwards. He had also recently lost his father, Marvin, with whom he had shared a mixed relationship over the years. Sometimes close, sometimes strained. But it was during this period, shortly after Marvin's passing, that his mother, Neva, chose to break the potentially devastating news to him that the man who had brought him up, whom James had always believed to be his natural parent, was not actually his blood father. That honor had fallen to a man with whom she had shared a brief liaison with during Marvin's absence overseas while serving his country during the war, a musician named Paul Brazil.

"He was a very handsome, wonderful man," remembers Carol Ann, James's sister. "My mother and father got married during World War II, before he went overseas. She had met Paul after daddy left. I don't think they had a long-term love affair or anything. I'm sure she felt very bad, but she was very young. She told Jimmy, and it really was a shock." James's future wife Kathy also comments that, "I think Jimmy wanted to believe that he was his dad in one way, but then didn't in another. But his mother said that's who he was, so he accepted it." It would be a few more years until James would actually meet up with his natural father.

Interestingly, during December of that year, Al Schlesinger received a letter from an agency in London, Harold Davison Limited, who had heard and were duly impressed with the debut release. "I have just heard their album…" it said, "and I feel that this group could do very well in England. However, the first tour would be purely promotional and there would be no big fees. I think the most important thing is for them to come here to do television and a few engagements. I feel we could probably make this group very big in this country." They *would* be... but not just yet.

Subsequently, the first official live concert that Bread were to perform, booked on the same bill as The Flying Burrito Brothers and Dillard & Clark, took place on July 14th, 1969, at the Aquarius Theater, situated at 6230 Sunset Boulevard, one week before fellow Elektra recording artists The Doors were to play a legendary set there. There are seemingly no records currently in existence of any further shows played locally over this period, and the next known live venture for the band, the first true test for them as a performing entity, came shortly afterwards, when they headed up to Seattle for four weeks' worth of appearances.

"We had thought of (ourselves) being a studio band," David was to tell *Classic Rock* magazine in 2002, "but the Elektra president, Jac Holzman, would have nothing to do with that. He said, 'You guys have gotta get out there and work.'"

The northern city of Seattle was a hotbed for breaking new bands at the time, and Bread's initial set lists comprised many of the songs taken from the debut release, although Robb recalls that, "We started with the album. It was all that we knew, but we were writing all of the time. It was hard to bring off 'Friends And Lovers' live, but we also worked up some Chuck Berry and some other stuff. It was 99 percent Bread songs."

Drummer Jim Gordon had reprised his role within the band for their debut performance at the Aquarius Theater, and was a popular enough choice among the band members that they now considered offering him a permanent berth within the ranks. Unfortunately, Gordon instead opted to join up with the Delaney & Bonnie Bramlett tour of that year, which ultimately led to the formation of Derek & The Dominoes with Eric Clapton twelve months later, along with Carl Radle (a former member of The Accents), and subsequent rock infamy as the co-composer of "Layla." David, James, and Robb clearly needed to find a swift replacement to occupy the drum stool in order to get out on the road in Washington State, but one who was capable of filling the void created by Gordon's sudden departure. The first call was made to Ron Edgar, who had assisted during the initial sessions at Elektra, but he had to decline the offer due to touring commitments with another band he was currently working with:

"I was playing with a group called Bandana, who were very popular in places. It was a showband, a covers band, and cover bands in those days did very well. We were in Denver, and David Gates had called my home phone and then my wife rang me to say that David had called wanting to know if I wanted to go on tour (with Bread), and I said 'I can't leave this band... just get up and walk off.' I just made the decision that I couldn't do it..."

Fortunately, for David, James, and Robb, despite the setback, one other drummer they also had connections with was available.

Chapter Six

He's A Good Lad

Michael Gene Botts was born on December 8th, 1944, in Oakland, California, eight miles to the east of San Francisco. Partly of Portuguese descent on his mother Mathilda's side, partly of Irish descent on his father Eugene's side, the family moved shortly after his birth to nearby Antioch where he spent the first six years of his life, although at the age of seven, the Botts family upped sticks and valuables once again, this time relocating to the state capital of Sacramento, where Mike settled into school life comfortably. With encouragement from the music facility on campus, the youngster developed an early fascination for percussion, and by the time he had reached his teens he was also fast developing a fervent interest in jazz music, and to a lesser extent rhythm and blues.

School friend Joe LaManno remembers: "Mike Botts was the first musician I ever met. That's a simple enough statement until I tell you that we met at age 13, in band class in our first year of junior high school. I played music... but Michael was a musician. We became instant brothers of the heart. We played the parades, school dances, rallies, and hung out at each other's houses listening to jazz for hours. He was particularly drawn to the hard-edged bebop of Charlie Parker, Miles Davis, Thelonius Monk, Charles Mingus, and Cannonball Adderley. He didn't have much use for lyrics, with the exception of the words of Lenny Bruce and Lord Buckley. His music and good looks also made him the envy of all the boys and the heart-throb of all the girls."

Mike took every advantage he could to discover more about the music he was now so avidly devouring, keen to learn at every opportunity. So keen in fact, that even at this early stage he'd go down to the dilapidated, derelict areas of the city, skid row, the undesirable parts of town, where a Latin percussionist named Armando Perazo used to live. Such was his willingness to learn that he used to head out, on his own, whenever he could get a ride, simply to study with this talented individual. Although unaware of his surreptitious activities across town, Mike's mother, and his new stepfather John (his parents having divorced a few years previously), also used to help him realize his ambitions by paying for regular drum lessons. While by no means an affluent family, they generously honored what was fast becoming their son's passion in life.

By the time both he and his friend Joe LaManno entered high school, Mike was beginning to play his music to a wider audience. The local musicians around town began to discover how good this kid really was and he began to get gigs at various social events, weddings, and dances.

"In high school I switched from trumpet to playing upright bass," continues LaManno. "That added another layer to our bond, for now we could be part of a rhythm section together. Already, Mike's single-minded focus and undeniable talent had earned him a reputation around town. At that time in Sacramento, in order to join the Musician's Union you had to be 18 years old. To no one's surprise, Mike was getting called for jam sessions and paid gigs with the local music royalty in early high school, and he was in such demand that he was issued a union card at age 16, just to keep it legal. The good news for me was Mike's persistence in bringing me along to these sessions and gigs to meet, observe, and learn from the best of the local players. Although I wasn't really a strong enough bass player to play (with these guys) he knew that just having me around would be good for me."

Such was his loyalty to Joe that on occasions when there was a gig to be played, and no bass player was available from the usual line-ups, Joe would often get the call from Mike to fill in and although, as he now admits, Joe would often be out of his depth he subsequently got a lot of "on the job" training thanks to such loyalty. In addition to these local gigs, and their work with the various high school bands, both Mike and Joe would also participate in the DeMolay Revue, a traveling variety show affiliated with the Mason's Lodge, that would tour up and down the entire western coast of America. Academically, Mike passed all of his school classes, doing just enough to achieve strong enough grades without losing the true focus of his attention. The same with sports and athletics. But it was all about the music.

With his radio often tuned into the local stations, his ears pricking up whenever he heard the sounds of Miles Davis or John Coltrane coming over the airwaves, he began to absorb all styles of music that he encountered. Rock'n'roll was also happening and, as with much of the nation's youth, the pounding sounds of Little Richard, Fats Domino, and Chuck Berry all held a strong interest for the young drummer. Initially, he appeared slightly reluctant to accept this new form of music, such was his purist jazz nature, but gradually, through being asked to play at various rock'n'roll shows around town, he began to appreciate what much of the nation already knew. Rock'n'roll was big news. Joe LaManno was also proving influential in some areas as he had recently become involved with a local folk group, playing bass in the line-up, and Mike often traveled to see him play, occasionally sitting in during rehearsals once the previously acoustic folk scene began to accept both electricity and drums. His intensity with pure jazz was now starting to ease up a little as he opened his eyes and ears to these outside sources. However, what was happening in California at the turn of the decade, the early staccato runs and the high harmonies of the soon-to-be burgeoning "surf music scene" held no interest for him whatsoever. He termed surf music as "pretty stupid stuff," but once the

Mike Botts (courtesy of Michele Botts)

Beatles touched down in America, a few years later, it became a whole different story. He was soon finding himself playing behind guitarists and singers who were cranking out the current hits not only by the Beatles, but also by the Rolling Stones and The Kinks.

Mike was later to say: "When I first began working, professionally, my first inclination was to go in the direction of jazz. It's a players' form of music. And then the Beatles came. A jazz piano player I was working with said, 'You should go see *A Hard Day's Night.*' Well, at that point, I had barely heard of the Beatles, couldn't care less, but I went to see it and it just turned a whole lot of things around in my head."

By the time he entered college, his standing among his musical peers was being graciously acknowledged, and it was to give him the opportunities rarely afforded to someone so young. Despite his age he was now on the lists of a number of local music agents and, even before he left his teenage years behind, he had managed to fit in performances alongside some of the jazz giants of the era. Guitarist Wes Montgomery and organist Jimmy Smith, both major influences among their contemporaries, benefited from the rhythmic patterns Botts was able to play behind them and, even so early in his career, Mike was deemed a player of such note that he was afforded a tryout in the acclaimed Miles Davis backing band. Unfortunately, just prior to his audition for the esteemed bandleader, the equally talented Chicago-born youngster Tony Williams also tried out for the position, passing with flying colors, subsequently depriving Mike of the opportunity to play before his jazz hero. Nevertheless, despite such disappointment, the city of Sacramento could only offer so much to the ambitious teenager, and after successfully avoiding the draft, sparing him the horrors of the Vietnam war, his thoughts began to head towards the coast.

According to Mike's own biography that ran on his website, prior to his all-too-early passing in the winter of 2005: "It was during my second year of college that I was offered a few casual summer gigs with a group based out of Los Angeles called the Travelers 3. A few months later they called me from Canada to say they were going electric, they needed a drummer, and offered the job to me. We all got along great. I enjoyed the music and besides, it was my ticket to Los Angeles and The Road, so of course I accepted. Being in L.A. soon gave me the opportunity to break into recording."

In a later interview he considered the opportunity now afforded him in more depth: "If I had stayed in Sacramento and remained a big fish in a small pond I may have reached age 36 or 37 and sat down in a chair, read the evening paper, and stopped for a second and thought, 'I wonder, if I had gone to L.A. would I ever have made it?' I would rather go to L.A. and succeed or fail but at least have the answer."[31]

The Travelers 3 had originally formed in Oregon, with Charlie Oyama, Peter Apo, and Dick Shirley meeting up at the State University. A love of folk music pulled the trio together and, after consolidating their sound, they moved out to Hawaii, Charlie and Peter's family home, and took up a lengthy residency at the famous Shell Bar in Honolulu. However, the early 1960s saw them relocate to Los Angeles, often attending the regular "hoot" nights at The Troubadour Club on Santa Monica Boulevard. It was here that record label boss, Jac Holzman, first heard the group, and signed them to his Elektra Records label, from where they issued three albums: *Travelers 3* and *Open House*, both in 1962, and *Live Live Live* the following year. By 1964, with the arrival of all things "beat"-related, and the traditional folk sounds of The Kingston Trio et al. gradually being consigned to the bargain-bins, the Travelers 3 decided to update their sound and move with the times. They signed with Capitol Records and issued the *New Sounds* album that year and, while maintaining their folk origins, the threesome added a drummer to the ranks.

Founding member Charlie Oyama recalled in conversation with the author: "In the summer of 1964 Michael was nineteen years old and on summer break from attending Sacramento City College. The Travelers 3 had a booking at the Cal-Neva Lodge in Lake Tahoe, I believe that Frank Sinatra still had some sort of ownership role in the place at that time, and the contract called for four musicians. It was a big lounge. The drummer from L.A. who we used in other Nevada lounge bookings became unavailable at the last minute, so we called the Sacramento agent and asked if she could get a drummer. She told us that none of her professional drummers had a four-week open slot, but she did have 'a kid on summer vacation who was pretty good.' We said okay. A couple of weeks later we arrive at the Cal-Neva Lodge, and see, sitting on the front steps of the casino, this skinny kid almost hidden by the cases of his full drum kit. They wouldn't let him in, because he was still underage! That was the (first) meeting. We had rented a beautiful home overlooking Lake Tahoe, so we just dragged him with us. Every night he had to get to the backstage area through the kitchen because he was too young to walk through the Casino. To say that we were impressed by his musicianship and eagerness to learn would be a huge understatement. It took him all of four weeks to go from 'college kid' to 'pro.'"

Following the conclusion of the Lake Tahoe residency, Mike returned to college, impressing his friends with his summer stories. Meanwhile, the Travelers 3 ventured back to their scheduled tours, filling in the vacant drum stool with another player. A few months later, in early 1965, they came to the conclusion that they had to move from acoustic to electric instruments in order to maintain their ongoing career. Traditional folk music was simply being swept aside in the rush to electrify: Dylan, The Byrds, The Lovin' Spoonful. They also decided to add a permanent drummer to the ranks and despite the succession of percussionists they had used on previous tours and residencies, there was no hesitancy in their choice. Maintaining the Hawaiian origins of two thirds of the band, their "choice" was to be invited to join their "family" as opposed to simply being referred to as the drummer. Charlie Oyama called Mike at home in Sacramento and asked him what he was currently doing, the answer he got: "flunking out!"

"When I popped the question, he was so happy I think he was yelling and crying at the other end of the line. He packed up and left Sacramento and met us the following week in Vancouver, Canada, and our opening line from then on was, 'Hi, we're the Travelers 3, all four of us!'"

Shortly afterwards, with the band now permanently based in Los Angeles, bass player Dick Shirley, who was keen to return to his native Oregon and be with his family, decided to opt out of the line-up and so Mike, naturally, placed a call back home to his longtime friend Joe LaManno, encouraging him to audition. Keen to participate, Joe packed up his suitcase and his bass, hitched a ride west, and auditioned before them at The Playboy Club on Sunset Boulevard.

"I got the gig," recalls Joe, "and you can only imagine how elated I was to now be making my living as a musician, and to be in a band with Michael. We were just thrilled, the both of us. It couldn't have been a better deal."

This band would spend the next year or so together, touring, writing, and recording, with the elder band members, Charlie and Pete, becoming almost surrogate fathers to the young Sacramento pairing. Indeed, Mike had become estranged from his father at a young age, and his new band mates, Charlie in particular, would remain a stabilizing force for much of his life. They toured across the country, far and wide, sharing the driving of the band's van between them, bonding as only four traveling musicians could. The music, the relationships, the emotions.

"It really set the bar for Michael and me as to how to function in the music business, and how not to get caught up in all of the trappings of all of that stuff," summarizes Joe of that period.

During time spent at home in Los Angeles, the Travelers 3 continued to solidify their standing in the community, appearing at a number of the new L.A. folk-rock clubs that were springing up around town, often appearing alongside The Nitty Gritty Dirt Band, The Association, or solo acts such as Steve Martin or Lily Tomlin. They even occasionally shared breathing space with rock royalty.

"David Crosby looked at us like, 'Who are you two nerds?'" laughs Joe, recollecting how both he and Mike came across The Byrds' guitarist in a Sunset Strip nightclub while both wearing matching capes, inspired by the look that Crosby himself had worn on the cover of The Byrds' debut album.

It was also around this period that Mike first met two new industry connections that would play a pivotal role in his development within the recording studios. The first contact was Dick Rosmini, who immediately took a shine to the young drummer and his explosive talents. Rosmini was a part of the original folk revival troupe of the early 1960s and was a highly respected guitarist and banjo picker. He later moved into production and session work once the initial folk-boom had begun to disperse, even appearing alongside the earlier incarnation of the Travelers 3 on some of their early album releases, prior to Mike joining up. His connection with Mike would prove to be an important factor in getting the drummer's talents acknowledged by a wider audience.

The second such connection came in the form of the six-piece (or seven-piece depending on which era one is referring to) pop-folk band The Association. With the Travelers 3 having supported this successful group at various local Los Angeles gigs, Mike was already familiar with their material and the various members of the line-up, particularly bass player Brian Cole, whom Mike was to become especially close to. They would spend a lot of time hanging out together and Mike would often stay at Brian's house, overseeing the property, while he was away on tour with The Association. Brian would also offer whatever assistance he could to his young friend, banding his name around whenever possible among the session circles, and The Association would also play a major part in Mike's next musical venture. However, the Travelers 3 were still the priority at this time, although all four group members were all too aware that their moment in the collective spotlight may be wearing thin. Bookings were slowing down. Times were moving on. So with Charlie Oyama's encouragement, the foursome decided to put together their own production company, A-Brah, managing other artists, and administering publishing. Mike wasn't particularly noted for his business skills at this time, having minimal interest in that side of the industry, other than undertaking much of the Travelers 3 musical arrangements for their shows, but he did harbor thoughts about becoming a record producer. However, his initial contributions to A-Brah were not really of significance, choosing instead to leave much of the business dealings to Charlie. One of the first bands through their doors and to be managed by the new company was another Sacramento act called Fourth And Main, later relabeled as The Aerial Landscape. Among their line-up was a young man named Larry Hansen, a talented songwriter and guitarist who had earlier been a part of Joe LaManno's folk quartet back in their hometown. He too was to become a future part in the developing story.

Meanwhile, the Travelers 3 continued working, despite the dwindling appearances that would eventually lead to the parting of the ways, and while the band were to release no more records during the 1960s, they did try to develop their new style within the confines of the studio environment, the first such experience for both Mike and Joe.

LaManno adds: "And so continued a lifetime of inspiration. As much as I loved music, the idea of making a living at it had seemed so remote. For Michael there was never a doubt as to his career path, which opened me to the possibility that it could happen, even for me. He led the way for me working around Sacramento, often-times together. He was the first to make it out of town, getting hired by the Travelers 3. Within a few months he had me in that band, traveling the country together, moving to Los Angeles together, being roommates for many years, all the while both of us living a dream. We even played our first record dates together. The producer of those sessions was a then-little-known string arranger named David Gates..."

Capitol Records, still keen to see new material on the market, authorized a recording session for them under the guidance of the upcoming producer David Gates, hoping to benefit from the combination and although a number of songs were worked upon during the session – "In The Early Mornin' Rain," "Let's Get Together," "The Times They Are A-Changin'," "Turn, Turn, Turn," and a composition based upon the JRR Tolkien novel *The Hobbit*, appropriately titled "The Hobbit (I Sit Beside The Fire)" – Capitol chose to pass on the final results. Nevertheless, Gates himself was suitably impressed with the band that he continued to utilize the four musicians as his "in-house" team on a further series of recordings he was working on, including some for fellow Capitol performer and country music star Jody Miller.

"With some networking and recommendations by a few close friends, I was able to do more and more session work in between the college and club tours with the Travelers 3," continued Mike, retelling his own story. "As the group started fading, my career as a session player started getting brighter. In fact, it was at a recording session for the Travelers 3 that I first met David Gates. David had been brought in to produce some recordings of us for Capitol Records. The record company passed, the group broke up, but I continued to run into David occasionally in various recording sessions around the city."

It was at this point that the connection with The Association reared its head once again. Jules Gary Alexander, one of the fellow founding members along with Brian Cole, had recently returned from a sabbatical in India, intent on putting a new group together alongside a songwriting friend named Richard Ellison. At Brian Cole's suggestion, Jules contacted Mike to see if he was available to occupy the drum stool. Mike in turn, having committed himself to the project, recommended Joe LaManno and guitarist Larry Hansen, the latter having by now left his previous group The Aerial Landscape. This new five-piece band labeled themselves Joshua Fox, and spent the next few months continuously writing and rehearsing, developing their own sound. All five members actually lived together in a loft on Hollywood Boulevard at one stage, referred to as "the foxhole," surrounded by equipment supplied by The Association, who even went to the extent of buying groceries and pot for their friends in order to sustain their minimal income. With his experience in the industry to date, plus a certain amount of financial input courtesy of Association royalties, Jules Alexander was thus seen as the undisputed band leader and it was therefore assumed that they would fall under the wing of The Association's own management arm. Instead, at the suggestion of Mike, Joe, and Larry, they opted to go with Charlie Oyama, their former Travelers 3 associate, who was still running the production and management venture.

During the initial period of writing, rehearsing, and jamming, the band gradually began building up a buzz around town, and the talk was that they were going to be the next big thing, in as much the same vein that The Millennium was promising so much during the same period. So Charlie Oyama set up an audition with Tetragrammaton Records, a label founded by comedian Bill Cosby back at the start of the decade (and most notably famous for "handling" the infamous Lennon-Ono *Two Virgins* album that same year). The band played a fifteen-minute live set at the loft in Hollywood for label heads Roy Silver and Artie Mogul, and they made an offer on the spot. After all of the negotiations were done, and the contracts signed, the band began working with one of the label's own producers, but with the actual recording barely started, the original band broke up; Jules Alexander deciding that it wasn't really working for him. He subsequently left, taking his friend Richard Ellison with him.

Charlie Oyama recalls: "It was not a bitter parting, just too 'chemically' influenced. But the company still wanted the remaining members to go ahead with the recording..."

So Mike, along with Joe LaManno and Larry Hansen, recruited additional guitarist Tom Menefee, an old high school contact from Sacramento, and they reconvened in the studio, pulling a successful gathering of twelve songs together for their debut album release.

Starting off with a minute of vocal harmonies, played in reverse, the album runs the gamut of country, rock, psychedelia, and folk across the featured twelve songs, including five songwriting credits for Mike, along with a surprising six lead vocals (and he even handled lead guitar on some of the sessions). "It's Just Meant To Be," the first of Mike's contributions, commences with a Grateful Dead-styled country/jug-band groove, before adding a brazen horn section and heavy guitar riff that takes the song in a completely different direction. The tight rhythm section that Botts and LaManno pulled together is also noticeably impressive on this particular cut, with the bass run prominently weaving up and down the frets as the track gets wilder. The more subdued "Goin' Down For Big Numbers," a Botts-Hansen collaboration including some pleasant tempo shifts, follows on with some nice Association-styled harmonies showing the influences of Jules Alexander. But of all of the songs on the album, it is the brief band-composed "We're All In It Together" that particularly highlights Mike's impressive drum fills and abilities, and his overall influence on the direction of the band. It really becomes apparent here that his contributions were the essential lynchpin in how the band so successfully gelled together, and while LaManno's ambitious offering, "How I Managed To Stay Off The Truck And Find Comfort In My Sanity," is perhaps just that one step too far in self-indulgence, it also shows the true capability that this still unknown four-piece had to offer, albeit sadly tailing off before they really hit the mark. In fact, it is only on two of the songs, "Monkey Song #1," and the lengthy seven-minute "Anne," both from the Botts-Hansen writing partnership, that they really have the opportunity to hit their stride, shifting time patterns with ease. However, the most impressive cut on the entire album comes in the shape of "Billy Goat Capricorn Lover," a composition that Larry Hansen and Jules Alexander had pulled together during the band's initial conception, and it shares its inspiration with the early themes that Crosby, Stills & Nash were also experimenting on during the same period. A delicate bass run, impressive harmonies, and inventive percussion combines into a truly majestic recording, and overall this was a remarkable debut offering from the quartet. Maybe it was a little too out of control at times, with no clear boundaries to work within, but praiseworthy indeed. Yet, ultimately, one that would take them nowhere together.

Issued on Tetragrammaton Records during 1968, but with little publicity, the record quickly sank without a trace, not helped by the record label folding shortly afterwards due to financial issues. Despite the buzz that Joshua Fox had initially created, and the promise the sessions had showed, the four members were left high and dry.

"It was tough enough to get it going," Mike stated in a 1970 interview with *Record Mirror*, a leading U.K. music publication. "But just when it started getting a few plays and stations wanted more copies, the company had this embezzlement problem and went bankrupt. There we were with a possible seller, no more company, and no more records. We did another thing, Dave Van Ronk's 'Young Man Blues,' which The Who also do, (but) it was banned for its lyric. So we split..."

Despite the obvious disappointment at the failure of this project, Mike continued with regular paid session work, focusing his boundless energies towards developing a permanent career along these lines. Appearances on releases by The Association, The Everly Brothers, some Ike & Tina Turner sessions, along with the debut release by folk singer Mary McCaslin, and a spot with former Blues Project vocalist Tommy Flanders, kept him busy, although he remained keen to utilize his close friend Joe LaManno as his rhythm partner whenever possible.

Joe: "We weren't in L.A. long before word had spread of 'the new kid in town,' and Dick Rosmini did for Michael in L.A. what Michael had done for me in Sacramento. A last minute call from Dick for Michael to cover a Bill Medley record date resulted in an offer to tour. Once again Michael shared his good fortune, recommended me for the bass spot and, in the time it takes to pack, we were touring together with Bill..."

Having met Rosmini following the Travelers 3's initial arrival in Los Angeles, Mike had crossed paths with him on a number of occasions since, often getting paid sessions at the recommendation of Dick, and they had worked together on Mary McCaslin's album. As with most who saw the drummer at work, Rosmini had been suitably impressed with what he both saw and heard, and so when he found himself without a drummer at a Capitol Records session for Bill Medley one Friday evening, Mike was foremost in his mind. Regular studio hand Earl Palmer had canceled due to ill health at the last minute, and as most paid sessioneers were already booked either on tour or at other sessions, the call was made to the new boy in town. Thus began one of the most enjoyable periods in Mike's long musical history. After the Capitol session had finished, and Mike was clearing away his kit, Bill Medley had called him up into the control booth from where he had been watching the young percussionist. Fearing the worst, Mike slowly made his way up the stairs to where the vocalist was waiting, only to be greeted with, "You know, kid, I like the way you play. Wanna go on tour?"

Clearly his connection with the booming vocalist was another stepping stone in Mike's now busy and burgeoning career, and for Joe as well, and together they headed out on the road with Medley and his band, although Mike actually missed the first show due to a prior session commitment. The duo ultimately became the regular rhythm section for the former Righteous Brother, playing in larger venues than either of them had experienced before, often supporting other established artists such as Dionne Warwick. However, Mike's connections with his first band also remained strong, and were ultimately to guide him back to the producer of the discarded Travelers 3 sessions.

Charlie Oyama remembers: "I guess we (the Travelers 3) officially disbanded in 1968, although I think we may have played a small group of West Coast college concerts in 1969. In 1968 we collectively formed a management and production firm, and everyone took on specific duties, but Mike and Joseph continued to work as clients, including the Joshua Fox band. One day I was leaving the Musicians' Union after a meeting and I ran into David Gates. He was into, or had just finished, recording the first Bread album. When he found out that we were no longer working as a group, he asked about Mike and the contact was made."

Keen to fill the drum stool, left empty by Gordon's departure, David contacted Mike, and despite the drummer's reluctance to get involved within a group scenario once more, following on from the unsuccessful Joshua Fox collaboration, and with a somewhat less than enthusiastic approach, Mike agreed to meet up with Gates and his two new musical partners. Yet, after hearing the debut album, and meeting James and Robb, he agreed to join up with the band and help them out with their current predicament, although his perspective was more philosophical, later commenting: "If the group failed I always had the studios and Bill Medley to fall back on."

He was also too aware that there would be no place for his loyal sidekick, Joe LaManno, on this project, seeing that the bass role was already filled by the instrumental prowess of the three songwriters involved. But, with Joe's encouragement, he took on the role as the drummer for Bread.

"Michael's rock heroes (by that time) were people like John Bonham, Keith Moon, Buddy Miles, the heavy rock players," recalls Joe. "I don't think anybody ever told him to play louder, it was always to play softer. He had so much passion for what he was doing. I think he was able to find a middle ground working for Bread. He toned it down a little bit, but maybe lifted them up a little bit. He brought a rock edge to some of what they did."

"Botts was in the orbit of The Association who had a lot of hits at the time," Robb remembers of his first meeting with the drummer. "He played terrific, he was a great, great drummer. We played 'Dismal Day' with him and just went 'Okay!'"

With Mike aboard, as an unofficial band member, the new four-piece line-up made the 1100-mile journey north to central Washington State to fulfill the month-long contract, performing in a number of clubs and high school halls around Seattle and the surrounding areas, including The Trolly Club, Lake Hills Roller Rink, Parker's Ballroom, and O'Dea High, often working alongside many of the local bands such as Trane, The Sundae Funnies, and the popular country rock influenced Bluebird. Being away from home for that period of time would certainly have raised the performing standards of the band, playing night after night, tightening the sound, and yet it was also to be a source of inspiration, albeit unintentional. During these early years, with families at home, Bread as a band never toured excessively, more often than not spending the weekdays at home in Los Angeles, either songwriting or recording in the studio, then come Friday or Saturday flying to whatever venue or city they were booked to perform. But this initial lengthy residency out of state was to bring out the very best in David's writing talent. Frustrated at being away from home, the unsettling atmosphere of the plush yet cold hotel room, the noise of the city traffic, to David he had simply been too long on the road.

"That song came out of being away from home with the band. The title hit me first, and then as I started writing the thing, it got more and more complex, and it turned out to be this five-minute epic. That was strictly just like it says. When you've been out there a long time you kind of wish you were at home. It was just some things that I put together from things I'd heard other people on the road say. It wasn't necessarily all my thoughts. It was sort of a compilation of all the things that we all think about. It was fun to do on stage, you can really get into the mood of it."[12 14]

"Been Too Long On The Road" would be one of the highlights of the band's second album, which they were to start working on once promotional duties for the debut release subsided. Yet it wasn't just David who found inspiration for writing while they were out touring the album. The gospel influence that ran through the Griffin-Royer composition "I Am That I Am" was initiated during a stay at an overnight Holiday Inn. Robb had opened up a Gideon bible that lay on the bedroom table, only for it to fall open upon the line "I am that I am." James already had a guitar part written out in his head, and Robb's accidental discovery was to fit the melody perfectly. "Don't ask why children, know that I know." Additionally, one of the very few occasions that David and James were to write together came courtesy of the extended Seattle visit. James later recalled: "We were sharing the same room together while the band was on tour in Seattle. I remember that I was sitting on the bed, having some coffee and strumming a guitar. David was in the other room and he heard me playing this riff, and he came out and sang a line or two, and it developed really quickly from there..."[14]

The gentle rhythmic chords of the finished song, "I Want You With Me," another number lyrically outlining the absence of loved ones, would grace the opening track on side two of their next album.

With touring commitments completed, the band returned to Los Angeles where they undertook a few further hometown shows in order to keep the momentum for

1969 Whisky-A-Go-Go ad

their debut album afloat, including a series of performances over the Christmas period at the popular Whisky-A-Go-Go, a legendary club situated on the northerly side of the Sunset Strip. They found themselves playing over six nights on a bill that also featured the hard-rockin' James Gang, originally from Ohio, and the hot L.A.-based garage band Smokestack Lightning, performing for (as Robb had previously noted) a "bunch of Coke freaks," which perhaps wasn't the easiest of opportunities to introduce their cross-pollination of rock and mellow ballads to the crowds who regularly haunted this infamous hostelry. Darryl Palagi, a close friend of Mike's who had recently joined up with the band during the Seattle excursion to assist with road-crew duties, and would remain a loyal member of the team for many years to come, recalled in conversation with the author: "My first tour with Bread was in Seattle, but I also worked the Whisky and I was disappointed in the crowd's response to the band, though I was not surprised. The club was really a hard rock club, and Bread certainly did not fit the bill. There were fans, Bread-lovers, in the crowd, but of all the shows I did with the band, the Whisky was a low point from my perspective. We were just getting our live show together when I came on board. Things were happening very fast. It was really fun..."

Nevertheless, the uncertainty of this new venture meant that the band members still had to find additional work to maintain a viable income. Mike Botts simply resumed his session duties outside of Bread, and one of the first projects he undertook was providing percussion on the debut release by Bengali musician Ananda Shankar, nephew of renowned sitar player Ravi Shankar. Released during 1970 on the Warner Brothers label, this was a wondrous fusion of Indian classical music with the more accessible western rock music of the day. While not overly successful, it was a stunning offering, with the mixture of east and west being interpreted nowhere better than with the opening "Jumping Jack Flash," a sitar-driven take on the Rolling Stones anthem. Needless to say, Botts' driving beat laid down a solid foundation for the mix.

Meanwhile, his touring colleagues were also avoiding the idleness of unemployment, with all three of them undertaking a series of songwriting jobs as security, while awaiting to see if Bread was going to develop into a permanent fixture within their lives. To a songwriter in the busy commercial city of Los Angeles, home of music, television, and cinema, the competition was great but the opportunities were there if the contacts were made. Jingles for commercials were one avenue that generated an income, and the three founding members of Bread were not averse to this particular street. During 1970, and in between album projects, they contributed a musical backdrop to a number of commercial products, with David once again utilizing drummer Ron Edgar on occasion as the supporting percussionist. Products that benefited from their musical abilities and talents included both Winchester Cigarettes and Cheerios breakfast cereals, with the Winchester commercial in particular containing a fine piece of music, a nifty blues guitar riff and an accompanying organ, with a familiar vocal gracefully layered on top: "A whole new taste is heading straight your way..."

Not that commercials were the only successful external venture for David, James, and Robb during 1970, for that year also saw them tentatively embark on various projects within the world of movie soundtracks. David had already worked on soundtrack recordings before, arranging and scoring on *Journey To Shiloh*, *Charro!*, and *Follow Me*, while James had even appeared up on the silver screen himself, performing in the 1964 movie *For Those Who Think Young*. Likewise, Robb had also toyed with film and soundtrack music during his college days, and so the three projects undertaken that year were not too far departed from the norm. However, for James and Robb, the subsequent results far exceeded their expectations...

Chapter Seven

Too Much Love

David Gates' 1970 re-entry into soundtrack production saw him take on the accompanying music to the Richard Rush directed movie *Getting Straight*, starring actor Elliott Gould (coming off the back of his phenomenal success with the smash hit film *M*A*S*H)*. The story of an ex-Vietnam veteran returning to college in order to gain a teaching degree, and co-starring Candice Bergen, the film was not a major box-office hit, despite getting favorable reviews. The lilting, laid-back theme song, written and performed by PK Limited, the duo originally produced by David the previous year, along with four other songs, all featured Gates back in his comfort zone, producing and arranging from behind the mixing desk. None of the featured tracks involved any compositional input from him at all, and although the results are relatively pleasant offerings, it was not the kind of work that was going to stand up against what David was now creating alongside his new partners.

It was within this new partnership that the next movie project of early 1970 came about. *Cover Me Babe* was to be a low budget Twentieth Century Fox production, with no major Hollywood stars in the line-up and, at times, seemingly little depth to the proposed plot. The soundtrack for the film included two brand new songs, both performed by Bread and duly credited on screen, although only one actually contained any band composing credits. Frederick Karlin, a Chicago-born former jazz musician who had broken into soundtracks three years previous, and had already earned four such commissions in the interim, was writing the music score for the project. However, the executives at Fox reportedly wanted one of the best new bands in the industry to assist Karlin with the featured songs, and they subsequently contacted Herb Eisman, who was currently head of BMI (the performing rights society), asking who were the hot new bands at that time. The response they got from Eisman, who had heard the *Bread* album and was an admirer of the product, was simply to recommend the talents of Gates, Griffin, and Royer.

Of the two recordings they contributed to the film, the title song was by far the less impressive. This was an endearing if somewhat soporific ballad, composed by Karlin in partnership with Randy Newman, himself a former staff writer for a number of publishing houses, and featured David and James in gentle voice accompanied by the band's trademark harmonies, and yet, much like the film itself, it simply washed past without making too much of a statement.

"We didn't write any of 'Cover Me Babe,'" recalls Robb. "Fred Karlin did the chords and I think we did a version of the lyric which was based on the first title of the movie, *Run Shadow Run*, and it probably took us fifteen minutes to write. But Fred always warned us there was a political situation on that song. We didn't care, we were working for the bucks and, since we were concentrating on Bread, we didn't see much of a future in the movie stuff anyway. Randy Newman ended up doing the lyrics on 'Cover Me Babe' and we just performed it."

The second song however, co-written by Karlin, Griffin, and Royer, was more in line with the new "sound" of Bread. "So You Say," which actually ran during both the opening title sequence and the closing credits, again with James handling the vocals, is far more upbeat, with the steady drum pattern holding down the rhythm, and the guitar line maintaining a solid riff throughout. Unfortunately for viewers of the film, those who did venture along to the poorly attended screenings, the song never really had an opportunity to develop. Two instrumental breaks during the introduction, necessary for the intruding dialogue sequences ("the whole point is that there is no point," which appears to sum up the film nicely), takes away the impact from the listener, although the clever bass run that develops towards the end is a nice flourish.

It is also worth noting however that, chronologically, this must register as being Mike Botts' first studio session with his three new colleagues, although he was still to commit to being a permanent fixture in the band. Unfortunately, neither of the new recordings were to see release anywhere else (a belated 2011 limited edition issue for the title track partly revised this oversight) and they soon both slipped under the radar into oblivion, although an alternate take on "Cover Me Babe" did see a 1970 release on vinyl. On the other hand, that too may have escaped the clutches of many a record buyer seeing that it was released as a single on the obscure Trump Records label, a small Memphis-based subsidiary of Capitol Records, under the name of The Sunshine Trolley. This version was recorded and produced by Tommy Cogbill and Chips Moman, both seasoned professionals in the Memphis recording industry, and while for many years it was rumored to feature David providing the lead vocals, neither he nor Robb can recollect having any involvement in this second cut, thus ending the Bread/Sunshine Trolley connection.

While all of this activity was going on, ABC Pictures, the new film division of the giant ABC Television network, was also in pre-production for a new movie, a comedy film based on a play written by Broadway actors Renee Taylor and Joseph Bologna, titled *Lovers and Other Strangers*. With Fred Karlin once again scheduled to score the soundtrack, and pleased with the combined results they had achieved with "Cover Me Babe," he once more requested the assistance of the James Griffin-Robb Royer songwriting team. Only too pleased to oblige, they started work on the project together, composing the lyrics to three of Karlin's melodies: "Comin' Thru To Me," "Keepin' Free," and the film's feature number, "For All We Know," recording a series of demos for Karlin to hear during March of

David in NY (courtesy of George Naumann)

that year. Later reissued on CD in 1996, the demo of "For All We Know" reveals the song in all its simplistic splendor. James and Robb, accompanied by guitarist David Cohen, turn in a truly wonderful version, although James was later to show displeasure at its eventual release, commenting that "it really was truly just a demo. I just sat there to get the words out. I wasn't really trying to sing it," which makes it all the more upsetting that the actual film soundtrack utilized the vocals of another singer, Larry Meredith, a relatively unknown performer. Despite Meredith's faithful interpretation it became so apparent, upon the release of the original demo, what the song truly had to offer. James would also later state that Bread considered recording their own version, but opted out due to a wealth of ballad material in their expanding catalog. However, such was the song's potential that, upon the original release of the film, the popular brother and sister act, Richard and Karen Carpenter, were so enamored by the tune that they immediately recorded their own version, taking it to #3 on the *Billboard* charts. And yet, songwriting credits on the three new songs were given to the unfamiliar sounding trio of Frederick Karlin, Arthur James, and Robb Wilson. James would later explain:

"We had our own publishing company to which we were signed exclusively and (the film company) retained the publishing for all songs in their movies at the time. Consequently, we decided to use pseudonyms in order to protect our exclusivity to Candlewyck Music, our publishing company, otherwise it would diminish the company's value if we ever wanted to sell it..."

Subsequently both James and Robb dropped their given surnames and utilized their middle names and thus, Arthur James and Robb Wilson were born, although in a 2009 online interview with *Country Music Facts & News*, Robb also suggested that David may have instigated the change, insisting that the band members shouldn't be seen writing outside of the "band" arrangement. By comparison, "Comin' Thru To Me" and "Keepin' Free," the two other co-compositions, are barely in the same league. Middle-of-the-road arrangements at best, with vocals supplied by another little known act, Country Coalition, who also recorded for the ABC/Bluesway label, achieving a #96 hit on *Billboard* that same year.

Meanwhile, back at Elektra Records, Jac Holzman was remaining faithful to his new band, regardless of the debut album's poor showing. "I was mighty upset because I thought the group deserved better. I immediately picked up their option and began to prepare for their second album."[12]

This album, released later that year, was to be the turning point in the band's history. It would be the start of an incredibly successful period for the trio, soon-to-be-quartet. An ascent that had, looking at the complete picture, taken almost twelve years to come about. The youthful innocence of the late 1950s, the halcyon days of the early 1960s, the heady, heavy days of the late 1960s; it would all pale into the Los Angeles smog of yesteryear as the next twelve months projected them into areas of success that they had only dreamed about. And all it would take to kick start it was a simple David Gates' composition. A gentle, graceful ballad that even David was later to recollect: "I got goose bumps while I was writing that song. I knew that I was onto something, that it was better than the run-of-the-mill song."[14]

Recalling Mike Botts back into the studio to take on the session drummer's role once more, David, James, and Robb reconvened at the Elektra Studios, hoping to recapture the essence of the first album. Unfortunately, initial attempts at recording the new songs they had compiled quickly proved fruitless. In their opinion studio engineer Bruce Botnick, who had overseen the previous sessions, didn't appear as receptive this time around.

Robb: "Rightly or wrongly, we felt that Bruce wasn't as into it as he was on the first album. So we moved over to Sound Recorders and worked with Armin Steiner, who was a semi-legendary, very technically accomplished guy. He'd been working with Neil Diamond at the time and had a lot of hits behind him."[14]

Over the years Armin Steiner has built up a list of engineering credits that are virtually second to none, including in excess of one hundred gold and platinum awards for major artists such as Glen Campbell, Neil Diamond, The Fifth Dimension, Heart, Dolly Parton, Barbra Streisand, The Turtles – and Bread. Built in 1965, Sound Recorders was one of the first commercial studios in Los Angeles to acquire an 8-track recording facility, and it quickly took off as one of the best new studios in the city. By 1970 its reputation was consolidated via a number of successful sessions and hits, and it was an obvious choice for Bread to relocate to, in order to restart work on the second album. Seeing that the three composers in the band had already started building up a backlog of new songs, a number of which had come about as a result of the lengthy Seattle trip, they were not in short supply of new material. But, as before, there was never a surplus of songs floating around during the actual recording sessions. They chose their selection carefully before the "record" button was pressed. Unlike most rock bands of the time, many of which often worked long hours through the night, a recording session for Bread was noticeably well organized, on a social and business level. Jac Holzman: "The way Bread went about recording was so civilized it attracted attention. Most groups would shuffle into the studio, if you were lucky, in the late afternoon, and nothing would happen until seven, and then you'd work until two in the morning. Bread would arrive in the morning at nine sharp, David with his attaché case, as if he was off to a downtown bank or Pacific Bell. They would record till lunch, break for an hour, work all afternoon, and David would go home to his family at five."[12]

Robb put a lot of this organization down to the simple facts of family life: "From my point of view, we were always a recording band. We went out and did live gigs, and we had hit records, but we were always a lot more comfortable in the studio. We were all married, you know. Do you just want to leave the wives at home? David didn't even smoke a joint!"

Studio work was shared evenly among the three songwriters, with the composer, or composers, of each number often taking the lead guitar duties alongside. On the majority of David's compositions, Robb would regularly provide the bass lines, James offering up rhythm support while David would take the lead. Likewise, on the Griffin and Royer compositions, it would more often than not be Gates taking over on bass, with Robb or Jimmy taking the guitar parts. Robb: "I enjoyed working with David because he could fill any hole. He could play a great bass part, excellent guitar, really good piano. He even did violin on one tune."

In the studio, as before, the band made use of a variety of instruments, although Robb preferred his distinguished Les Paul guitars – in particular the "Gold Top" model – despite David trying to convince him to switch to the ever-popular Fender Telecaster. James meanwhile tended to favor the distinctive red Gibson ES335 he had initially purchased back in 1968 from a dealer on Larchmont Boulevard. The Fender bass was the preferred instrument for the lower range although, once again, Robb held preferences towards another model, particularly for live performances,

Robb in Phoenix (courtesy of the Malcolm C. Searles collection)

feeling that he lacked the required "bang" on the strings of a Fender. Hence his choice of the Hofner violin bass, so distinctly popularized by Paul McCartney the previous decade. As for the role of the drummer, Mike Botts certainly had a hot seat to fill, sitting down to take over from the amazing talents of Jim Gordon, and yet it was a position he was to fulfill admirably. David Gates: "Mike was put in control of the drum parts, and he was pretty innovative in trying different things. He made a significant contribution on the percussion side, and he sang an occasional harmony once in a while."[14]

However, the role of the producer within the previously unified setup was one early cause for unrest, and one that would ultimately have a long-term effect among the principal band members. Clearly, the amount of experience David had gained in the producer's chair over the past decade gave him good reason to want to maintain his sole studio control, and he believed that at the time he was doing the major share of the production duties, despite the valuable input of his two songwriting comrades. This may well have been so and yet, despite the debut release having the role evenly shared among the three members, somewhere along the line Elektra began officially utilizing the "produced by David Gates" tag without the consent of all three parties. Naturally, the Griffin-Royer axis objected to this unquestioned move, believing their contributions to be equally valid and that they should be credited accordingly, with the subsequent result being that a band meeting was hastily called. With manager Al Schlesinger also in attendance, the arguments were tossed back and forward for a number of hours, with James, Robb, and David all given opportunity to air their concerns, and out of this came the "produced by David Gates, together with James Griffin and Robb Royer" credit, reportedly to the satisfaction of all. Robb: "David wanted the sole producer position but we felt that we were contributors. When we collaborated together I always tried to keep the sweetness down. That was my role. But David had hit his streak, he was writing unbelievably great songs..."

How could James and Robb compete with such a proficient writer as David? Simply by producing some of their best collaborative work to date. The sessions that the second album was built around were to feature some of their finest work, and yet it was still to take just three minutes and fifteen seconds of David Gates' magic to define the ultimate success of the release.

The first few songs recorded for the album seemed to pass smoothly, but by the time the fourth song was nearing completion, the presence of label head, Jac Holzman, threw a wrench in the works of the recording process. David recalled: "(The song) was the fourth or fifth one that we were in the process of recording. Jac came in, and he absolutely flipped – 'I must have this record out right away.' Then the discussion began. 'But the album's not done, and if you put this out and it does well, there'll be no album on the street.' Jac says, 'I don't care, that's a high class problem.'"[12]

The composition in question was "Make It With You," a simple ballad, one that James initially referred to as being "pretty schmaltzy," and yet one that David knew was something special even before he had finished writing it. He already knew how the arrangements should sound. "I realized while I was writing that it was meant for just a solo vocal and that a string section was appropriate for it. I wanted a fairly bare bones rhythm track, and we had a hard time getting it to work. I ultimately ended up going in with just Mike Botts, and he sat there playing drums while I played acoustic guitar to start the track off right. Then I added the bass and electric guitar afterwards, because that was the only way I could control the emotional feel. I had done a lot of string arrangements prior to being in the band, so it seemed natural to put a string part on there."[14]

In another interview David suggested that the initial foundation of this particular tune is somewhat representational of his regular writing method. "That was a big phrase at the time. I was sitting on the bed watching the evening news when I started that little trill melody and those major 7th chords, and it just kind of flowed out. I don't picture a song that I want to write, like some people do. You know, 'Let's write a song called "Sad September,"' then sit down and structure it. I just start playing, and looking for an interesting melody and chord changes to build on. Something that's infectious. It might just be a ten second thing. Like the opening line of 'Make It With You.' Then you develop from that start, rather than from a finish. That's the only way it works for me. You chase it down a little further, then maybe a line comes to you that you can build on, or it suggests a title.

"Exactly where the title goes in the song is one of the most critical things," he stresses. "When I finish a song, there's a culmination point in a melody or verse or someplace where the title belongs. It needs to go right here. So I concentrate on trying to make the title land in the right place."[17]

The actual title of the song itself, and some of the lyrical content, perhaps didn't sit as comfortably with areas of middle America as it did with other more liberal views, a theme that David touched on when talking to *Zig-Zag* magazine during the album's initial promotion. "'Make It With You' worried me for a bit. It fit so perfectly. I'm not a puritan, but I found myself thinking, 'Is it decent?' I concluded by thinking that any reasonable person would realize that it meant 'we can make it through life,' which I was pleased about because the song would lose everything without that line. In 'Family Doctor' (from the first album) there is a reference to 'he gave me an artificial you'... that's not intended to conjure up visions of life-size plastic females! It's just a take-off of 20th century life. Robb, who wrote it, thought it was funny. He certainly had no intention to be offensive, and as a group we make no attempts to be risqué."

This use of only himself and Mike in the studio on this particular track perhaps gave justification to David's claim for sole production credit on the song, and although there was seemingly no involvement from either James or Robb, the credits, as agreed, were to feature the names of all three on the finished product. Nevertheless, the same could be said for some of the works that James and Robb were to bring aboard for the recording sessions, although none of these were to be released as stand-alone singles. The united front was clearly not so united underneath. With Elektra Records keen to issue "Make It With You" as the first release from the sessions as soon as possible, and with the remainder of the album still incomplete, the sprint was on to complete the remaining songs. In the end, it took them just 120 hours from start to finish...

"Five years ago it was unheard of to spend 120 hours in a studio," David was to say to the British press shortly after the album's release, "but today I suppose it's quite a short time. I just don't understand what groups do with the vast amounts of time they spend in studios. We believe this is an improvement on the first album. It's a little heavier for a start and we've used an orchestra on three tracks. But the point about the strings is that all three numbers can be played live on stage without suffering from the loss of the 10-piece string section."

Of the finalized selection, "Been Too Long On The Road," "I Am That I Am," and "I Want You With Me" were all fairly well worked out in advance, having been conceived a number of months earlier during the stay in Seattle, but added to the mix were the rock-influences of "Why Do You Keep Me Waiting" and "Call On Me," along with the upbeat "Easy Love," and the prophetically titled "Coming Apart," all compositions from James and Robb. David additionally chipped in with the delicate "The Other Side Of Life" and the more adventurous "In The Afterglow," while also suggesting he could rock-out as well with the lively "Blue Satin Pillow." It was a full sounding collection, offering up a wide variety of blues, pop, rock, and ballad, although, as Robb suggests, he in particular was keen to keep them away from the standard quick or slow formula:

"I was trying to get the band off this thing that it was either an up tempo or a down tempo, and trying to get more of a lilt into the melodic stuff. That was kind of where I was heading, but lost influence at that point. When 'Make It With You' came along, David phoned in himself as producer without telling us that was what he was going to do. In fact, the original credits of 'produced by Bread' were already (scheduled) on the album, but he changed them, and there was a huge crisis."

At this point the meeting with the band members and Schlesinger took place in an attempt to settle their widening differences. Clearly, a mutual understanding was achieved, however delicate the balance or amicable the result, for listening to the album today, once the initial hard opening chords of "Why Do You Keep Me Waiting" kick in, accompanied by the heavy thud of the accompanying solitary drumbeat, one is struck by the diversity the twelve songs have to offer, and yet the band truly sound as one. David's impressive "Been Too Long On The Road," featuring James on lead guitar, shifts and modulates through various time signatures and yet at no point does the band sound at odds with each other. At the opposite end of the scale, "Coming Apart," often perceived as a comment on the factions within the band itself, but in reality based more within the confines of a love affair, is a beautiful composition, highlighting the amazing vocal capabilities of James for the first time since the trio came together. Filled out with a delicate string arrangement, solid percussion, and some subtle piano flourishes, this is the band reaching a peak together, and then some. Yet, the combination that they brought to the mix was still subject to the influences of outside parties, and none more notable than on the Beatle-esque guitar riff that introduces "Easy Love," or on the heavier drive of "Call On Me," both songs that James and Robb brought to the sessions. Robb: "There were groups like Grand Funk Railroad out at the time who had their songs with big minor licks, so we wanted to make sure we had one too. 'Call On Me' was a fun song to play live."[14]

Rounding out the album was a composition that James and Robb had attempted during earlier sessions for the debut release, but had felt that the first attempt wasn't quite right. The song had been put on the backburner for the time being but, during sessions for the second release, now with Armin Steiner engineering the board, they resurrected the song. "Look What You've Done" would go on to become a firm favorite among Bread followers, and was without a doubt one of the highlights of the second long-player. "Jimmy and I wrote this song in its entirety in his apartment on North Gordon Street in Hollywood at the same time we wrote all our other songs on the first Bread album," recalls Robb. "We wrote it in the usual fashion; jamming chords back and forth, both guys throwing in ideas, 'til we had a melody. Then I wrote the entire lyric. There never was any part of a song before we started jamming. It was expected to go with the first batch and I know we sat down with it – pretty sure the red light went on so there's probably an eight-track somewhere. Remember, we were cutting with Bruce Botnick who had just cut 'Light My Fire' for God's sake, but somehow it didn't seem hip enough for the moment, too victimy. It didn't start working 'til we got over to SRS and Armin Steiner. Armin worked better with that solid middle of the road sound we came to have and 'Look...' started working."

With the sessions now hastily completed, drummer Mike Botts, still not committed to a full-time position in the band, returned to other work, resurrecting his role in Bill Medley's touring band. However, all that was about to change as, true to his word, Jac Holzman swiftly issued "Make It With You" as the next Bread single. Released on May 7th, 1970, coupled with "Why Do You Keep Me Waiting," the record swiftly garnered radio play, something that was a completely new concept to the band. After just a couple of weeks, people were requesting the song in record stores across the country, many of which were still awaiting delivery. Initially hard to find, gradually, the record took off and on July 11th, 1970, it made its debut in the *Billboard* Hot 100, swiftly climbing to the very pinnacle on August 22nd, where it displaced The Carpenters' "(They Long To Be) Close To You" at pole position. The hard work had finally paid off, but naturally the band now had some serious promotional work to undertake, and they needed a serious commitment from the man they wanted permanently in the line-up.

Botts: "There I was, in paradise, working with Bill Medley of the Righteous Brothers at a major hotel in Honolulu for a three week engagement. It was TOO MUCH FUN! Bill had a burnin' R&B band and I was having a ball playing with the band at night, and soaking in paradise, mostly at the beach, during the days. It was on one of those tropical days that I got a call from David. He told me that, in his words, 'I think we've got a hit on our hands' and that I should get back to the mainland as soon as I could. There were offers for concert dates coming in and it looked like we would have to start to do some serious touring to support the record. Of course, this meant Bread was going to be a 'working' band and that presented a problem. Up to that point, I had been successfully able to work with both Bill Medley and Bread but 'Make It With You' changed all that. I had been with Bill Medley for two years and had no desire to leave. He had become a good friend and playing with that band was a drummer's dream. Yet, I knew that I could no longer balance the two. I had to choose. It was going to be Bill Medley or Bread."

Mike was encouraged in his decision by another musical friend who, at the time, like himself, was perhaps not so enamored with the prospect of the music they were to be making, but could identify with it as a wise career move. Brian Cole from The Association had been friends with Mike for a few years by this stage and, along with Jules Alexander (Mike's previous working partner in Joshua Fox), was one of the driving forces behind the success of that popular band. Upon hearing of the opportunity that now presented itself to Mike, Brian had responded: "Well, I don't much care for the music... but I smell money in it."

Mike continued: "Later on that day I ended up at the beach. I was thinking about David's call and still trying to get it through my head that we actually had a hit record. It all seemed somewhat surreal until I heard 'Make It With You' coming out of several portable radios on the beach. That's when it really hit me. We've got a hit record!! I had to control myself from jumping up and screaming to everyone on the beach, 'Hey you guys!! That's me playing on the radio!!' Of course, since no one would know what the hell I was screaming about and would probably think I was a nut case, I wisely resisted the urge. At that point I knew I had to make the choice. So, with the understanding and encouragement of Bill Medley, I flew back to L.A. to be a full time member of Bread."

One of his first duties was for a series of publicity pictures, taken to adorn the sleeve of the forthcoming album. Alongside his three new band mates Mike posed on the shoreline of the mighty Pacific Ocean while acclaimed photographer Ed Caraeff snapped the shutter. Now known for his work with The Rolling Stones, Hendrix, Linda Ronstadt, The Beach Boys, Elton John, The Carpenters, Frank Zappa, Creedence Clearwater Revival, Eric Clapton, Tom Waits… and the Beatles, Caraeff is recognized today as one of the most respected rock photographers in the industry and his stunning picture of Jimi Hendrix, encouraging the flickering flames to rise from his burning guitar at the Monterey Pop Festival, is one of the most iconic images ever taken.

With the second album, now titled *On The Waters*, hastily pressed for release in the wake of the success of "Make It With You," the band geared up for a series of promotional activities. However, it is worth noting that the accompanying sleeve notes, prepared for the album's imminent release, appeared to push James to the forefront of the band, with his boyishly good looks clearly seen as a positive factor. The notes state that "Jim is the group's lead singer," despite his sharing equal billing on the final song selection, while also suggesting that Robb is "lead guitarist," despite the shared duties among the band members. Clearly the label was trying to create an image for the band, while attempting to heal over any burning wounds. And yet it is also at odds to point out that David is "the leader of Bread," confirmation that, despite the warring over production credits, Elektra Records still viewed David as the true driving force, especially in light of the sudden success of the single.

The album officially hit the shelves on July 21st, 1970, and the following month the new four-piece band spent time in rehearsal in preparation for an upcoming mini-tour, due for late summer. However, they still allowed themselves leisure time between the extensive rehearsals, and on August 25th, 1970, Robb and James attended a performance at The Troubadour Club in Hollywood to see the debut of a new singer/songwriter who was being promoted in Los Angeles. Dressed in hot pants, white-stacked boots and a tee shirt with the words "Rock'n'Roll" emblazoned across the chest, Reginald Dwight had arrived in America. The rocket man had landed...

Then, during September of that year, Bread accompanied another of the new "rock" sensations of the time, Santana, out on the road for a short series of shows during the San Francisco-based band's lengthy summer touring schedule. Fresh from their previous year's appearance at the Woodstock Festival, and basking in the glory of their debut album, the Carlos Santana-led outfit were promoting a new album themselves, *Abraxas*, destined to reach multi-platinum status, and were fast becoming one of the most exciting bands on the circuit. To many, Bread would not have seemed the obvious choice as the support band, with their mellow acoustic melodies seemingly at odds with the stoned crowds that were known to frequent the 'Frisco band's Latino-tinged performances, but it gave David, James, Robb, and Mike the perfect opportunity to highlight the diversifying wealth of material they had at their disposal. For every "Make It With You" there was a "Call On Me," for every "Look What You've Done" there was a "Blue Satin Pillow," for every "Look At Me" there was a "Last Time," plus they also continued to feature a number of rock'n'roll classics in their set, with reports of "rip-roaring" versions of "Johnny B. Goode" being included.

The Santana summer tour zigzagged its way through eight states, although Bread only joined up for five shows mid-way through the trek, linking up with the tour in Denver, Colorado, where they played the Mammoth Gardens over two nights, September 16th and 17th, along with Country Joe McDonald. They then worked their way via the 10,000-seat Salt Palace in Salt Lake City, and the Arizona Coliseum in Phoenix, before finishing up at the Swing Auditorium in San Bernardino, where Boz Scaggs was added to the bill.

"I do remember Country Joe & The Fish on that tour," laughs Robb today, recalling these early dates. "He had the 'fuck' cheer... you know... gimme an 'f'... gimme a 'u'... what's that spell? And the whole audience got to yell 'fuck' which, apparently, in the '70s was a ton of fun. He got arrested every night, which stood out in my mind more than anything else on that tour. The cops would show up every night and dutifully wait till CJ performed the cheer, then arrest him!"

What is also worth considering is the fact that to the majority of the audience in attendance, very few, if any, would realize that during Bread's set they were watching a band that already featured a songwriter with two Top 3 credits and a former actor who had appeared alongside Sinatra. Even though the band members were still only in their mid-late twenties they had already seen fame close-up.

"That was our first hit tour," continues Robb. "It was all kids, teenage girls... It was business, but all of the accompanying stuff that goes on during a tour was visible." Although, when remembering how the band came across he adds, "David wasn't really a lead guy, Jimmy didn't have the hits. He sang great, but I always thought there was a bigger hand for David when the song started and a bigger one for Jimmy when the song ended."

However, it wasn't solely concert appearances that were to take the band to a wider audience, and on October 3rd the quartet appeared on the highly-rated NBC weekly TV program, *The Andy Williams Show*, fronted by the easy listening crooner and featuring a regular succession of popular artists and performers interspersed

James in NY (courtesy of George Naumann)

with various variety and novelty acts. Introduced by Williams in seemingly comedic style, Bread appeared against a palm tree laden backdrop, surrounded by a set burdened with overwhelming shrubbery, with the mustachioed David performing a live solo vocal of "Make It With You" while his three band mates played alongside. Unfortunately, it was an all-too-rare television performance, and although Royer today recalls a number of similar televised guest spots, the music-buying audiences would often be unaware of the band's actual appearance. None of the U.S. single releases to date had featured picture sleeves and, although the debut album had featured images of the three founding members, the slow sales, in the aftermath of a relatively low-key launch, had hardly raised their profiles. Indeed, the sleeve for the recent *On The Waters* album had also featured darkened images of most band members on the front, James being the exception, with mere silhouettes appearing on the rear... and yet, for a band who prided themselves on the quality of the music, the image and public appearance was clearly not always foremost in their minds.

Despite all of the summer concerts, and the occasional television spot, David still found the opportunity to share his time with his family, back in Oklahoma. A local newspaper from Tulsa ran a small article commenting on his return visit to the family home, prompted by a telephone call from his mother. It featured a photograph alongside picturing him, Jo Rita, their four young children Ricky, Angelyn, Craig, and Lorilee, and his mother, while a second article saw fit to comment that he had just composed and written the lyrics and arrangement for a record with his group Bread, that had gone on to sell 250,000 copies, and that the title of this song was "Naked With You." A story David would recall humorously in concert many years later.

Ironically, by the time that the Andy Williams' show aired on national TV, Elektra Records had already issued the follow-up single to the chart-topping hit but, such was the delay between filming and airing, presumably the band had not prepared the second release at the time of the studio appearance. In order to capitalize on the success of the gentle ballad, and deeming that nothing else on the album was of a similar nature (despite the album peaking at the credible #12 position), the label put out a re-recorded version of a song that had appeared on the debut release, choosing to overlook the quality and single potential of the other songs on the new album. Maybe they felt they were too "rock." Maybe the vocals didn't have that same gentle, lilting melody. Maybe the new audience who had purchased "Make It With You" wouldn't connect with a totally "different" sound of Bread that, say, "Call On Me" or "Coming Apart" would bring. Maybe... whatever. Clearly Elektra Records wanted more of the same and so, with David once again leading the direction, the band opted to record a new version of "It Don't Matter To Me," with James providing a new lead guitar line. This was the song David had originally composed three or four years previously, and although both company and composer were keen to follow the formula, the decision didn't sit comfortably with all.

"There was a big controversy over the choice of the next single, but it was 'no, no, no,' follow it up with another David single," says Robb today, "and when the second one happened it was pretty much David's band. We tried to pull 'It Don't Matter To Me' by putting that kinda screaming section in the middle and guitars and all that, but it was in a 'Make It With You' approach. But I would say that's my favorite Bread song."

David: "We recorded that hurriedly on the first album without strings. After 'Make It With You' was a hit, we went back and re-recorded 'It Don't Matter To Me' in the key of D instead of E, did it slower, and added strings to it. Basically, I think we got it right the second time. The record label had this committee where they'd get all these people together to hear the songs. I had some input, as had James, and as had the management, but it was just whichever was the best song at the time that was chosen as the single."[9]

Possibly by way of appeasement, James and Robb once again had one of their compositions placed as the accompanying flip-side, and the combination of "It Don't Matter To Me" and "Call On Me" hit the shelves on September 7th, 1970, peaking at a respectable #10 position in the charts, much to the satisfaction of Elektra. The writing was clearly on the wall.

October 1970, saw the foursome make their first promotional visit overseas. Following the letter Schlesinger had received the previous December, the band had waited until they had a new album on the market before making the journey across to the U.K. but now with two Top 10 hits under their belt, and a new LP on the charts, they figured the time was right to expand their horizons. David made the journey across to the U.K. first, undertaking some radio promotions along with a brief, non-performing appearance on the BBC's flagship music TV show, *Top Of The Pops*, which had been featuring "Make It With You" during its initial climb up the U.K. charts. The single had gone on to reach #5 in the official U.K. *Music Week* lists and was still riding high in the Top 100; *On The Waters* had also just been released (hitting #34), so the entire band then headed over the Atlantic to meet the U.K. press, and perform a number of promotional shows, with the intention of filming the tour for a one-hour TV documentary for the U.S. market. Unfortunately, and despite footage being filmed, overseen by British director Michael Wale, nothing ever came of this, and the reels have not been seen or heard of since.

Supported on this brief visit by a new band named Osibisa, a group of African origin who, very much like Santana, fused a number of worldwide influences into their sound including Latin and Caribbean jazz, the tour began with a show at the infamous Revolution Club in London's Mayfair on October 1st. This was one of London's most "hip" joints of the era, popular with many of the city's fashion-conscious and socialite elite, and was certainly a good way in which to introduce themselves to the U.K. media. The following night they played at the London Central Polytechnic College, where they were received equally enthusiastically, despite the onstage failure of the electric keyboards, which restricted them to a standard four-piece instrumental backing, and a hastily revised set list. Reviews reported on David's particular disappointment with this occurrence, seeing that they couldn't perform "London Bridge" as anticipated, but nevertheless they still managed to highlight a number of songs from both albums to date, including "Call On Me," "Don't Shut Me Out," "The Other Side Of Life," and, of course, "Make It With You," before culminating in a raucous rock'n'roll medley.

The influential music press dedicated a number of paragraphs to their visit, with *Melody Maker*, one of the leading exponents of U.K. music journalism, offering up a short article:

> *"Bread guitarist, singer, and songwriter Jim Griffin looked out across London from his hotel room window, commented that there was no fog, 'I was led to believe it was always foggy,' and talked of the group's lack of experience on stage. 'Performing live is now very important to us, and*

we've found that it's a tremendously rewarding experience. You get immediate gratification if you play well. This is obviously not so with records. This British tour we are doing is one part of a year's heavy date work we have now decided to do, and we'll be playing everywhere.'"

The article then went on to comment on James's view of the band's philosophy on their songwriting:

"Well, we go for a good harmony, an honest lyric. We're not preaching anything, just singing about living emotions and feelings. I attach tremendous importance to the lyric, about 50 percent of the number in fact. But it's the music that comes first. I agree that many American bands have maybe forgotten about lyrics, but this is because they have turned on to some other facet of their music. We've always tried to keep our sound uncomplicated, but if strings and brass might make it sound better, then we put them in."

Following a number of further appearances, including a second show at the Revolution Club on October 8th, plus visits to Sutton Coldfield and Newcastle, with an earlier show in Reading being canceled, the group headed back to the warmer climes of California to reflect on the journey.

"Our U.K. visit wasn't Beatlemania," jokes Robb, "but we always turned out a good crowd. We had pretty good parties afterwards. I thought it was a blast. Some of the stories were pretty salty. We went and played Manchester and Jimmy got himself into a series of complications, and Botts did too, and they almost got into a fistfight with a guy. We played football with an uncompromising team of English drivers and managers in an Alice in Wonderland garden, all carved with hearts. It was amazing..."

"We couldn't play (the scheduled gig) in Reading," remembered David. "I remember that because there was some kind of a riot on the campus! We couldn't play, everybody had to get out of the building. It was some sort of political thing. It had nothing to do with us!"[13]

Upon their return Stateside, Bread made a scheduled three-day appearance at the legendary 5000-seat Winterland Ballroom in San Francisco, commencing on October 16th. They were due to perform alongside the new golden rock pairing of John Mason & Cass Elliott, along with John Fahey and Joy Of Cooking but, when Mason, Elliott, and Fahey dropped out, soul legends The Four Tops, along with Merry Clayton, stepped in to fill the bill. Following this, they once again returned to where they were most comfortable, the recording studio, putting down tracks that would ultimately become the third Bread album... and the last to feature the original line-up.

Chapter Eight

What A Change

By the end of 1970, strong divisions were starting to show among the principal songwriters in the band. Guitarist Robb Royer was finding it increasingly difficult to communicate with David Gates over songwriting and production issues, and David's own domineering presence in the studio, especially in the role of producer, was having a negative impact on James Griffin as well. For the most part, drummer Mike Botts was separate from the downbeat feeling that permeated the studio setting, seeing that he was universally given responsibility for the percussive role within the band, and saw no immediate reason for dissension with any of his musical partners, although he too was now becoming aware of the unsettling factions that were forming. Nevertheless, the band settled once more into their comfort zone, again under the watchful eye of Armin Steiner, and the coming New Year was to bring them a series of both incredible highs and depressing lows.

The success that the two David Gates ballads had brought to them would, in most cases, have been cause for celebration. Two Top 10 hits in a chart listing that was constantly changing in style from month to month. The Jackson 5 alternating places with Shocking Blue, the Beatles swapping with Ray Stevens, Three Dog Night passing ships with The Partridge Family, and among all of this varying success was the groundbreaking, heart-rendering delivery of Paul Simon and Art Garfunkel's exquisite "Bridge Over Troubled Water," featuring a piano introduction so sublime that it duly went on to receive a prestigious Grammy Award the following year. Hats off to Larry. Yet in the proverbial Bread bin, it wasn't all sweetness and light.

"We had pressure from the label, from our management, from the radio, from everybody, to keep putting ballads out. I was sort of resisting that, and after a while it became a point of contention between David and me. He said, 'This is really paying off, let's roll with it.' Jimmy and I were in other areas, exploring, whereas David was just powering down the middle of the road," Royer was to tell Barry Alfonso in 1996.

In David's eye, Robb was often the antagonist in the disagreements due to his attempts to roughen up the edges, and take out the overwhelming sweetness that often permeated many of Gates' own compositions, and something had to give sooner or later. Despite this, they persisted with the studio sessions, pulling together another fine collection of work, once again evenly split between the two writing camps. The resulting album appears darker in comparison with its predecessor, and the acoustic element that had infused much of the previous releases was not so apparent this time around. There were also no obvious external influences and, save for the light country feel that ran through the Griffin-Royer "Too Much Love," the commercial sound of *On The Waters* was counterbalanced by a moodier, more serious tone.

"(That album) has a unifying theme running through it," Robb was to state later in an article that appeared in the June 1971 edition of *Cash Box*. "Everything is tinged by it. The title itself, the cover shots, and the music. The song 'Take Comfort' really sums up the feeling we wanted to get across in the entire album. Whatever gives you comfort is a religious experience..."

Yet, in spite of the intended conceptual tone that ran throughout the final release, and to the detriment once again of some wonderful contributions from both James and Robb, the focal point was to shine on just one particular song; yet another masterful ballad conjured up by the magical wand of David Gates. If a picture paints a thousand words...

By early 1971, the rewards for their previous laboring were beginning to be seen. The songwriting trio had set up Bread Enterprises to take care of all the business arrangements and to distribute the royalty payments that were now coming in. Al Schlesinger and fellow attorney Michael Dave, now in partnership, were instrumental in the founding of the company, with the three principal band members taking an equal slice of the corporate shares. Mike Botts, now considered an equal within the band itself, was seemingly omitted from the board due to his non-songwriting status, although he was still entitled to his performing rights settlements. But for the four members, business details aside, it was still all about the music. Each member felt strong enough about the band that they all committed to the album sessions, still keen to pull together to provide the best product they could, regardless of warring factions.

"Jimmy and I felt pressured to write ballads like David did, but we didn't do it," Royer says of this period. "We were looking into other musical areas. What we were trying to do was expand on *On The Waters*, and for some reason, at that time, we were verging kind of orchestral. I felt that some of our best things were being overlooked, even some of David's stuff. We were locked within a trend and couldn't change it, and David realized that and only wrote love songs. But we were capable of a wider variety of things than that..."[14]

However, in retrospect, David believes that these current sessions were "an extension of what our strengths were. It had a consistent flow to it. We felt that we knew who our audience was by that time. We had an identity and we had more confidence."[14]

Certainly, while many of David's songs may well have contained a theme of love and relationships, musically he was to be found building on his strengths, and with some of the new songs he was contributing, reaching new pinnacles of composing ability, although not all of his compositions reached such levels of expectation, or were deemed appropriate for the band. February 1971, saw him register one such song, "My Heart's At The Cleaners" (originally composed back in 1967), a hokey little number with its influence in goodtime country roots:

Baked beans and wieners, my heart's at the cleaners
And my love's hung out to dry

that was to remain in the catalog, but not the studio. For the first time, it also became apparent how much composing time David was now undertaking sitting at the piano, as opposed to writing on the acoustic guitar. Use of the keyboard was taking his vision, and the structure of his songs, into previously unchartered waters. One only has to listen to the ambitious "Come Again." Sounding far more suited to a stage production, or the Hollywood screen, it leaves one with a sense that he was outdistancing himself from the confines of the band. Stretching himself to see how far he could go, but ultimately omitting the united front that had brought the band together in the first place. But with "Let Your Love Go," he was clearly prepared to simply let rock'n'roll take over, and show what the band could do if it was left to the basics. Deemed by David as what he would begin to term "Bread Zeppelin," this is a great song, and yet it notably highlights with obvious clarity that his voice just wasn't as well suited for rock'n'roll as it was for the ballads. The grittier, raw tonal qualities that James could bring to a rock tune would often outshine David's attempts at the genre, although such was the emphasis that Elektra Records was now placing on David that it came as no surprise that once again they opted to issue one of his songs as the next single. What is surprising however was the choice. Pushed into the Christmas market of 1970, the upbeat "Let Your Love Go" was selected as the first release from these sessions, paired with the gentler "Too Much Love," a country-styled song that was much more identifiable with the formulated Bread "sound" than the heavier lead side.

"Everyone thought that song ("Too Much Love") should've been a single, but the intro was too long," recalled James. "David set up a good mood at the beginning with his guitar playing, but it was just too much to get on the radio..."[14]

If ever there was a case of the Griffin-Royer partnership having the opportunity to feature on the A-side of a Bread single snatched from them, then this was it. "Let Your Love Go" remains a fine song, a great "rock" number with which to open their concerts with, as was now their wont, but having had success with two ballads, then surely the melodic "Too Much Love" would certainly have been the obvious choice. But, alas, no. Despite the faith that Elektra put upon the audience favoring David's recognizable vocals, the single was to stall at a lowly #28. Maybe the public just couldn't, or wouldn't, accept Bread as anything more than a ballads band after all.

Recorded over the winter of 1970, the album was deemed completed and ready for release on March 1st, 1971, issued under the title *Manna*. Packaged in a lavish tri-fold cut-out sleeve that, for the first time, gave the public the opportunity to see, close-up, the faces of the four band members, complete with full printed lyrics within, the cover clearly indicated the investment that Elektra was prepared to put into the band. The pictures that adorned the cover, and the overall concept and presentation, were placed in the hands of one Robert L. Heimall, one of the youngest and most talented art directors in the business, hired by Elektra at the recommendation of The Doors' Jim Morrison. His subsequent handiwork suits the serious nature within. Heimall was also responsible for utilizing the image that adorned the rear of the sleeve: "The Gingerbread Maker," a rare 17th century Nuremberg print, although he appropriately "adapted" it to include four loaves of bread, not previously featured within the original piece of art. He also chose to remove the text that accompanied the original work:

God smartly measures and weighs
the gift of sweet hours in life,
wherein we are seeking almonds of joy.
The hand of love is never foreshortened
and if my time is seasoned with grief;
then I will also kiss the gingerbread.

In addition to the two tracks issued as the advance single, highlights abound. From the driving, bluesy-rock edge kicking off the Griffin-Royer composition "Take Comfort," down to the David Gates bouncy and commercial tune "He's A Good Lad," reportedly written for son Ricky. And from the wonderful production values on David's soaring "What A Change" to the subtle lyrical sniping that is suggested on "I Say Again."

"'I Say Again' is one of my favorite songs," Robb stated in the *Cash Box* interview. "Usually Jim is the one to come up with the lyrical phrase that starts a lot of our writing, but I had this image in my mind of a guy on his last legs with a chick. He knows there's still something there, but he can never get together with her. 'I Say Again' popped into my head as the phrase he uses to strike home to her that he's been talking but she's not been listening..."

Almost 40 years later however, Robb recalls the song in a different light. "*Manna* was starting to show the strains of David putting pressure on Jimmy, and Jimmy putting pressure on David. On the first Bread album I wrote a lot of the music, but by the time *Manna* came along there was only room for Jimmy's music and I just moved over to lyrics to make things accommodating," he says today when reflecting on his final album with the band. "That song is about non-communication and drifting apart, trying to connect with someone and not being able to do it. You get this sense of frustration flashing in the lyrics' pictures."[14]

The musical performances from each member appear flawless. The solid rhythms, the driving leads, the ambitious flourishes, all accompanied by Mike's intricate fills and rolls, beats, and breaks, make the release one of the more ambitious collections in the Bread catalog. However, much like the preceding album and the ensuing focus around "Make It With You," most of the media attention for *Manna* was directed towards one particular tune. Issued simultaneously as a single, coupled with "Take Comfort," this was the David Gates ballad "If."

David recalled how this particular tune came about during his interview with *NetMusic*: "The ideal situation on composing would be if you're trying to write a ballad, that you were just in a wonderful frame of mind that matched the kind of song you're trying to come up with. I've had that happen a number of times. My best songs have come out of situations where I was in the correct frame of mind, I had a little time, and I had some peace and quiet. 'If' was like that. I started at 9:30 one night after my wife and kids had gone to sleep. By 11:00 I was done with the song. Everything just worked. It clicked."

At Robb's suggestion, they called in Paul Beaver once again, a recognized pioneer in experimental electronic music, to add a synthesized effect to the recording of the song. "I called Paul up and said 'help us cut this tune' and he said 'sure,' but when we came into the studio that day there was this huge equipment everywhere, on every surface! It was an immense experiment..."

David continues, "That was one of the very first times a guitar had been played through a synthesizer. Up until that time you could only use a keyboard, but I wanted to run this electric guitar through the synthesizer, and the effect on 'If' is of two synthesizers going back and forth, two tone generators bouncing off each other to get that little sort of tremolo effect. I remember when Paul packed it up and went home, he said, 'I hope you liked that because I could never get that again!'"

"Ironically," James later added, "the sound we ended up getting, after all that huge bank of synthesizers and tone generators, sounded remarkably like a wah-wah pedal, which we used live and was much more manageable!"

The single raced up the charts, peaking at an impressive #4 in the *Billboard* Top 100, and actually topping the alternate Adult Contemporary lists, thus wiping out any disappointment that Elektra may have felt with the relative failure of "Let Your Love Go." While the band members themselves must have been equally thrilled with the success, underlying feelings must no doubt have cast further shadows on any hopes that James or Robb had for maintaining an equal balance within the band's output. Three ballads, three top 10 hits. "Ultimately 'soft rock' was what we did best, and you can't really argue with success," was David's summary.

February 1971, a traditional occasion each year when the pride of Hollywood, and the accompanying worldwide film industries, receive their combined moment in the spotlight, and the results from the previous twelve months are accordingly announced as to whom will be permitted their due time on the red carpet. Each year the nominations for the Academy Awards, the yearly highlight of the movie industry, are announced a number of weeks prior to the actual event, and among the prestigious best movies, the best producers, the best actors and actresses, some of the lesser reported awards are still given to those who make the magic that is the movies. Without the make-up artists, editors, and costume designers, there would be no golden age, or modern age of Hollywood, and very much a major factor of cinema, even since the days of the silent film when only music accompanied the images on screen, is the accompanying original score, or the big featured musical number. Needless to say, even to receive a nomination for an Academy Award is an honor in its own right… but to win one? Such moments have often left even the greatest of screen gods and goddesses babbling incoherently among a jumble of tears, running mascara, and scribbled thank you notes, often for far too long.

So it was that during 1971 both James Griffin and Robb Royer were very much in the headlines, but not solely for their achievements with Bread, for they too were announced during the February nominations as potential Academy Award ("Oscar") winners. The song they had composed alongside Fred Karlin for the 1970 movie *Lovers and Other Strangers*, which had subsequently become a huge pop hit for The Carpenters, "For All We Know," was up for the honor, chosen by the voting members of the The Academy of Motion Picture Arts and Sciences, alongside songs featured in *Scrooge* ("Thank You Very Much"), *Pieces Of Dreams* ("Pieces Of Dreams"), *Madron* ("Til Love Touches Your Life"), and *Darling Lili* ("Whistling Away The Dark"). On the night of the awards ceremony, the 43rd such occasion, held on April 15th, 1971, at the Dorothy Chandler Pavilion in Los Angeles, James and Robb, along with Karlin, donned their tuxedos and patiently sat in the audience alongside the famous and not-so-famous, waiting to hear the nominations and winners read out.

"I had a weird hostility towards that song, because I knew how perfunctory it was made. But it really did turn out to be a good song, and that night was just an outrageous high. We put on the tuxes, and the limousine flung us in there, and they interviewed us…" Robb remembers with a laugh.

Due to the request from the producer of the ceremony that all performances on the night be made by singers who had previously appeared in a film, British-born singer Petula Clark was given the responsibility of performing "For All We Know" at this special occasion. While she didn't quite bring across the delicate emotion of the song, as had either James's original demo or The Carpenters, or for that matter Larry Meredith, the vocalist on the actual movie soundtrack, the reception the song received by the gathered audience was suitably polite. Husband and wife team Burt Bacharach and Angie Dickinson were then given the honor of announcing the winner for "best song" and, upon their reading out the names of Fred Karlin, Robb Wilson, and Arthur James, the three writers leapt out of their seats, shook hands,

Multi-imagery at the Oscars (courtesy of Robb Royer)

and made their way onto the stage to collect their awards. James later jokingly commented that "they had me tucked so far back, and so deep in, that I had to step all over Henry Mancini to run up there and get it!"

Suitably humbled, in his role as Arthur James, Griffin stepped forward first and spoke into the microphone: "I was not really prepared for this. I would just like to thank not only Robb Royer but of course Fred Karlin for the wonderful music and, most of all, the Academy members for making this song a winner. Thank you." Robb stepped up next: "Like James, I'm a stranger to all this but I'd like to thank James Griffin and Fred Karlin and everyone involved. Thank you." Finally, the third member of the partnership, Fred Karlin, moved forward and interestingly chose to thank both the director of the film and The Carpenters, for making the song a hit, but notably omitted to mention the two men standing next to him. Despite this oversight, it remains doubtful that it would have hindered the enjoyment of the moment for the two musicians who, clearly, had not experienced such an occasion before.

Robb: "The press interviewed us going out and we sat at the party, with the 'thing' sitting on our table, cheering! That's the way it's supposed to be..."

It was during this ceremony that George C. Scott became the first actor to reject an Oscar, claiming that the Academy Awards were "a two-hour meat parade, a public display with contrived suspense for economic reasons," but nevertheless, to those lucky recipients who did accept the golden statuette it was a small blip in an otherwise memorable night, although James and Robb were both due back out on the road the next day.

While Robb and James were enjoying the fruits of their labor, David himself undertook a slightly different approach to the movie industry, and for the first time appeared on screen himself, albeit in a minor uncredited role. Described as the "ultimate car chase movie" the film *Vanishing Point* was a vehicle for Barry Newman, labeled in the screenplay as the "last American hero." Essentially a hippy-styled road movie, in *Easy Rider*-meets-*Two-Lane Blacktop*-meets-*Bullitt* fashion, David appeared briefly as a part of a traveling band of faith healers, with vocalists Delaney and Bonnie, Rita Coolidge, and a very young Bekka Bramlett wildly singing praises to the Lord, "You Got To Believe," off the back of a truck in the middle of a desert. Meanwhile, David sits stoically behind an upright piano, with barely a hint of emotion, pounding out at the piano keys for a full five and a half minutes, while dialogue and dancing goes on around him. It was not a particularly successful film, and would hardly raise a glimpse among Academy members, but it was a nice entry into this favored cult genre, and an interesting footnote on David's resume.

Mike too kept himself occupied between stints with Bread, returning to session work and appearing on two further studio albums during the year. Firstly, he provided the percussive duties on the debut solo album for Cyrus Faryar, a founding member of the Modern Folk Quartet who had signed a solo deal with Jac Holzman at Elektra Records. He followed this by assisting on the eponymous third studio release for Linda Ronstadt, sharing the drumming duties with Don Henley and Roger Hawkins. Although neither were particularly triumphant ventures in the chart listings, Mike's introduction to Ronstadt was to prove particularly beneficial to him in later years.

"It was the first time I worked with her," Mike would tell Ronstadt's biographer Peter Lewry. "It was plain to see then that she was going to have a huge music career. She was not only physically gifted with a great voice but she also had an amazing musical sensibility in everything from her vocal delivery of a song to the material she chose to record. She was amazingly adept at a number of styles and genres of music..."

With *Manna* riding high in the *Billboard* album charts, although one may consider a peak position of #21 disappointing in relation to the sales of *On The Waters*, the band reunited and headed out on a promotional tour during April, May, and

June. Accompanying the four-piece line-up for a number of shows was a 15-piece string section, brought in to add to the onstage presentation, and in particular to the "hit ballads" that had originally featured a string arrangement. One of the early shows was held in David's hometown of Tulsa on April 16th, the night after the Academy Awards ceremony, but it was David who was in the mood to party that evening, surrounded by family and friends backstage at the Tulsa Municipal Theater, and the show went down a storm, as did much of the ensuing tour. One review of the show held at Santa Monica's Civic Auditorium on May 21st summarized it neatly by simply stating: "Flawless. Better than on record..." and subsequent appearances saw them perform at the Circle Star Theater in San Carlos and at The Coliseum in Portland. One of the final shows on the tour, in more ways than one, came about on June 26th when they appeared alongside The Beach Boys, Alice Cooper, and Steppenwolf at the Beggar's Banquet Festival, held at the Borough Of York Stadium in Toronto, Canada. It had been a long time since James had last performed alongside The Beach Boys, seven years previously, although interestingly, with the legendary Californian band's career in a comparative slump during the early part of the decade, it was James and his group who were now in the ascendance. Bread were on the rise, although for Robb Royer, things were soon to take a downward turn.

Following their return to Los Angeles, they once again booked a series of sessions at Sound Recorders, with the intention of recording the next single, a follow-up to the Top 10 smash "If," and started initial work on the fourth album. Having recently been awarded the prestigious honor of "Best New Rock Group Of The Year" by *Record World* magazine, one of the three main music industry trade publications in the United States, the band should have been in buoyant mood as they reacquainted themselves with familiar surroundings, but these early sessions provided mixed results.

David: "I'd had two, or three, or four of the first Bread singles, songs I'd written and sung, and it was now time for James and Robb to go home and come up with something. It was to be their single and they just didn't have anything, and we needed to have a song ready for the next single. So the night before the session I sat down in my living room with a Telecaster guitar and wrote 'Mother Freedom.' We went in the next day and recorded it.

"My recollection is that I played the bulk of the instruments. I did the two electric guitars, and James played the solo guitar part. James and I sang it together to give it a little more punch and power."[9 14]

With Mike's solid playing laying down a tight groove, and Robb filling out on the bass once more, Bread made a further attempt at releasing a "rock" number as their next single. Ultimately a heavier sound than "Let Your Love Go," with a Zeppelin-styled riff during the introduction, and a surprisingly confident-sounding Gates still supplying the upbeat lead vocals, this was truly a credible attempt at bridging that now widening chasm between what they wanted to do as a band, and what the record-buying public were expecting to hear from them. The production also sounds a lot fuller than on previous rock numbers, although lyrically it remains a fairly unchallenging composition. Nevertheless, it was the overall heavier style that once again failed to win over the radio stations and their audiences. Despite being issued at a time when The Moody Blues, Grand Funk Railroad, Deep Purple, The Allman Brothers, and a similar mix of bands were running riot with their heavier or more progressive offerings, Bread could simply not win over the affections of such a key market, the all-important radio programmers, with songs such as this. The committed Bread fan, those who relished everything that the band put down onto vinyl, may well have lapped up this change of direction once again, and they were the ones who appreciated equally the diversity that the two songwriting camps brought into the mix. But overall, the band just did not have that large enough a following that would give all varying styles an equal opportunity. Core loyalty was one thing, crossover appeal was another thing altogether. "Mother Freedom" coupled with "Live In Your Love," a simple piano-based ballad taken from the *Manna* album, and composed by James and Robb, fared poorly in the singles market.

"That, to me, was a big question mark at the time. It really started to make me realize the power of radio," Mike Botts later remarked. "Because our fans were the ones who were raving about the song, they loved it in concert, and we thought, 'They can't be wrong, let's go ahead and put it out as a single.' Then we got some notes from various radio station chains who said, 'We're not going to play "Mother Freedom." Send us a ballad and you'll go on an automatic playlist.'"[32]

As for the accompanying "Live In Your Love": "I wasn't crazy about that one," James was to recall. "I started it on the piano, and I don't think we worked long and hard enough on the lyric. I think the lyric is kind of whiny."[14]

While the Rolling Stones' anthemic "Brown Sugar" ruled at the top, this new Bread release barely scraped into the Top 40, peaking at a lowly #37. The band even made an appearance on television to promote it, performing the single, along with "Too Much Love" and "It Don't Matter To Me," on the 1971 show *California Sound*, but to little effect. Ultimately, this became the very last time that Bread would issue an upbeat "rock" offering as a single.

With "Mother Freedom" struggling to gain a foothold in the charts, David, James, Robb, and Mike continued with the early sessions for their next album, although David did take a short break during this period and made a fleeting solo visit to the U.K., performing a live rendition of "If" on *Top Of The Pops*, and then taping a 35-minute *In Concert* performance for a forthcoming BBC broadcast. Once he'd returned home the foursome worked on two new compositions in the studio. The first, which remained unfinished, was a new Griffin-Royer song titled "Try," while the second was another new David Gates ballad. Initially composed on the piano, and with Robb providing bass once more, and James on guitar, this song simply wasn't developing in the way the composer had envisaged. Instead,

David opted to call a halt on the session until he figured out a new approach for the song. "I had written the song on piano and when we recorded it on piano the track had no life. I went home demoralized because I knew it was a good song..."[14]

However, what was perhaps most fascinating about the new song in question was how the strange phrasing of the title came into being. After all, "Baby I'm-A Want You" was not the most grammatically correct of song titles. Drummer Mike Botts was later to explain: "David came in one morning and he started playing 'Baby I'm-A Want You' on the piano. He sang the first line, 'Baby I'm-A Want You…' and I couldn't help it. I said, 'David, what made you say that? It sounds like baby talk' and he said, 'Y'know Michael, I wrote the melody and I didn't want to change it, and I had one note left over, so I added the extra syllable!'"[32]

David confirms: "I had struggled with a lot of different phrases and had to add 'I'm-A' to match my melody. I was not going to give up that melody!"[32]

This song would ultimately reappear a few weeks later, with a new acoustic arrangement similar to "Make It With You," although there would be one further change in its eventual construction – that of the band personnel.

The sessions were not going as smoothly as they would have wished. Neither "Try" nor "Baby I'm-A Want You" were finished, and the growing animosity between David and Robb, initially born out of David's dominance in the studio, but also widened by David's belief that Robb and James were conspiring against him, was becoming intolerable to both. Musically, they still maintained the utmost respect for each other and their individual abilities, but when in the same studio tensions ran high. Robb also found himself, much to David's annoyance, often diverting his focus to a reoccurring interest in writing screenplays, an interest carried over from his college days. He would often arrive at Sound Recorders carrying a satchel laden with books, only to spend valuable studio time scribbling notes on ideas and plans for scripts. Ultimately, this became the centerpiece of one of the final fallouts between the pair. To David, Robb clearly had other interests more important to him than the music. The unfortunate result of all this in-house arguing and internal friction was that, following a further band meeting, Robb was removed of his responsibilities within the line-up, a situation that caused James much unrest over the coming months, aware that perhaps he had not supported his friend and partner to capacity. Did Robb leave willingly or was he pushed? Stories continue to circulate, subject to who is telling them.

David recalls, rather diplomatically: "We always felt Robb was just biding his time with the music in order to get where he wanted to be, which was the movie business. At a certain point there was a noticeable lack of camaraderie, and he just about got into a fight with Botts one day. He and I got along all right at first, and then it began to bother me that his loyalties lay elsewhere. He began to drift away mentally from the band, so in the end he stepped aside."

Robb however, had this to say in conversation with the author. "The (final) conflicts began around June or July, 1971, and I wouldn't have left the band were it not that things came to a point between David and I where it couldn't go on. It wasn't like I said 'I quit.' I didn't quit. I got pushed out by David who decided I was conspiring with Jimmy. In a way, I was defending David from Jimmy and for the most part we were giving a lot to David and we were getting a lot back from David, even though it was an uncomfortable relationship. But, for the most part, I defended David from Jimmy and I never made that clear to David. I wasn't happy I was out of the band."

With one of the band's founding members now gone from the line-up, this was clearly a major issue for the remaining trio. James was still intent on keeping his songwriting partnership with his friend alive, albeit away from confrontations of the Gates/Royer scenario, but with Robb removed from the recording and performing entity of the band, they simply couldn't function as a three-piece, especially if they were to remain a self-contained unit without the obvious answer of bringing in faceless sidemen. However, it was an issue that was swiftly resolved. David immediately turned to one of the musical associates that he had worked alongside on countless occasions during the previous decade as a hired session musician. One who would, ultimately, increase the musical abilities of the quartet and raise their performing barriers to new levels. Enter Larry Knechtel...

Chapter Nine

Picture In Your Mind

It is only just over 20 miles from the golden sands of the Pacific shoreline to the center of Bell, an easterly suburb of the great sprawling metropolis that is Los Angeles County. Lawrence William Knechtel had been born in Bell on August 4th, 1940, the eldest of three sons hailing from Germanic roots, and an early interest in music resulted in all three boys undertaking rudimentary piano lessons before they had even reached their teenage years. As the most musically talented of the threesome, Larry reportedly took to them swiftly, sight reading with ease, and, as one who was seemingly gifted with perfect pitch, he started playing by ear soon afterwards, thus avoiding many arduous hours hunched in front of sheet music. His younger brothers, Don and Bob, while also keen to learn both piano and violin, soon trailed in the wake of their elder sibling.

Although trained classically on the piano, his early forays into a teenage lifestyle at Bell High School developed another early interest for Larry, in the form of electronics. Through an inquisitive nature, he soon found the ability to build his own crystal radio, one that successfully brought the sounds of the local radio stations into his home, thus introducing him to the then-popular rock'n'roll and rhythm & blues artists of the mid-late 1950s. A proportion of his Bell High year was of Hispanic descent, and his Chicano classmates shared his love for the raw sounds they heard, dressing themselves out in the "bad" styles of the day: khaki pants with turned cuffs, long-sleeve dress shirts, and greased back ducktail hairstyles.

"L.A. had a healthy R&B scene, with three black radio stations and a lot of independent record labels," Larry later recalled in conversation with Dick Stewart, editor of the popular *Lance Monthly* music magazine. "I didn't like white rock and roll. It sounded like rockabilly music to me, and I hated Pat Boone, Patti Page, Georgia Gibbs, etc., doing bad covers of black records. Once you heard the real thing, there was no going back. If you lived where they played the black artists, down south or a large city, it was no contest. My personal choices were blues and jazz. As for Buddy Holly, I liked 'That'll Be the Day' and 'It Doesn't Matter Anymore,' but, overall, I didn't like rockabilly much."

Clearly struck by the inventive sounds of the black artists he was hearing across the airwaves, he spent untold hours purchasing, listening to, and dissecting the arrangements of each melody that came out of the grooves. At the tender age of fourteen he joined up with a number of like-minded young teenagers, including future session stalwarts Michael Deasy and Jim Horn, as part of an inner-city youth band, populated by musicians from several local schools situated in and around the central Los Angeles area. Larry's immediate presence on the piano helped him slot in comfortably, and it was to prove a positive breeding ground for these young talents, developing their instinctive love of music, and just two years later, aged sixteen, Larry entered the recording studios for the first time and cut his debut single. In partnership with another young musician, known locally as Murl, the duo formed a band they named Murl & Larry and The Dynamics, and alongside saxophonist Jim Horn they taped the self-composed instrumental "Pidgeon-Toed," which actually achieved a modicum of local success when issued on the small Delta label, earning Larry around $800 in royalty payments, before it swiftly disappeared into rarity status. The band also played at a number of dances and hops around the city, favoring their instrumental prowess over any attempts at a vocal approach.

"Pidgeon-Toed" 45 (courtesy of the Malcolm C. Searles collection)

"I had no ideas of going any further than playing weekends in a band. I didn't know of the existence of studio musicians, and I always thought I would someday have to get a real job."[21]

Nevertheless, despite his youthful uncertainties, alongside his new musical peers he began to seek out opportunities to perform wherever he could, often supporting more established performers such as Ed Townsend, Bumps Blackwell, and Sonny Knight at any number of local venues around the vast city, or even supporting the likes of Johnny Otis at demo recording sessions.

During the late 1950s, he hooked up with fellow Californian rock'n'roll enthusiast Kip Tyler, one of the leading exponents of the local rockabilly sound. Larry's initial resistance to this style of music was now gradually easing as he began to participate further among fellow like-minded musicians. By joining Tyler's backing band, The Flips, as the piano player, and working alongside his close friend Michael Deasy who played guitar, with Mike Bermani on drums, and Steve Douglas Kreisman on saxophone, Larry began to integrate himself within the genre. Tyler himself was as wild as they came in those days, often arriving onstage on his motorcycle, clad head-to-toe in black leather. He was originally the singer of The Sleepwalkers, who were Union High School's toughest rock'n'roll band, and members from this group were later to combine forces with the best musicians from rival Fairfax High School to form an early version of Kip Tyler & The Flips. Besides the usual shows at high school dances, and parties, the group's wild sound and stage performances soon made them the most popular band on the legendary shows at the El Monte Legion Stadium. Once Larry linked up with them, they virtually became the house band, as they often provided the backing for other artists appearing at the venue. On more than one occasion, once school was through for the week, Larry and his friends would jump in their low rider 1950 Chevys, tune into to the Art Laboe radio show, and head off either to the El Monte, the Long Beach Municipal Auditorium, or the Pasadena Civic Auditorium to support the current top stars of the day, including Ritchie Valens, The Everly Brothers, and Little Richard.

Larry recalled, "I had to join the musicians' union when I was 18. All the gigs with these bands were paid gigs and I played piano back in those days. Kip Tyler was my first local taste of the big time. He had a couple of records out in L.A., but the main thing was we were the backup band for local TV personality and deejay, Art Laboe. We played shows in auditoriums all over the L.A. area, backing up acts such as Marvin & Johnny, Don, and Dewey."[21]

Disc jockey Laboe, who was the organizer of many of these stadium shows, knew potential when he saw it, and he subsequently signed Kip Tyler & The Flips to his newly created Starla label. They released one single on the short-lived Starla, "Let's Monkey Around," in the fall of 1957, before signing with the fledgling Challenge label, from where they issued "Jungle Hop," the following year. Unfortunately, neither of these two releases saw any significant sales, although the band also played on numerous demo sessions for other local artists or songwriters, many of which actually received radio airplay time on their own merits.

Upon completing high school, Larry enrolled at college, intent on taking his interest in electronics to higher levels of education and keeping his musical activities as a sideline, but, after deciding that, just maybe, his heart wasn't really in it, he soon quit the arduous college timetable and chose instead to pursue the musical direction full-time. When, in 1959, a popular new guitarist named Duane Eddy made contact and offered him a job, touring as a part of his Rebels backing band, Larry quit The Flips and, along with Steve Kreisman and drummer Mike

Bermani, hit the road as a Rebel. Of note, Larry's replacement in the Flips line-up was future Beach Boy Bruce Johnston.

It was also during 1959 that Larry got one of his first tastes of success as a burgeoning songwriter. Following on from his initial attempts at composing with his band The Dynamics and their recording of "Pidgeon-Toed," another instrumental composition he had written, "So Fine, Be Mine," this time with fellow musician Michael Deasy, was picked up by Eddie Cochran and his friends, and released on Silver Records under the guise of The Kelly Four. Although not one of Cochran's more familiar offerings, the release, reportedly using Larry and Michael's demo version as the basic backing track, was another early rung on the ladder of success. Meanwhile, now an essential part of Duane Eddy's touring band, Larry began to see the far wider reaches that his music had to offer, traveling the breadth of the country, and indeed the world as, for the next three years, Eddy's popularity began to rise swiftly. The band was strictly instrumental, highlighting the growing influence that its leader was having among his peers, and, in Larry's own words, was "probably the best caliber rock band out there."

In 1960, Eddy and his band set out on a three-week tour of the United Kingdom, accompanying Bobby Darin and Clyde McPhatter. Although listed down on the bill as the opening act, The Rebels literally rocked each venue to the foundations every night, far outstripping the response to the headlining acts, much to their chagrin, with the British public loving The Rebels so much that, immediately after the tour was finished, they started another run of European shows, this time acting as the headliners.

Upon their triumphant return home, they joined up with a series of Dick Clark "package tours," a run of concerts across the country that featured short sets from a number of popular and upcoming acts, often featuring a variety of musical genres, including both black and white artists, a somewhat revolutionary approach for the times. With everyone crammed aboard tour buses, these diverse acts zigzagged across the country, performing one night stands from city to city.

"We played a package with B.B. King, James Brown, Hank Ballard & The Midnighters, Jerry Lee Lewis," remembered Larry. "These were mixed shows in a segregated south, and we saw racism in our faces. In L.A., it was there, but not amongst the musicians. I watched every show! I remember the great ones, but most were mediocre. The one real bad one was the time we played the Cotton Bowl on a rainy night, and the stage was wet. We were being shocked by our own instruments because of grounding problems. They brought flattened cardboard for us to stand on, but it got wet and was useless. A two-inch, blue spark hit anyone who approached a microphone. They finally shut the show down, and we all went to a bar and got drunk."[21]

It was during this period touring with Eddy that Larry first picked up a bass guitar, and was soon utilizing his new found skills on the tour. As a naturally gifted musician, it was a relatively easy progression for him and, subsequently,

Eddy reduced his band down to a four-piece with Larry taking up the bass position full-time.

During a break from the endless touring, while in Arizona, the band took the opportunity to participate in the filming of *A Thunder Of Drums*, a western movie being shot for MGM Pictures featuring Richard Boone, George Hamilton, and Luana Patten in the lead roles. Duane himself had a minor role in the film, albeit a more prominent one than his band mates, but Larry and his colleagues still managed to fit into the filming as extras. However, it wasn't all just life on the road and, as Eddy continued to build on his successful recording career, releasing a series of albums including *The Twang's The Thang* and hit singles such as "Pepe" and "(Dance With The) Guitar Man," Larry began to gain further experience working in the studio, supplying either piano or bass. And yet, tiring of the constant demand for live performances across the vast country, away from home for extended periods, Larry chose to leave The Rebels during 1962 in order to spend more time in his home city, close to family and friends, claiming he didn't want the lifestyle to run or ruin him. Instead, he began picking up with a number of local club groups such as The Gene Connors Band, a previously all-black line-up, for whom he filled in on electric bass.

Then, during the summer of 1963, he received a call from his former Rebels band mate Steve Kreisman, now known as Steve Douglas, who was establishing himself as an in-demand session player and contractor for the L.A. studio circuit. He wanted Larry to play on an upcoming seasonal album for producer Phil Spector, the result of which was the now acclaimed, but at the time relatively unsuccessful *A Christmas Gift For You* album, a collection of festive offerings from Spector's stable of performers (The Ronettes, The Crystals, Darlene Love, and Bob B. Soxx). This notable moment in turn led to Larry becoming one of Spector's regular session team, helping develop the "wall of sound," and appearing on numerous sessions and releases over the coming months. The summer of 1963 was also the time that the vocal surf-sound became the recognizable voice of California, having evolved out of the staccato instrumentals of two years earlier. Artists such as The Beach Boys and Jan & Dean were taking their vocal interpretations of the sound to the mass market, with Larry often contributing to their instrumental work, most notably at this stage with Jan & Dean.

"I never surfed. We smoked pot, cruised the freeways, and ate hot fudge sundaes. I didn't like surf music," recalled Larry, again in conversation with Dick Stewart, "(but) because I played on Spector's early stuff, Brian Wilson and the other artists wanted to use the same guys that Phil did and it kind of snowballed. I had done a lot of demo recordings when I was playing with Johnny Otis and, therefore, I was not bothered by the 'red light' going on as some great players were. I knew what was required; for example, a good performance, no mistakes, good time, and feel, and being able to fit musically into the arrangement. I also have perfect pitch, which makes me quick on my feet musically. And I was easy to get along with, and would try something else if they didn't like what I first offered. I never tried to schmooze the artists and producers, was polite, but I kept a certain professional manner and distance. Personally, I liked Jan & Dean a lot, working for them. They borrowed a lot from The Beach Boys, but not enough!"

In addition to working with Jan & Dean, Larry contributed to a number of other recordings from the surf and hot-roddin' genre, and the subsequent sunshine-pop phase that followed, including the second album by The Hondells, Paul Petersen's "She Rides With Me," The Rip Chords' version of the Brian Wilson composition "Help Me Rhonda," the Gary Usher-produced *Silly Surfers* novelty album, Bruce & Terry's "You're So Good To Me" and "Four Strong Winds," The Bandits' *Electric 12* album, and the soundtrack collections for the *How To Stuff A Wild Bikini* and *Skaterdater* movies.

Then, in 1964, Larry was offered a spot as the bass player in the house band for the TV music show *Shindig!*, a show that, as previously mentioned, went on to become one of the defining moments in American music history. Numerous artists passed through the *Shindig!* studios over the two years it ran for ABC television, and Larry was in the fortuitous position of performing alongside many legends, including one notable date in May 1965 when he found himself backing one of the greatest blues artists of all time, Howlin' Wolf. For someone who grew up listening to the great rhythm and blues recordings of the '40s and '50s, this must have been a particularly satisfying moment.

As the 1960s progressed, and the demand for session musicians increased, Larry became one of the first call players. The successful period he had endured as one of Phil Spector's leading men had given him a key role in the burgeoning L.A. industry, and producers of the caliber of Brian Wilson and Terry Melcher were now utilizing these same A-list players on their own sessions. This elite band of performers, a close-knit bond including bassists Carol Kaye, Joe Osborn, and Ray Pohlman, drummers Hal Blaine, Jim Gordon, and Earl Palmer, guitarists Glen Campbell, Billy Strange, Tommy Tedesco, Al Casey, and Mike Deasy, keyboard wizards Leon Russell and Don Randi, and assorted percussionists and horn players, along with the multi-talented Knechtel, and occasional associate David Gates, were now very much in demand, often pulling eighteen-hour days as they jumped from session to session, studio to studio. Western Recorders to Sunset Sound to the Capitol Tower. More often than not, they simply turned up, plugged in, and performed whatever was on the chord sheets laid out before them, and, having pulled off a near-perfect take in the first few attempts, it was across town to the next booking, without even realizing or hearing back how the eventual finished track would sound.

However, on regular occasions, the producer would often rely on these talented individuals to add their own flair to an arrangement. A full-blown drum fill, a bass riff, a guitar run, or a keyboard flourish. Not that they were ever credited for this added "extra," but it was an acknowledgment that if anyone could add a mo-

Larry during the mid-'60s (courtesy of Lonnie Knechtel)

ment of sparkle to a production it was these guys. And then, it was only when the completed song appeared on the L.A. radio stations, often weeks or months later, blaring out of the in-car stereos while *en route* to the next gig, that this team heard for the first time the completed song, often recognizing it by no more than the familiar riff or pattern they had laid down a few weeks previous. It was constant, but the rewards were notable, with many of the top-rated players pulling in earnings equivalent to the highest paid show business stars. Drummer Hal Blaine, who often jokingly referred to Larry as "Prince Valiant" (due to his flowing golden locks, styled in a "bob 'n' bangs" fashion), lived in a Hollywood mansion, with numerous cars in the driveway and a yacht in the marina. Bass player Carol Kaye, the only female member of the "crew," once commented that during one particular year, so busy was her schedule, that she earned as much, if not more, than the President himself. Larry, too, was appreciative of the income that these sessions could bring him, choosing to live in an impressive mock-Tudor house in North Hollywood with his wife Vicki, whom he had met while on tour with Duane Eddy in Florida, and their young son Lonnie.

"We never gave discounts in order to get work," remembered Larry. "In fact, we were soon getting double and sometimes triple scale, as we couldn't do all the work offered us. That's not to say we wouldn't sometimes help someone we liked get a break now and then, but once that person got a deal or had a hit, we were fully compensated and got our regular rate from then on. I remember many times the road bands would be in the booth staring at us through the glass, just waiting for us to die or make a mistake. The pressure was on us, not them!"[21]

The Byrds, The Fifth Dimension, The Beach Boys, The Monkees, Johnny Rivers, The Mamas & The Papas, Frank Sinatra, The Turtles, Sonny & Cher, all famous names that benefited from having this established team performing on their records. And just to scratch the surface of Larry's individual resume from that heady period would include such huge hits as "Mr. Tambourine Man," "Mrs. Robinson," "MacArthur Park," "Eve Of Destruction," "Good Vibrations," "River Deep Mountain High," "Never My Love," "You've Lost That Lovin' Feeling," "San Francisco (Be Sure To Wear Some Flowers In Your Hair)," and "Stoned Soul Picnic," along with The Beach Boys' *Pet Sounds*, The Doors' debut release, and The Monkees' first two million-selling albums. The Mamas & The Papas' undisputed leader John Phillips, who had also utilized Larry on the phenomenally successful hit "Monday Monday," even had his own affectionate nickname for the popular musician, simply referring to him as "Third Hand."

Larry's simple opening bass slide during the first few bars of "Mr. Tambourine Man" remains such a distinctive moment in rock history and yet, for Larry, it was the recording of the 1966 *Pet Sounds* album that was to remain a particular cherished memory for him. "All throughout *Pet Sounds* I felt it was a special project. We all did. I would go home and play some of the sequences just because I loved the way they went. And at this point we hadn't heard any vocals. I'm proud of it. Period. The album had a lot of impact. I don't take credit for anything, but I was part of it. After *Pet Sounds* came out, I went and bought it, which was something I never did. And I had him (Brian Wilson) sign it. That meant a lot to me. I learned a lot. I was pretty much a four-chord rock'n'roll nightclub player when I started."[22]

Unfortunately, such was the extensive use of Larry's musical abilities, and those of his session partners, that no official logs have ever been recorded of every session they worked upon, and most likely never will be. Many recordings were scrapped, abandoned, or unfinished, AFM contracts misplaced, credits undocumented, and thus a definitive listing is now nigh on impossible.

Two releases that are certain, however, were among a series of albums that appeared on the World Pacific label during 1965 and 1966. The first was entitled *In Harmonica* (WP-1836), comprising of 12 instrumentals (including covers of "The Universal Soldier," "All I Really Want To Do," and "The In-Crowd") featuring Larry as the principal player on harmonica, albeit with the album credited to Larry *Nelson*. The second appeared under the credit of "The Carmel Strings featuring Larry Knechtel." This latter instrumental collection went by the title of *Boss Baroque* (WP-1838) and again featured Larry leading the instrumentation, this time on harpsichord, offering up 18th century-styled classical interpretations of 20th century compositions. An interesting concept, and one that was clearly inspired by the mid-'60s need for all-things-British, with the baroque "sound" originating from the long-gone years of European history. The arrangements featured on the record highlighted Larry's all too evident fluency on the keyboard, with the accompanying sleeve notes stating that:

> *"America was hearing the top tunes of the day in a style hundreds of years old. The marriage worked. Enter World Pacific with a concept to expand the modern baroque idea even further. Assembling such top-notch arrangers as Billy Strange and Buddy Prima, harpsichordist Larry Knechtel and top-flight pop producer Andy DiMartino, the company set out to devise a program of pop entertainment, broadening the baroque sound to include the modern, contemporary rhythms of today's top songs."*
> —Eliot Tiegel, *Billboard*

Engineered by Bruce Botnick, who was also utilizing Larry's uncredited bass playing on The Doors' debut album at the same time, the ten featured tracks included versions of George Gershwin's "Rhapsody In Blue," Paul McCartney's "Yesterday," the Jagger-Richards composition "As Tears Go By," Linzer and Randell's "A Lover's Concerto," Holland-Dozier-Holland's "I Hear A Symphony," and five pieces from the Billy Strange-Buddy Prima arranging team. Needless to say, such was the specialization of these releases that neither were major successes, and yet they remain nice period pieces, particularly the latter with its elegant old English charm coupled with a dash of 1960s Mediterranean Riviera.

One year later, on June 16th, 1967, Larry, along with roughly 100,000 other young people, journeyed north to the small coastal city of Monterey, Northern California, where the first International Pop Music Festival was being held. It promised to be an exciting event, with a number of the top stars of the day making the same journey to the sunny western coastline of America. Indeed, it was even rumored at one stage that the Beatles themselves would be making an appearance, and, while this was never genuinely a possibility, the subsequent line-up, pulled together by John Phillips, leader and principal songwriter for The Mamas & The Papas, was truly an impressive bill. The Who, Simon & Garfunkel, The Byrds, Otis Redding, Buffalo Springfield, Janis Joplin, The Jimi Hendrix Experience, Ravi Shankar, Jefferson Airplane, and Phillips' own kaftan-clad quartet gave those in attendance a truly memorable three days of music. Essentially, it was an amalgamation of the Southern California L.A. pop-sophistication, and the Northern Californian Haight-Ashbury free approach to peace and love. Maybe the at-odds mixture didn't appeal to all, but the flowers bloomed and the drugs flowed...

"I wore my hair long but, by that time, I was married and had a child and already a fiscal conservative, so no hippy ways for me," said Larry, when asked to reminisce on those halcyon times. "I did smoke pot, but I started that back in high school in East L.A., way before you ever heard of hippies. We all knew drugs were involved, but they were everywhere and with pretty much everybody. I was in 'Frisco a couple of times, working with Jerry Garcia, and Simon and Garfunkel. I didn't like the town and I wasn't a fan of the 'Frisco music either… too folky, and, while they recorded a lot of self-contained bands, there wasn't a studio musician scene there."

Having been an essential part of The Mamas & The Papas' studio band, it was logical that certain members of the Los Angeles studio crew, notably Larry, Joe Osborn, and drummer Hal Blaine, would supply the backing music for the band onstage at Monterey as well, particularly as the eyes and ears of the world would be upon them as the headlining and closing act of the festival. And while it certainly wasn't the most explosive of performances – that honor would be fought over by antics of both The Who and Jimi Hendrix – it was an accomplished if somewhat anti-climactic finale. The supporting trio of Knechtel, Osborn, and Blaine were, in fact, such a recognized rhythm section during this period that they were now known among their peer group as the "HGT," referring to their status as Hollywood's Golden Trio and, in addition to playing alongside The Mamas & The Papas, these famed sessioneers also acted as the "house-band" at Monterey for any other artists who needed support on the stage, Johnny Rivers included.

It appeared that Larry's approval among his fellow musicians could barely get any higher, such was the demand he now found himself in, and as the year progressed, yet more sessions followed. Dean Torrence, The Mamas & The Papas, Richard Harris, Spanky & Our Gang, Johnny Rivers, and, before the decade was out, there would be at least two further notable occurrences in his illustrious career.

June 20th, 1968, found Larry to be working at the familiar location of Western Recorders in Hollywood, although on this particular date the King of Rock'n'Roll was also in residence. Elvis Presley was working on a proposed 1968 TV Special for NBC, initially to be simply known as *Elvis*, but these days, more often than not, referred to as the *'68 Comeback Special.*

"Elvis was a great guy. I had met him in Memphis years before when we were doing a Dick Clark Caravan of Stars tour and he invited us to his brand new home, which became Graceland. When I played bass on that comeback TV Special, he remembered me from then..."[21]

Larry had been recruited to supply bass guitar for a series of backing tracks, to be used for the TV Special, that Elvis could then perform to, "live," during the actual taping of the show. Sitting alongside him in the studio that day were such familiar names as Mike Deasy, Tommy Tedesco, and Hal Blaine, and over the course of the next week the team committed to tape the tracks for such notable Presley classics as "Guitar Man," "Memories," "Trouble," and the song chosen to be the show's big closing number, "If I Can Dream." This wasn't the first time Larry had sat in on a Presley session. Indeed, three months earlier, on March 7th, he had played bass at Western Recorders on a session that had resulted in "A Little Less Conversation," along with a couple of other tunes for the forgettable *Live A Little, Love A Little* movie soundtrack, but such was the focus on the NBC-TV Special, the first time that Elvis had performed before a live audience since 1961, that this was a significantly far more important tracking session. Needless to say, the 1968 *Elvis* TV Special, airing on December 3rd, was a phenomenal success, almost single-handedly resurrecting Elvis' ailing career overnight, and paving the way for him to resume regular recording and concert duties.

"He also twice asked me to join his band," Larry was to say. "First on bass, later on piano for the Vegas gig, but I didn't want to leave town at that time so I didn't even ask what the gig paid. And as the soundtracks involved arrangements and a pretty good-sized orchestra, horns, and strings, there were not a lot of takes. Time be money..."[21]

Time was money indeed, and eighteen months later Larry was to achieve equal, if not more significant, acclaim for another studio project. In this case, taking four or five days of expensive studio work to complete just one track, admittedly an expansive five-minute offering, that would go down as one of *the* greatest popular songs of all time.

In the interim, he spent session time in L.A.'s Sound Recorders studios working alongside Beatle George Harrison on the Jackie Lomax debut offering *Is This What You Want?*, and also assisted in the recording of a new project by two other rock'n'roll greats. *Roots* was the 1968 album issued by The Everly Brothers, two of the founding lights in rock harmony, and this new offering, despite its relative failure at the time, garnered critical praise throughout the industry, setting the benchmark for the flurry of country rock releases that was to follow. One of which, the 1969 *Longbranch Pennywhistle* album, featured future founding-Eagle Glenn Frey in the singer-songwriter chair (alongside JD Souther), with Larry helping out on piano duties once more. In addition, as a songwriting sideline for himself, Larry also composed and arranged both sides of an obscure 45rpm release for Magic Lamp Records, a small independent label run by fellow session regular Joe Osborn. This particular issue, released by Mickey Jones & The Triumphs ("I Can Live Without You" b/w "I Thought I Could"), was notable for also featuring a young, pre-fame Karen Carpenter as a backing vocalist. Nevertheless, it was his work the following year that was to afford Larry his most notable success as a session performer. Composed by New Jersey-born singer-songwriter Paul Simon for the fifth studio album he was recording with his musical partner, Art Garfunkel, "Bridge Over Troubled Water" came together during the summer of 1969 and was perhaps most significant, not only for being the title track for the popular duo's million-selling final album, but also for exposing the underlying tensions that ran between the partnership. Tensions that ultimately came to a head and pulled them apart a short time later.

Simon had originally written the emotional ballad, a simple two-verse song, on the guitar, envisaging a gospel-sounding piano accompaniment as a counterbalance to the vocal. With the initial tracking sessions being held at the Columbia Studios in Los Angeles, and utilizing both Hal Blaine and Larry Knechtel from the established core of top-flight West Coast session musicians, Simon entrusted the

The Jackie Lomax sessions (courtesy of Lonnie Knechtel)

responsibility for coming up with the required piano work to Larry. They told him they needed an intricate gospel arrangement, and it was one that would ultimately take Larry four days to work up – but they were four days well spent. Working alongside vocalist Art Garfunkel, and co-producers Roy Halee and Paul Simon, Larry came up with an ambitious yet inspiring solo, including the now-famous introduction, while Garfunkel also contributed to the intermediate piano chords between verses. However, because Larry was elongating the piano part, it became apparent that a third verse was required, which necessitated a hasty additional rewrite from Simon, who came up with the memorable, "Sail on silver girl, sail on by..."

Later, when speaking to journalist Kim Nowacki from the *Yakima Herald*, Larry commented that "Simon & Garfunkel took exacting pains, but it was all overtime for me. They're East Coast intellectuals, I'm a West Coast ruffian," while also confirming to author Dick Stewart that "Simon & Garfunkel were the pickiest, but they were paying well for it, and they were a prestigious act with which to be associated."

Following the initial sessions for the song in Los Angeles, the track was finally completed when the vocals were added in New York during the first week of December, 1969. Paul Simon was later to admit regret at his decision to allow Garfunkel to take lead vocal duties, as it pushed his partner to the fore, leaving him in the shadows during, what is perhaps, the duo's finest moment. Certainly, at initial concert performances, the rapturous reception that Garfunkel received, having performed the song, was a sight and sound to behold, and for a while Larry, too, was to bask in that glory, being requested to accompany the duo on tour during some of the album's initial promotional outings. In the spring of 1970, with both the album and single topping charts all around the world, Larry accompanied Simon & Garfunkel on a short visit to Europe, appearing onstage in Amsterdam, Moscow, and London.

"We brought our piano player friend out from Hollywood to play 'Bridge Over Troubled Water' with us..." ran the introduction, whereupon Larry would saunter onstage as the only accompanying musician during the entire concert, and pick out the now-familiar chords to the chart-topping track, to enthusiastic applause from the appreciative audiences.

However, despite the acclaim this was to bring him, the turn of the decade was a difficult time for the Los Angeles studio session musicians. A new crop of performers was now replacing the hardworking teams of the 1960s, and new bands were being built around young, enthusiastic members who wanted to play the music for themselves. Artistic integrity they called it. The kids were now all right. Not that the work was to dry up for the likes of Hal Blaine, Tommy Tedesco, and Knechtel. There were still the industry-creations such as The Partridge Family and The Brady Bunch who needed a session team behind them, or the MOR approach of The Carpenters, Streisand, Andy Williams, and The Fifth Dimension. But the demand for established rock'n'rollers was certainly on the wane. Sure, there was always a need for an experienced sessioneer, but nowhere near as much as when Spector was on call twenty-four-seven. The Wrecking Crew era was all but over, and yet the individual musicians still had a living to make, and not all of them could simply hang up their instruments and turn to face the audience, microphone in hand, as Glen Campbell had so successfully done. New opportunities were needed.

The beginning of the 1970s saw Larry continuing with his session activities, accepting paid work where it could be found, and the first twelve months or so saw him appearing in the studios with Jesse Davis, Billy Joel, John Phillips, Mason Williams, Poco, John Stewart, Dory Previn, Harry Nilsson, Lalo Schifrin, and Seals & Crofts among others. He also undertook a few production duties as well, working alongside Johnny Rivers behind the control booth, and even continued to develop his occasional songwriting flourishes with "Burnin'," a recording by the band Spider. Yet, it was "Bridge Over Troubled Water" that once again was to thrust him into the spotlight when, on March 16th, 1971, the annual Grammy American Music Awards took place at the Hollywood Palladium in Los Angeles.

Larry's contribution to the success of the Simon & Garfunkel hit was rewarded with a nomination for "Best Arrangement Accompanying Vocalist(s)," and was placed up against The Carpenters' "(They Long To Be) Close To You," Ray Stevens' "Everything Is Beautiful," and Blood, Sweat & Tears' "Lucretia MacEvil." Still, given the sheer quality and beauty of Larry's contributions, it surely came as no surprise when the prestigious gilded award was placed in Larry and Paul Simon's hands for their efforts. In total, "Bridge Over Troubled Water," either the album or single, won six awards that evening, confirming its status as one of rock's truly legendary recordings and, while this occasion was to follow Larry for the remainder of his career, regardless of all other notable contributions, it was one of which he was unduly proud. However, he was all too aware by now that many leading artists and performers were reaping the financial rewards far better than before, and whereupon, in the previous decade, it had been the studio musicians who were pulling in the big bucks, now it was the turn of the headliners. Priorities change when money is involved, especially when it is not in as much supply as five or six years previously, and so when David Gates, a session musician from the early 1960s who had played alongside Larry on a number of recordings, called him up one day, enquiring whether he would be prepared to fill in the gap in his band Bread left open by the departure of founding member Robb Royer, it appeared an ideal opportunity for Larry to link up once again as a part of an established line-up.

It was a wise move from the astute David Gates...

Chapter Ten

Games Of Magic

With a fourth slice now back in the rack, Bread resumed their position on the promotional circuit. A September 28th appearance on *The Glen Campbell Goodtime Hour*, the phenomenally successful CBS-TV variety show, hosted by David's former session partner, saw the revised line-up performing a rendition of "If" before a live audience. Shortly afterwards they returned once again to their touring schedule, finishing up the promotional *Manna* tour. Larry clearly added that extra edge to the band, assuming the onstage bass duties as well as filling in on keyboards when required, and this in turn allowed David to remain center stage, switching between acoustic and electric guitars, remaining in the focal spotlight, and supporting James when the light switched to stage left. However, some of the reviews from the tour suggested that the positive elements that Robb had initially brought to the live sound were now notably absent, to the detriment of the shows.

> *"Royer is a bright innovative performer who added an unmistakable touch of cerebral class to Bread. He not only wrote good and occasionally excellent lyrics to Jim Griffin's music but also contributed greatly to what was at the time one of the tightest and most outstanding three-guitar blends in popular music. New member Knechtel is a fine studio musician who helps his colleagues come very close to duplicating the original Bread sound... however, the group's sound during the 50% that Knechtel is on keyboards, particularly organ, is more than different. It's a cut lower than before since the keyboard tends to overpower the melody lines of those strong guitars. Give the group a few more months to get their sound together and they'll doubtless be back to their usual all-out performances."*
>
> —Review of Long Beach Auditorium concert, November 26th, 1971
> *The Register*, Orange County newspaper

The October and November schedule took in a variety of venues across the country, culminating in a show at the Long Beach Auditorium on the 26th where, alongside the usual hits and choice album cuts such as "Easy Love," "Truckin'," "The Other Side Of Life," and "Too Much Love," they highlighted a new, as yet unrecorded Griffin-Royer composition entitled "She Knows." A delicate ballad in the mold of David's hit recordings, this surprise added bonus to the set list would not see a studio release for a further two years, despite its obvious quality, and yet the song that many of the audience were waiting to hear was often chosen to feature as the closing number of the show, and would do so for many a Bread concert hereafter. The recent Top 10 single, "If," would always receive a huge cheer, and loud screams from the many teenage girls present, once the initial quivering guitar chords rang out over the vast arenas and concert halls, and with Mike often appearing on bass for the song – what else could the drummer do on this final ballad? – it would draw the performance to a tumultuous conclusion after seventy or so minutes onstage.

With the 1971 tour completed, the band was once again free to go back into the recording studio, picking up from where they had left off prior to Robb Royer's departure. For the next few weeks, and possibly even in between the final scheduled dates of the *Manna* tour, they toiled daily in the studios, choosing to work between the more familiar Sound Recorders studios and Sound Labs, a new complex created by Armin Steiner, across the street in Hollywood. Once again, Steiner himself was also on hand to control the board. Despite James continuing to compose alongside Robb, only two of the songs chosen to appear on the next album came as a result of this established partnership, although without doubt they remain two of the album's progressive highlights. Instead, for the first time, James came up with two new compositions on his own: the gentle "Just Like Yesterday" and the funky-blues of "I Don't Love You," the latter reportedly being inspired after a costly losing visit to the craps table during a visit to Las Vegas. Additionally, David and James resurrected their all-too-brief songwriting partnership for only the second time, adding another couple of tunes (one new, one old) into the mix, one of which, "Nobody Like You," was in joint collaboration with their new partner Larry. All in all, this was a refreshingly diverse collection of material, attempting to broaden the boundaries away from the previous 50-50 sharing of responsibilities. And in order to assist their creativity, or more often than not, to avoid hindering them, they were extremely fortunate in that Elektra Records, and Jac Holzman in particular, left them to their own devices, trusting the four individuals, along with Armin Steiner, to create commercial material that would generate the sales they had previously experienced to date.

"That's one thing I will say about Jac Holzman and Elektra Records," reminisced David. "They never, never tried to tell us what to do. We were free to go in and do pretty much what we thought was best."[9]

And best was what they managed to do, for the resulting collection stands as, perhaps, the finest combination of material to appear on any Bread album. From the opening driving chords of the preview single, "Mother Freedom," notably without any credit given to Robb, despite his bass duties, through to the raw edge of James's "I Don't Love You," this was a slick production from start to finish and, more importantly, gave the band their most successful run of chart positions to date.

"In the studio everything is really under the microscope. Little time discrepancies, or little things where you buzz or hit the string with your finger. Little bad habits that you never hear in a live concert. On a record they just stand out. Everything must be smooth and perfect," David was to comment later when questioned about the band's tendency to strive for studio perfection.[31]

Following on from the relatively unsuccessful release of "Mother Freedom," had come the next single, a newly re-recorded version of "Baby I'm-A Want You," abandoned earlier in the summer but now re-arranged in a different key with an acoustic guitar accompaniment instead of piano, and featuring Larry Knechtel's debut appearance on bass. James provided the lead guitar lines, using his favorite Gibson model. "I did the solo with my Gibson ES 335. I think I used a chorus effect on 'Baby I'm-A Want You' from my Roland amp, or maybe a separate chorus box through my other amp. It was a famous bass amp that Gates and I used for guitar as well as bass because it was warm sounding."[18]

Released as Elektra 45751 on October 23rd, 1971, the single stormed into the *Billboard* Top 3, while making the U.K. Top 20 at the same time, ultimately confirming what was already clear: the public wanted to hear a David Gates ballad. The song would also go on to receive a Grammy nomination the following year, sadly losing out at the 15th Grammy Awards ceremony (which were not actually held until March 3rd, 1973) to Roberta Flack & Donny Hathaway's "Where Is The Love."

Gates: "One song led to the next, which led to the next, and we became a soft rock group. We did try a bit of rock and roll and up-tempo things, but when 'Make It With You' was the big million-seller hit it sort of forced us to consider that. We had to remember these ballads were what got us where we were and we needed to come back to them from time to time. My strength as a writer has always been the ballads."[9]

The flip-side of the single was an edited version of "Truckin'," the Griffin-Royer fun-filled offering taken from the *Manna* album. Robb was to later recall: "It was kind of a country rock song. It grew out of the lick to 'Move Over,' a song on our first album. Jimmy and I were sitting around trying to write, we were stuck, and he started playing that riff with a different feel. He started singing a new melody to it and we sort of finished the song on the spot as a gag. Gates wasn't sure about the tune, but Botts really drove the song when we recorded it. Gates played some harmonica on it. It turned out to be the most popular song that Jimmy and I ever wrote for Bread."[14]

With a Top 5 smash in the bag, and the single going on to garner the band's second gold award for record sales, they prepared the fourth album for release. Photographs taken in preparation for the album launch show an image change for the group, and perhaps more so for one member in particular. David had by now shaved off his familiar moustache and grown his hair out, combing it forward with a fringe/bangs style along the front and, with his tall slim figure, both he

Soundcheck on tour (courtesy of Ken Bank)

and James now cut a suave dash at the forefront of the band. Subsequently, and despite their relatively elder statehood in comparison with a lot of the popular acts in the early 1970s – two members were now over 30 – it was a line-up of four handsome faces that appeared on the front of the album cover, bordered by a dark brown hue, and also that of the expansive spread inside the gatefold sleeve. Image was a lot more important in the entertainment industry during the 1970s, far more than it had been during the closing years of the previous decade when a number of bands simply let the freak flag fly. But for the record buyers that Bread were clearly intending to appeal to, how they came across to their audience was vitally important. Polished and professional, and yet in any number of photographs from that era, it is noticeable how the foursome, with James in particular, were becoming more and more stylishly flamboyant and fashion-conscious.

In order to capitalize on the success of the recent single, Elektra naturally named the new twelve-song album after the hit, and the *Baby I'm-A Want You* album appeared in stores around the globe during January of 1972, accompanied simultaneously by the follow-up 45 release. As with its predecessor, "Everything I Own" b/w "I Don't Love You" raced up the *Billboard* charts, topping out at #5 and giving David yet another successful ballad, albeit one with mixed emotions for him.

"That was written in memory of my father. I worked on the lyric so that it could be taken in a general sense and not be real obvious. Recording the song went really well, I was quite motivated to get that one done right. Larry played a real interesting and complicated part on the harpsichord, and we doubled the kick drum to get that thick sound. I just tried to put as much emotion into it as I could."[14]

This particular song stands out more than others, perhaps for the raw fragility in David's tone during the opening bars. One can almost feel the emotion of his thoughts as he sings the first four lines, dedicating his pain on to vinyl, before the chiming unison of the acoustic guitars and the gentle bass riff introduce his colleagues' accompaniment into the sound. The delicate string arrangement adds further texture to the song, while Mike's drums and cymbals brings a certain amount of 'rock' emphasis without overloading the drama, keeping the sentiment of the ballad at a premium. Although the original inspiration behind the lyrics was not hidden away, many were to take the song at face value with a number of successful cover versions appearing in subsequent years, leading much of the listening public to remain blissfully unaware of the song's true meaning.

With the record also peaking in the Top 5, Bread's highest placing for an original album release, the group were at an all time high on a professional level. The quality that came out of every track on *Baby I'm-A Want You* gives justification to the perfectionist attitude, and diligence, over what could have been a difficult period of transition for them. David still maintained the lead production and arrangement duties, with James now listed as 'associate producer,' while additional credits went out to Armin Steiner, photographer Frank Bez, art director Robert Heimall, and Michael Manoogian for his elegant lettering. Also worthy of appreciation and acknowledgment were Jac Holzman, Al Schlesinger, and two of the band's loyal touring crew, tour manager Willie Leopold (co-founder of Concerts West Promotions) and Darryl Palagi. However, it was the abilities of Larry Knechtel that were the most impressive additional factor to the new release. Even his predecessor was totally praising of his replacement, acknowledging the positive edge that Larry now brought into the band.

"I was thrilled with what Knechtel was doing," says Robb Royer. "I wasn't happy to be out of the band, but I wanted that element in there too. We could all do solos but Knechtel was just unbelievable. To hear that applied to our music, I was really thrilled. I was really happy that I could feed in almost any song I wrote with Jimmy into that band and get those kind of recordings and those kind of sales. *Baby I'm-A Want You* was a celebration of Larry's instrumental talent."

Following on from the opening riffs of "Mother Freedom," the album weaves its way through a series of further rock-orientated numbers, with the equally impressive Gates-Griffin combination of "Down On My Knees," featuring some dynamic Botts percussion, and the progressive tones of "Dream Lady," a wistful melodramatic composition from James and Robb that is highlighted by an amazing organ solo from Larry and a heavy wailing guitar break. The aforementioned "Down On My Knees" was yet another song that the band had been keeping in storage for a while. Co-written by James and David, it had initially come together back in October 1970, during Bread's first promotional visit to the U.K., while they were staying at the Royal Lancaster Hotel in central London. James had conceived the title phrase and then, with David assisting, the remainder of the song came together swiftly although, in James's opinion, it doesn't hold together too well lyrically.

"I think we were each writing about different things," he was later to comment, "but the song got a lot of airplay and people seemed to like it."[14]

Further highlights came in the form of James and Robb's second contribution to the release, "Games Of Magic," which proved that the duo could come up with some wonderful ballads themselves, as could James on his own with the delightful piano-based "Just Like Yesterday." However, as was to be expected, much of the focus fell once again onto David's contributions and, alongside the first two "hits," three other compositions bore the sole credit of David Gates. Both "Daughter" and "This Isn't What The Governmeant" were lively songs, but in more of a pop vein than the heavier offerings elsewhere on the album. David's own two daughters, Angelyn and Lorilee, were clearly the inspiration behind the former, although the song was nicely balanced by the dueling voices of David and James, one of the rare occasions where they would each share the lead. With Larry's breezy piano styling and Mike's clever drum fills, the "pop" approach of this song is highly infectious, whereas the bright, country overtones of "This Isn't What The Governmeant," resplendent with David's violin mixed to the fore, disguises the thinly veiled dig at the U.S. tax system and the ongoing war in Vietnam. They may have simply been a successful adult pop group in the eyes of many, and not a lot else in the notes of the heavy "rock" press who were beginning to balk at their clean-cut soft rock, but they still managed to sneak out the occasional political opinion among the lovelorn ballads and wistful melodies. It may not have been what the "governmeant" ... but their audience loved it.

The fourth single taken from the album sessions, the first time that Elektra had issued so many from a Bread album which ultimately goes to show how pleased they were with its quality, was the final inclusion from the solo pen of David Gates. A song that had been filed away for almost six years, having first appeared in David's ever-increasing catalog during a demo session for producer Gary Usher back in the mid-1960s, "Diary" was to give the band their sixth Top 20 hit when, in April of 1972, and accompanied by "Down On My Knees," it reached the #15 position in *Billboard.* Interestingly, this release was actually chosen by the radio controllers themselves, having been approached by Elektra to see what song from the album they would like to see released next. Clearly their stance hadn't changed, they wanted another David Gates ballad.

David's catalog of compositions from the mid- to late-1960s included a vast number of works that seemingly never saw a release of any note, such as "Peddler Man," "I Knew You Well," "Summer Of No Regret," and "Goin' Back To The Land," but "Diary" remains something special by any standard, and it was only right that this particular song was resurrected for the new album. Remaining faithful to David's original demo recording (a tape of the original acetate survives in the hands of the collectors' circuit), with a lone acoustic guitar, accompanied by a simple bass pattern, some delicately wavering electric guitar chords, a soft string arrangement and some gentle Griffin harmonies, this is one of David's most sentimental offerings. Subtly saccharine, but not overly so.

"I just made that one up," he was to remember. "A lot of people asked me if I'd really found a diary and I'd say 'sorry to disappoint you, but I didn't.' I probably would have turned it in without reading it anyway. There's an unusual word in there: 'disconcerting.' It just fit. I used a guitar run through a synthesizer of some sort on the track."[14]

Around the same time the *Baby I'm-A Want You* album appeared, Elektra also pressed up a 13-track promotional album, simply entitled *Bread* (catalog #BRD-1), that compiled a selection of tracks from all four group albums to date. Essentially an early "hits" collection, this was pressed for radio promotional purposes, and came complete with picture sleeve and in limited quantities. Naturally, this particular collection was soon to become a much sought after release among audiophiles.

With *Baby I'm-A Want You* fresh in the stores, it goes without saying that the band undertook some further heavy promotional work in support of the new studio release, with three prime-time U.S. TV slots scheduled over the first few weeks of the year. On January 15th, the long-running *American Bandstand* show chose to devote an entire one-hour episode to Bread, the first time the popular ABC-TV program had done such a thing. David, James, Mike, and Larry performed eleven songs for the cameras, including three from the new album. This was followed on February 8th by performances of "Baby I'm-A Want You," "If," "Let Your Love Go," and "Make It With You" for a Valentine's Day NBC-TV Special, *Love Love Love*, filmed for Hallmark Television from The Troubadour Club in Los Angeles. In addition, they also taped an appearance on the syndicated *Tommy Smothers Organic Primetime Show*. Meanwhile, across the ocean, the British public was also given the opportunity to see the band represented on television, albeit with just one member in front of the cameras. On January 15th, the same day as the *American Bandstand* show appeared on U.S. screens, the 35-minute *David Gates In Concert* recording, taped the previous July, was aired on BBC2, featuring him performing a selection of his own compositions, starting with a wonderful version of "It Don't Matter To Me," and running through "Look At Me," "The Other Side Of Life," "She Was My Lady," "He's A Good Lad," "Come Again" (a phenomenal solo rendition performed at the piano), "Make It With You," "Diary," "Baby I'm-A Want You," and finishing with a delightfully delicate "If." An interesting onstage comment by David confirms that, at the time of recording the show, he hadn't as yet committed a version of "Baby I'm-A Want You" to tape.

"Well, there's probably some of you wondering who I am. David Gates. I am more well known through the group Bread, of which I'm leader, but they turned me loose tonight to do some things on my own and I'm appearing here as a composer and so perhaps if you've ever read some of the fine print on our records you'll have seen my little name down there. This is the latest song that I've written... I'm gonna try it out on you, see if you like it tonight. Hopefully

I'll record it when I get back to the States." He then proceeded to play the early piano-based arrangement of the new composition.

Supported by a four-piece British backup band, along with a fourteen-strong string section, this well-received solo performance was recorded especially for the British viewing audience, and would go on to become an essential foothold in re-establishing the group with the British press later in the year. Such was their current concentration on the American market that the initial impact they had made with "Make It With You" in the U.K. charts had now lost much of its impetus, and a fresh assault on their British audience would come the following year. This particular appearance would certainly start the ball rolling once more, with a *Radio Times* review commenting that this was "every pop fan's dream." Unforgivably, the recording was returned to the BBC vaults after the initial airing where it remains, virtually untouched, to this day (Author's note: during research on this book David was approached and asked as to whether he would ever permit a release of the recording. Unfortunately, his response was that under no circumstances would he consent to this. The show, in his opinion, was ill prepared, the harmony singers were mediocre at best, and overall the show was of poor quality).

Further activity during 1972 also came along in the shape of a second promotional release, this time issued by the United States Naval Services as a recruitment drive. *Sounds Like The Navy* was a series of record releases, tying in interviews and music from some of the more popular artists of the day, while also encouraging recruitment for the Navy via a number of featured advertisements. The Bread release (SLN-723336) featured a collection of short interviews with David, James, and presenter Sam Riddle, clearly heavily scripted, interspersed with a number of the band's recordings, including "It Don't Matter To Me," "He's A Good Lad," and "Games Of Magic." Pressed in limited quantities, this one-hour release also swiftly moved on to achieve collectable status among followers of the band.

By the time all of this promotional activity was actually ready for public consumption, be it of an audible or visual nature, the foursome were already heavily into their American promotional tour to support the *Baby I'm-A Want You* album. The 1972 outing was an extensive 47-date tour, commencing with a preliminary three dates in Illinois and Wisconsin during January, then kicking off with three full months on the road, starting in Bloomsburg, Pennsylvania, on February 18th, and culminating three months later at the Academy of Music in Philadelphia. In between, the band traveled the width and breadth of the country, performing to sellout crowds nightly. The set list, naturally, was heavily reliant on material from the new album, with "Mother Freedom," "Everything I Own," "Down On My Knees," "Dream Lady," "I Don't Love You," "Just Like Yesterday," "This Isn't What The Governmeant," "Diary," and the title track all featuring among the mix, which kicked off with "Let Your Love Go" and then followed with earlier favorites such as "It Don't Matter To Me," "Make It With You," "Easy Love," "Been Too Long On The Road," "Truckin'," and "Take Comfort."

In addition, it was on that tour that the band first began to perform the classic Simon & Garfunkel hit, "Bridge Over Troubled Water," with the intricate piano introduction recreated note for note by its originator. The set would then culminate each night, just before the band broke into the opening chords of "If," with the four musicians inviting the audience to liven up with a rebel-rousing medley of old Chuck Berry favorites, a trick they had been doing since the band's early shows with Robb Royer. "Johnny B. Goode," "Too Much Monkey Business," and "Reelin' And Rockin'" would be churned out, night after night, proving that, when they truly needed to, the band really could rock'n'roll with the best. One fan review, taken from the April 15th show in Portland, Oregon, noted that it actually started at 10:00 pm after a long opening act, and a lengthy intermission, with the eighteen songs running at seventy minutes in total. In between numbers there was also a bit of light-hearted banter between the band members, with Mike referring to David as the winner of a Donny Osmond lookalike contest, and David retorting that at least he "doesn't take drumming lessons from Karen Carpenter." James also joined in the fun, teasing David about his many guitar switches and waving a baby rattle in his face. These "off the cuff" moments were usually initiated by Mike who, having experienced such a close rapport with his audience during his spell with The Travelers 3, always believed there should be more interaction with the fans in attendance. He truly believed in the value of entertainment. Sadly, for the most part, his suggestions fell on deaf ears, which ultimately resulted in an ongoing sense of frustration for him.

Support on the tour varied from location to location, with upcoming soul singer Bill Withers performing in his home state at one of the early shows in Hampton Roads, Virginia. A concert also notable for the band having to borrow instruments due to their own equipment truck being caught in a Pennsylvania snowdrift where they had played two days earlier. The following month Bread was joined on the tour by a young acoustic duo, out to promote their debut album *Off The Shelf*, released on Atlantic Records under the supervision of the label founder Ahmet Ertegun. John Batdorf and Mark Rodney were gradually building up an impressive following among the elite Los Angeles music industry and Atlantic were keen to promote the duo to the nation. Batdorf recalled when asked to reminisce by the author: "We did tour the U.S., opening up for Bread who were huge at the time. We were all so young, none over twenty and Bread seemed much older than us. They had such a string of hits and the venues were big and packed most nights. We didn't have much interaction with them other than with Jimmy Griffin who was friendly. David and the rest of the guys pretty much stayed to themselves. It was great experience for Batdorf and Rodney. We'd never been on the road before for such a long tour. The only thing that was kind of a hassle for us was that Bread had a particular way they liked to set up on stage. They set up in a very tight semi-circle and wouldn't let us move any of their gear. We had two sidemen, drummer John Mauceri and bassist Rick Carlos, so we had plenty of gear. We had to set up all our stuff, three amps and a set of drums and the four of us in a semi-circle within their semi-circle, and needless to say it was very tight, but somehow we managed. We were very fortunate to get on that tour and it helped expose Batdorf and Rodney's music to a lot of people…"

The impression the duo left behind during their short set was particularly memorable for many members of the audience, and, despite the unfortunate lack of commercial success that was to come their way, Batdorf and Rodney built up a small cult following that continues to this day. Listen to either "Oh My Surprise" or "Can You See Him" from their debut release and understand why.

As the tour wound its way across the continent one notable stop off point *en route* included an evening at the prestigious Carnegie Hall in New York City. Fabled for its wonderful acoustics, Bread made their sold out appearance on the hallowed stage on March 18th, 1972, with both David's mother and the band's business manager, Al Schlesinger, also flying in to see the performance. Backed by a twelve-strong string section for part of the set, the band ran through 24 songs, including "Let Your Love Go," "Coming Apart," "Easy Love," "Make It With You," "She Was My Lady," "Too Much Love," "This Isn't What The Governmeant," "It Don't Matter to Me," "Could I," "Look What You've Done," "I Don't Love You," "Just Like Yesterday," "Truckin'," "Diary," "Down On My Knees," "Family Doctor," "Take Comfort," "Baby I'm-A Want You," "Been Too Long On The Road," "Everything I Own," "Nobody Like You," "Mother Freedom," and "If." The foursome were reportedly on strong form that night, occasionally even turning their backs on the audience, facing and feeding off each other.

Nashville '72 (courtesy of Dennis McGee)

Two weeks later *Billboard* magazine ran a review of this particular concert:

> *"Just when you think that Bread is no more than a well-packaged middle of the road rock group they surprise you. In the middle of several melodic but unexciting tunes, lead singer James Griffin sits down at the piano and delivers a startlingly impressive blues vocal. And gradually the lyrical wonder of Bread's compositions overcome your resistance and you are entirely won over."*
> —Dan Bottstein

After an arduous three months, the tour finally began to wind down, firstly with a show at the Hawaii International Center in Honolulu, followed by dates in Arizona, Ohio, Utah, and finishing in Pennsylvania. It hadn't all been continuous, and there had been a number of short breaks between some shows, but it was still the longest tour that the band had undertaken to date, and subsequent sales of the album showed that the constant days on the road were paying dividends. In total, *Baby I'm-A Want You* was to remain in the Top 40 album listings for the entire run of the tour. The overall response was one of phenomenal success, with many local reviews praising both the performance and musical dexterity of each of the individual band members.

> *"Each song is artfully arranged and flawlessly performed; the vocals are sure, true and polished while the group's instrumental work is clean, crisp and light."*
> *—Los Angeles Times*

> *"The only problem with the four-man group is that they were too perfect..."*
> *—UCLA Daily Bruin*

> *"They play what might be classified 'hard rock', loud, intensely rhythmic and which, through sheer force of sound, imprints itself on the listener's mind. The music is colorful and tangible, like a piece of varicolored cut velvet..."*
> *—The Denver Post*

> *"The music here is superb. Instrumentally too, Bread excels. This quartet knows their musical ropes."*
> *—Oklahoma City Times*

In addition, a number of the influential national music business magazines also wrote in favor of their performances:

"They played a very tight, very solid instrumental sound; no ego-inspired solos. They played and sang with remarkable precision."
—Cash Box

"Thank you, thank you, thank you, thank you... I'm just thanking four marvelous musicians for bringing me a little bit of happiness."
—Showcase

An early 1972 edition of the popular *Teen* magazine ran a lengthy article on the trip, with "celebrity editor" Maureen Donaldson accompanying the band during their initial three-date run in Illinois and Wisconsin. The million-plus readers of this monthly entertainment magazine had previously voted Bread as one of their Top 10 favorite acts of 1971, and so a lengthy article seemed in order to please the subscribers. The first show Donaldson attended had been held at the Arie Crown Theater in Chicago, followed by a short flight in a rickety old prop plane to Quincy, 300 miles south of the windy city. After a performance at the local college, with the student audience huddled closely together on the floor, the band managed a short night's sleep before another flight and drive, this time to Kenosha in Wisconsin, location of the third show. Although readers of *Teen* would find nothing of real significance over the three featured pages, pulled together under the banner "Bread: A Slice Of Rock Life," it was good to see the band receiving a positive, lengthy response from the media.

Unfortunately, some of the more illustrious and "hip" publications of the era – *Rolling Stone*, *Creem*, *Bomp* – had little to report on the band, despite having offered praise on the debut release, and were now choosing to devote their pages to the more serious and heavier rock acts of the era, and to the increasing focus on the "new wave." Although, even *Rolling Stone*, the daddy-mag of them all, once again had to acknowledge the vitality of the *Baby I'm-A Want You* album, with staff writer David Lubin confirming in print that it was a "full-bodied album, exuding health and vigor," yet he also felt compelled to sneak in a snobbish byline, adding "even in the thick of its most exaggerated sentimentality..."

"Many songwriters today spend hours contriving words to fit music for the sake of commercializing," wrote Donaldson, "their goal being to produce a product that sells something to the public. The core of Bread's success, however, is the genuine portrayal in song of their heartfelt endeavors, growth and approach to life's endless search by man for fulfillment. This is vividly conveyed in the blending of lyrics with melodic moods which their listeners subscribe to through personal identity and feeling, a kind of human bond in which commercialism finds no place. Bread has found its place among people's hearts, for collectively and individually, their music is the continual story of their souls."

As to whether the youthful readers of such teenage fodder were quite ready for these philosophical thoughts is a debatable point, for it was the commercial characteristic of Bread's music that truly found a home within their hearts, and within their record collections. Certainly the songwriting aspect of the band, David Gates in particular, maintained the emotional characteristic within the core of their songs, but to compress such emotion into the melody of a three-minute pop song required the necessary adoption of commerciality in order to achieve significant radio play. And radio play meant record sales, and record sales meant success. Bread were a commercial force to be reckoned with, and despite the attempts by James and Robb to sway the balance towards a more progressive sound with tunes like "Games Of Magic," "Dream Lady," or their earlier contributions to the first three albums, all three principal songwriters understood the concept. The emotional commerciality was what made "Make It With You" so successful. It wasn't to the degree that the bubblegum "teen-pop" songwriters of the late 1960s-early 1970s were deemed to stoop to, and "Baby I'm-A Want You" was certainly no "Sugar Sugar" or "Chewy Chewy," but Bread had far more in common with Led Zeppelin and Steppenwolf than it did with The Osmond Brothers or The Partridge Family. They knew where the line was drawn and David, James, and Robb, along with Mike and Larry, stuck to their principles, however disparate they may have seemed to each other at times.

Nevertheless, despite the overwhelming grandiosity of her writing, Donaldson did manage to gain a small insight into life on the road, and in the sky, with the foursome, and it remains one of the more noteworthy articles from this particular era. She continued:

"Each member of the group projects a separate identity. They all, however, have a positive outlook on their lives and their music, and this common bond is perhaps the key to Bread's success. David Gates is the acknowledged leader, taking care of most of Bread's business arrangements. He seems like a man who knows exactly what he is doing and why at all times. Jimmy Griffin appears to be the 'flashy' member of the group. He wears the brightest clothes and seems to have the most outgoing personality. When you get to know him, though, you find a serious, kind and emotional person who would never hurt anyone. Michael Botts' fun-loving personality projects a love of life and a friendly warmth when you first meet him. He is the type of person you want to tell all your problems to, because you know he will be genuinely interested in all you have to say. Larry Knechtel is definitely the serious musician of the group. He's forceful, quiet and shy, keeping pretty much to himself. He seems easy to please as he keeps away from the business aspect of Bread and concentrates fully on his music, which is obviously his life…"

To the young female fans of the group, the concert "screamers," this was the kind of gossip column writing that they would lap up, along with their glossy pin-ups plastered to the bedroom wall, although to the more discerning follower of the group, those who listened to every lyric, every musical nuance, there was little to mull over in the serious rock press, such was the passing over of this new "soft rock" genre. Too hip to be square, too square to be hip. Newcomer Larry Knechtel was made all too aware of the diversifying lines of the genre's differences during these shows, later remarking to Barry Alfonso: "I'd look out into the first three or four rows of the audience and I'd see these romantically enchanted girls, and next to them would be their boyfriends, sitting there with their arms folded, kind of pissed-off. As far as (the girls) were concerned, we didn't need to put any up-tempo things on our albums at all."[14]

All the same, regardless of genre or demographics, Bread fans had little way at all of keeping tabs on the movement of their favorite band. Judy Donofrio, who had held together the Jimmy Griffin Fan Club back in the 1960s, briefly took on the role of running a Bread Fan Club, and she recalls: "Jim suggested I could take this weight off Schlesinger's office list but the rest of the band were not so keen. But it happened. This was in early 1972. There was not all that much mail really. I doubt most folks knew where to write. I'd say I answered 1,000 letters in a year, all personally, and then I started doing newsletters. I named them *The Breadwagon, The Daily Bread, Breadbox,* and *Breadboard,* things like that. The newsletters were three or four pages long and gave reports from the fans who attended concerts as well as info on new releases. There was no membership fee and the idea of a fan club did not appeal to anyone except Jim..."

Despite the band's seeming reluctance to step into the spotlight, out of the shadows of privacy and into the media frenzy, they remained keen to develop the group's music to higher levels of public acceptance, to keep pushing back their own boundaries even if, following the departure of Robb Royer, they had lost a little of the bravado. With Larry's admission into the inner circle, the arrangements of the newer songs appear far more advanced, and richer in resonance. His distinctive organ playing, the swirls and keyboard runs that feature throughout the *Baby I'm-A Want You* album, bring a fuller sound to the mix that was distinctly lacking before, and it was with this newborn confidence that, having completed the tour, the four musicians settled once more in the recording studio to work on the follow-up album to their Top 5 success.

Meanwhile, elsewhere in the vast city, their erstwhile colleague Robb Royer was also hard at work. Despite his dissatisfaction at being out of the band that he had helped put together, his attentions now lay elsewhere, and he was spending much of his time working on a particular project that had been simmering on the backburner for many years...

Chapter Eleven

Fly Away

Although he was now no longer a third of Bread Enterprises, Robb Royer continued to reap the rewards of the increasing record sales and royalties, courtesy of the songwriting and performances he made while a member of the group and, more recently, his contributions to the success of the *Baby I'm-A Want You* album. At his request, these payments were made directly to him from James and David, although the confusion over such payments, notably for all five band members, was to continue for a number of years, even reaching the Superior Court during the latter part of the decade when even their record company became unaware exactly to whom and where payments should go. Nevertheless, with a relatively steady flow of income, it now allowed Robb the breathing space to diversify his interests, and to develop the ideas he had begun to work on during the *Manna* sessions.

Immediately after his departure from Bread, Robb went back into the studio to work on some of his own material. "I did a couple of things, and I said,'Let me sing on this,' but I really didn't like the result... and nobody else did either," he laughs today. Even so, the concept of writing screenplays had always held a fascination for him since his college days, and such was his apparent passion to explore this route, it ultimately became one of the reasons for his downfall within Bread. Back at Northridge, alongside Tim Hallinan and other college friends, he had helped conceive the rock musical *The Plastic Sibling*, and although this particular project had never seen full development, Robb had kept ahold of the idea, along with a number of others, and now, with more time on his hands, seized the opportunity to develop these further.

"When we were in college there was this guy named Michel Levesque, a wonderful fellow, and another talented, crazy playwright named David Kaufman, and they did this play called *The Plastic Sibling*, based on conversations with us, so it all started with an idea that I was involved in. They wrote this play and the deal was that I was going to write the lyrics for it with Jimmy. Tim Hallinan and Richard Blakeslee were also involved. Had we had the time to finish it and do it in this little theater at Valley State College it would have been sensational. It's hilarious…"

The concept of the "rock musical," certainly at the time that *The Plastic Sibling* had been conceived, was virtually an unknown phenomenon waiting to happen. "Rock" music as such had made brief appearances during stage shows on

Broadway, but they had often been as lone examples of the genre, interwoven with the more established show tunes that featured throughout the productions. It wasn't until the 1968 arrival of *Hair* in the established theater district of Manhattan that the terms "rock" and "musical" were so indelibly fused together. Created by lyricists James Rado and Gerome Ragni, in partnership with composer Galt MacDermot, the show was a genuine product of the sexual revolution of the mid-to-late '60s, with profanity and nudity accompanying the unforgettable rallying cries of "Let The Sunshine In," "Hair," and the uplifting anthem "Aquarius." Signifying the rise of the hippie counterculture, this truly was sex, drugs, and rock'n'roll. By contrast, Andrew Lloyd Webber and Tim Rice's conceptual *Jesus Christ Superstar* approached the same medium of the rock musical, as did Pete Townshend's *Tommy*, but *Superstar* was perhaps the first such example to take it out to a wider market. Financed and adapted for the stage from the proceeds and sales of an initial 1970 record release, the show was living proof that the rock musical was here to stay.

The Plastic Sibling, in comparison, while never aiming for the same lofty heights, maintained the same ideals. A conceptual storyline, the tale of a mismatched family of siblings, enhanced by being told through a varying sequence of rock-orientated songs, but not the standard fare of three-minute verse-chorus-verse compositions. The music of Robb Royer and James Griffin demanded far more serious listening. Within each individual composition, the tempos were often found to be changing mid-way, the chord structures were alternating, the balance was shifting. Commerciality was still evident, right from the opening introductory lines, but at times it stepped away from the expected, even venturing towards a more operatic theme at times, albeit with tongue firmly in cheek.

The complete storyline revolved around the crazed family of a Hollywood Lothario from the 1930s, with three illegitimate sons in tow. These three, having now grown to adulthood, were each developing differing career paths: one of them earning his living as an inventor, while another was a plastic surgeon, and the third was working as a salesman. Ultimately, the focus of the plot was that the inventor built a robot, the plastic surgeon made her beautiful, and the salesman marketed the product. Much hilarity apparently ensued, and yet the collection of imaginative scriptwriters, Kaufman, Levesque, Royer, Hallinan included, completed their college studies before the original play was fully finished, resulting in its being placed on the collective backburner. Keen to keep the project alive in some form, Robb had continued to work on the music right up to, and even during, his period with Bread, utilizing James as his co-writing partner on the project. It has even been implied that some of the songs completed for *The Plastic Sibling* were later adapted for the band's debut album, although aural evidence suggests otherwise. And while the song "Family Doctor" certainly contains the theme of "an artificial you" incorporated into the lyrics, Robb is keen to convey the connection between the two was really "only in a mindset... at the time I was only thinking about such stuff."

Another project that this talented group of writers and musicians began to develop together was entitled *Black Angel*, and this particular venture came about following a visit to Michel Levesque's house, with both Robb and David Kaufman in attendance. At the time, Kaufman and Levesque were also working on an early idea that they had titled *Werewolves On Wheels*, a potential film script that incorporated two then-popular movie genres; that of the biker flick and the horror movie. This idea eventually went on to completion, giving the duo their first cinema release during October, 1971, and co-starring Barry "Eve Of Destruction" McGuire in one of the lead roles. However, during the film's formative planning stages, with Robb sitting in, another idea thrown about was taking the concept of Shakespeare's *Othello* and developing a biker script around it. Black biker, white chick. Thus, at Robb's suggestion, came *Othello On Wheels*. With a script written by Royer and Kaufman, the idea was even sold to Larry Gordon at American International Pictures during 1972, now under the working title of *Black Angel*. But, unfortunately for the two budding scriptwriters, the company wasn't taken with the initial screenplay, despite press in the trade papers announcing the forthcoming project, and they rejected the opportunity to develop the proposal.

Still, knockbacks aside, the model they had maintained for *The Plastic Sibling* continued to build momentum. Following Robb's departure from the ranks of Bread, the idea for the musical was taken one step further and a full demo recording of the proposed music was recorded during 1972. Conceived by both Robb and James, it has even been mooted that Elektra Records was offered the opportunity to release the work, ultimately passing on the project.

With the music itself performed mainly by Robb and James, and with vocals from fellow Elektra recording artist Ronee Blakely and Kerry Chater, formerly the bass player for The Union Gap, the demo recordings offer up a clear indication as to the serious approach that Robb was taking with the project. It is hard to see why, with Bread being such a notable money-spinner for the label, Elektra chose not to pursue this, although Robb, in his own words, was perhaps already viewing the work on a grander scale.

"After I left Bread, I think it was a conversation with my dad actually (about *The Plastic Sibling*), he said it shouldn't just be this little thing in a living room, it should be this really big thing."

Far more than a simple gathering of songs, the thirteen proposed compositions incorporated a variety of styles and themes: ballads, synthesized heavy rock, folk, comedy, 1930s pastiche. And while the vocals of Blakely and Chater featured heavily to the fore, there was still one opportunity for James to step forward and take lead vocal duties on one of the new songs, a tune entitled "New Steps," that crossed the borders of both balladry and heavy rock.

If I'd learned the new steps
Don't want to do the two-step again
So tired of living then

Wondering when I might see her again...
If I'd learned the new steps
Wouldn't always be a few steps behind
Why should I wait in line for what was mine
I'd just take up her time..

"The New Steps" (Music by James Griffin and Robb Royer / Lyrics by David M. Kaufman, Timothy Hallinan, and Richard Blakeslee). Reproduced with permission

The distinct Griffin-Royer musical arrangements that had so dominated much of Bread's early works were still in evidence, and on occasion one could detect similarities between the riffs on "Do The Harold" and the earlier "Take Comfort" from the *Manna* album. Or the guitar refrain on the delightfully lilting "This Famous Face" which bore a distinct resemblance to the closing bars on David Gates' "Been Too Long On The Road." Other highlights came in the form of "Elementary Shuffle," the folksy "My Mother Doesn't Know Me Anymore," and the whimsical vocals on "A Day You Will Remember."

However, despite the demo recordings going no further, and not wishing to give up on the overall concept, Robb continued to expand the work, developing it alongside the original scriptwriter David Kaufman, gradually evolving the theme of *The Plastic Sibling* into a new project altogether. With the shared writing credit of Royer-Kaufman, the initial revised script was completed during April of 1973. They called this new variation *Cosmo & Robetta.*

The basis for this revised storyline was a science fiction tale, set in the future, whereupon a brilliant young motor engineer, Cosmo, builds a female robot as a friendly companion to keep him company in his lonely world, dominated by computers and machines. A freak radioactive storm brings his robot, Robetta, to life, and the trouble starts as she learns more about his world. She desires the beauty that she sees while watching the Miss Universe pageant on television. The fun-filled fantasy continues as Robetta then visits a beautifying treatment center, intent on becoming the vision she has seen on the small screen, and goes on to seek stardom in Las Vegas, only for her dreams to come crashing down around her courtesy of a power crazy entrepreneur named Benny Doomsday. Cosmo, meanwhile, in trying to rescue his metal maiden, falls foul of his bosses at the motor factory, and it all ends in tears, loose nuts and bolts – and a rocket to a new life. Humor remains prevalent throughout the script and, while the concept is one of drama and of undying true love, the tongue-in-cheek comedy aspect is never far away, and perhaps nowhere more so than in the ultimate finale for Doomsday, voiced admirably by James Griffin. This whip-laden fiend foolishly lashes out at the unfortunate Robetta, only to suffer the consequences himself.

Benny learned too late. You must never strike an electric person. He was shocked into the fourth dimension and was never seen again. Wise words indeed.

In order to promote the project, and to seek the development he hoped for, Robb put together an audio version of the story, this time complete with both the musical and spoken narrative on which he'd been working, recorded in his own 8-track home studio. Once again, Robb and James performed nearly all the musical interludes themselves, with guitar, bass, piano, and synthesizer shared between the two of them, even using a children's toy piano at one stage in the musical arrangement. Meanwhile, drummer John Mauceri, formerly with the Batdorf and Rodney band, sat in on percussion. With a number of fully-fledged compositions, all polished productions co-written by the Griffin-Royer partnership, featured throughout the 46-minute presentation, it all came together into the complete concept recording, with James himself supplying the vocals on a number of the songs.

"Jimmy was nearly all of the singing voices," says Robb when recollecting the *Cosmo & Robetta* story. "I sang 'Miss Universe,' while most of the voices of Cosmo and the announcer were done by Shadoe Stevens who was a very popular L.A. DJ, who I knew through Tim, and he came out and did it. His wife Linda was the voice of Robetta, and Cliff Potts, who was a wonderful actor and was a friend of ours, was there as well."

Potts was, in fact, now in a relationship with James's former wife Maria, and while the rapport between James and Cliff was friendly, Robb never had them in the studio together. Maria herself would also contribute to the ongoing recording sessions when, along with Robb's wife Anabel, she helped add dancing sound effects into the mix. Despite the breakdown of their marriage, James and Maria had remained on close terms.

"Jimmy and Cliff got along great, both were charming, easy going guys," Robb continues. "They seldom met but when they did they liked each other fine from what I could see. They never recorded together, I brought them in at separate times for different kinds of sessions, and I think I remember that Cliff did all his parts in one session. I always liked Maria. She eased the way for us in a number of capacities: Jimmy's wife, our introducer, encouraging our relationship with Schlesinger… and much other stuff. She was really the unsung hero of Bread, if you have to pick one."

The written narrative for the musical is a wonderful parody of a science fiction drama, full of laughter and pathos, while the accompanying music fits perfectly alongside. The instrumental excerpts, including "Cosmo's Theme," "Robetta's Theme," and "At Dr Claude's" that run in conjunction with the script, intermingle freely with the characters, adding drama, tension, and breathing space. While a number of the actual songs that appear, ranging from the lampooning of "Miss Universe" (featuring a rare lead vocal from Robb) and the witty "Elementary Shuffle" (the only survivor from the original *Plastic Sibling* songs), the heavy rock on "Doomsday Child" and "Get Strange," to the pop-simplicity of "March Of The Savage Robots," are near-Broadway perfection and would grace any musical or stage play with ease. Infectious, melodious, downright feel-good. However, the best is left towards the end, firstly with the Griffin-Royer composition "I'll Be Here With You," which brings the heartbreak of Cosmo's loss and the rediscovery of his love to life. One of the duo's most tender compositions, and one of James's finest vocal readings, this ballad strikes directly at the heart, before we are finally lifted up again with the closing number, "Fly Away," another Griffin-Royer tune that elevates the positive aspects of their partnership. Sadly, in the ensuing years, "Fly Away" was to remain as the only song from the *Cosmo & Robetta* project to see an official release. But even that would take a further three years from its original concept.

Having come out of Bread, and the subsequent success and recognition that came with it, Robb still had an enormous amount of contact with people within the industry. Hollywood executive Michael Ovitz, one of the leading lights at the Creative Artists Agency, was the first connection Robb made having completed the rewrite, taking on the representation of the new project for him, and that in turn led to meetings with such up-and-coming heavyweights as Jerry Weintraub, Michael Eisner, and Michael Apted, who were all keen at one time or another to see *Cosmo & Robetta* developed into a fully-fledged media project. The general consensus among its creators at the time was that it would be developed into a spectacular animated film, and for a number of years it continued to gather momentum and interest but ultimately, as time moved on and little headway was made, enthusiasm began to wane…

When questioned for this book during 2009, Shadoe Stevens had this to say:

"I met Robb through one of my closest friends, Tim Hallinan. I spent a lot of time in Robb's little home studio; at the time it was incredibly impressive to me but by today's standards it was quite humble. We worked on the narration and characters together, although it was really Robb's vision. I've always been good with writing and helped polish and refine his script, and I brought in my then-wife Linda to play Robetta. I always felt the story and music had a kind of magic that was touching and engaging. We spent a lot of time on it and when it was finally mixed we were all quite proud of the results. And then, after some disappointing efforts to bring it to life, Robb inexplicably shelved it and didn't want to work on it, try to do anything with it, or even talk about it. No one could ever understand why. I still think it's charming and I'm surprised that nothing has ever been done with it. Oh well..."

Certainly, at that time, Robb had tried to push it as far as it would go, and with the various studio executives and big Hollywood players also pushing in a similar direction, it had every opportunity. But therein lies the issue. A similar direction is not always the right approach. Those involved have to be pulling in the same direction, and those who attempted to assist Robb with fulfilling his vision clearly had visions of their own. That was ultimately the true reason why Robetta was never to walk and talk during this particular period.

The final word goes to Robb:

"*Cosmo* was just this big... God knows what. I don't know what word to put on that. It was just seminal, but we couldn't quite find the center. It was just one of the huge "almosts." I think it would have made a great movie. It's been riddled with things coming out later like *Star Wars* and *Blade Runner*. All of those angles were in *Cosmo* in a much more humorous context. We got it up to a pretty high level. We got a call from Michael Eisner and we thought we were going to sign contracts. Then we were taken to Broadway, all expenses paid, and we tried to put it on Broadway but I never saw it as a Broadway piece. Michael Apted and I never agreed. He wanted to do a very realistic thing about the real day problems of roboteering or something, and I wanted to do a far more psychedelic musical. I guess you'd say it was one step more literal than *Tommy*. It was highly interpretive. We didn't attempt to tell the story with the songs, they were set in the story in a different way than the stuff that had been up to there. That, I think, was the problem with getting producers at the time. There was this wildly varied view of how to do it, and in fact what I kept trying to describe to everybody, including Eisner and Weintraub and all of these guys, was that we needed to do it as an animated thing. We needed to do it so that we (could) pull the cell off a film and then we process the cell. That was the argument I was making at the time. Well, unfortunately, that was 30 years ahead of its time. You could only do that in a Disney-esque fashion which was insanely expensive, but it was written in my mind to be done that way…"

With the master tapes placed firmly back on the shelf, and the years rolling by, fans and followers of Bread, those who were aware of the project, were left wondering if *Cosmo & Robetta* were ever going to take flight.

Chapter Twelve

Coming Apart

The fifth studio album to be released by Bread followed in the wake of their monumentally successful spring 1972 tour, and the preceding gold award status of *Baby I'm-A Want You*. The band themselves were, by this stage, enjoying the fruits that success had brought them, each benefiting in their own way from the rewards of their hard-earned labors. Both David and Mike had developed a love for sailing, each purchasing lavish boats with which to sail up and down the warm coastal waters (Mike's a Santana 35 sloop, David's a 90-foot ketch), while expensive cars and houses were another way of outlaying the large income they were now generating. Larry, financially independent due to his previously successful session career, remained in his large family house in North Hollywood with his wife Vicki and their two children, while Mike lived in the shadow of the Hollywood sign itself, high up in the hills off Mulholland Drive, from where he would race around town in his new red Ferrari, beautiful women in tow. Jimmy, too, now separated from Maria and also living off Mulholland, was not averse to sharing his own passion for cars, owning a 1972 black Porsche Targa. "He only knew of two speeds, bat out of hell and stop," recalls a former family member. "The first rule getting in a car with Jimmy driving was never show your fear or he would feed on that and make you even more frightened. He loved driving fast!" David, meanwhile, ever the family man, opted for an open ranch-styled house in Calabasas, an affluent area situated to the north of Malibu and Mulholland Highway.

The new release was to follow a very similar pattern to its predecessor: slick, polished, melodious, but perhaps a little too safe in some people's eyes. The formula had been very much created and molded and by now it was too late to be seen shaking it up and demolishing what they spent the previous ten years building up. Without Robb Royer in the band, James or David no longer appeared to have that extra spark to ignite the harmony, or disharmony, by way of pushing and questioning the boundaries, despite the clear intention of developing their sound further. Robb's contributions were very much still within the album structure, with two of his co-compositions appearing in the final track line-up, but what the band had gained musically and professionally by adding Larry to the ranks they had maybe lost a little in the experimental value. Indeed, the subsequent release of the record was not universally accepted by everyone.

"They were pretty much repeating the formula," believes Royer with hindsight. "In retrospect it was probably good that I was to leave by *Baby I'm-A Want You*, but I should have come back for *Guitar Man*. They were starting to really repeat themselves…"

Nevertheless, to many others, including their thousands of fans around the globe, the 1972 *Guitar Man* album stands high as one of their major accomplishments, going on to notch up the band's third Top 20 *Billboard* placing, and it still ranks among one of David's personal favorites.

"I think it's a toss-up between *Baby I'm-A Want You* and *Guitar Man* because they both had so many strong songs in them."[9]

Needless to say, James was undoubtedly all too aware as to where the focus of the public attention was to be, aimed squarely at the quality of the material that his band partner was to conjure up. But to his own credit he delivered another strong set of accompanying tunes although, notably so, the final selection was significantly less than a 50-50 split. The overall Griffin-Gates division was to yield in David's favor on this occasion, although two numbers were, once again, the result of a combined composing credit, a partnership that was, perhaps, never fully explored to its full potential owing to the diverse nature of the two contrasting characters. Also of interest was the fact that Mike received a co-credit on one number, his first Bread billing, while Larry was also to contribute a further solo offering.

Clearly, it was a relatively united band that re-entered the studio during the summer break from touring, full of confidence and support for each other after three steady months on the road. Any frustration James may have been harboring over the constant overlooking of his songs for single release was amiably curtailed once they reconvened for studio sessions at Sound Recorders. And, taking the final record purely on a performing basis, the diversifying vocal abilities from James were to receive prominence throughout the twelve featured songs, albeit not on any of the chosen singles. During the previous tour he had wistfully commented to journalist Maureen Donaldson for *Teen* magazine: "Dave and I choose the material that we record. We respect each other's opinions and bounce ideas off each other. I hope that in the future I'll do the lead vocals on one of our singles. Time will tell, I guess."

In following the pattern of the previous release, the title of the new album was already a foregone conclusion as, even by the time they neared completion of this fresh collection of compositions, they already had another Top 20 smash on their hands. Recorded and released as Elektra single 45803 during June of that year, with "Diary" having barely dropped from the Hot 100, this new song, accompanied by a rare promotional film featuring the quartet, climbed steadily to the by now familiar higher reaches of the charts where, coupled with James's "Just Like Yesterday," it settled at the #11 slot.

"Guitar Man" was yet another David Gates classic. A song firmly in the familiar mold of his previous successes, albeit with a slight twist this time around. As the title suggests, this new offering was dominated by the interweaving of the lead guitar lines, prominently mixed throughout the relatively lengthy 3:40 timescale. David recalls:

"(That song) is about the guy that just can't quit, he doesn't care how many people come along… just got to keep playing and being on the road forever. I didn't have any particular person in mind. It was supposed to be about many, many people who've been involved in that situation, of just wanting to keep reaching out and touching people with their music. It took me two or three days to write it, to get the thing just how I wanted. After we got the track down, we started playing the guitar work. I couldn't get a good guitar solo on it, and James went out and tried to play a solo that wasn't sounding right. Larry plays a little guitar and he said, 'Well, give me a try at that thing.' He hooked up a little wah-wah pedal and he came up with all those things on the spot. I'll bet that wasn't more than two hours of work on his part!"[9] [14]

Later commenting on his approach to capture such a spontaneous moment David was to add: "During the time Larry goes out to set something up to record something, I've got the tape rolling from the beginning, because his rehearsals… half of the solo on 'Guitar Man' he didn't even know I was recording because the free-thought process is most open in the very beginning, and then after you play something a number of times you begin to form patterns, and the more you form patterns, the worse it is."

Paired with Knechtel's sublime guitar breaks, the building string arrangement, and the cheering audience as the song reaches its climax (taken from a live recording of a Doors concert and overdubbed during final mixing), this composition rates as good as anything David had written before, and would go on to become a firm favorite among both record buyers and concertgoers for many years to come. It also gave the band a firm foothold with which to release their new album, guaranteeing a positive return on the strength of the single's success. However, regardless of the quality of the composition, the key to the song's worldwide success lies in the arrangement. Unlike many tunes whereupon there is the odd bar or two between verses, or verse and chorus, "Guitar Man" has the audience enraptured during every passing second. Each bar has a noted point of interest, be it David's vocals, the slide guitar effect, or Larry's solos. It is, quite simply, a flawless recording from a listening perspective.

The remaining album sessions brought about a variety of styles to the new release, as well as some interesting surprises, and perhaps none more so than with the David Gates offering "Tecolote." Notably far heavier than anything David had come up with before, this mid-tempo atmospheric mystical pounder saw the band taking some tentative steps into a "serious" heavier rock vein, and it could almost be seen as a progression of the style that they had attempted on the Griffin-Royer offering "Dream Lady," featured on the previous album. James provided a gritty vocal and Larry, once again, came up with one of the album's musical highlights with another scintillating keyboard solo, while all around him David and James's guitars weep and wail away, with Botts' heavy tom-toms driving them on. Although lyrically the song fell short of what it was attempting to achieve, with the simple naivety of a voodoo theme coming across as overly lightweight in comparison, it made a nice change to the formularized "Bread" sound, but ultimately one that, for fear of alienating their audience, they could little afford to attempt again. Subsequently, the more familiar sounding newer ballads from David, such as "Aubrey," "Didn't Even Know Her Name" (co-written with James), and the lovely "Sweet Surrender," the latter composed during the heavy spring touring schedule and arranged with the assistance of Mike's distinctive rhythm track, were once again prominent on the final song selection.

"That may be the best melody I have ever written," David was later to comment on "Aubrey." "I hardly ever write any 'name' songs, but I loved that name and the way that it flowed in that particular melody. I had been watching the movie *Breakfast At Tiffany's*, a very moody, sensitive picture that I didn't totally understand. When it was over I wrote 'Aubrey,' even though it had nothing to do with that film, the moodiness that it had kind of set me up to write that song."[14]

Maybe the song bore no true relationship to the storyline of the film, but spiritually the influence it had on David is there for all to see, especially within the lyric "catching all the words but then the meaning going past." There also remains the possibility that the star of *Breakfast At Tiffany's*, the glamorous Audrey Hepburn, subconsciously aided David's thought process in the composition, such was the similarity of name.

"The random nature of it catches you by surprise as it moves along," he says of the song today. "It takes off and goes wherever it wants, and that's what makes melodies. It's the unpredictable nature, the surprises and the twists and turns. It helps, too, if there's a somewhat repetitive phrase or passage in it so that you can hear it three or four times to make it more easy to remember when the record is over."[17]

With only David's acoustic guitar as accompaniment, other than a single keyboard line, the lone vocal is strikingly bare throughout and, as the string arrangement builds up around it, the singular emptiness of the vocal track highlights the honest and emotional impact of the song. It genuinely is a delightful composition but once again, as with "Diary" six months earlier, the cloyingly over-sweet production threatens to envelop the simple delight of the song and it maybe just lacked the textures that the group as a whole could have added on top. Not that it halted the runaway success when issued as a single the following year, as it justifiably continued with the band's pattern of hits. It also brought about a multitude of cover versions, including a cloying 1974 cabaret rendition from the Vegas-era Elvis Presley, that strips away all the delicate sentimentality that the song ever suggested and offers up an horrific aberration in its place. One can only wonder what David thought of Presley's interpretation of his work.

On the other hand, in contrast to the ballads, David also provided the lively "Yours For Life," a cheerful country number that brought a distinctly light-hearted flavor to the album, complete with a Larry Knechtel harmonica solo that showed the band didn't take themselves too seriously, and it would go on to become a concert favorite, highlighting onstage the close harmonies of David and James. Likewise, the Botts-Griffin combination of "Fancy Dancer" was a breezy rocker along the lines of "Down On My Knees" that the talented drummer had initially conceived while toying around on a guitar. The song was virtually complete in the mind of Mike when he played it for James, but with Griffin's minor additions it went on to become another live highlight, although it is a notable observation that Mike was still considered the "timekeeper" by his partners in the band, and thus didn't justify handling the lead vocal on his own song, despite his ability. James Griffin remembered: "He'd worked on this one lick for a long time. We'd heard it so much every time he'd pick up a guitar that David said, 'Get with him and write to that.' So I started playing rhythm guitar along with him and we wrote the lyric together in an afternoon."[14]

Of the two Griffin-Royer contributions to the sessions, the first was a moody ballad, "Let Me Go," which sat as an impressive contrast between the differing rhythms of "Tecolote" and "Yours For Life" on the final track line-up. Lyrically downbeat, and sadly all too prophetic at times ("If I'm to meet my maker, if I'm to rule my fate..."), this composition was ongoing proof that the duo could still provide quality material, even though they were no longer a part of the same band. If anything, the distance between them had reignited some of the spark of their earlier efforts. Unfortunately, however, the second song from the prolific duo, intended as the album's final rock'n'roll moment, didn't quite hit the mark. "Don't Tell Me No," although rocking along in fine style, doesn't quite match the traits of their previous offerings. Well crafted in the studio, with polished performance and production, it comes across as somewhat forgettable and is probably the album's weakest moment.

Elsewhere, the Knechtel composition, "Picture In Your Mind," the longest song on the final album, was a stark reminder that the band could also dig deep into the soul, away from the overtly lovelorn ballads. Lyrically complex, heavily keyboard driven, this was the only occasion that Larry really got the opportunity to prove his solo compositional abilities, and James's affecting vocals truly do the song justice. However, this wasn't the only chance that record buyers had to purchase one of Larry's compositions during the year. The debut solo release by his former high school friend, now regular session player, Jim Horn, titled *Through The Eyes Of A Horn*, featured composing contributions from Larry on the track "Shake 'n' Bake," co-written with Horn and singer Rita Coolidge, although, needless to say, this didn't get as much public exposure as his Bread offering.

With sessions drawing to a close, David, James, Mike, and Larry resumed their concert schedule during the final two weeks of August, fitting in a number of dates across the Northeast of the country before the release of the new album. The set list contained the usual variety of songs, both old and new, with "Move Over" and "Family Doctor" from the debut release still featured among the selection, which was now interspersed with offerings from the forthcoming release, including the current hit single and title track from the album, and the crowd-pleasing harmonies of David and James on "Yours For Life." The majority of the jaunt was a sell-out success although Larry Knechtel, despite being an integral part of the band for almost a year by this stage, was still finding the resulting acceptance by the adoring crowds a little difficult to connect with, later admitting his discomfort over much of the band's mellow output. "Whenever somebody in the back of the hall would yell, 'Boogie,' I'd feel damn miserable," he admitted, "because I knew there was no way that this band was gonna get up and boogie."

Such was the professionalism within the four members, particularly from the principal songwriters, that it was always their intention to reproduce their studio recordings as closely as possible for the paying concert audiences and, despite the undeniable abilities of all concerned, and particularly those of Knechtel who could spin and jam at the flip of a coin, there was no place for improvisation on a Bread set. They could rock'n'roll within their structured planning, but the crowds didn't pay to see random "improv" or boogie.

Kicking off at the Blossom Music Center in Cuyahoga Falls in Ohio they worked their way through Rhode Island, Maryland, North Carolina, Louisiana, Missouri, Arkansas, Illinois, and Michigan during a ten-day period, even playing two shows a night in some venues, accompanied this time by another promising duo as support act. Dan Seals and John Ford Coley had already released two moderately received albums on A&M Records the previous year (*England Dan & John Ford Coley* and *Fables*) before being dropped by the label, and by 1972 they were to be found attempting to keep their flagging partnership alive. In his previous role as session musician for hire, Larry Knechtel had participated in the recording of these early releases, but true acceptance and success for the duo would still be a further four years away.

> *Britain and Bread have had a strange affair. Two years ago they caused considerable excitement when their beautiful melodic single "I Want To Make It With You" hit the charts, but since then little has been heard of this Los Angeles-based quartet. Their follow-up record "Baby I'm-A Want You," which was equally as good, never reached the heights of their first and Bread faded into obscurity, apparently content to develop their careers in America without pressing too hard for further successes in this country. Now Bread are happening again. Their new single "The Guitar Man" is at #19 in the MM charts this week and a couple of albums are being issued. One, already released, is a compilation of their better-known numbers, and the other, a new album, is shortly to be released. And Bread are likely to be over to capitalize on their new success next spring.*

"Our careers have been doing pretty well over here," David Gates told me this week on the transatlantic line when I asked what Bread had been doing for the past two years. "We have had nine straight hit singles in this country since 'Make It With You.' We are happy pursuing our career here before we start to seriously look outside our own country. Now, probably, the time is ripe. The new single must be better for the British market."

The group have recorded a new single, "Sweet Surrender," which has been released in the States and will probably be their next record over here. A new album too is on the way. "This will be out in about a week here and early next year in Britain. The best way to describe it is by saying certain tracks are recognizable as Bread and others no one would think are Bread. It's as good as our last one, if not better.

"We have tried to do some soft numbers, which people expect from us, and some rock numbers too. I have written about half the numbers on the album and Jim (Griffin) writes most of the other half, but everybody gets a say in what's going on the record. We always play our own songs and never anyone else's. That's why we formed Bread in the first place, to do our own things..."

—Chris Charlesworth, *Melody Maker*, October, 1972

The U.K. release of *Best Of Bread*, a full six months before the American equivalent, confirmed that the band's record label believed that they could be an equally commercial success overseas. Certainly, in the U.K., while three Top 40 singles, and two Top 40 albums were not comparable to the heights they had reached in their homeland, the band had generated enough interest early on in their career to mount a further assault on the charts, and with the release of the new collection they hoped that the British audiences would once again reconnect with the quartet. And so it proved. This release, comprising of "Make It With You," "Too Much Love," "If," "Let Your Love Go," "Everything I Own," "Been Too Long On The Road," "Baby I'm-A Want You," "Down On My Knees," "It Don't Matter To Me," "Mother Freedom," "Look What You've Done," and "Truckin'," put Bread right back at the forefront of the British rock scene, peaking at #7 on the U.K. charts and remaining a fixture in the lists for 100 consecutive weeks. Tastefully packaged with a new Frank Bez color photograph of the foursome on the front sleeve, it was the perfect stepping stone, both home and abroad, with which to foist the new studio album upon the public.

October 1972, saw the release of *Guitar Man*, and for the following seven months the band would tour to promote the album. While most of the dates would still be around the United States, plans were put into place for a full U.K. tour the following spring, a tour that the thousands of new British fans were keenly waiting to see. However, just before the release of the new studio collection, fans of Bread also had the opportunity to hear two further new recordings featuring the distinctive vocal talents of James Griffin. During the fall of 1972, two episodes of the successful NBC-TV detective series *Ironside* (the second such link between Bread and this particular show, following The Pleasure Fair's previous guest appearance) featured brand new songs composed by the established arranger and conductor Marty Paich, and his equally talented son David (later co-founder of hit band Toto). With James providing the uncredited lead vocals, "Yesterday's Love" and "The Other Side" were both sensitive ballads, registering at barely one minute in length, and simply utilized as settings for the subsequent plotlines. Unfortunately, following on from their short appearances on the show, and despite the obvious quality of both works, the recordings remained unreleased on any other media and were subsequently lost in the TV archives of time.

The brief excitement upon catching James's vocals coming from the muted television speaker was soon forgotten with the imminent arrival of *Guitar Man* in the record stores. And the song that would open up the new album, one that would go on to be the introductory number for many of the following shows, was yet another David Gates solo offering, a funky composition that included another wailing Knechtel harmonica solo, along with a number of lyrical references to the previous tour, notably mentioning the legendary Carnegie Hall show in the process. "Welcome To The Music" was to be a fine introduction to the new collection. In keeping with their total support for the release, Elektra Records once again invested heavily in the presentation of the new product, featuring a full color inner sleeve, resplendent with an artistic "bread-inspired" photograph, over which the song lyrics were presented, and a new glossy picture of the four-man band once again caught on camera by the acclaimed photographer Frank Bez.

Promotional merchandise (courtesy of Cindy Meger-Ramsey)

"Bread was the most courteous and responsible group I worked with," comments Bez today. "As compared to The Byrds or The Doors, they were a dream, and while they seemed to be more comfortable working outside, rather than in the studio, they were always prepared and on time. Both Larry and Mike were on the quiet side, David seemed to be the organizer, but Jimmy always had an opinion.

And they seemed to have a friendly back and forth going on. Since I'm an amateur musician, I've always been in awe of Larry's ability to play any type of music and David's skill in writing the simplest but harmonically beautiful music. I guess I'm a fan and loved every time I had an opportunity to shoot the boys."[34]

However, it was the image that graced the outer sleeve that impressed most. Printed onto a grainy, heavily textured card, the soft-colored images of the four faces, hair intertwined, stared out from the cream background. Illustrated by New York-born artist Bob Ziering, this was a stunningly beautiful piece of artwork, created solely from a collection of photographs and a set of colored pencils. Ziering recalled in conversation with the author during research for this book:

"I remember it as if it were done yesterday. It is a piece of work that is still remembered today by younger artists and students who identify me with the portraits. Unfortunately, as is often the case, I wasn't given the opportunity to work directly with the group, taking my own photos and studying my models in person. I did however request lots of photos so I could pick, choose, and compose. I remember making a number of preliminary sketches before the final drawings. The medium was colored pencil.

"Some years later I was vacationing and I was confronted by a young fellow with my cover art printed across his sweat shirt. How'd that happen? Not in the contract with Elektra. I stopped the guy and identified myself. He was so surprised and delighted. Actually we both were, but he couldn't, and nor could I, determine the source of the printing. For sure, I was happy to see my artwork exhibited across someone's chest. That assignment was a wonderful and exciting opportunity for me early in my career, that's for sure."

The rear of the sleeve featured another magnificent work by the same artist, appropriately picturing the movements and dexterous finger positioning of a guitar man and his instrument. Ziering would go on to achieve much credit and acclaim in the subsequent years, accepting prestigious commissions and displaying his work all over the world, including projects for the New York Opera Company and the Cirque du Soleil. He has also been the recipient of several "ANDY" awards, the highest honor awarded to commercial illustrators.

Unlike the previous release, the Bread touring schedule for *Guitar Man* was not so intense this time around, despite the seven months of proposed bookings, with initial shows during November and December mixed with days and often weeks of rest in between venues. With "Sweet Surrender," backed with "Make It By Yourself" (the latter being the second of the Gates-Griffin co-compositions on the album) issued as the follow-up single, and peaking at #15 in *Billboard*, England Dan & John Ford Coley were again enlisted as support act for many of the shows, while the set list once more contained a broad mix from across the catalog. An appearance at the imposing Daughters of The American Revolution Constitution Hall in Washington D.C. saw the band offer up the following selection: "Let Your Love Go," "Coming Apart," "Don't Tell Me No," "Make It With

You," "Anyway You Want Me," "It Don't Matter To Me," "Fancy Dancer," "Baby I'm-A Want You," "Diary," "Yours For Life," "Tecolote," "Guitar Man," "Let Me Go," "Nobody Like You," "Sweet Surrender," "Down My Knees," "Everything I Own," "Mother Freedom," and "If." Surviving audio from the venue reveals a very rock-orientated show. Certainly, the hits are in evidence but the song selection, and the live arrangements, are truly exemplary. To those who attended this show, and any other on the tour, thinking it was to be a collection of David Gates ballads, they were to be well and truly shaken up with the first trio of numbers, all featuring James on lead vocals, giving the audience no doubts as to how serious these musicians were about their craft. Commencing with a wild opening vamp, "Let Your Love Go" rips it up, "Coming Apart" then contains an amazingly spiritual arrangement revolving around Larry's organ playing, while "Don't Tell Me No" contains a rawness and drive sadly missing from the studio version. Needless to say, "Make It With You," "Baby I'm-A Want You," "Everything I Own," and "If" all receive rapturous applause, and even wild screams from the teenage girls in attendance, much to the amusement, and seeming bemusement of others. But it comes as no surprise to read once again the reviews afforded to the band's live performances from the local American press circuit.

> *"Bread is a very warm group, reproduces its albums with amazing precision. If anything the show was not long enough for me. I could have stayed all night."*
> *—The Denver Clarion*

> *"Bread is without qualification one of the finest groups now playing in America. The group has the ability to either be soft and sexy or hard and heavy, but it always goes. The group's versatility is remarkable."*
> *—Oceanside Blade-Tribune*

> *"One of pop music's finest male vocal groups is Bread. The four singers have created an even balance between their firm masculinity and a gentle, warm delivery. They demand more of themselves than a good beat and fancy vocal techniques. They use intricate vocal patterns and churn out rich phrasing."*
> *—Milwaukee Journal*

Indeed, such was the strong crossover appeal of Bread by now that, in late 1972, Grammy Award-winning vocalist Jack Jones released an entire album on RCA Records of Bread cover versions. Cleverly entitled *Bread Winners*, this ten-track release also was given the seal of approval by David Gates himself, who provided his own sleeve notes on the reverse of the cover.

However, this wasn't the first, and certainly wouldn't be the last time that a cover version of a Bread recording would appear. One year previously, back in 1971, former vocalist for Paul Revere & The Raiders, Mark Lindsay, had taken David's "Been Too Long On The Road" into the Hot 100, while British-born songbird Petula Clark had included a version of "It Don't Matter To Me" on her 1970 *Memphis* album, and then a recording of "If" on *Petula '71*. The Sandpipers also issued a version of "If" on their *Gift Of Song* album from 1971, as did Scott Walker on his 1973 offering *Any Day Now*, and Olivia Newton-John on her debut album. Newton-John would then follow it up with a cover of "Everything I Own" during 1972. 1973 would see the emergence of a number of established easy listening crooners covering their own Bread versions with Johnny Mathis and Perry Como performing "Baby I'm-A Want You" and "Aubrey" respectively. Meanwhile, Dusty Springfield issued a recording of "The Other Side Of Life" on her *Cameo* album and U.K. pop veterans The Searchers taped a version of the more obscure "Don't Shut Me Out," initially a track on Bread's debut release. Heck, even glam-rockers The Sweet, still masquerading under their guise of Brit-bubblegum purveyors, also turned in a reasonable assault on the same Gates tune early on in their career, as did Slade with a cover of the Griffin-Royer tune "Could I." The following year would see the status taken one step higher when the "chairman of the board" himself (and James's former silver screen partner), Frank Sinatra, recorded his own take on "If," while, across the Atlantic, international reggae star Ken Boothe would push a lively version of David's memorial to his father, "Everything I Own," right up to the peak position in the British singles charts. A feat that the popular TV and movie actor Telly Savalas would match during 1975 with yet another rendition of "If." In more ways than one were these compositions, mostly from the pen of David Gates, becoming Bread winners.

As the winter of 1972 receded, and the first weeks of 1973 began, the band enjoyed a brief break from traveling around the country, taking the opportunity once more to reconnect with Armin Steiner in the recording studio. On January 29th, three members of the band finally committed to tape a version of the James Griffin-Robb Royer ballad "She Knows," a song that had been debuted over twelve months previously during the final dates of the *Manna* tour. With James providing the vocals along with electric guitar, David on 12-string guitar and bass, and Larry sitting in at his Baldwin keyboard, this delicate offering had no place for Mike and his drum kit in the arrangement, and it was just the threesome that, with take 23, eventually cut a satisfactory recording. In addition, at least two other songs were reportedly taped during the session: the gospel-influenced "Don't Give Up On Me Now," and the infectious, hook-laden "Before Long," both Griffin compositions. The latter was certainly filled with trademark Bread harmonies, but neither was to see completion, and were shelved immediately afterwards. Clearly, the band was now looking towards the next album.

February 1973, saw the third single issued from the latest record, "Aubrey" b/w "Didn't Even Know Her Name," continuing Bread's ongoing presence in the Top 20 of the *Billboard* singles charts, finally topping out an eight-week run at the #15 position, matching the achievements of its predecessor. Then, just before the quartet resumed their *Guitar Man* touring schedule during March of that year, they took the opportunity of recording a number of television appearances, scheduled for the upcoming spring season. CBS Television was taping an 80-minute pilot episode of a new variety show, tentatively titled *Hotel 90*, with featured performers including Diahann Carroll, Tim Conway, Alan Alda, Sally Struthers, Joyce Van Patten, and Donna McKechnie. The concept was simply for a series of comedy sketches, songs, and dance routines set against the background of "Hotel 90," a luxurious mythical hotel. Bread were chosen to provide two of the musical sequences within the show and, although the pilot was completed, the show was sadly not picked up by the network, despite Bread turning in an impressive performance of "Welcome To The Music," followed by an exquisite solo rendition of "Aubrey" from David. The band's second appearance reached a far wider audience, seeing that their host on this particular show was former '50s/'60s swinger Bobby Darin, who, despite his ailing health, was still actively seeking to achieve the creative heights of his early years. *The Bobby Darin Show* (initially airing as *The Bobby Darin Amusement Company*) ran on NBC between 1972 and 1973, just months prior to the host's early death, and Bread featured during one episode of the show's second season, appearing on April 13th, joking with the host and miming to "Baby I'm-A Want You" and "Fancy Dancer" (with the latter featuring Larry "playing" the lead guitar riff).

Such was the success that the U.K. edition of *Best Of Bread* was currently receiving during this period that Elektra Records in the U.S. was keen to replicate the impressive sales figures at home. Subsequently, the American equivalent of the collection was issued during March of 1973, reaching the Top 40 within the space of a few weeks, and finally culminating at the #2 position during a 28-week run. It was to be Bread's highest ever album placing in their home country and, while the track selection was sequenced slightly differently from its British counterpart with "Diary" replacing "Been Too Long On The Road," and the front cover presented with a more subdued monochrome Bez image, it still contained many of the early highlights from the band's initial four albums. Plus it was to be the only location for completists at the time to pick up the single version of "It Don't Matter To Me" from 1971, seeing that it had never appeared on any of the band's studio albums. In response to the collection, even some of the industry's heavyweight press finally relented in their acknowledgment of the band, with the following excerpt taken from a review that appeared in the June edition of *Creem*:

> *"THIS IS IT, this is it, this is it! The wimps rule; there's no doubt about it. AM critters like Steely Dan and King Harvest and Christie and the Rowan Brothers and even your old standard favorites like the Hollies and*

the Guess Who have nothing, absolutely nuttin', in comparison with this shimmering tribe. Bread beats 'em all..."

began the lengthy review, before culminating with the thought-provoking image of:

"And hopefully, soon they'll conquer the whole world and smother us all with their syrupy spit."
—Robert A. Hull, *Creem*, June, 1973

In order to ensure that any subsequent collections contained the same track line-up, and for ease of marketing both home and abroad, with a Volume 2 presumably already in mind, the original U.K. pressing was withdrawn and replaced by an exact replica of the U.S. release, color replaced with monochrome, and complete with "Diary"... but still retaining the original U.K. catalog number.

On March 3rd, the band attended the 15th Grammy Awards ceremony, held for the first time in Nashville, Tennessee, where they were nominated for an award in two categories. Unfortunately, the single "Baby I'm-A Want You" lost out in the "Best Pop Vocal Performance by a Duo, Group, or Chorus" category to Roberta Flack & Donny Hathaway's hit "Where Is The Love," whilst the *Baby I'm-A Want You* album, nominated under the "Best Engineered Recording" category (a tribute to the work of Armin Steiner), also failed to pick up the prize, with Neil Diamond's *Moods* coming out tops. However, five days later, they were back in Los Angeles to be honored during the *Billboard* magazine "Number One Trendsetter" ceremony, held atop the Continental Hyatt House, where they were awarded the "Top Singles Award" for 1972. A notable accomplishment, such was the prestigious position that *Billboard* held within the industry, although the band had little time to reflect on their continuing success story with the closing section of the *Guitar Man* tour now back in progress. The final push saw the band once more work their way across the states, from Washington to Colorado, Texas to Arizona, California to Georgia, Virginia to Utah, although the proposed visit to the U.K. during April was postponed, and rescheduled for June of that year.

One other act that appeared alongside them during much of the April/May leg of the tour centered around the promising pairing of jazz-influenced rock duo, Walter Becker and Donald Fagin, out on the road to promote their all-important second album. Accompanied in the band by guitarists Denny Dias and Jeff "Skunk" Baxter, drummer Jim Hodder and singer David Palmer, they were out to take Steely Dan's upcoming *Countdown To Ecstasy* release, featuring such notable moments as "Bodhisattva" and "My Old School," to a wider market. Clearly succeeding, the album topped out at number 35 on the *Billboard* charts.

The song selection for Bread this time around covered a slightly wider spectrum from the band's five-album career. Although the most recent release was still heavily represented, notably with "Welcome To The Music" appropriately added as the opening number, they also resurrected the spotlight on Larry's acclaimed piano arrangement for "Bridge Over Troubled Water," with James stepping into the footprints of Art Garfunkel, and reviving their nod to the inspirational days of rock'n'roll. Then, in April, confusion began to reign…

The U.K. tour, scheduled for June, having already been postponed once, was canceled again. The band, having almost completed the U.S. leg of the tour, had reconvened in the recording studio to pick up sessions from where they had left off in January, but it quickly became apparent that not everyone in the band was pleased with the quality of the material.

"When you consider two albums a year, that's 24 brand new songs," Mike Botts was to comment diplomatically. "That's got to be two good, really good songs every 30 days. Now on top of that you're gonna go out and tour half a year, sporadic dates, two weeks here, two weeks there, and all the other goodies. Finally, it drained us emotionally and physically and, probably for the first time in their careers, David and Jimmy were coming in to the studio with songs that were (only) 70 or 80 percent completed. When we started there was a backlog of maybe 20 or 30 songs that had yet to be tapped. I don't want to wince, or apologize when I play a record for somebody and I'm on that record. If my name is on it I don't want to have to say, 'Well, I like it but you have to understand it was a bad day'…"[31]

David, having brought in a selection of his new songs such as "Clouds" and "Sail Around The World," was reportedly not happy with the standard of James's new offerings. The band had committed to tape two of the new Griffin compositions, one of which was a raucous blues-rock number entitled "Love You 'Til The Cows Come Home" but, in David's words, "Some of the material was not of sufficient quality. It was starting to get poor in my opinion. We were unable to match the quality of songs, top to bottom, that we'd had on our first five albums and I didn't like what James and Robb were bringing in. And yet I had no right to ask them to go back and rewrite, because we had an agreement that we'd each be responsible for 50 percent of the album. Maybe my songs weren't as good that time either. We finished four cuts, I listened to them and thought, 'We've lost it here.'"[13]

Unfortunately, in addition to David's dissatisfaction, James was also voicing his displeasure over his continued absence from the composing credits on the A-side of all Bread singles. And, as the band were about to re-sign with Elektra for another contracted period, he was allegedly refusing to put his name to paper unless he got a single release commitment. It was all beginning to unravel, resulting in the U.K. concert dates, a lucrative 24-venue schedule including a proposed performance at The Royal Festival Hall in London, being canceled. On April 7th, Elektra Records issued an official statement commenting that the reason for the cancellation was "internal difficulties," but just three days later a further statement was issued, apparently overruling what had previously been said. The second statement was worded: "Both David Gates and James Griffin of Bread are signed personally to Elektra as well as the band. There are no problems at all between the musicians and Elektra. Even if the band should split, which is uncertain at the moment, both David Gates and James Griffin will continue solo careers with Elektra."

Clearly the ongoing status of Bread was in dire straits. After fulfilling the final few concert bookings in May of that year, with memories of the final show in Salt Lake City tainted by the destruction of much of their touring equipment when one of the tour trucks overturned en route, and faced with the choice either to continue and, as he saw it, put out an album that could potentially destroy the reputation of the band or quit, David chose the latter.

"You can get into the trap where you stay together just for the money," he concluded. "Then people begin to fight and pick at one another, and ride to the concert in separate cars and all that nonsense, and I just didn't want any part of that."

"We broke up in 1973 because David had refused to support me having a single release after him having had ten in a row," James was later to state. "Elektra was about to re-sign us for another term and I told our manager that if I didn't get a single release commitment, we would not re-sign. I didn't hear anything back from David or the manager as David had decided to go solo ..."[18]

Once again, it was a case of two sides to every slice of bread, and regardless of whose opinion holds more weight, with both offering valid reasoning, the truth of the matter was that both David and James had their issues working within the confined structures of an equal partnership. Both had had to tolerate so much, and perhaps give so much, that it had stretched their abilities to harmonize further than they were prepared to go and, while David denied there was any friction between him and James, he admitted that when they re-entered the studio in the spring of 1973, "we were exhausted creatively." Creatively and mentally...

In an interview with *Sounds* magazine three months later, he summarized the reaction of his fellow Bread associates to the breakup. "I remember the day I phoned the others. They just said 'Yeah, you're right.' Everyone understood, record company people, management, so there weren't the usual hassles. We just ran out of things to do. It was getting pretty boring and everyone wanted a new challenge. We were suffering from certain musical limitations that were holding us back. We got to the stage where we were really dragging ourselves out on the road, playing the same things over and over again. It became kinda meaningless. Everyone knew we'd have to end the band."[20]

"I just remember David calling me and saying, 'I've got a bombshell to drop on you,'" James was to continue. "It kinda surprised all of us that David chose that time to go solo, I don't think the rest of us wanted to hang it up, but we all were burned out a little bit from being on the road. The creativity was waning, and the interest was dying. It wasn't as much fun to be in the studio together, though there was never any acrimony or fistfights or anything like that. We always conducted ourselves in a pretty business-like manner."[18]

Wishing to defuse the situation, and while unclear himself as to how it would all unfold, Jac Holzman went on record as stating: "At the moment, all I can tell you is that the group are in a state of flux, to use an official term, which either means that they will continue to make records or they won't. In the latter case, we will make records with David Gates and probably Jimmy Griffin separately. Larry Knechtel is not an Elektra artist, he is involved in the group for recording and live performances, but is not a signatory to the original Bread contract. The original three signatories were David Gates, Jimmy Griffin, and Robb Royer. Robb left, leaving Jimmy and David as the original two signatories, and our claim is to those two artists only. In fact, we have asked Larry to make an album for us, indicating that we think he might find it interesting to do. Larry feels very close to Elektra, and he is a great musician and craftsman, one of the rare ones. He is the guitar man on the 'Guitar Man' track. We couldn't get that thing right, and he just picked up the guitar and played it. Also he is a great bass player, as well as a formidable keyboard player and the arranger of 'Bridge Over Troubled Water,' which is not a bad claim to fame. He's a much in-demand session musician in Los Angeles."

Clearly, to all concerned, while Mike was deemed very much an essential part of the performing band, it was simply believed he could always fall back on his in-demand session duties and, along with Larry, he was a subsequent victim of the dissatisfactions that ran between the band's two front men. It was a cruel indictment that Mike warranted not even a mention in Jac Holzman's statement, as if justifying the status of the two songwriters to the detriment of those who stood behind. Neither part of the rhythm section appeared to have any significant say in the day-to-day running, nor a decision on the future of the band, such was the overwhelming control of the songwriting duo. And unfortunately, the breakup had a harder effect on both Mike and Larry who, without the profitable songwriting royalties coming in, still had to make a living to survive.

The rhythm section, along with Robb during the band's formative years, may well have been seen by many as the "background" players, mere supporting roles to the two prominent lead singers out front, but cast no doubt over the fact that Bread was a four-man band. David Gates, James Griffin, Michael Botts, and Robb Royer/Larry Knechtel. Two performers may have been lately pulling the strings of the band but without the contributions of the remaining two members, it would never have gelled to the standard it reached. Maybe even the two front players themselves were guilty of overlooking the importance of their silent partners, but they were the counterbalance to the individual egos out front, and when Bread officially called it a day at the end of May 1973, they were left to their own devices. For everyone involved, it was a rather dismal day.

Band manager Al Schlesinger summed up: "The reason they broke up was that it just wasn't happening in the studio. They went in to make an album in January of 1973 and by some time in the middle of March they had had bits and pieces, but the feel wasn't there, the romance wasn't there. They were laboring and they decided that rather than come up with something that is forced and really isn't giving the public what they expect from Bread, they'd best call it a day."[31]

Chapter Thirteen

Clouds & Rain

Elektra Records now had the careers of both James Griffin and David Gates on their books. Whereas before, with a united band, they had one career with one amount of record sales to handle, they now had two potential best-selling artists to hand. One of 1972's most successful bands had become two of 1973's most promising artists. The remaining half of Bread, as was to be expected, reverted back to their previous livelihoods, re-entering the world of paid studio session musicians, although their hectic life on the road with Bread had stood them in good stead for the years to come, with Mike Botts in particular becoming both a favored session and touring musician with a succession of performers.

Shortly after the disbandment of Bread, Mike once again joined up with Linda Ronstadt's touring band, bringing his seasoned talents to Ronstadt's ever-increasing crowds at venues across the country. Linda was on the verge of breaking big across America, and such was her willingness to have Mike sit behind her on the drum stool that she told him to "name his price" in order to secure his services. Her constant touring schedule would subsequently keep Mike occupied for over two years, balancing gigs with regular studio sessions and musical projects in and around Los Angeles whenever the touring band rested. The first of these projects was *The JBL Sessions*, a rarely heard vinyl collection of studio recording techniques, including various drum patterns from Mike, compiled by the JBL sound system specialists and designed as an instructional tool for loudspeaker technicians. This was then followed by *Islands*, the second Elektra release from Cyrus Faryer, along with the self-titled debut Motown offering from former Pleasure Fair guitarist Stephen Cohn.

"When The Pleasure Fair broke up, it was a major turning point in my life," recalled Cohn. "I lost the main focus of my work and also broke up with a girlfriend with whom I had been quite passionately involved. My reaction was to get very depressed and, in reaction, to go into one of the heaviest growth periods of my life. I moved to Venice, California, which was one of the epicenters of the 'hippy movement.' The Doors and Canned Heat were based there as well as many other musicians. There were 'happenings' on the Santa Monica Pier and psychedelic drugs flowed freely. It was in this environment that I became a serious artist, in that I consciously developed a creative lifestyle aimed at being a productive composer.

At that time, this meant writing songs and living a life that gave me something to write about. I spent two years doing this and wrote a large volume of songs that were of a personal, singer-songwriter nature, typical of the late '60s. Over the course of eight or so months, I self-produced a master of sixteen of my songs at 'The Farm,' Cyrus Faryar's legendary home studio.

"One day, I walked into Motown, which was on Sunset Boulevard. Much to my surprise, (my music) got a good reception there, however it took almost a year before a contract was completed. I did some further recording and a great deal of mixing before I finished the album. The work I did with Michael Botts was done at The Farm. Michael was a very solid professional. I was working with a top studio pro. He read well, learned quickly, and played takes that were perfect. There was very little, if any, to criticize in his playing or his work ethic…"

One more important event that occurred in Mike Botts' calendar during this period took place during the early summer of that year, a few short weeks after the dissolution of Bread. On this particular day, a friend of his brought someone new across to his house to visit, an extremely talented 22-year-old aspiring actress and songwriter named Michele Dalcin, who was currently singing on studio sessions for artists such as Kenny Loggins and Michael McDonald, in-between trying out for various acting roles around the city. She had previously been in a band named Friends, alongside Mike's high school partner Joe LaManno and so it was only a matter of time before they would cross paths. She now recalls:

"The minute he opened that door I was like, *oh crap*! It was instantaneous. He was looking for a female singer to produce in the studio. My music was everything to me, but the minute he opened that door my heart sank, and after spending the entire rest of the day with Michael and a mutual friend, I knew he was a rare human being. No arrogance, much humility, and so much humor and intelligence. That was it for me…"

And so began a friendship, and then a lifelong partnership, for Mike, much the same as it had for both David and Larry many years before, one that was to see him through the traumatic years ahead. He had found his soul partner. Michele and Mike dated for eight years before marrying on January 24th, 1981.

In the aftermath of the disbandment, the focus was obviously going to fall on the band's principal songwriters and singers, and both James Griffin and David Gates immediately went about recording songs that would kick-start their subsequent solo careers for Elektra Records. Al Schlesinger had no concerns as to how he saw David's career developing as a result: "He's certainly going to be interested in doing meaningful film work. I think he's probably got some very fine musical works in him, be they concertos, suites. Something more than popular songs, without in any way knocking the contribution of beautiful, popular standards. I think that he probably wants to go on musically..."[31]

Following the short hiatus, James immediately resurrected his studio partnership with former band mate Robb Royer. As well as continuing to work on the still-unfinished musical project *Cosmo & Robetta*, the duo gathered up a collection of new compositions and a couple of songs from the abandoned Bread sessions and settled in at the Wally Heider Studios on North Cahuenga Boulevard in downtown Hollywood, utilizing the skills of in-house engineer Ed Barton. Bringing in session musicians in the caliber of bassist Leland Sklar, drummer Russell Kunkel, guitarists Jeff "Skunk" Baxter and Denny Lardin, and a wind section comprising John Miles and Curtis Amy, the band established themselves during mid-June to commit the new tracks to tape. String arrangements were undertaken by Marty Paich, who had previously worked with James the year before on the soundtrack to *Ironside*. Also contributing to the sessions on one new Griffin and Royer composition was keyboard virtuoso Michael Iceberg (listed as Iseberg on the subsequent sleeve notes), famed for his extravagant solo performances at Walt Disney World, where he regularly performed on his "Amazing Iceberg Machine," a bizarre amalgamation of various keyboards and electronic devices. The track he appeared on, a rich ballad entitled "Goin' Back To Boston," highlighted a lovely vocal melody accompanied by two acoustic guitars, James overdubbing both a six-string and a twelve-string on top of each other. Over this, Iceberg began his synthesized wash, utilizing his complex creation to capacity. The track then broke for a brief baroque interlude before it climaxed with the revisited chorus, once more enveloped with mellotron-sounding overkill. Despite its less-than-subtle grandeur, this was to become one of many highlights to evolve out of these sessions and yet, it is unfortunate to note, the highs that James was achieving in the studio were sadly now being matched by the new lows, and alternate highs, appearing elsewhere in his life. Regardless of the possibilities that his solo career had to offer, this period also marked the beginning of his slide into chronic substance abuse, a slide that had commenced during Bread's final decline, and one that, for the next few years, would prove to be a considerable reason for concern.

In spite of these recreational distractions, work on James's projected album continued at the Heider studios, with further Griffin-Royer co-compositions, including "Father And Son," "Only Now," "Melody Maker," "Lifeline," and "Love To Light The Way," mixed with a solo offering from James, "Someday," a lone composition from Robb that would ultimately give the album its title, "Breakin' Up Is Easy," and a track resurrected from 1969, "Beachwood Band," initially proposed for Bread's debut album. In addition to these songs, two further numbers were also brought back into the studio, both having initially been recorded during the abandoned sixth album sessions for Bread. "She Knows," featuring David Gates on acoustic guitar and bass, and Larry Knechtel on organ, was revitalized with a string and oboe arrangement, while "Love You 'Til The Cows Come Home," featuring all three of James's former compatriots, was built up with an additional slide guitar track from Jeff "Skunk" Baxter, the lead guitarist of Steely Dan. Also in attendance during at least one of the sessions, whilst on a visit to the U.S. to promote his upcoming *Foreigner* LP, was acclaimed British-born singer-songwriter, Cat Stevens, although he didn't contribute in any way to the recording process.

Recalls Robb: "Oh yeah, Cat Stevens! I remember him well. He was quite amazing actually. Only person I ever met that actually did have an aura. He seemed to be backlit all the time. Very nice guy and what a vibe!"

While James and Robb were ensconced at the Wally Heider studios, David was also to be found recording, returning to the Elektra studios with engineers Bruce Morgan and Armin Steiner, and cutting a series of tracks that would ultimately become his debut solo release. Like his erstwhile partner, David also brought in a number of songs that had previously been worked on during the abandoned Bread sessions, with "Clouds," "Sail Around The World" (reportedly featuring an uncredited James), and the lively "Soap (I Use The)" already having been partially completed. "Soap," in particular, was akin to a number of his previous Bread contributions, molded in the distinctive up-tempo vein of "Yours For Life" and "This Isn't What The Governmeant." Bringing in a stellar session crew around him, including drummers Jim Gordon, John Guerin, and Russell Kunkel, in addition to the previous contributions that Mike Botts had laid down, guitarists Larry Carlton and Louie Shelton, woodwind virtuoso Jim Horn, string man Jimmy Getzoff, and jack-of-all-trades Larry Knechtel, David worked up enough new material to complete the collection over July and August of 1973.

"I knew exactly who I wanted to play what on this album," he recalled in conversation with *Sounds*. "Larry has helped me out on the production and I'm very pleased with the outcome of the sessions. The first day of recording was pretty strange because I hadn't recorded with session musicians for a long time. But after the first day I got back into the swing pretty quick. It was like the days before Bread when I was working with session people all the time.

"I'm not worried about the commercial quality of my music, but more about stretching myself to my natural limits musically. Now my responsibilities are to my record company and my management. I'm no longer concerned with goals like having a series of monster smashes. I just want to make records that I'm pleased to go home and play."[20]

By way of an advance release, David chose to issue his reconstructed rendition of "Clouds" as a single on Elektra Records during July, coupled with "Soap," resulting in a #47 position on the U.S. charts. While not as successful as either the artist or the label would have liked, it was a firm foundation on which to schedule the album's release the following fall. The single was not as immediately accessible as some of his previous "hit" records, and that lack of commerciality may well have contributed to its lower position. On its own merits the composition never really develops, void of any immediate hook line or chorus, but all that was to change once the album sessions progressed into the summer.

Rounding out the proposed album were seven new Gates' compositions: "Sight & Sound," "Help Is On The Way," and "Sunday Rider," all songs with an underlying rock flavor, the gospel-driven "Do You Believe He's Comin'" featuring some wonderful guitar from the featured musicians, the delicate and distinctive balladry of "Ann," and the silky-smooth "Lorilee," the latter highlighted by another of Larry's amazing keyboard solos. However, the main focus of attention was on the final number, "Rain," which was the second portion of a lengthy "suite," in partnership with the aforementioned "Clouds."

David: "The suite is something that runs for nine minutes. I had to do it in three different installments to be able to put it together. I spliced it together and tried to make the piano match..."

Filled out with sound effects, crackling thunder, and pouring rain, this lengthy opus was central to the intended success of the album, showing that David could break away from the simplicities of the three-minute "pop" single and could provide his audience with a work of substance. As an individual piece, "Clouds" had failed to live up to expectations. After all, it was simply *not* a three-minute "pop" song. But once integrated into a longer concept, the emphasis of the composition shifted, for "Clouds & Rain" as a combined work is an exceptional piece of music, taking the listener through a sequence of alternating tempos and mood swings, never easing up, never letting the listener down. Lyrically, some of the couplings and phrasings were not David's strongest. "Come on rainbow, I can't let you go, before I reach the end of you someway," was certainly not going to win him any awards, and yet one cannot take away the ambition of such a piece, and it remains one of the most musical accomplishments from his vast catalog.

"Lyrics for me are the most difficult. The music comes easy. I've got five melodies for every set of lyrics. My lyrics are a sort of summation of things I see around me, or that I read about, or how I feel about those things. It's best for me to try and get it all said in one sitting, too, because it's very hard to recreate the mood out of which the song originally grew."[19]

Surprisingly, and despite the quality of the music that ran throughout, upon release by Elektra during October 1973, the album, issued under the title *First*, failed to achieve the success that both artist and label had anticipated, despite heavy advance publicity. David had originally planned to take the album out on the road, employing a fifteen-piece band, including a horn and string section, for ten shows in 3,000 seat venues. However, a suitable schedule couldn't be organized due to the number of concert venues pre-booked over the winter period. In addition, the availability of his chosen players, including Horn, Gordon, and Kunkel, was always going to be a further issue due to their heavy demand on the studio circuit.

"It'll have to be planned around their work on sessions, so it'll be fairly intermittent..." David had commented to *Sounds* during his initial planning. Subsequently, in lieu of the concert appearances, David went out on two heavily planned radio promotional tours, along with a televised guest spot on *American*

Bandstand performing "Sail Around The World." Unfortunately, even the radio visits were significant cause for concern, failing to find the full support needed to help the singles culled from the album.

"At one of the most important Top 40 stations in the country, the program director didn't even know Bread had broken up eight months ago," David was to comment at the time. "I'm afraid that kind of ignorance isn't uncommon in the business, and it's this attitude that worked against us when building the airplay to break these first releases into the Top 10. If the same record had had Bread on it, it would have instantly been on the playlists and when that was taken off, it wasn't, and yet it was basically the same voice. The same songs. The same everything."

Peaking at a lowly #107, *First* also received mixed reviews from the music press on both sides of the Atlantic. In the U.S. it was one-time Bread supporter, now aggressor, *Rolling Stone* magazine, who were only too happy to dig the barbs in, citing the album as the "same old slick rock & roll muzak, often very pretty and doubtless commercial, but devoid of identity. Produced and arranged by Gates, the album comprises ten attractive formula tunes, the best of which have the professional gloss of filtered airbrushed nude centerfolds in which nothing is revealed..." Although *Phonograph Magazine* was quick to balance out such negativity, referring to the release as an "exceptional experience." Meanwhile, in David's newly rediscovered U.K. market, the varying reviews ranged from "recedes into the background" to the more positive "a winner that draws the listener into the grooves." Reviews aside, the overall lack of success undoubtedly hurt David. But, undaunted, he issued a second single from the album, "Sail Around The World" b/w "Help Is On The Way" which, although garnering some of the more favorable responses from the nine-track collection, once more failed to gain significant airplay and limped to the equally unimpressive #50 position.

This surprising lack of success wasn't the only change to David's musical status at the time, for 1973 also saw a significant alteration to his arrangements with his record label. One of the key reasons for signing with Elektra, back in 1969, along with the ongoing support that Bread had received over the years had been the unquestionable endorsement from the label's founder and head, Jac Holzman. Jac had played a major part in laying the foundations for the band, often being the dominant voice when hearing the album playbacks, and in selecting the most appropriate songs for single releases. In 1970, the previously independent Elektra Records had merged with the larger Warner group with Holzman, still operating as label head, taking a three-year term of employment to continue developing the company, with a two-year option following on.

By the time 1973 came around, Jac was tiring of the business, longing for a simple retirement to the islands of Hawaii and when, unbelievably, the New York offices of Warner forgot to pick up on his two-year extension period, he took the opportunity to call it a day. Steve Ross, the head of Warner, immediately met with Jac and attempted to get him to change his mind. And maybe it was his loyalty to his own company, the baby he had founded back in 1950, that made Jac hesitate on his planned retirement, instead agreeing to take on a consultancy role as Senior Vice-President and Technologist with Warner, providing he could undertake this position from his beloved Maui. But, of more significance, he agreed to relinquish the running of his company, suggesting the amalgamation of Elektra with upcoming music mogul David Geffen's Asylum label, under the leadership of Geffen himself. For those who were a part of the Elektra roster it was a tortuous decision. Jac Holzman had cared and nurtured his stable, and had been like a father to many, while the brash, business-minded Geffen ripped through the Elektra offices like a hurricane, tearing down those who stood in his way. Declaring Elektra a disaster zone, he immediately began to cut out the artists who didn't figure in his plans and, while David Gates survived the cull, Elektra Records, or Elektra-Asylum as it was now known, became a very different label.

In the years to come Elektra would see further changes, including Geffen's own departure due to ill health, but back in 1973 it felt like the revolution was here, and as Elektra in-house producer Russ Miller so eloquently put it: "The day Jac left, the butterfly died..."

"This album is dedicated to Jac Holzman. I shall miss him," ran the credit on the reverse of the sleeve to David's *First* album.

Shortly after the release of *First*, James Griffin's solo album also appeared but not, as was to be expected, on the Elektra label. Upon completion the finished product was submitted to, but ultimately rejected by, Elektra and, unlike David, James was not fortunate enough to escape the hurricane that swept through the offices on North La Cienega Boulevard. Though it has been suggested that others felt that there was not enough room on the label for both former members of Bread, and, from the label's perspective, who had the more commercial viability?

Instead, James signed a solo deal with Polydor Records, a German-founded label that had achieved considerable commercial success across the U.K. and Europe. During 1972, the label had merged with Phonogram, to create PolyGram Records for distribution across America, although Polydor America continued to run as a smaller subsidiary to its larger partner. Credited to "James Griffin & Co.," and housed in a gatefold outer sleeve with the inside picture featuring a lavish photograph of him, partly silhouetted by candlelight, taken in his Mulholland Drive house, and with lyrics and session details listed on the inner packaging, this was a relatively expansive outlay for James's Polydor debut. But one befitting a slice of one of the 1970s' most successful acts to date. The title track of the album, "Breakin' Up Is Easy," was issued as the lead single, paired with "Melody Maker," but it met with little success. Ironically, despite all of James's hassles with getting one of his own compositions to feature on the A-side of Bread's singles, even on his own debut 45 release he went with the work of another. "Breakin' Up Is Easy" was a solo composition from Robb Royer, and while it features all of the distinctive qualities of a Griffin-Royer composition, James's name was notably absent. Nevertheless, the accompanying "Melody Maker" did feature the name of the artist on the label, being another Griffin-Royer combination, but this was a much looser recording, almost sounding like the result of a jam session between the musicians present. "I think it was Botts," recalled Robb when asked who supplied the funky drum rhythms, but it wasn't just the impressive backbeat that made the track work. The bass riffs, the rhythm guitar, both interspersed with the lead patterns, the chorus of female backing singers, all topped with James's enthusiastic lead vocals, made this a rare combination within the Bread circle. Even with "Fancy Dancer," the band had never tapped quite so far into the R&B groove but clearly, despite the unqualified success of the completed track, this was new and unexplored territory, and the song was inexplicably left off the album release, destined to appear simply as a single B-side. Much like "Mother Freedom" had been for the earlier radio programmers, this was almost one step too far from the recognizable sound and, regardless of James's new found freedom as a solo artist, it simply would not have fit comfortably within the album structure. It would remain as a lost, forgotten gem.

Robb with engineer Ed Barton, overseeing the Breakin' Up Is Easy *album (courtesy of Robb Royer)*

One other track that appeared on James's album, recorded within a much safer framework, had actually been taped after the majority of the work had already been completed. Three months after the sessions at the Wally Heider Studios had been finished, James and Robb ventured 1,100 miles north of Los Angeles to record in the famed Kaye-Smith studios in Seattle, Washington, the northerly U.S. state that was now home to former band mate Larry Knechtel. Together, the threesome taped what would become the opening track on side two of the final release. "You'll Get Along," written solely by James, featured some lovely keyboard flourishes by Larry and a series of flute overdubs from Larry's old school friend, seasoned session player Jim Horn. Certainly, the second side of the album contained the stronger collection of songs with the gorgeous "Love To Light The Way," initially titled "Love Could Light The Way," culminating in some wonderful harmonies and arrangements, bringing the album to a satisfying climax. Yet, despite some glowing reviews in the rock press, the album fared poorly, failing to chart whatsoever.

> *"Every song is constructed with the craftsmanship Griffin and Royer have employed in the past, the string arrangements by Marty Paich are unobtrusive and the performances maintain a high standard throughout. An album that's easy to listen to, and one that proves that breaking up is easy... if you've got talent."*
> —Fred Dellar, *NME*

Robb: "Jimmy was limited by his struggle with drugs at that time. He had several opportunities (to promote the album) that we couldn't fully cash in on, plus I have to say that Polydor America was kind of a skeleton label. We never knew where the hell they were, they just had a message machine going, and it was a major label! We never felt that the Griffin album got anything like the kind of release it deserved..."

Nevertheless, James did manage to promote his album in the U.K., undertaking a brief trip to London during the latter part of 1973, where he was to first encounter another talented singer-songwriter, Terry Sylvester, guitarist and vocalist for the popular U.K. act The Hollies. Sylvester had joined the band during 1969 as a replacement for Graham Nash, who had quit for fame and fortune Stateside, and by 1973 had established himself within the role, his vocals and songwriting meshing alongside fellow Hollies front men Tony Hicks and Allan Clarke. Reportedly, James and Terry first met in the offices of a music publisher in London, struck up a friendship and, as The Hollies had also recently signed with Polydor Records, it seemed a logical arrangement that, upon undertaking the next Hollies tour in the U.K., James would be signed as a "Special Guest" to open up each show, in order to promote his own new product.

That early 1974 U.K. visit, coinciding with the U.K. release of "She Knows" b/w "Father And Son" as the next single, saw a 10-date tour around the provinces, along with a brief sojourn across to the European continent, with one notable show at the grand Theatre Royal in the heart of London. The Hollies, by that time, were past their popularity peak but were currently to be found basking in the afterglow of a current worldwide Top 10 hit, "The Air That I Breathe," and so were still pulling in an audience of considerable size. James's appearance, as opening act, was his first solo tour to date (excluding his venture with The Beach Boys ten years earlier) and yet, despite his personal demons at the time, his popularity among the U.K. crowds was still evident and he was well received as he included covers of a number of his Bread songs among the set list. Most venues saw him accompanied by a four-piece British backing band, playing between eight to ten songs each night, with "Melody Maker," "Dream Lady," "Someday," "You'll Get Along," "Just Like Yesterday," "Take Comfort," "Breakin' Up Is Easy," "Truckin'," and "Love You 'Til The Cows Come Home" all featuring at one stage during the short tour, before finishing off each night with the then-current single, "She Knows."

Then, on May 15th, he appeared on the popular U.K. music show *The Old Grey Whistle Test*, one of the few "serious" rock programs on British television, as opposed to the light-hearted "pop" content that dominated much of the U.K. media of the time. Fronted by the grizzled, long-haired presenter, "Whispering" Bob Harris, James's appearance on the show, recorded the previous day, was a calculated move to be seen among the rock elite as a serious artist in his own right and, performing live in the studio alongside heavy rock band Nazareth, James's solo spot included delicate interpretations of "Just Like Yesterday" (mistakenly referred to by Harris as taken from the new album) and "She Knows." The former track, a solo composition from the *Baby I'm-A Want You* album, saw him alone at the piano, while "She Knows" featured James on his favorite Gibson guitar accompanied by a solitary bouzouki player. Unfortunately, despite this TV appearance, and the relatively successful U.K. tour (along with further promotional work in France, Germany, and Holland), neither the single, nor the album, achieved chart success in Europe.

It was a similar story back home, whereupon the second single release from the album to be issued on American shores, "She Knows" b/w "Beachwood Band" also bombed, despite the A-side essentially being performed by three-quarters of Bread. Another track left over from the debut album sessions, "Beachwood Band" was named after the Hollywood community to the north of Los Angeles where seemingly everyone, at the time, was trying to get into the music business. Back in 1969, during the song's formation, Robb and James simply figured it an amusing anecdote that everybody from the block should simply join this one big band, the "Beachwood Band," hence the title. Today, Robb Royer cannot recall as to whether the release featured the original 1969 track, embellished with 1973 studio overdubs, or was a totally new recording, but he does clearly recollect engineer Ed Barton chasing the session musician bestowed with bagpipes around the room, attempting to keep the wailing pipes within microphone distance, as the musician marched back and forth. Having unsuccessfully attempted a saxophone overdub, the addition of the distinctive reed bagpipe sound added a new dimension to an otherwise melancholy acoustic track.

"Jimmy really wanted to do it," comments Robb on this unique addition to the studio setup. "I kept saying 'great idea, but hate the sound!'"

While both James and David were busy promoting their recent solo releases, and Mike was watching the endless miles of scenery pass him by as he worked his way across the country with Linda Ronstadt, Larry Knechtel was again easing himself away from the constant battles of the Los Angeles music scene. Having worked with David on his *First* album, and more recently assisting James in the studio, he was now more often than not to be found out of the Golden State, losing himself in the wilderness surrounding his new cattle and timber ranch in Maple Falls, upstate Washington, away from the grind and pressures of band life. He had recently suffered a severe health scare, and while it was one from which he was fortunately to recover, his life in the backwoods gave him pause for thought. Here, away from the minute-by-minute chaos that was Los Angeles, he was in his element. Living off the land, reconnecting with nature. Living the dream. Not that he was avoiding the industry altogether, but the daily demands of the studios he had experienced in the 1960s and early 1970s were something he no longer had the desire to repeat, especially while recovering his health. Nor, if truth be told, was the opportunity quite so available anymore. Such was his notable and respected talent that his telephone would never stop ringing completely, but the great "session" days that both he and his fellow studio musicians of the 1960s had experienced during the heady rush of rock'n'roll and "beat music," when the Wrecking Crew were the most in-demand session team around and it was constant bookings day in, day out, were now long gone.

The fall of 1973 saw a number of less obtrusive projects bearing the Knechtel name among the credits, including the October release of Asylum artist Rod Taylor's eponymous album, John Kay's *My Sportin' Life*, Chi Coltrane's *Let It Ride*, *Compartments* by Jose Feliciano, and Barry McGuire's *Seeds* album. In addition, he continued developing his writing credits, contributing to the song "Captain's March" alongside Jim Gordon, Mike Deasy, and Lee Sklar, while also performing on the sixth and final album by the Partridge Family, a series of record releases that he had intermittently been involved in since the inception of the popular TV music family back in 1970. But, to a man for whom the music was his life, it mattered little how successful the works he appeared on became. It was simply all about the music. Period. It always had been, and would be until his final days, despite his willingness to disappear into the rural woodlands around his new home, where he could chop wood, build with his bare hands, fish, and pan for gold in the unspoiled rivers and streams that flowed from the Cascade mountain range. As long as there was always a piano at hand, black and white keys on which his fingers could dance across...

During 1973, and into 1974, the music of Bread continued to be a regular feature on the radio stations across America, the U.K., and beyond. But once again the focus of the band's legacy, in the aftermath of their breakup, was always going to be on the hit singles. David Gates' hit singles. It may have been James Griffin supplying harmony vocals and rhythm or lead guitar, but Bread was becoming synonymous with the sound of David's delicate, distinctive vocals. The considerable wealth of material that James and Robb had written and, along with David, Mike, and Larry, had created in the studio, was becoming forgotten but to the faithful few who remained the dedicated fan. The failure of James's solo product only heightened the misguided belief that David was the sole driving force behind the band's earlier success, and this erroneous myth would grow in the years to follow. What is surprising is that David's solo career also faltered in its aftermath. He would never again quite recapture the magic of his early compositions, although anthems such as "Make It With You," "Baby I'm-A Want You," "If," and "Everything I Own" would make him an exceedingly wealthy man in years to come. And while, just maybe, he had set out to achieve all he had intended to during that brief, three-year summer of success, the legacy he had left with his songwriting would continue, even while the band itself, along with the varying solo careers, were all but forgotten by the general music-buying audiences. His compositions would go on to dominate the subsequent "hits" and "best of" collections, and when *Best Of Bread Volume 2* appeared during 1974, eight of the eleven featured cuts were from David, although, unlike the earlier release, this collection had to settle for a modest #32 placing in the American charts, and an even lower #48 in the U.K.

During the fall of 1974, David's composing talents again enlivened the British charts, although this was due to a pleasing cover version of one of his earlier successes. Jamaican-born artist Ken Boothe was to take "Everything I Own" all the way to the top of the singles charts with his light reggae rendition of the song that David had written in memory of his father. Although, interestingly, Boothe chose to reword the lyrics as "anything I own," retaining the original phrase in the song title only. Nevertheless, the radio stations were again awash with the gentle melody that permeated the song's very essence.

In the meantime, Mike continued with his commitment to Linda Ronstadt and her touring band, forming the backbone of a stellar line-up that included Andrew Gold, Kenny Edwards, and Waddy Wachtel. He was in his element surrounded by such an established team.

"It was a physical workout for him every night. They were playing incredible music," says Michele, Mike's wife, of his period with Linda's band. "He used to tell me he never even broke a sweat playing 'weenie rock' as he often referred to Bread's music. When Michael was touring with Linda, she was just hitting her stride; she had her best band ever. They were touring constantly. Mike had it made. He was paid handsomely when touring, and on a retainer while at home. This left him free to do the studio work he loved with many fellow musicians."

On a commercial level, Mike was probably now having the most successful career of his former band mates, and was again playing to huge audiences night after night. It was on this tour that they started performing a version of the old Buddy Holly hit, "That'll Be The Day," that, as yet, Linda hadn't attempted in the studio.

As 1974 drew to a close, David Gates attempted to put aside his disappointment at the relative failure of his debut album and re-entered the studios to start work on the follow-up release. *Never Let Her Go*, when it finally appeared in January of

1975, was a marked improvement on its predecessor, containing a number of notably more accessible songs, void of anything as bold as the expansive "Clouds & Rain" suite. Unfortunately, the overall length of the album clocked in at a mere 26 minutes, and record buyers may well have been justified in claims of being shortchanged. Nevertheless, the quality of the production and performances lived up to the usual high standards that the artist himself set and demanded. Partway through the recording sessions, David took a short break in order to make a televised appearance on the syndicated *Bobby Goldsboro Television Show*, surprisingly performing "Clouds" as opposed to any of his newer material. But focus was swiftly drawn back to finishing the album sessions, and once again, Larry Knechtel was on hand to assist with the production duties. The pleasing title track from the new release harked back to the previous decade, when David had written and arranged a version for Glenn Yarborough in 1965.

"That song comes from my pre-Bread days," he later recalled in conversation with Barry Alfonso. "I'd written it back in 1964 and had forgotten about it. Years later I was looking through my archives for some tunes and I stumbled across it again."[14]

Other highlights came in the form of "Part Time Love," "Light Of My Life," and the impressive "Playin' On My Guitar," and it's immediately noticeable how, despite the distance David now placed himself from his former band, the "rock" influences he had previously felt so uncomfortable with appeared to be flowing far easier from him now. "Light Of My Life," "Chain Me," "Angel," and "Watch Out" are all compositions with a heavier rock base than one would have anticipated from the acknowledged balladeer. While the nostalgic "Greener Days," the lively final inclusion, was another leftover from David's prolific 1960s songwriting sessions, first appearing during the early months of 1967 when recorded by the Mississippi-based band The Gants.

Released simultaneously as the first single from the album, "Never Let Her Go" b/w "Watch Out" climbed steadily up the *Billboard* charts, peaking at a comfortable #29, justifying the faith Elektra Records still held in David. And while the album itself only reached #102 in the charts, a mere five places higher than its predecessor, a second single, "Part Time Love" coupled with "Chain Me," also achieved a modicum of success, reaching #34 on the U.S. Adult Contemporary charts, an alternate *Billboard* list that featured the most popular songs on the adult and light-pop radio stations across the country. Additionally, that same year, soul singer Gladys Knight would turn in a sizeable hit with her own unforgettable cover version of the song.

> *If there's a single behavioral pattern which has emerged over the last four years of pop music, it's the reinstatement of the song, not the singer, as the primary element of a successful record. The succession of stylistic explosions which rocked the middle and late sixties served to elevate performers and personalities high above such conventional musical com-*

ponents as composition, arrangements and style; any number of hit acts, from Eric Burdon through Cream and Hendrix, fashioned careers out of performing intensity and a corresponding abysmal lack of songwriting talent. The turnaround, to an emphasis on matching competent performers with exceptional material, has defined the '70s charts more than any other single trend.

David Gates' contributions to Bread from 1970 to '72, songs like "Everything I Own," "It Don't Matter to Me," "Guitar Man," et al, fit so precisely into seventies pop to serve as its major cornerstone. Gates' commitment first of all to the craft of composition, not to slight his professional involvement in all aspects of production, is what made his Bread work and his solo album of 1973 such exceptional experiences. Despite the fact he missed having his own hit single as a solo a year ago, the news is good about Gates' prospects for success this season. As demonstrated by Never Let Her Go, the writer-singer-guitarist-producer is in better shape than ever.

The hit bound title track is no surprise. Sounding like a skillful fusing of "Make It With You" and "Wichita Lineman," it's not exactly what you'd expect Bread '75 to come across as, containing a bona fide super pop verse such as "True love takes a little longer – Your heart beats a little stronger." Easy. The remainder of the set is the most interesting for it discloses, in a much more effective way than his first album or any of the Bread LPs, Gates' breadth as a writer. As adept as he is at crafting winsome ballads, he's no slouch at hard rockers and medium tempo tunes, tearing off a clean yet tough, percussive "Angel," wiring up an offbeat vaguely Dave Mason-ish rhythm track on "Chain Me."

"Part Time Love" is an expressive melodic exercise that smarts with all the style and grace of the wounded Todd R. of years past. "Light Of My Life" does the unthinkable, matching a typically evocative Gates lyric to a rough-hewn guitar riff borrowed from Hendrix's "All Along the Watchtower." "Watch Out" bumps along like comfortable Santana singles used to, right down to the mock-psychedelic filigree on the intro.

Which shouldn't be interpreted as ascribing to Gates a fine sense of plagiarism. His sense of taste, of knowing how and when to use which musical elements, is so comprehensive as to be uncanny. The album's two high points in fact point to Gates' new direction, toward perfecting rather specific mood pieces; both the bouncy "Greener Days" and the cool, subtle "Strangers" give indication of his mastery of form, and natural growth will soon extend even beyond the wide boundaries of Never Let Her Go. Gates' special gifts are consistently well handled, and it's to the music audience's advantage that he persists at his craft.

—Gene Sculatti, *Phonograph Record*, March 1975

For the next few months, David worked hard on both touring and promoting the album, appearing on a number of popular U.S. television shows such as *The Smothers Brothers Show*, *The Bobby Goldsboro Show*, *The Mike Douglas Show,* and *Dinah!*. However, promotion for the album wasn't just restricted to his homeland and, having re-established his musical credentials over in England, David then undertook a short series of radio, television and concert appearances across the Atlantic during April and May of that year.

Accompanied by a healthier Larry Knechtel on keyboards and bass guitar, David assembled a touring band comprising of Jim Gordon on drums, Texas-born session guitarist Dean Parks on lead guitar and Parks' fiancé, Carol Carmichael, singing backup vocals. Together they performed four sold-out shows to his ever-increasing U.K. audience, featuring "Make It With You" as the show's opening number, swiftly followed by "Baby I'm-A Want You" and "Guitar Man." The set was then interspersed with more recent offerings including "Greener Days," "Never Let Her Go," and "Ann" before he brought it to a climax with "Everything I Own" and "If." Yet, for many of the subsequent press reviews from the tour, the highlight of the performances came not from the singer himself but from Dean Parks, the fluent-fingered guitarist who had previously backed Steely Dan, Carole King, and Marvin Gaye in the studio.

"Guitarist Dean Parks, frankly, stole the show. He was a magician. He soloed with simple logic touched with flashes of inspiration that lit the stage. One lost count of Parks' stunning contributions to the evening," wrote journalist Geoff Brown in *Melody Maker*.

As well as performing before a live audience, much of David's 1975 U.K. promotional visit was taken up with radio interviews and television appearances, starting off with a live guest appearance on the BBC *Round Table* radio broadcast to help review that week's new record releases. This was followed with BBC Radio 2's *Open House* and then on May 1st, he also appeared on the popular BBC radio show *My Top 12*, an hour-long slot devoted to one particular guest each week, with David talking about his career throughout the years and choosing twelve of his personal favorite recordings. The wide variety of his chosen styles included Chuck Berry's "Sweet Little Sixteen," Maria Muldaur's "Midnight At The Oasis," Jimi Hendrix' "All Along The Watchtower," the Beatles' "Yesterday," Led Zeppelin's "Stairway To Heaven," and his own composition "If." The television appearances lined up for him included guest spots on *Rock On With 45* (performing "Make It With You," "Sunday Rider," "Part Time Love," and "Never Let Her Go"), *Musical Time Machine*, *The Moira Anderson Show,* and, following on from James's appearance the previous year, a prestigious slot on the BBC's *Old Grey Whistle Test*. Appearing on the same show as the popular duo Seals & Crofts, David's *Whistle Test* appearance saw him and his four-piece band perform faithful renditions of "Soap (I Use The)," "Angel," and "Baby I'm-A Want You" live in the BBC studios. One final show on which he appeared while over in the U.K. had far more personal relevance for him, as this was hosted by his longtime friend and musical sidekick, now a major international recording star in his own right, Glen Campbell.

Glen was recording a series of variety shows for the BBC, *The Glen Campbell Music Show*, each week featuring a different guest in the studio. In addition to David, the subsequent weeks would see Seals & Crofts, Anne Murray, Jimmy Webb, Wayne Newton, and Helen Reddy appear on the stage, but for David's appearance Glen seemed genuinely delighted to have his old friend back alongside him. However, it is clearly noticeable, when viewing tapes of the show, the stark contrast between the two men. Having been a regular host on American television for a number of years prior to this recording, Glen Campbell is so overly confident in front of the cameras that his self-assured personality dominates over the shy, somewhat uncomfortable demeanor of David. Glen is loud and brash, David is quiet and gentle, although the affection is clearly in evidence. Performing solo versions of "Everything I Own," "Playin' On My Guitar," and "Part Time Love," David is then joined by Glen for a medley of "Make It With You," "Baby I'm-A Want You," and "Never Let Her Go," both taking turns in harmonizing with each other. Glen then takes the lead for a truly wonderful rendition of "If," commenting, "Boy, I wish I could write a song like that." David meekly responds with a huge smile on his face, "I wish I could sing like that..."

Nevertheless, all of this promotional work across the U.K. was to prove successful when the *Never Let Her Go* album broke into the Top 40 charts while David was still in the country, culminating with a #32 position, a reasonable placing considering the rocky start David had made in launching his solo career.

Upon his return to the United States, David continued with the promotional jaunt, undertaking a few headlining slots (and on at least one occasion sharing the bill with Emmylou Harris) before taking on the supporting role on a month-long tour with Olivia Newton-John, the Australian-born vocalist who was touring on the back of two huge #1 hits in America. While it may seem surprising that David was reduced to the opening position for such a tour, this was the first time he had really been out on the road in his homeland since Bread had disbanded two years previously, and it proved an arduous slog for him at times.

"Your biggest problem when you're touring is keeping your voice in shape," he told one of the many reporters who covered the tour. "It's really your whole show. I used to smoke and I couldn't hold notes so well. You've got to want to quit smoking. I decided to do it. Now I've got my wind up better..."

Despite the tiring schedule, the overall acceptance for the album was proving it had all been extremely worthwhile. After all, by deciding not to tour for the previous release, he had seen it disappear barely after it was released, despite the immaculate quality of the product. This time around, while the album had again failed to match earlier chart heights, the success of both the title track and of "Part Time Love" as singles, and the British chart placings, had proven Elektra's faith in their artist.

Could it be that the specter of Bread was finally behind him?

Chapter Fourteen

Change Of Heart

And so it was, that in 1974 James Griffin found himself in the unfortunate position of recovering from a faltering solo career, and a faltering ability to rid himself of the substance abuse on which he was now beginning to depend upon. Unfazed by the reaction to his *Breakin' Up Is Easy* album, he had returned to the studios during late 1974 to commence work on what he hoped would be his next album release. During September of that year, while his former partner was also starting work on his own second solo project, James had returned to the familiar surroundings of the Elektra Records studios to commit to tape a lovely new song that Robb Royer had recently written. What made this particular session so notable was that assisting James in the recording of the composition was Mike Botts on drums, Larry Knechtel on piano and synthesizer and, taking a break from his own recordings, David Gates on bass duties. Putting any ill feelings aside, harbored from the initial breakup, Bread was back together again in the studio for the first time in almost sixteen months, and even more notable was the fact that Robb Royer was also in evidence at some of the sessions.

"By then David and I were talking again," remembers Robb. "I showed him 'That's All I Need' and he really loved it, and he made a nice little change in it. I wasn't there when they cut it, but I was there with David for the three of us to work it up, like we cut an old Bread song."

It appears unlikely that there was ever any serious thought given to reuniting the band on a permanent basis, but the results from this particular session certainly showed that, given the right material, the four essential components of Bread still gelled as only they could. The dexterous piano flourishes and swirling synthesizer strings of Larry Knechtel essentially hold the ballad together as he weaves a delicate pattern on which David and Mike underpin the rhythm track, and James adds his rich resonating tone and a searing, yet brief, guitar break. Sadly, the foursome chose not to continue the collaboration further, and David departed to resume his own career. As did Mike and Larry, although three months later James called again on both of them for another composition on which he was working, this time bringing in established studio guitarist Dean Parks as the fourth musician. This session resulted in "Blood From A Stone," another new work from James and Robb that was distinctly reminiscent of some of their earlier work together. Before the year was out, James had added two further completed tracks to his upcoming project, both composed alone and taped back in his home town of Memphis at the Audio Dimensions recording studios, a complex owned by producer Ted Sturges. James had returned to his home state to visit his family, and while there he had taken the opportunity to record some new material in one of the local studios. Ted Sturges himself acted as engineer on these new recordings and the first song cut was a simple, lonely-sounding piece featuring just voice and acoustic guitar, "How Do You Say Goodbye," while the second featured a very spiritual arrangement and went by the title of "I Repent."

"He had a very spiritual side to him," recalls Carol Ann Jones, James's sister. "If you listen to many of his songs you will see how spiritual they are. 'Love To Light The Way,' 'I Repent.' He was a poet and a minstrel. He just had a song in his heart..."

"I Repent" was also notable for featuring the Memphis Horns, the legendary brass section featuring Wayne Jackson and Andrew Love that had so memorably added their collective talents to previous recordings by Elvis Presley, Al Green, Otis Redding, and Aretha Franklin. However, music wasn't the only thing on James's mind at this particular time. A number of months before, during this lengthy spell back home in Tennessee, he had been introduced to a 19-year-old southern belle by the name of Mary Katherine Collins, whose father was a devoted follower of Bread and who had become acquainted with Neva, James's mother. Charles "Dick" Collins let it be known that he was keen to aid James's wavering career and, with Neva's encouragement and concern for her son's health, he offered to assist in rejuvenating the sudden downturn in fortune. In turn his daughter, the young Mary Katherine, was also introduced to the family and it was then, during James's homecoming visit, that he and Kathy, as she was known, were first introduced. Following a relatively short period of dating the relationship became more serious and love blossomed, culminating in their marriage on December 14th, 1974, at the Highland United Methodist Church in midtown Memphis. Shortly afterwards, with his new wife in tow, James once more packed his bags and headed west, California bound, to resume his career, following the same route taken twelve years previously.

Kathy: "From the very beginning we had been looking for a home together in Tennessee, but it had always been a plan to have a house in both places…"

"Blood From A Stone" was the first track completed upon his return to the Los Angeles recording studios, with James, Larry, and Robb all sharing the production duties. Shortly afterwards, he cut a (still unreleased) version of the Larry Knechtel composition "Aphrodisia," along with a heavy rock number entitled "Step Outta Line," the latter co-written with Robb that inexplicably remained unreleased for over 30 years.

Robb: "Jimmy was battling addiction during this period even though, in my opinion, it was when he did some of his best work. 'Step Outta Line' was written from me to him, telling him to go ahead, be spectacular, you can do it and for God's sake don't kill yourself..."

This was followed by "My Love Is Mine," again featuring Mike Botts on drums, but this time accompanied by Mike's old friend and music partner Joe La-Manno, who supplied some impressive bass playing on the introduction. Then, in February 1975, the bulk of the remaining sessions were completed at Sunset Sound Recorders, situated on the corner of Sunset Boulevard and Cahuenga. With Jim Gordon sitting in on drums, Dave Budameyer on bass, Dean Parks on guitar, and David Paich on piano, the line-up committed "Hanalei," "Treat Her Right," "Goin' Back To Tennessee," and "Laura Lee" to tape. Keyboard virtuoso David Paich, along with his father Marty, took production and arrangement responsibilities on these particular tracks, the first time James had used the talents of an external producer, David Gates aside, for many years.

"On the second album Jimmy decided they should go with hotter guys, and I'd write a couple of songs for it, but I wouldn't try to produce it," says Robb of the new studio arrangement, "and that's when David Paich came in."

Paich would later go on to achieve phenomenal success as one of the founding members of the rock band Toto, but back in the mid-'70s he was gaining major kudos for his studio talents, both behind and in front of the mixing desk.

"David Paich would come over to our house. He was pretty good friends with Jimmy. He wrote 'Laura Lee,'" says Kathy, picking up the story. "'Goin' Back To Tennessee' was written for me about two weeks after we married and 'Hanalei' was where we honeymooned."

While the down-south feel of "Goin' Back To Tennessee" was clearly inspired by his new wife and his recent visit back home, it was the remaining three tracks from these February sessions that were to define the cleaner, slicker production that was to shape the final album. "Laura Lee," as composed by Paich, was an outstanding addition to James's repertoire, and while such a delicate ballad is often deemed a 'mood' piece, predominantly placed mid- or end-sequence to gain the most effect in any final line-up, this particular offering was believed strong enough to be the proposed album's opener. "Hanalei" was another pleasing number, written alongside Robb, but it was "Treat Her Right" that was to have the most emphasis placed upon it. This was a rocking, upbeat song with some wonderful rhythm guitar riffs from James that also included horn player Jim Horn and session vocalist Carol Carmichael, adding their considerable talents to the mix. A full-bodied production, with Horn and Carmichael well to the fore, it was with this track, also composed by Paich, upon which the success of the album was to hinge. Without doubt the completed line-up was notably superior to James's debut album, certainly on a commercial level, and the overall sound and mix was far richer than the earlier work. Although one wonders if a little of James's own personality was lost in Paich's polished production. It was not so instantly a "Griffin album" in comparison to his own productions with Bread, and of those on the *Breakin' Up Is*

Easy album. Nevertheless, with faith in the product, Polydor Records chose to release "Treat Her Right" as a single (Polydor 14282), paired off with "How Do You Say Goodbye" on the reverse... only to see it instantly disappear. Despite all of the wonderful sounds that emitted from the three minutes of professionally produced vinyl, it was an unceremonious commercial disaster, failing to chart at all, and one that would have far reaching effects.

Dismayed at the lack of success, Polydor chose to scrap plans for releasing the album, regardless of quality, and the remaining cuts were shelved in the vaults. No second single, no promotion... and James left pondering his career prospects. Plans to go out with his own band, "Griffin," reportedly featuring Larry Knechtel and bassist Kerry Chater, were abandoned, and he opted to part company with manager Al Schlesinger who had, in one capacity or another, overseen the career of Bread since its inception. Instead, against the advice of others, and listening to the concerns of his mother, he installed his new father-in-law, Dick Collins, to administer the managerial side of his work, under the banner of Griffin Enterprises, a partnership company set up between James and his new wife Kathy. With little or no experience in entertainment management to date, Collins undertook the role with gusto, advising and encouraging as he saw appropriate.

By contrast, Mike Botts was still on a roll during this period. His position with Linda Ronstadt's touring band was reaching new heights as the genteel country rock vocalist, prone to bouts of rock'n'roll, consolidated her growing reputation with sell-out tours and steadily increasing record sales. Early 1976 saw the band base themselves in the Sound Factory recording studios in L.A., working on what would become her seventh studio release, *Hasten Down The Wind*, and her third consecutive album to sell in excess of one million copies. Also out of these sessions came the Top 20 hit "That'll Be The Day," a one-take cover of the Buddy Holly classic.

Mike: "As I recall, Linda was the one who was saying she wanted to do it the way Buddy Holly would have done it. It was one take, because the one thing I do remember about that session was that I was amazed that Andrew (Gold) and Kenny (Edwards) were going to be in the vocal iso-booth and not only sing the backgrounds but play their instruments at the same time, and I thought this is how Buddy Holly had to do it. When we did the first take we went in and listened to it, and none of us could believe it. That was a (big) hit for her."

Mike's partnership with Ronstadt, and also with that of her arranger, songwriter, and guitarist Andrew Gold, was to stand him in good stead throughout the industry, widening his acceptance as an acknowledged session and touring player. Gold's own eponymous 1975 debut solo release also benefited from the talents of Botts, as did his later 1977 smash hit "Lonely Boy," and their partnership was to continue throughout their intertwining careers. However, while Mike was ensconced in the studios with Linda, rebuilding his career, another opportunity was slowly building momentum...

Likewise, although the heyday for the session musician had passed, in addition to his ongoing work with David, Larry Knechtel was also keeping himself fairly busy. A more sedate, private family lifestyle up in Washington State kept his feet firmly on the ground, but his love of the music couldn't keep him away from the studios for any extended period of time, as 1976 appearances on releases by Joan Baez, Jerry Garcia, Stephen Bishop, and Neil Diamond would testify. Two years previously, he had also come into contact with the Texas-born singer-songwriter Patti Dahlstrom, when he stepped in to offer his support on sessions for her third album, *Your Place Or Mine*, and over the subsequent years a strong working bond developed between the two.

She later recalled: "I actually began working with Larry in 1974. He came into my life when I was deeply heartbroken, as I had lost a great love and my piano player. He stepped in with compassion and patience and we quickly became good friends. He played piano and bass on *Your Place Or Mine*, as well as producing, arranging, playing piano, harmonica, bass, and supplying background vocals with me on my next album, *Livin' It Thru*. On that one, which came out in 1976, we had a song we wrote together called 'Changing Minds.' Larry titled both of these albums. Besides being stunningly talented, Larry was a deep person, someone who saw things much more comprehensively than most people. He had a profound philosophical attitude towards life. He loved music, and his family was his foundation. I was blessed to have him play on my albums and even more blessed to call him my friend…"[26]

Larry's contribution to Dahlstrom's two releases remain distinctive throughout, and "Changing Minds" featured some of his most intricate playing to date, void of any hindrance that often came when playing along to someone else's composition. His beautiful, yet complex, accompaniment to Dahlstrom's husky melody is a startling reminder of how restricted he could be within the confined structures of a band. However, as his occasional rhythm partner, Mike Botts, was also to find, the studio session work was still in another league to the big bucks that could be found from headlining sales and touring, and just around the corner was a further, unexpected event, awaiting to be awakened from slumber.

Elektra Records, still in control of Bread's back catalog, were acutely aware that the band's records continued to bring in vast revenue for the label, especially in light of the huge success that the *Best Of Bread* release had achieved, and they were keen to see it continue. David too, was aware that the band still owed the company two or three albums under their initial contract agreement and despite his reservations, and efforts to develop a successful solo career, he agreed to discuss plans to reunite the group for a new studio album, and subsequent concert tour. He'd recently purchased a vast 3,000 acre ranch in Northern California, and initially had little desire to return to the treadmill, but as he was to later comment: "I said I would give it one more try, but with no guarantees. Money wasn't a factor, but I was perfectly willing to give it a try. But only once."[13]

James, too, had to be convinced that a reunion would work. He maintained some ill feeling towards the band following the initial breakup and the disappointing development of his solo career, and his manager and father-in-law Dick Collins had to persuade him to consider the prospect of reuniting. Yet, it clearly wasn't going to be all plain sailing, and certain obstacles had to be overcome before the proposed reunion could become a reality. Reportedly, early talk revolved around the trio of David, James, and Larry being the core of the reunion, and it was even muted at one stage that a session drummer be brought in to allow any lucrative income to be split three ways instead of four, but Elektra Records stood loyal to the original band, insisting that Mike be involved in the project.

Then there was the issue of James's health. By this stage, he was trying to wean himself away from the substance abuse he had endured during the previous twelve months. He was using prescribed methadone at the time, in order to reduce his craving for the harder elements he was prone to using, so his overall ability to give total input to the reunion was brought into question, and was a cause of concern for all involved.None more so than Al Schlesinger, who was still acting as the band's manager and lawyer during this period. Schlesinger had contacted Mike during initial talks, and had requested that he keep a keen eye on James, ensuring that he was kept away from alcohol and drugs. But, during the summer of 1976, while Mike was visiting his band mate in Memphis, initially planning some songwriting alongside James, a particularly concerning incident had taken place, where James had been found slumped unconscious in the bathroom, various drug paraphernalia alongside, and it had quickly become apparent to Mike that James was still out of control, regardless of all his promises and intentions.

Nevertheless, despite these unsettling distractions, the quartet was still able to sustain a period of songwriting activity, with James managing to fly between the new family home in Memphis, which he shared with Kathy, now expecting their first child, and their house on Mulholland Drive in Los Angeles, where the whole band would often write and rehearse. James and Robb Royer would also often meet there to pool their resources and compose a number of new songs for inclusion, although James opted to sell the house shortly afterwards to Don Henley of The Eagles, choosing to make Memphis his permanent base. In occasional moments of peace, in between the general mayhem of life in Los Angeles, Larry's farm up in Washington, complete with its own recording studio, was also used as a home away from home for the foursome. Using the time between Mike's commitments to Ronstadt, they eventually all came together at the Elektra Sound studios during the late summer-fall of '76 to lay down a number of new tracks. In addition, the various compositions that Robb and James had conceived for the *Cosmo & Robetta* musical, which were now gathering dust on the shelf, were revisited and at James's suggestion, the striking "Fly Away" was proposed for inclusion on the new album.

With Bruce Morgan sitting alongside as engineer, David acting as producer, and James once again submitting to the role of "associate producer," the quartet taped ten new songs, six of which were written by David, three by the Griffin-Royer partnership, and one by the frustratingly underused combination of David and James. As well as the featured four band members, a number of additional sidemen were also brought into the sessions, including guitarist Dean Parks, from David's touring band. Dean was rapidly developing into one of the leading session players from the new breed of studio performers, and his credits to date had not only included the first three Steely Dan albums, but also work with Joan Baez, Rita Coolidge, Glen Campbell, Stevie Wonder, and Randy Edelman. Performing alongside Dean for the new Bread album were saxophonist Tom Scott and synthesizer player Michael Boddicker. Boddicker himself was also a working colleague of Robb Royer, and the two had recently put a new band together they had named Baby Grand. Although Robb was not actually a performing member, he was instrumental in getting the full line-up of Boddicker, drummer Pat Mostelato, and bass player Eric Nelson together. Following a label showcase, with both Warners and Portrait showing interest, they had added guitarist and vocalist Chuck Cochran to the mix, but, despite the immense talent on display, Boddicker and Cochran clashed on personal levels and the band went no further.

It was also during this period that James reacquainted himself with the talents of the Liverpool-born guitarist for The Hollies, Terry Sylvester, who was recording a solo album at the famous Abbey Road Studios in London. James contributed a familiar harmony vocal to the Paul Williams and Roger Nichols ballad "Travelin' Boy," which ultimately appeared on the U.K. version of the album, issued as *I Believe*, that same year. While not a particularly memorable song, James's distinctive high harmony adds a certain depth to the track that was noticeably absent when the album was later issued in America, with the song remixed, polished, and James's contributions removed. He was also to offer vocal support during 1976 on the debut album from Mike Finnigan, another renowned studio keyboard player who had previously gained much praise for his work on Jimi Hendrix's *Electric Ladyland* album, before going on to aid both Joe Cocker and CSN. Finnigan would reappear in the Bread story at a later date.

While the actual recording sessions for the upcoming Bread reunion had been ongoing, the quartet had refrained from making any official announcements to the press regarding their comeback, preferring to concentrate and to complete the intended album to their satisfaction before going public. However, speculation among the music media had begun early on during the process and before long it was certainly a case of not "if," but "when," they would step back under the spotlights. Finally, after a long six-month haul, with the tracks now completed, the official announcement was made to the world media, with a scheduled preview single due to pave the way on December 3rd. As reported in the U.K. press at the time:

> *"After much speculation throughout the whole of this year, it is now officially confirmed that Bread have reformed with their original line-up. A spokesman said this week that there are no immediate plans for live dates, because the various members of the group are still fulfilling outstanding solo commitments. However, negotiations are already in hand for Bread to headline a series of British and European concert dates in the spring. Meanwhile, Elektra are mounting an extensive advertising campaign in connection with the band's comeback release."*
> *—Melody Maker*

Clearly, this was not the *original* line-up, regardless of what the press releases would have us believe, as Robb Royer was nowhere in sight. But it *was* the four-piece band that had achieved the most success during the band's initial chart foray, and thus, it was assumed, would reclaim the mantle of popularity they had previously worn during the height of their run.

Following the completion of the revitalized sessions with Bread, Mike had once more returned to his committed schedules as a part of Linda Ronstadt's band, undertaking a November tour of the U.K. and Europe, even flying across the Atlantic on the supersonic airliner Concorde, such was Linda's new found "rock royalty" status. Four successful shows were played in the U.K. before the band headed out to the wider pastures of Europe. However, due to her popularity, two further U.K. dates were added before the band headed home.

"I had toured the U.K. with Bread," Mike was to recall. "So I knew what to expect. However, it was all new to Linda and I think she was overwhelmed at the positive reception she got from her European fans."[24]

They arrived back in the United States in time for the press announcements regarding the Bread reunion, and Mike's partner Michele flew out to New York soon afterwards to meet up with him there, in order to help celebrate his 32nd birthday. In her luggage she carried the rough cuts of the new Bread album. "Peter Asher (Ronstadt's producer) flew me out to New York, where they were throwing a big birthday party for Michael at this local club, and I brought the cassette tapes of the album roughs with me," she remembers. "There was no artwork or anything, it was a 'rough,' and I remember putting it on and thinking 'Oh my God! This is incredible!'"

Unfortunately, despite Mike's intentions during his summer songwriting sojourn with James in Memphis, there were no composing contributions of his included, nor those of Larry, on the final release, and the first single from the project was, as perhaps to be expected, a new David Gates ballad titled "Lost Without Your Love."

"I wrote that one night on the piano," said David in conversation with Barry Alfonso. "During the entire Bread era, James and Robb wrote so many songs on the piano that, to balance out the albums, I wrote almost exclusively on the guitar. When Bread broke up, I suddenly found I could write songs on the piano again, which is a totally different experience for me. 'Lost Without Your Love' came out of that."[14]

Coupled with a new Gates and Griffin composition, "Change Of Heart," the single received heavy promotion from Elektra, keen to see their faith in the band justified. With the media focus understandably on the lead side, "Lost Without Your Love" climbed into the Top 10 with ease, re-establishing the band with style. This was David Gates back at his very best, sitting comfortably alongside his previous gold records and hits, and showing that he had lost none of his balladeering abilities, despite the switch to piano. Even the up-tempo guitar bridge that breaks away from the familiar sway of emotion only adds to the impact of the song. Radio play for the release was also good, and the band further highlighted their comeback with an appearance on the popular *Captain & Tennille* TV variety show, performing the single. Not surprisingly, a huge amount of publicity was generated surrounding the reunion, with two or three significant radio broadcasts being devoted entirely to the history of the band and their music. At least one of these, the popular ABC-Watermark syndicated broadcast of Robert W. Morgan's *Special Of The Week*, even appeared as a promotional vinyl release much to the delight of the Bread audiophile.

1977 had the promise of a fresh start for Bread: a Top 10 hit on the *Billboard* charts and Top 30 placing in the U.K., a brand new album ready to hit the shelves, and a potentially successful tour lined up. Despite the initial concerns of all involved, particularly David, at the start of the reunion project, it looked as if the band might just pull it off, and maintain the run of success they had achieved at the start of the decade. The new album, also labeled *Lost Without Your Love*, arrived in the stores during January, immediately making an impact during the first few weeks, swiftly climbing into the Top 30 album listings. But, somewhat surprisingly, there it stalled, reaching no higher than #26. And why was that? The quality of the featured work was undeniable, although a number of reviews did noticeably make reference to the lack of heart that ran through the grooves. But 1977 was the year that adult-oriented rock – AOR if you will – was taken to new levels of expectancy. It was the year that produced two of the biggest selling albums ever, and *Lost Without Your Love* came nowhere near the benchmark that these albums were now setting. The Eagles' *Hotel California* ruled the roost for eight of the opening weeks of the year, followed shortly afterwards by the definitive example of the genre, *Rumours* by Fleetwood Mac, which remained virtually untouchable for over half of the entire year. Bread, who had been right at the forefront of AOR, or soft rock as it was initially referred to just six years earlier, were left trailing in the slipstreams of the Lear jets that now ferried these mega-bands across the country. Maybe if David and James had seen the changes coming, had tried a different approach to the new album as the Eagles had done before, moving on from their country rock roots to a more rock-based approach with the arrival of rock-rebel Joe Walsh in their midst, or as Fleetwood Mac had done once the *tour de force* of the Buckingham-Nicks axis arrived on their doorstep, then Bread could have moved with the times. But, sadly, it wasn't to be. They stuck with their own tried and tested formula of success, wavering very little from the well-trodden path, and while the new album certainly contained moments of beauty and a number of impressive works, it lacked a vibrancy. It lacked the heart that the reviews had picked up on. It was... safe.

The opening number, David Gates' "Hooked On You," the second single to be released (peaking at a lowly #60), was initially written with James's vocals in mind, but the songwriter had ultimately taken the lead himself, delivering a catchy little number, but one that was sadly overladen with strings, and giving Mike little opportunity to drive the band into an early groove. This was followed by James and Robb's "She's The Only One," one of the true successes on the release, albeit one that slides into the country rock feel that The Eagles had just vacated. Dean Parks' effective lead guitar effortlessly brings home the correct counterbalance between an underused accompaniment and overproduction, and his subtle fretwork justifies the faith the band had in bringing him into the sessions. But then, after "Lost Without Your Love" makes its appearance, the remainder of the album slips between the disparaging variables of highlights (Griffin and Royer's impressive and full-on production of "Fly Away," and David's unquestionably silky-smooth "The Chosen One") and lowlights (the "Aubrey"-esque emptiness of "Belonging" and the half-hearted attempt at a rock number with "Lay Your Money Down"). All told, there were no tracks, other than the hit single, that really reeked of "Top 10" status, and while some of the remaining fillers, such as "Today's The First Day" and "Hold Tight," were acceptable by the standards of many bands of the era, one was left feeling a sense of regret that there was no "Dream Lady," "Been Too Long On The Road," or "Fancy Dancer" to lift up the proceedings. The songwriting strengths of Gates, Griffin, and Royer, were sadly not gelling in sufficient quantities this time around, and, despite the initial promise of the reunion, the band knew it.

Gates: "*Lost* was a pretty tentative album. We tried not to step on each other's toes, but after we were halfway through it, I got the feeling that we were going to stagger to the finish line with this one."[14]

The album was presented in another lavish gatefold sleeve, complete with a carved wooden frame pictured on the front cover, designed especially for the project, while the inner spread, complete with lyrics, showed the band photographed by Frank Bez walking up a steep hill, surrounded by lush green pastures. Without intention, this shot was an unforgiving symbol of the uphill struggle that both band, and label, had to face with the album.

Even so, despite the difficulties that faced them, the band agreed to tour in order to promote the release. Following Mike's concluding duties with the Ronstadt band, including an appearance at President Carter's Inaugural Concert, March 1977, saw Bread kick off the first leg of the *Lost Without Your Love* tour in Kansas, performing at the 14,000-seat Ahearn Field House on the State University campus, incorporating some of the newer songs such as "Lay Your Money Down," "She's The Only One," "Hold Tight," and "The Chosen One" into the set. However, it was immediately noticeable to those in attendance how James's role in the performing unit was under scrutiny from his partners and management. For the first time, he stepped down in his role of sharing lead guitar duties, and Dean Parks accompanied the band for the duration of the tour, bringing a notable stage presence to the performances. While Parks' wild guitar solos certainly added to a number of the more upbeat numbers, his presence also led to James being reduced to banging the tambourine, or simply supplying backing vocals on a number of the songs when his rhythm or acoustic guitar wasn't required.

The opening show in Kansas was followed by a series of successful performances over the next few weeks, including slots at the Anaheim Center in Los Angeles and the Honolulu International Center in Hawaii. Then, after taking a brief mid-tour break, the band resumed their schedule for the extensive second leg of the tour, although not before David had taped a solo guest appearance for a forthcoming Canadian TV Special with the South African-born vocalist Roger Whittaker (airing during the following December). Both Mike and James had also scored moments of significant solo satisfaction during the intervening weeks in the schedule.

April of 1977 saw Mike's drumming patterns and arrangements play a significant part behind the success of Andrew Gold's Top 10 smash hit "Lonely Boy." Having befriended Gold during the lengthy tours with Linda Ronstadt, a close bond had developed between drummer and the multi-instrumentalist, singer, and producer, the result of which, as Gold himself freely said, was that Mike was extremely influential in the development of this particular best-selling track. "In the rehearsals (Mike) was organizing the whole drum part which was a very big part of it, especially in how it starts. He was very instrumental in the arrangement. He and Waddy (Wachtel) and Kenny (Edwards) were interested in keeping the middle section rock and rolling, as opposed to how I wrote it, soft ballad-like in the middle. We kept the music, but made it rock."[23]

Certainly, much of the pleasure on listening to the finished product hinges upon the timescale and rhythms laid down by Mike, and one can feel the passion in his playing. With it peaking at #7 in the U.S., and just missing out on a Top 10 placing in the U.K., the song would always receive standing ovations whenever the duo performed it, often as Linda Ronstadt's opening act.

At the same time, James was also to be seen diversifying his talents, moving away from his familiar position in Bread, and undertaking a role that gave the American public the opportunity of seeing an alternative side to him on their television screens. *They Said It With Music: Yankee Doodle To Ragtime* was a two-hour salute to America and its musical heritage, taped during the fall of the previous year while the Bread reunion was still in its infancy. Airing on the CBS network during the July 4th, 1977, celebrations, the show starred a host of well-known performers, including Tony Randall, Bernadette Peters, Jason Robards, and Jean Stapleton among others, and featured a vast collection of songs that, in the words of the show's creator, Goddard Lieberson, "have stirred the nation. Music that is intertwined with significant moments in the American experience."

Among his various appearances throughout the show, James portrayed the role of a young confederate soldier back in the American Civil War, a role that came courtesy of the show's musical director and researcher, Fred Karlin, James's 1971 Academy Award-winning partner. With a combination of live action, vintage photography, animation, and original historic film, the varying segments covered all areas of American musical exploration. However, as Karlin himself was keen to point out, this wasn't just a chronological history of America, but "a study of the relationship between American popular music and the social elements of the times. What it shows you are attitudes toward a specific topic." James's contributions were certainly some of the more impressive musical highlights, and none more so than with the beautiful mid-19th century ballad "Lorena," a brief solo number filmed directly to camera, while his vocals were also prominent on several other featured songs: the stirring "Bonnie Blue Flag (Hoorah!)," "The Preacher And The Slave," and "Get Off The Track." He also contributed background vocals to "My Old Kentucky Home," the official Kentucky State song.

"The first thing that comes to mind was the costume Jimmy wore and the way he looked at the time," his former wife Kathy recalls. "When singing the Civil War tunes he wore an authentic Confederate soldier's uniform. His hair was longish, and he had a scruffy-looking beard. A number of the songs were very touching, especially 'Lorena,' as he sat alone in his uniform. He made friends with Jean Stapleton, and was very fond of her. However, the male lead, Tony Randall, insisted on a non-smoking set, and during that time people smoked everywhere, so that was considered to be very overbearing. Jimmy would come home from working and complain about that guy, because he was so rigid!"

Despite the credit his appearance on the show was to bring, albeit below those of the headliners, by the time the show had aired, James's attentions had returned to his revitalized commitments with Bread, and that of the ongoing tour. And yet, the personal issues that he was now carrying around, most notably with his recurring use of drugs, were starting to weigh both him and the band down, and the inclusion of Dean as principal guitarist was also proving a cause of concern for him as an individual, leading to beliefs that certain members of the touring party were colluding against him; reducing his role within the set-up. And worse was to follow.

Dallas, 1977 (courtesy of Bill Anthony)

Still under prescribed methadone to reduce his debilitating needs, at one point towards the end of the second stage of the tour, he vanished one night from his hotel suite, simply leaving a note behind that read, "Gone back to Memphis. Out of methadone." To some members of the band this was deemed unacceptable, a breach of contract. You simply cannot walk out mid-way through a tour with bookings still outstanding, and they demanded action be taken against him. But Al Schlesinger, along for much of the tour himself, reportedly made light of the potentially volatile situation, reassuring them that this was a one-off occurrence, and despite James's absence they should continue with the tour, fulfilling their obligations to the promoters, and rework the set list to cover for their errant partner. Clearly Dean Parks was already playing all the required lead guitar roles, and David simply handled all the vocals for the shows that James was missing, reworking the song selection as appropriate. But the harmony within the band was now rapidly unraveling.

"Jimmy just disappeared one night," recalls Kathy. "They called me. I would often go out on tour with them, but Jamey was a baby so I would try to stay home a couple of times, then go back and meet them. This particular event he just left, and nobody knew where he was, and the next morning he showed up at home. But we got him right back out there…"

Traveling across the country in a series of luxury tour buses, with James now back on board as if nothing had happened, the band was also accompanied for at least two of the shows by a camera crew, including one performance in David's home city of Tulsa on May 9th, where they had singer Stephen Bishop added as support act. Six thousand fellow Tulsans came to see the concert that night at the city's Assembly Center Arena, hearing a mixture of both old and new songs. Although local reviews noted that David appeared nervous at times, forgetting the words to at least two of the tunes he had written, clearly the Oklahoman population maintained an affection for the "local boy done good," and he was subsequently afforded the "key to the city" during a county commission meeting the previous afternoon, when an official "David Gates and Bread" day was also declared.

Captured on celluloid for some of the performance, along with the sound-check and an "access all areas" pass behind-the-scenes, the accompanying film crew compiled footage for a 30-minute Elektra promotional film to be titled *Bread Is Back*. The band is shown performing "Fancy Dancer," "Baby I'm-A Want You," "Guitar Man," "Look What You've Done," "Lost Without Your Love," and "Mother Freedom" before a rapturous audience, with the increased instrumentation notably benefiting some numbers, particularly with "Fancy Dancer" where the heavy twin rhythm guitars of David and James lay down a driving pattern for Dean's impressive fretwork, while Mike keeps solid time from behind his kit. Larry, meanwhile, stands slightly behind the leading line, solidly supplying the underlying bass. Nevertheless, it also makes for uncomfortable viewing at times, seeing a newly-permed James giving his all, striking various "rock" poses, against the mellower sight of his sequined-jacketed partner, grinning broadly, strumming his favored Telecaster as he delivers his high-pitched vocals to a screaming audience. One can almost sense something *not quite right*, and despite the off-stage relaxed atmosphere at times, with Mike laughing and fooling for both camera and teenage fans from the rear seat of the tour bus, one gets the feeling of a band ultimately delivering their last hurrah.

It was at this stage, during the second leg of the tour, that they also made an appearance on the NBC-produced *Midnight Special* television show, airing on 3rd June. With a line-up that still included Dean Parks, the expanded five-piece band hosted the show, and introduced guests England Dan & John Ford Coley, Valentine, Johnny Rivers (with a wonderful comic introduction from Mike and Larry), Eddie Rabbitt, and Mike's good friend Andrew Gold, while also performing five numbers before the live studio audience, representing the new album with scintillating versions of "Lay Your Money Down," "The Chosen One," "She's The Only One," and "Lost Without Your Love," along with a rendition of their debut hit "Make It With You." Using the stage set-up that they were currently using on the tour, complete with flora and palm fronds, the band's performance defied the odds that were working against them. They turned in a fine short set, with "She's The Only One," featuring James strumming on his acoustic guitar – with David and Larry stepping up from behind to offer vocal support – and "The Chosen One," being particular highlights. Regardless of internal friction, and the personal problems that now surrounded him, James's amazing vocal prowess was still intact, and that rich tone and professionalism on stage, from an audience viewpoint, was still one of the reasons why the band continued to draw an appreciative crowd. One simply cannot argue that despite the questionable studio quality of the rocking "Lay Your Money Down," when the band performed it live, James, reduced to his tambourine contribution, vocally nailed it.

However, the brief respite wasn't to last, and although the positive united front they had displayed before the television cameras and the film crew seemed genuine, when the third, and final leg of the *Lost Without Your Love* tour was announced, it was missing one vital factor: James Griffin.

Chapter Fifteen

That's All I Need

Mike Botts recalled that, "We tried to ignore it, but it eventually became too much for any of us to deal with,"[18] which ultimately summed up the feelings from within the band as to how they saw James's ever-increasing dependency on drugs. He had tried to quit, and they had tried to support him, but for some reason he just couldn't curb his errant ways. He was also tiring of David's revitalized attempts to control the band. After taking advice from his new management team, who were keen to see that he receive all due credit, the subsequent outcome of both health and business concerns was that ten days before the final leg of the reunion tour was due to take place, James called in, informing his band mates of his decision to pull out. He expected them to do the same. Without him in the line-up there was no Bread. He co-owned the brand name.

"Michael's analogy of this was always, 'it's my football, and I'm going home, and I'm takin' the ball and that means game over,'" recalls Michele Botts, with a sense of bemusement over the scenario. "But God knows what was going on with Jimmy and David. I'm sure there was a lot of jealousy. Jimmy also had people talking in his ear, saying 'you're better than them,' and he got a lot of coaching from people, and that's what fuelled it."

However, with a huge schedule already booked, and thousands of tickets already sold, the three remaining members of the group, David, Mike, and Larry, along with manager Al Schlesinger, chose to go against James's wishes and proceeded with the third leg, completing the U.S. tour as a four-piece, with Dean Parks retaining his lead guitar role, and performing a set that now featured two of David's "solo" numbers mixed in among the assortment of Bread songs. David's "Sunday Rider" now kicked off the shows, followed by "It Don't Matter To Me," "Been Too Long On The Road," "Make It With You," "Daughter," "Lorilee," "Diary," "Yours For Life," "Everything I Own," "Lay Your Money Down," "Baby I'm-A Want You," "Guitar Man," "Hold Tight," "Aubrey," "The Chosen One," "Long Tall Sally," "Lost Without Your Love," "Sweet Surrender," "Mother Freedom," and "If." Without James on the tour, one other change to the revised list was that Mike now got his opportunity to shine in the vocal spotlight when, still seated behind his drum kit, he provided the lead vocal to a version of the Little Richard rock'n'roll classic "Long Tall Sally," while also contributing backing vocals throughout the remainder of the set. Bread had nearly always acknowledged their rock'n'roll roots at some stage during their concert performances, but this was the first time that Mike had been given his opportunity, relieving David from the lead vocal duties, and proving that the drummer could also take his moment with cool ease. He had always been one for singing, both offstage and on the tour bus, but this was the first time the audiences were given the chance to see his previously restrained talents.

Alas, not everyone in attendance was pleased to see the band still playing without James in the line-up. Some fans were understandably annoyed that it was essentially no longer a Bread show, but more in line with a solo David Gates concert, despite it being predominantly made up of Bread songs and, potentially, promoted as such. It was by no means the fault of those playing onstage, they were simply fulfilling previously booked obligations, but to the paying customer, the true Bread fan, what they were getting was not a true Bread concert. At one particular moment during the set, the four touring members would gather around the microphone, offering up a four-part harmony on the country-influenced "Yours For Life," and despite their best intentions, and with Dean taking on additional responsibilities he clearly hadn't signed up for, to many fans the resulting sound just didn't gel as it should. The vital ingredient was absent. And James also recognized the fact. Clearly unhappy that his partners had continued with the tour, regardless of his own decision to quit, he still ultimately owned the rights to half of the band's name, and the familiar group logo that still adorned the many concert posters. The tickets, the billboards, the concert hoardings, none of these should have had the word "Bread" on them without him in the line-up. With the encouragement of those standing behind him, and with the assertive presence of Dick Collins pushing hard to give Griffin Enterprises rights and recognition, the decision was made to issue individual lawsuits against his former colleagues for breach of agreement. When the band had first been formed back in the winter of 1968, a mutual arrangement had been made between the founding members that it was to be an even partnership, and once Robb Royer had departed it was a straight-down-the-line 50/50 split between James and David. Mike and Larry had no say in the brand itself. It was a co-owned Griffin and Gates property, and David, Mike, and Larry were now deemed in collusion to represent "Bread" as a band without his consent. Night after night during the tour, after the band had finished each show, a representative from James's company was waiting in the wings to issue subpoenas against unlawful use of the band name, the name he co-owned.

"He and David had their differences," says James's sister Carol Ann, "but he had a lot of respect for the members and their talents and musicianship, but this caused a lot of hard feeling and heartache."

All of the members were served with papers, as well as Elektra Records, and upon receipt, Elektra froze all of the band's assets, future royalty payments, and even their individual pension funds, another area of dispute.

"It was based on some technicality or theory that he had," David was later to state in conversation with *Classic Rock* magazine. "He felt that *we* had left the group and therefore lost our rights to the pension fund. So the rest of us had to go to court to get our share. We had to pay all these attorney fees just to get our own money."

One person unaffected by the case was former associate Robb Royer. Upon his departure from the line-up back in 1971, he had an arbitration clause inserted into his agreement, thus avoiding him from being pulled into the mire that was now swallowing them. The remaining members of the group however, had no such foundation in their contracts, and now found themselves, legal papers thrust into their hands, without the hard-earned, guaranteed flow of income. They had little option but to unite, fight together, and continue touring to generate cashflow, but each show was costing them thousands of dollars in legal fees, and, while David had accumulated a sizeable portion of wealth due to his previous songwriting royalties, for both Larry and Mike it was an extremely tough period. And it would get worse.

Such was the nature of the ever-changing music industry that, during the late 1970s, the new wave of dance music, "disco," was very much the flavor of the day, and the bookings for a rock'n'roll studio musician were few and far between. If a band wasn't out on tour, or had no new material to record and sell, then requirements for an established session team were virtually nil. Computer programming had taken away much of the core business. What had been the order of the day for Larry earlier in the decade had now come full circle for his drumming partner.

"It virtually killed us," recalls Michele Botts of that period. "I think Michael was in a state of disbelief. Everybody had their own agendas and he was just caught up in the muck and mire. He was not a bitter person, but he was devastatingly disappointed."

In October, David made an offer to James's representatives to buy out his former partner's shares in Bread Enterprises for an undisclosed sum, but later that same month James responded by making a counter offer to David, suggesting he take $250,000 for his 50 percent of the shares, plus 2 percent on future Bread records, those without his participation. He also asked for a solo recording deal with Elektra, requesting a $75,000 advance per album, matching the previous payments Bread had received. Further affidavits were heard once the suit eventually reached the court, and all of the dissent back and forth ultimately brought about the resignation of band manager Al Schlesinger, once Griffin Enterprises also filed suit against him for misrepresentation. The case against Schlesinger claimed poor investment of real estate, dissuading of any audits of the Elektra books pertaining to the group's finances, and of contriving significant favor towards David when negotiating the percentage cuts for the reunion album. It was rapidly crumbling apart.

Nevertheless, through all of this negativity, there were still some positive signs to be found when, in November 1977, two brand new record releases appeared in the stores, both becoming significant hits, although due royalty payments again found themselves tied up in the Elektra accountancy files. One record was a successful worldwide single release, the other an album, initially issued solely in the U.K., but one that would go on to establish a whole new listening audience for the band, and give them their most successful overseas venture to date.

Despite the fact that the single had initially been conceived as a Bread release, the label on the new disc, when it appeared in the stores, ultimately featured the solitary name of David Gates, appearing under the Elektra caterpillar logo. Recorded the previous July, before the lawsuits were flying from every corner, this new recording had been initiated when the director and producer for an upcoming new movie, a big-screen adaption of the Neil Simon screenplay *The Goodbye Girl*, had contacted David asking him to contribute a song.

"I'd gotten a call from Herb Ross and Ray Stark, and they wanted a song in the film that was something similar to the style in which I write," David recalled in his interview with *NetMusic*. "I went in and looked at the picture and came back to the ranch. I started writing while I was out raking hay and driving my tractor around. Then I came rushing in at lunchtime and finished it off. I'd gotten some pretty good inspiration while I was out in the field."

Styled in typical Gates' ballad fashion, this latest offering was yet another credible notch in his ever-increasing folio, and another that demonstrated his now reliant use of the piano in his newer compositions. Accompanied by some scintillating guitar riffs from Dean Parks, and with Mike and Larry also contributing to the sound, this features one of David's more memorable choruses, with his vocals rising to new heights of maturity each time he hits the opening line: "So remember goodbye doesn't mean forever...." The film itself went on to receive a number of notable achievements, including five Academy Award nominations and five Golden Globes, while David's contribution was also a hit, giving him his highest ever "solo" chart position of #15 in America. Sales of the single were no doubt aided by two U.S. television performances of the song over the winter season, both on *American Bandstand*, while further guest spots on *The Mike Douglas Show* and *Dinah!* during early 1978 were also focused towards the soundtrack release.

By way of acknowledging the renewed interest in the band, as a result of the recent *Lost Without Your Love* tour and of David's current success, Warner Brothers in the U.K. then packaged together a new compilation featuring 20 of Bread's greatest and most successful recorded moments. Following on from the phenomenal U.K. success of the previous year's *20 Golden Greats* from The Beach Boys, issued on EMI, Warner took a similar route with their collection, *The Sound Of Bread*, concentrating on a British TV-advertised market. And it worked. With a byline of "Their 20 Finest Songs," and including hits and choice tracks from across all six Elektra albums, the record reached the very pinnacle of the British charts during a lengthy 46-week run in the Top 100 and while, naturally, it was heavily weighted in favor of David's hit recordings, it was pleasing to see such moments as James and Robb's "The Last Time" and James's solo composition "Just Like Yesterday" being given due credit. Indeed, such was the success of the release that it prompted the British Broadcasting Corporation to request that Bread come across to the U.K. to record an hour-long television special. Needless to say, it was a moot point as to whether there *was* still a 'Bread' at that point in time, but this sudden revived interest in the group from across the waters prompted the current touring band to schedule a number of concert dates in the country, as well as accepting the offer from the BBC. Unfortunately, that too was to generate further ill-feeling between the band and their recently isolated partner.

"The next I saw was an article in *Billboard* describing an upcoming tour in the U.K. by David Gates and Bread as well as another in Australia. David and I had formed a corporation, which gave us both ownership of the name. David disregarded this when he set the tour. I phoned him to let him know that I was available and willing to participate in the tour, but he refused my offer," James was to comment in later years.[18]

So with Dean still in the line-up, the band arranged to go ahead with the trip, without inviting James to participate. By rejecting his offer, and still clearly smarting over the lawsuit that had been instigated upon them during the U.S. tour, the dividing lines had now been drawn. With eleven dates booked at varying venues, including two nights at London's prestigious Royal Albert Hall, this was to be the band's first serious tour of the U.K., having previously cancelled at the height of their popularity, and, with the new compilation album still riding high in the charts, was seen as an ideal opportunity to revisit distant shores for the first time in over eight years. And while to some it appeared perfectly understandable to go ahead without James, especially in light of recent activities, to others, it appeared as betrayal. By including the band name in the advance promotional activity, using that distinctive logo, it implied that it was the very same line-up of Bread that had recorded all of the hits and albums. There were two main focal points fronting the complete band, both of them sharing equal rights to the band name, and by simply adding 'David Gates' in front altered nothing in the eyes of the Griffin camp. No Griffin, no Bread.

However, before the group headed out across the ocean, David, Mike, Larry, and Dean pulled together in the studio once again, where, along with a number of sidemen, they completed five new tracks for an album, compiled to capitalize on the recent success of the "Goodbye Girl" single. The plan was to fill out the album with a mixture of newer songs, along with half a dozen tracks taken from David's previous two solo outings.

"It will either be a David Gates album, or an album by David Gates and Bread," David was to say in a press interview. "We want to use the latter name, but there may be a legal roadblock. Everything was fine, but (then) James got some lawyers and said he didn't want to tour. I can't do anything without his permission, and he can't do anything without mine. It's a silly corporate game. The problem is, people change, and James has changed quite a bit. I don't know what he wants to do."

Referring to the ongoing state of the touring band, David continued: "I don't think James can stop us from touring without him, but he could tie up the concert receipts. We're going ahead and touring England, that's a whole different legal structure…"

Of the new songs that were prepared for the album, all were David Gates solo compositions, except "Took The Last Train" which also gave Larry Knechtel a co-composing credit. "I love that song," David recalled in conversation with Barry Alfonso. "I worked on it with Larry Knechtel up at his place in Washington. He wrote the bridge for me and helped me with the chorus. I didn't do it fast enough, though. If I had recorded it at a much faster tempo I think it would've been much more successful."

Dominated by Larry's Moog bass and the saxophone soloing of his long-term friend Jim Horn, this new composition is a pleasant enough MOR number, but it sadly offers up little resistance before falling headlong into the murky mid-tempo mire and lyrical naiveté of the French terminology that runs throughout, and, while it did manage a reasonable chart position of #30 when issued as a single the following June, it surely did so solely on the merits of the disco-dancing qualities that the rhythm suggests, more than the actual quality of the composition itself. Certainly, it came nowhere near the standards that David had previously set so highly, and it perhaps wasn't even the strongest of the new additions to the catalog, with the delightful "Overnight Sensation," featuring some crystal clear solos emitting from Parks' guitar, claiming that particular position. The third new number, "California Lady," a breezy rocker that still paled against Gates' upbeat numbers from the early Bread-era, would have been far more effective with a gritty James Griffin vocal, but, of course, that wasn't to be, while "Drifter," a gentle swaying affair, featuring the fiddle playing of the popular studio sideman David Lindley, comes across as too laid-back, suggesting nothing more than an album filler. By contrast, the final new song, "He Don't Know How To Love You," complete with Mike's thunderous fills, a chugging rhythm guitar, and some strong harmonies, is one of the few times where the quality of the new songs matches the older ones. And therein lies the problem. The six songs taken from *First* and *Never Let Her Go* were, potentially, the strongest cuts on both those albums and they simply dominated this new collection. Comparing the composition or production qualities of either "Clouds Suite," as it is re-labeled here, or "Ann" against, say, "Drifter" or "California Lady," the older cuts win out each time, which ultimately makes for a slightly uneven listening experience.

With the new product now being prepared for release, the four-piece line-up of "David Gates and Bread" headed over to the U.K. to record the BBC TV Special, although David did manage to squeeze in an appearance at the annual American

Music Awards just before their departure, where he presented Barry Manilow with the Best Male Artist award. Once over in London, the group turned in a polished fourteen-song performance for the cameras, based around the recent touring set list. Filmed in the distinctly antiseptic environment of a converted BBC theater, on a small stage, void of any warmth or atmosphere bar a pleasantly receptive audience, David eloquently navigated his way through the selected tracks, offering comments and wit with apparent ease. The band commenced with "Make It With You," then followed up with "Sunday Rider," "Hold Tight," "Everything I Own," a fun-filled "Yours For Life" (with Mike supplying tight harmonies), "Diary," "Lorilee," "Goodbye Girl," "Baby I'm-A Want You," "Guitar Man," "Long Tall Sally" (Mike's own moment to shine vocally), "Lost Without Your Love," and "Mother Freedom," before winding down with "If." Staying faithful to the original recordings, albeit with Dean Parks' now-wife Carol Carmichael assisting with the off-screen backing vocals, the only notable moment out of the ordinary came during "Goodbye Girl," when Mike's use of the distinctive new syn-drum sound, an electronic pitch-changing addition to his kit, caused raised eyebrows among the Bread purists.

Having completed the taping for the BBC, the band returned Stateside to oversee the final production duties on the new album while the show, simply titled *The Bread Special*, received its official airing on the BBC's secondary channel, BBC2, during the evening of Friday, March 10th, 1978. Once the completed album was pressed and released, appearing in the stores during June, the band then crossed the Atlantic again to fulfill their concert bookings although, needless to say, the Griffin Enterprises lawyers were not far behind, still intent on stopping the unauthorized use of the band name.

The *Goodbye Girl* album, officially issued by Elektra under the David Gates banner, was to achieve reasonable success in the U.K., going on to reach a credible #28 position, which, in comparison to the lowly #128 placing in the *Billboard* charts, was due in no small amount to the success of the sold-out U.K. tour, and the viewing audiences for the BBC TV Special. In a subtle variation of the marketing, the U.K. release had a transparent "David Gates of Bread" sticker placed on the front of the sleeve, styled in the same artistic font as the familiar Bread logo. Clearly the record label was missing no opportunity, aware of the modest acclaim the previous David Gates "solo" affairs had received back in the homeland.

The U.K. tour kicked off on June 2nd, 1978, in Birmingham, before winding up twelve days later at London's Hammersmith Odeon (with a brief mid-tour stopover in Amsterdam) although, without doubt, the highlight was a two-night residency at the famous Royal Albert Hall in central London, where the members delivered an impressive sold-out set in this unique yet intimidating venue. As before, however, there were still detractors in evidence, clearly dissatisfied with James's continued absence, complaining that this was not the "Bread" they had expected to see on stage. In fact, such was the furor surrounding the ongoing battles, and with the lawyers continuing to hand out writs at each venue, that part-way through the tour, following a temporary High Court injunction obtained in London, the announcement introducing the group at the start of each show was changed to "David Gates and his band."

Following the completion of the tour, now with both *The Sound Of Bread* and *Goodbye Girl* albums positioned comfortably in the U.K. charts, the band headed home to the United States, although had they found the time to visit the record stores during their brief sojourn across Britain, they would have also found one further new addition to the collection nestling within the 'Bread' category on the shelf.

1978 UK tour poster

During late 1977, Dick Collins, James's father-in-law and recently appointed manager, had negotiated a deal with Polydor Records (with whom James had signed back in 1974), to issue his unreleased second solo album in Europe. The arrangement sadly didn't include distribution across the United States, the market where James would have benefited most, and there was no promotional activity scheduled to link in anywhere with the release, but at least, for his many fans around the world, the album was now out there... somewhere. Unfortunately, while the few media reviews that picked up on the release were favorable – comparisons with Warren Zevon were mentioned – the record swiftly disappeared.

"He has a warm and gritty voice that smacks immediately of the Deep South. But Deep South white soul and not country so, at the very least, James Griffin's debut album has a modicum of class to it," wrote a clearly misinformed Chas De Whalley in the U.K.'s *Sounds* newspaper. James's second album (or third if the early 1960s release is included), comprising of nine songs initially recorded back in late '74-early '75, certainly deserved far more attention than it received, and, despite Polydor also choosing to add the obligatory "member of Bread" sticker to the front of the color sleeve, the lack of promotion on James's behalf certainly hindered any potential it had to offer. The subsequent success of the far less coherent *Goodbye Girl* album highlighted how important promotion was to raise public awareness, and, while David's release was also built upon the success of a hit single, and a promotional tour, track for track the Griffin album wins hands down. However, as if to add further insult to injury, the front sleeve featured a photograph of James during an earlier Bread performance, and in the lower left corner one can also make out the head of David Gates.

Live in Amsterdam (courtesy of Wim Boekhooven)

Upon returning to California, with the successful sound of a tumultuous U.K. reception still ringing in their ears, the touring band undertook a further few concert dates on their home soil, supported at one stage by British-born folk musician Ian Matthews. Interestingly, and despite all of the negative attention and costs that the name was bringing them, the final few shows of 1978 were still being promoted as "David Gates and Bread" or, as was the case for at least two concerts held in West Virginia and Texas during November and December that year, as "Bread" only. The tour posters may have been showing the solitary face of David alone, but the band name was still there for all to see. As 1978 drew to a close, and with the last contractual concert obligations fulfilled, along with David's final appearances on *The Mike Douglas Show* and *American Bandstand*, Bread, as a band, retired from the circuit. One of their last public appearances was actually a televised guest spot during the November two-part airing of the ABC-TV series *The Hardy Boys Mysteries*, where they undertook small cameo roles, miming to five of their own songs in front of the cameras, pivotal to the light-hearted storyline. David was even afforded a number of lines within the script, debuting his acting abilities, and he received the honor of being beaten up Hollywood-style, off-screen, with plenty of grunts and groans, while both Mike and Larry also joined in, dancing with a bevy of beautiful ladies during a party scene. But by that stage, having filmed the episode a number of months earlier, Bread were realistically no more. The few solitary live shows that David would play the following year would see only *his* name in lights, and while he, Mike, and Larry would continue to work together, the ongoing lawsuits made it financially impossible to continue under the Bread banner. It was time to call it a day, for the second time. James Griffin himself, over the coming few years, would end up spending an extraordinary amount of money as he pursued his rights on the band name. On a number of occasions he was actually advised against proceeding with the case by his lawyers, but such was the strong counsel of his management, often undertaken while he was too incoherent from drug abuse to handle the situation himself, that lawyers who doubted the case were simply dismissed and replaced, which, in turn, only added further to the increasing costs raining down on him. Furthermore, the effects on his former colleagues, as a result of James's inability to direct proceedings for himself, would cause considerable, and some may say irreparable damage as to how he was perceived. In many quarters he was now being viewed as the bad guy. The one who pulled it all apart. But was he? Or was he just the haunted face, unable to fight for himself, an unfortunate company figurehead for those unfairly pulling the strings?

On the other side, David, Mike, and Larry would also be pushed financially to defend themselves over supposed misrepresentation of the group name. Encouraged by the various attorneys to stay united, all against one, the members, some more so than others, would have to dig deep into their resources to survive. Mike would have to sell both his beloved Ferrari and his 35-foot sloop, and would even remortgage his house in order to meet the legal costs, also offering at one stage financial support to Larry who was finding the costs, amid the laws of Washington State which disallowed remortgaging farmland, even tougher. Larry was later to tell a friend that he even sold the title to his wife's car seven times in one year to keep the cashflow going. "It was horrible," concurs Michele Botts, of the impact all of this had on Mike and his fellow band members. "Because you have to consider that at one point these boys were bunking two to a room and he (Mike) always used to bunk with Jimmy. And now, so many years later, they've had all of these hit records, and now the only way they communicate is through a $400-an-hour lawyer. You go through anger, denial, and all of these stages."

Not that the offers of work dried up completely. Despite the advance in both studio and computerized technology, essentially devaluing the need for actual musicians, late 1978 and early 1979 saw Mike contribute once more to Andrew Gold's new studio album, *Whirlwind*, supplying backing vocals to the recordings as well as offering up his usual reliable percussive support. That period also saw Botts' performances on works by Olivia Newton-John, Eric Carmen, Michael Murphey, John Stewart, Dan Peek, and John-David Souther. Likewise, a rejuvenated Larry Knechtel also maintained his notable presence in the studios following the dissolution of Bread, with appearances on Art Garfunkel's *Fate For Breakfast* album and Hank Williams Jr's *Whiskey Bent And Hell Bound*, along with a reunion of sorts with former employer Duane Eddy on the original guitar man's self-titled 1979 release.

Additionally, there were two further projects that Larry undertook during this period, the first of which came about when he joined up with guitarist Chuck Cochran, bassist David Miner, and drummer Bo Siegel to form "Bandit," a new group that managed to spend some time together in the studio under the production guidance of none other than Robb Royer. However, nothing of note was to come out of the sessions, and when Larry's insistence that he collaborate from the far reaches of Washington became an issue for the line-up, the band folded, and he instead focused his attentions on a partnership with one of his close Washington neighbors, a talented young musician just starting to find his way in the industry. Todd Smallwood would go on to become one of America's most innovative producers, working alongside Jackson Browne, Mick Fleetwood, Gladys Knight, and Carlos Santana among others, but back in 1979 he was only too happy to learn from, and share time with, such a talented individual as Larry.

Todd recalled in 2010: "He was my mentor in many, many ways. I don't think I've had as much respect for another musician. My place was only about ten minutes from his, and he would come over and play on my recordings. There's never been a better Hammond organ player. But further than just his talent as a musician and a player was the man himself. What really got me was that I could have this friend who was not only a superstar talent guy, but he never wanted to be up there in the limelight. For him, I think, fame was just kind of a hassle. We were neighbors as well as musicians, we played volleyball... he was just a regular person."

Along with two of Todd's friends, drummer Bobby Kelly and Scott Anderson on bass, Todd and Larry put together another new band, one that they called Silver Lake, named after the large expanse of water that divided their two properties in upstate Washington. "The four of us ended up going on these misadventures, playing around the area. We started playing the clubs, doing cover versions, and we did some really cool stuff. The band got really good and we were the big sensation up in Bellingham, which doesn't take a lot!" he adds with a laugh. "I remember Larry came into the dressing room once and said he just fell through the floor! That's the kind of dives we were playing. We used to play at the Maple Falls Tavern and it would just be packed, because everyone from the Silver Lake area would come to see us. We were doing, maybe, half of my original material and it would start out as a dinner set, but by the end of the night it was a rowdy bar! We would just keep playing 'til they made us quit..."

The new four-piece even managed to lay down some tracks in Todd's home studio which to date remain unreleased, although before long the band simply dissolved when priorities elsewhere took over. Mike Botts also managed to play on some of Todd's later recordings, with both Larry and himself contributing to some of Smallwood's sessions for the small Encore label during 1985, although unfortunately the label collapsed before these sessions could be released.

However, with James currently to be found treading a seemingly directionless path, it was once again David who would step up to the mark to release the next solo album, although he too was finding that the shift in direction within the music industry was taking him a step further out of his usual comfort zone. The disco dance craze that had enveloped the industry during the late 1970s was, fortunately for some, now on the wane, and some of the higher profile disco acts, Donna Summer, KC & The Sunshine Band, Gloria Gaynor, and, most surprisingly, a rejuvenated Bee Gees, to name but a few, were all now spreading their wings and moving on to develop their music further, intent on leaving the strobe lights in their wake. Unfortunately, the music and rhythms they had left behind were still influencing a number of both lesser and far greater acts. Artists who, perhaps, should have known better were still feeling the misguided urge to follow the bouncing mirror ball, and the end of the glam decade was to see established rock and "pop" acts such as Chicago, The Beach Boys, ABBA, and Rod Stewart all release albums with a distinctive "dance flavor" running throughout. The 1979 solo album by David Gates was no exception.

Falling In Love Again, David's final release under his contract with Elektra Records, was issued at the tail end of this phase, during the festive period of 1979. But it still featured three songs which were undoubtedly enhanced with the disco feel, and while it was a bold move for the man who was renowned worldwide for his ballads, one feels that, just maybe, it was an ill-advised attempt at updating an established sound. Particularly in light of the fact that of the remaining seven cuts gracing the final product only one of them, the pleasantly acoustic "She Was So Young," had an arrangement that even sounded reminiscent of the Bread-era. Pictured on the front cover dressed in shiny 1970s satin, with a studio team of nine other musicians credited on the final sleeve notes, including the familiar surnames of Botts, Knechtel, Horn, Kunkel, and Lindley, the album changes direction needlessly throughout the song selection, with the skittish groove of the opening "Can I

Call You," blending uneasily into the heavily string-laden ballad "Where Does The Lovin' Go," one of the few true successes on the release. The album then winds through the instantly forgettable "20th Century Man," the delicacy of the aforementioned "She Was So Young," the lyrical crassness of "Silky" ("roller-skates and satin"), a confusing mix of rock and dance with "Starship Ride," the latin-feel of "Chingo," a watered down attempt at rock'n'roll with "Sweet Desire," before ending with the truly delightful "Rainbow Song," a track that ultimately highlighted the fact that, underneath this bewildering mixture, the artist had lost none of his melodious songwriting abilities. He'd just lost his way a little. Nevertheless, following the completion of the recording sessions, David appeared optimistic about the new collection and the diverse approach, especially once the first single lifted from the album, "Where Does The Lovin' Go," became his fastest breaking solo single to date.

"I'm really excited about this one," he went on to say. "I like it a lot. I'm stretching out more. I'm not really going outside my area, but there are some surprises on the album. You do get stereotyped in this business. When you step outside your area you sometimes meet resistance. I'm definitely more comfortable and consistent in my area. But when the outside things come to you, you have to grab them and work on them."

However, not everybody in the band was so instantly taken with the disco sound that hovered uneasily over the proceedings. Larry Knechtel, who would go on to work with both Diana Ross and Thelma Houston in the dance/R&B field, had this to say about the period when questioned during 2004 by Dick Stewart for *The Lance Monthly*:

"I played on some Motown disco shit in L.A. It was like working in de salt mines of yore. I guess I am a musical snob, but so be it. I like a lot more variety of music now, except I still hate disco and rap…"

Yet, even with David's best intentions in updating the sound, his efforts mostly fell on deaf ears, and the release saw a muted response, failing to chart either side of the Atlantic, and, though the single had shown promise, that too failed to connect with a listening audience. This was despite David appearing once again on the syndicated U.S. television show hosted by Dinah Shore, performing both "Where Does The Lovin' Go" and "Guitar Man," followed by a further visit across the ocean during May of 1980 to promote the release in the U.K. with a short 13-date tour. His loyal fan base in the decidedly smaller U.K. market had remained faithful to him since Bread had reconnected with their audience during the middle years of the previous decade, and his records had always achieved a certain amount of success over there, yet even this 1980 tour couldn't help the ailing sales of the new record. With Britain still gripped in the vice of the new wave and punk explosion, David's soft, mellower approach simply couldn't hit home with the middle-of-the-road audiences. Accompanied by both Mike and Larry as before, but with the added instrumental power of bass player David Miner and lead guitarist Hadley

Hockensmith, replacing Dean Parks, who by now was one of the most in-demand studio session players in America, the tour was fairly low-key in comparison to previous years, and a number of the venues were smaller. With support from fellow American songwriter Gerard Kenny, there were certainly no Carnegie or Royal Albert Halls filled to capacity.

While in the U.K., David continued to promote the new album, offering press interviews and appearing on both television (*The Lena Zavaroni Show*) and radio, even stepping in as a guest disc jockey on BBC radio's *Star Special* where, for ninety minutes he sat alone in the studio, playing some of his favorite songs from the previous decade, reminiscing into the microphone. It made for a fascinating listen, as music from Rod Stewart, Billy Joel, James Taylor, Cat Stevens, Led Zeppelin, Loudon Wainwright III, and Gordon Lightfoot emitted from the turntable across the airwaves. Unfortunately, despite a favorable response from his fans, the total sales for *Falling In Love Again* failed to match the enthusiasm David had for the project, although perhaps one significant reason was due to David's faltering relationship with Elektra Records, his recording home for over ten years. The label was moving away from its singer-songwriting base, and had already lost the services of Carly Simon and Harry Chapin before David began questioning its commitment to him.

"My relationship with Elektra was excellent until the last couple of years, during which I was kind of the forgotten kid," David would go on to say to journalist Rob Hoerburger. "I didn't want to do my last album there because I knew it wouldn't get much attention. But I went ahead and completed it to fulfill my obligation."

The 1980 schedule for the Elektra-Asylum label in America saw not only faithful Californian singer-songwriter releases from the likes of Jackson Browne, Warren Zevon, and Linda Ronstadt, but also a wider catalog of issues from Queen, The Cars, Tangerine Dream, and The Doors, and sadly David's work was simply lost in the midst, passed over in the promotion budget in favor of a number of higher profile artists. Since signing with Jac Holzman back in the early weeks of 1969, David had seen the label flourish and flounder, Jac step away from the forefront, and David Geffen blow in and blow out. Now it was his turn. With the subsequent failures of the two follow-up singles taken from the album, firstly "Can I Call You" b/w "Chingo," and then the title track, paired with "Sweet Desire," David's contract with the label expired. It was time to move on.

Chapter Sixteen

The Other Side Of Life

The new decade commenced in a slightly subdued mood for the former members of Bread. David Gates was to be found unsuccessfully plugging his recent album, before signing off from his contract with Elektra Records. Likewise, James Griffin was also at a crossroads, having alienated himself from his former colleagues, and having seen his two solo releases sink swiftly into obscurity. Mike Botts and Larry Knechtel, meanwhile, again pushed themselves back into the daily grind of finding paid session work in order to keep the money coming in. The pending court case would drag on for a further four years before any agreeable solution was found and, for a team of musicians to whom the music was their life and livelihood, it was an extremely difficult time.

Meanwhile, their former colleague, Robb Royer, still had a steady flow of work coming in, despite being out of the spotlight. He achieved a reasonable amount of success during this period, writing songs for films and various television companies, clearly developing the passion that had partly driven him out of the group in the first place. Certainly, his workload wasn't quite comparable with what he had achieved as a member of Bread, but away from the pressures of such a band, he was able to develop his own niche within the industry. In addition, his previous songwriting credits with James continued to bring him acknowledgment, perhaps most notably back in 1978 when singer Ray Charles covered a version of their composition "She Knows" for his *Love & Peace* album.

Nevertheless, with the ghost of Bread now having been finally laid to rest, except in the minds of the attorneys, diversifying careers began to develop. For Mike Botts, the paid session work was always going to be his personal breadwinner over this period of time. Peter Cetera, lead vocalist for Chicago, used his services on some of the tracks on his debut solo album, as did Albert Hammond, The Ozark Mountain Daredevils, and Australian singer-songwriter-producer John Farrar. In addition, he continued in his quest to develop his own songwriting and production skills, contributing to one new song, "Here Come The Runner," on the 1980 album by Waddy Wachtel's new band, Ronin.

"That period was really when Michael started writing," says Michele Botts today, "and tapping into the fact that he was really more than just a drummer. He was always playing music at home. He had his guitar, he had his keyboards. He was always writing lyrics. But when the band totally broke up he had a lot of time on his hands, and in our upstairs room he put together a recording studio..."

Unfortunately, despite the strong music he was now beginning to create, Mike had no surefire channels for getting it out to a wider audience at that time, and a number of recordings from that particular period would remain at home, waiting for a future opportunity. The previous year he had briefly diversified, appearing in front of the cameras for the first time away from his former band mates, taking on a small acting role in an episode of the popular television series *Wonder Woman.* Airing on February 16th, 1979, the episode, entitled "Amazon Hot Wax," saw Mike feature alongside fellow rock'n'roller Rick Springfield in a spoof music-biz story, appearing as the drummer in an imaginary band named AntiMatter. Handed the opportunity by director Ray Austin, who had worked with Mike and the band during the filming of *The Hardy Boys Mysteries*, it should be noted that this wasn't the type of role that one could base a career in the movies upon, but it was certainly a small step.

Then, in 1982, he accepted an offer to join the touring band of another former employee of the Linda Ronstadt band, vocalist Karla Bonoff. Building up a career as a burgeoning songwriter in her own right, Karla was now taking her music out on the road, supporting such major artists as Jackson Browne and, with Mike Botts now as a part of her band, a summer tour with James Taylor. Mike and Karla had actually worked together in the studio before, during the recording of her debut album back in 1977, and his playing was also later featured on the track "Somebody's Eyes" that Bonoff had contributed to the 1984 soundtrack for the popular teen-movie *Footloose*. Alongside Andrew Gold, Waddy Wachtel, and Kenny Edwards, Mike was now very much a part of the Ronstadt-Bonoff core of friends and musicians that played, recorded, and associated together.

It was also with Andrew Gold that he was to create his next project, the 1983 formation of a new band, initially labeled Houdini, but ultimately renamed Yanks once the approach from a lawyer representing Whodini, a popular R&B group, became known. Alongside a third member, singer and guitarist Alan Graham, this new trio briefly ventured into the recording studios, cutting a number of demo tracks under the guidance of former Beatles engineer Ken Scott, including "Marilyne," "Good Things Take Time," "Don't Make Me Love You," and "Guilty." But the venture was not to see public acclaim, and the tracks remained unreleased as the project fell apart after just three months. Andrew Gold recalls: "Alan decided suddenly he didn't want to be in a group. I think he felt that even though he was a real strong singer and songwriter, he couldn't really contribute too much to my songs, instrumentally anyway, and was really more of a solo artist. It was also because of the constant bickering between Botts and him. He didn't want to sign anything, yet Botts had just come outta Bread, and they had some awful problems, legally, which kept Botts from money that was his for years, so he wanted everything in writing up front. I agreed with Mike, but Alan just didn't like the feeling he was signing his life away. He was a good-looking chap, with very melodic songs, and a great voice, but I think he became semi-paranoid he was gonna lose his songs and his identity, between me, who was more experienced, and Botts who was pressuring him a bit too heavily. It was slightly ironic, but it broke up for good one night soon after we began…"

On his own website Mike summed up the experience: "Although we had all the ingredients for commercial success, the group became a victim of what I call a spontaneous internal combustion. Unfortunately, it never got off the launch pad."

He continued, "By 1985, drum machines and computers had been introduced to the music scene. It soon became evident that this was not a fad or novelty, and that they would be incorporated into all areas of music. Consequently, I had to become a computer programmer as well as a drummer. Becoming at least somewhat computer literate not only helped me in studio work, but was also an enormous help in developing my songwriting and production abilities over the next few years. From 1985 through 1990 I was almost totally involved in recording as a player, singer, writer, and producer. The only exception was a short tour to Japan with Richard Carpenter in 1989. But other than that, I stayed in L.A. and concentrated on expanding my talents and abilities in other areas of music including some video production and direction."

This new excursion into video first came about when a thirteen-year-old family friend, Rachel Dunlap, the daughter of an acting colleague of Michele's, contacted him, asking if he would score the music for a new short that she and her father had produced. As with most things in his life, Mike accepted the new opportunity with enthusiasm.

"Michele and I were with the same modeling agency, and we did a couple of jobs together," recalls Robert Dunlap. "Rachel and I had just completed filming *Art Or Crime*, and we were exploring the idea of a unique soundtrack with a strong beat. Rachel said, 'Hey, how about Michael Botts on drums? I'll call him, he likes me and my film's concept.' She convinced him to do the score *and* negotiated the agreement, all at age thirteen. We gave him a rough cut screening in our garage studio, and gave him carte blanche for the sound design."

Pleased with the outcome, the working partnership developed from there and, during the mid-1980s, Mike worked on a number of projects with Dunlap. "Michele had the idea of doing a TV program on fashions in Hollywood. The concept was to film all of these fashions, like bathing suits and beachwear, on Michael's sailboat. While filming the project at sea, Michael sang a (new) song, 'Sailin' Shoes.' It was sort of an idea that he had involving our 'all girl crew.' When the footage was processed and we were looking at it, I thought, 'Wow! Let's make this into a music video!' Thus the birth of the short film *Sailin' Shoes*. Michael and I spent two days animating the shoes for the film, and I had the idea of making the shoes dance and board his sailboat. Michael also later scored my short film *Merry-Go-Rounds...*"

Of the various projects that Mike worked upon, *Art Or Crime* went on to win a series of awards for the Dunlaps, but it was never sold into distribution or syndication, and although *Sailin' Shoes* and *Merry-Go-Rounds* were also submitted to a number of film festivals, they never quite achieved the same success and were never marketed. "They really became 'lost' so to speak, for another big reason..." summarizes Robert Dunlap today, "...MTV. Short films and animations were being produced and distributed as music videos for 'free' by bands, groups, and record labels. It's very hard to compete with *free*!"

Staying with "Sailin' Shoes," Michele Botts also recollects a story involving the creation of the song: "I came home from a very long day, and it was a long drive from Beverly Hills, where I was working, to the Hollywood Hills where we lived, and I get home and Michael says, 'Come upstairs, Michele, you've got to hear this. I've been working on it all day.' He was so excited, and he played me 'Sailin' Shoes' and I looked at him and said, 'Well, I don't hear any money in that!' He was stunned! Now it's one of my favorite pieces that he's ever done, but he loved telling people that story years later. But the fact that he did it all, that's all him. He wrote it, recorded all of those voices. That's when he started writing, in earnest."

This astonishing track, a short *a cappella tour de force* inspired by the gospel and harmony groups of the 1940s and '50s, would eventually find a true home some fifteen years later on Mike's debut solo album.

Life for James Griffin during the early 1980s was based around the family home situated on Center Drive in the heart of Memphis, just a few miles from where the city merged with the banks of the Mississippi river. Home was a large, imposing building, surrounded by lush greenery and ever-flowering blooms, which James shared with his wife Kathy, their two young children Jamey and Katy, along with various extended family members. It was from here that he based himself in order to rebuild his musical career. Shunning the opportunistic lifestyle that Los Angeles had to offer, cutting himself off from the very hub of the industry that had turned its back on him, his forays back into the recording studio were initially intermittent, although he was by no means idle in his quest to rediscover his true musical identity. He linked up with an old musical friend from the 1960s, a Memphis-based songwriter and producer named Ray Chafin, and they would occasionally perform together at Chafin's popular nightclub, The Horseshoe Café. The two would later go on to collaborate on a series of anniversary "musicards" for the commercial market, featuring a series of joint compositions such as "Happy Birthday," "Happy Anniversary," "Congratulations," and "Heart On Heart," all featuring James's vocals. Unfortunately, due to lack of finance, this concept never took off, and neither did the next project they worked on together, a short-lived record company they named Centaurus Records, conceived with the idea of promoting some of Jimmy's own material. Nevertheless, these musical ventures only heightened James's desire to refuel his musical tank. Not that he ever stopped writing either, and the comforts of home were often accompanied by the image of him sitting around with his guitar in his hand, young children playing nearby.

Now finally clean from the drugs that had haunted him for the past five or six years, James also held on to nostalgic memories of his time with Bread, and even of his solo career before. The walls of his office, situated outside in the guest house, were filled with framed images from scenes in which he had appeared during his brief excursion into the Hollywood movies, along with the numerous gold records, and, of course, his Academy Award statuette. He purchased a number of scrap-books and asked his mother-in-law to go through the enormous pile of trade and music magazines he had accumulated over the years, compiling all the articles and advertisements relating to his former glories into one vast collection.

The ongoing lawsuit over the "Bread" brand was still unresolved at this time as James, still under the forceful guidance of Dick Collins, continued to fight for his beliefs. Attorneys were hired, and were subsequently fired. Settlements were refused. Negotiations were cut short. During 1980, Griffin Enterprises took former manager and attorney Al Schlesinger to court, along with Schlesinger's business partner in Bread Enterprises, Michael Dave, seeking $5 million in punitive damag-es. They contended that following increasing sales of the band's first two albums, Schlesinger had told James that "confusion of an unspecified nature" stymied the retroactive royalty hike that he understood would be renegotiated once the band established itself as a successful commodity. In addition, it was at this stage that James was dissuaded from viewing the auditing books by Bread's management team, with Schlesinger reportedly stating, "audits never disclosed anything bene-ficial to acts." The subsequent outcome was kept away from the prying eyes of the public, these were private matters, but it was quite clear to all concerned that this wasn't simply going to go away, and these final years of litigation seemed to drag on... and on.

With his recording contract with Polydor seemingly undemanding, James now began scouring around the studios of Memphis, looking to find a suitable loca-tion from where to base his next project. Despite the quality and size of locations such as Ardent Studios or Phillips Recording, or the original legend that was Sun, James instead focused his attentions on a small set-up, barely three blocks from his home on Center Drive. Shoe Productions was a small dual-room location that was not even big enough to accommodate a string section, but one that had a larger, 24-track studio named The Daily Planet, created by local producers Bobby Manual and Jim Stewart, located in an adjoining part of the building. The original Shoe studio, lacking in business, had closed down its recording facilities, and was simply being used as rehearsal space, while all projects were subsequently shifted into the updated studio attached.

By coincidence, while scouting the building, James encountered another Memphis-born industry insider, Phillip Rauls, who had spent a large portion of his career within music promotions for established labels such as Stax, Atlantic, and 20th Century Fox, but was now running his own marketing and consultancy company. Rauls was at Shoe that day, song-plugging for a number of his clients, and he immediately struck up a mutual friendship with James, who in turn hired the use of Rauls Music to review his own career, working together towards revitalizing the James Griffin profile. They also made a commitment to add fresh input into the ailing Memphis music industry. The city was going through a notable slump during the beginning of the new decade, with a lack of fresh, rising music talent breaking through to national success. The city's main musical focus, Stax Records, was experiencing tough times too, having recently filed for bankruptcy, and Hi Records, home of artists such as Al Green and Ann Peebles, had folded in the aftermath of the disco era, so James and Phillip set about using their experiences to aid the tired economy by encouraging the use of local musicians.

"My first thought was, 'What the hell is he doing here?'" recalls Phillip Rauls today, wondering why someone who had experienced such highs was now scouting around a tiny, independent studio. "I thought it was a step backwards, but he was wanting to revitalize his career, and help Memphis music. He had a real deep passion for blue-eyed soul music. He was a very gentlemanly person, soft heart, soft spoken..."

The first new project undertaken, using the core talents of local musicians as support, was a reunion with his friend from over the waters, Terry Sylvester. Instigated by a trans-Atlantic telephone call from Terry's manager, Robin Britten, during June of 1981, asking whether James would be interested in re-establishing their working partnership, the duo reconnected during the summer months of that year, with Terry flying in to Memphis to set up camp at The Daily Planet studios.

Over the next few weeks, the two singer-songwriters co-wrote more than a dozen new compositions and, even when prior commitments took them out of the city (on one occasion all the way back to Terry's home in Cheshire, England), they still managed to forge ahead with the project. Having composed enough material to their mutual liking, they kicked off the recording sessions at The Daily Planet studios during August, accompanied each day by in-house engineer Andy Black, and a team of local musicians, including drummers Ty Grimes and Steve Mergen, keyboard players Carl Marsh and Swain Schaefer, bass guitarists Steve Cobb and Dave Smith, and guitarist Gene Nunez. Southern blues'n'soul singer-songwriter Tony Joe White also made an appearance at the sessions, supplying harmonica on one track.

"Jimmy was kind of the driving force of the Griffin-Sylvester record," Andy Black says today. "But the way I remember, it was Terry would produce Jimmy, and Jimmy would turn to me as to who to play on which song, and then I would organize the session. But when the session would begin Jimmy was the director..."

Using their own musical abilities on both acoustic and electric guitar, and supplying all vocals themselves, the duo pulled together an impressive collection of recordings with their eyes set on a worldwide release, courtesy of James's contract with Polydor, although unfortunately, as had befallen his 1977 solo album, the deal didn't include distribution across the United States.

"Jimmy and I then went to New York, knocking on doors," continues Rauls. "We went to Capitol, Atlantic, Warner Brothers, sat with their A&R directors and vice-presidents, played them the album, but there was a major youth movement taking place. Thomas Dolby, Soft Cell, Cyndi Lauper, and The Human League were all hitting MTV, and Jimmy and Terry's music was considered behind the loop on that. There wasn't a youthful luster to it, and we got turned down. That type of music just wasn't dominating the charts. It did get some North American airplay but it was via bootlegs or copies that were not actively promoted by Polydor, they just ended up in the control rooms of various radio stations and they played it."

The ten songs that graced the 40 minutes running time were split fairly evenly between the duo, each handling both lead vocals and harmonies throughout. From the opening delights of "Please Come Into My Life" (released as the advance single in Europe), the infectious rhythm of "Till Midnight," the MTV-AOR-inspired rock of "Rozanne," and the dirty-soul of "Wolf River," the harmonic quality simply oozes from the grooves, regardless of the direction that the industry was heading in at that time. And the arrangements and performances from the local musicians are, at times, inspirational, albeit contentious.

Rauls: "Jimmy really wanted that Memphis grit, that Memphis soul in the drum sound. I didn't agree with it. He, more than Terry, was insisting they use it. A real muddy, dirty sound. But it wasn't what was in the charts and when we got to New York I could see what they (the record execs) were saying. It really stood out."

The duo also showed a more compassionate nature in their work, notably on the lengthy seven-minute closing number, "Did You Hear The News Today," which pre-empted the Live Aid/USA For Africa charity productions three years later, by raising awareness of the plight of the world's poverty-stricken children. Certainly, the two-minute closing instrumental refrain, with some wonderful guitar work from James and Gene Nunez, showed that they were not afraid to take risks, abandoning the restraints of the three-minute pop song that had restricted both their former bands. A number of additional songs that didn't make the final selection were also written during these sessions, including the still unreleased collaboration "Ain't It Nice," while three others would later make an appearance on a CD re-issue set, but, unfortunately, all their hard work was relatively in vain and the lack of an American release stifled the opportunities for the record. Despite some European promotion following an overseas release, traveling to Germany for a TV appearance on one occasion, it saw little success abroad either.

Undeterred, James returned to the small studios near his home, often walking or jogging there each day, while he worked a further series of new recordings. He was initially looking to buy a studio for himself and he had recently enquired about the availability of the successful Ardent Studios nearby but was told they were not for sale. Instead, he offered financial support to the Shoe/Daily Planet complex who, like many of the Memphis facilities, were struggling to keep their heads above the water. By funding much of his own session time, James recorded a number of demos and tracks there, including "Moon Over Memphis," while others, such as the unreleased "Baby Maybe This Time," were cut at various other established local studios, including Cotton Row. He also did some work in the small facility that keyboard player Swain Schaefer had installed in his own home.

Working in the studio (courtesy of Swain Schaefer)

"I had a 3,600 square-foot home that Frank Lloyd Wright and my mother designed," says Swain today, "and Jimmy just loved it. I had a studio there where we cut the songs 'Blown Away' and 'Angel In My Eyes,' among many other tunes. 'Honey Why' was one of his favorites (cut at Mastercraft Studios), as well as 'The Healing Has Begun.' He brought me the music to 'The Healing Has Begun'... my mom had just died, and I told him I'd have it done before I slept again and I called him with the lyric a few days later. I re-wrote the second half of the chorus for Jimmy but he didn't use (the new lyric)..."

My heart still hangs on to ya, my soul gets spirit through ya
Glory Hallelujah
The Healing Has Begun...

(Words & Music by Griffin-Schaefer)
Reproduced with permission

Swain was also present during the meetings that James had with his natural father, Paul Brazil. Having been informed of his true parental lineage by his mother a few years previously, James had now taken it upon himself to meet up with his blood father now that he was back in his home city. Perhaps unsurprisingly, given James's prolific musical ability, Brazil was also an extremely talented musician, while also prone to donning leathers and spending much of his time on his beloved motorcycles.

Swain continues: "I probably knew Paul better than Jimmy did unfortunately. I met Paul doing gigs, he played bass, and then one day he says 'Jimmy Griffin is my son.' By that time they had reconnected but were not what I'd call close. I was with Jimmy and Paul together, but for the life of me I can't remember exactly where in Memphis. Paul was a very upbeat positive kat. He used that word 'kat,' everybody was 'kat' all the time. He was so proud of Jimmy and they were on good terms. He beamed with pride over him and any animosities were forgotten."

"The first visit that Paul had was when he came to visit us at home on Center Drive," adds Kathy, James's then-wife. "He looked like Jimmy, played music, rode a motorcycle. They had a lot in common and I believe Jimmy wanted to believe he was his real dad…"

For James, regardless of the many distractions that had ebbed and flowed through his 39 years in this world, the music was now running freely once more. Having recently formed a new publishing company, JARP, with a group of like-minded musicians, his varying musical partnerships over this period brought forth dozens of new compositions, many of which would never see the light of day, but that never stopped him. At one stage he compiled sixteen of these new Memphis recordings onto a promotional cassette he jokingly referred to as *James Griffin's Greatest Hits (A Legend In My Own Mind)* and circulated them among friends although, unfortunately, the collection never reached an official status. He was also not averse to stepping out under the spotlight once more, performing solo, around his home city. One such occasion, on December 19th, 1982, saw him appear at The Madison House in midtown Memphis, performing a set that featured, "Blood From A Stone," "Honey Why," "If You Gotta Make A Fool Of Somebody," "Lonely Girls," and "Goin' Back To Tennessee" among others. Clearly, the ability to combine his rich, resonating tone with guitar, piano, or any other voice was his lifeblood. It surged through him. JARP was named after James, along with three other musical acquaintances who had recently enriched his life. The first was Andy Black, the studio engineer at The Daily Planet, while the others were Rick Yancey, a talented singer-songwriter that James had met by chance at a local festival, and Paul Compton, an old school friend he had recently reconnected with. JARP was equally an outlet for all four talents (and jokingly renamed PJAR for Compton's composing affiliation with ASCAP), with Andy Black in particular retaining fond memories of the songwriting sessions. In conversation with the author Andy recalled: "I loved working and singing with Jimmy. As a songwriter he had a way of bringing out the best of everyone in JARP. No idea was too bad to explore, and even though he was an incredible singer, we all could feel comfortable singing with him. We would usually write at his place and he was never a prima donna."

Compositions to come out of the newly-formed JARP partnership included "All I Need," "Stop And Think It Over," "I Love My Girl," and "I'm A Fool For Ya," and while these particular tunes were among those never to see an official release, James did actually issue one further record from the small site, the one and only single release to appear with the Shoe Records label attached. Such was James's devotion to assisting the local music scene that, for this one-off release, he chose to promote the works of a number of local songwriters, ignoring his own catalog of compositions, although personal issues also potentially aided the reasoning behind this. "Lonely Girls" was a lovely mid-tempo song written by John Paul Daniel and piano playing friend Swain Schaefer, himself a former member of a successful band, having been a latter-day member of the Memphis-based Box Tops, while the funky sound of the accompanying "Heartbeat" was the result of a collaboration between Tennessee tunesmith Wayne Crook and James's JARP partner Paul Compton. Released as SHO-1, and credited to Jimmy Griffin, the record slid swiftly into obscurity, despite achieving a certain amount of local success thanks to Rauls Music who were hired to promote the release.

"Jimmy was known to have deep pockets," laughs Phillip Rauls. "He held a number of parties at his large house, and he was always entertaining people. When the nouveau wine came in, he would have a party. When the New Orleans crayfish came in, he would have a party. When 'Lonely Girls' came out, he had a big party..."

And yet, despite the positive approach that he was feeling among the Memphis music fraternity, his home life was currently being turned upside down. His relationship with Kathy was now faltering and a new face had recently come into his life.

Martha Rodgers, fresh out of college, had been hired as both receptionist and phone operator for Shoe Productions, but as the adjoining Daily Planet studio couldn't actually afford a receptionist, she had become the gate keeper of both facilities and was subsequently placed in charge of booking studio time. A lot of her day was naturally spent talking with James, and what had started out as a professional friendship had gradually developed, and a strong bond blossomed between the two of them within the confines of the small building. The mixed emotions, caught up between family matters and business affairs, reportedly influenced James's reasoning to use outside songwriters for his new record release, thus affording him the time to sort out these personal issues.

"It was apparent that Jimmy was the eternal optimist, but during this period you could see the pain beneath his pleasant smile," summarizes Phillip Rauls.

However, it wasn't just the world of James Griffin that was being rocked during this turbulent period. Indeed, the entire music industry was shaken to the core on June 3rd, 1983, when, back in Los Angeles, acclaimed session drummer Jim Gordon, the same drummer that James, David, and Robb had used for their debut release, was arrested by the Los Angeles Police Department, having violently battered his mother to death with a hammer. After a phenomenally successful career as a session player and touring drummer, supporting artists such as John Lennon, George Harrison, Eric Clapton, Jackson Browne, Joe Cocker, Barbra Streisand, CSNY, and Frank Zappa, Gordon had suffered from the same fate that had befallen many of the original '60s "crew:" that of a lack of work in the indecisive '80s. And having started complaining of hearing "voices" in his head, misdiagnosed as alcohol abuse, alongside constant heavy drug use, his mental health had deteriorated rapidly. Only too late was it properly diagnosed as acute paranoid schizophrenia. Unable to use the insanity defense, which California had recently removed, Gordon was convicted of second-degree murder and sentenced from sixteen years to life in prison where, to date, he remains.

In 1984, finally, after a long drawn out battle, the court case between James Griffin, David Gates, Mike Botts, and Larry Knechtel drew to its conclusion. Seven years of bitter fighting had not only left bank balances teetering on the edge for some; personal belongings had been sold, family homes put in jeopardy, individual prides had been hurt, and friendships had also been destroyed. It would take many years for the wounds to heal. At the eleventh hour, just before the case was to be heard in trials, an agreement was reached between James and David, both reluctant to see the case brought before a judge, and a settlement was made. James, acting against the advice of his own management team, took the initiative and offered a last minute resolution, to which David was reportedly amicable to, wishing for a swift conclusion himself. As to whether either could claim true satisfaction was a moot point, but James ultimately stood victorious in his claim that the name "Bread" could not be used without the consent of both the surviving founding members.

But it was a hollow victory. The band "Bread" was essentially no more and, while the legacy they had created would live on, it was a legacy heavily fortified by the success of their hit singles – those same singles that David had composed. Unfortunately for James, despite the lawsuits ultimately giving him the voice he desired, and the rights that the initial formation agreements had intended, the unforgiving "David Gates and Bread" headline would be one that would constantly re-appear, time and time again. Thus reminding him that, despite his contributions and co-ownership, it was David's own compositions that the world would remember, featuring endlessly on the numerous re-issues and collections appearing around the world. At what price was victory?

James's health was now recovering, despite his continued smoking, and he had a new partner with which to move his life forward, but his income was still lacking the impact on his bank balance that it had in previous years, despite the potentially vast royalty payments now being freed up by Elektra. This was partially due to the unfortunate parting with Kathy and the subsequent dissolving of their marriage that year, but also to the fact that his relationship with Dick Collins had collapsed beyond repair and he would find himself back in court shortly afterwards, fighting to recover monies, including the newly freed up royalty payments, along with his musical rights, that he believed his management company had appropriated without true justification. A vast proportion of his hard-earned wealth had seemingly been lost to him. It was from one court battle to another, and it would take him the good part of another thirteen years of soul searching, reaching as high as the Tennessee Court of Appeals, before his claim was finally vindicated, his rights were returned, and he was freed from all financial constraint.

But there was always his music. His career had taken a battering with the demise of Bread; his solo releases had been met with little success, and to add further insult to injury, none of the group members ever fully received all of the monies still owed. Their assets, frozen by Elektra Records during the lawsuit, comprising back payments, royalties, and pension funds, were freed, but the four musicians had never had a contingency plan drawn into their contracts. Clearly an oversight from their original management arrangement, thus securing increasing interest benefits should payments be withheld for whatever reason. Subsequently, seven years of owed payments built up a vast amount of interest on the royalties due, potentially six-figure sums for each individual, but this was never added to their released funds, Elektra Records benefiting instead from the windfall. How could friendships be rebuilt from such a mess?

"We couldn't forgive and forget that easily," Mike Botts was later to say. Clearly, for all concerned, it was time to move on.

On May 18th, 1985, James Griffin and Martha Rodgers were wed in Memphis, and while James was intent on reconstructing his career, running alongside his ongoing court battles, one of the first moves he made was back to California once more.

"I found I liked doing group work instead of solo work," James was to say in a later interview. "It was a lot more satisfying, and a lot more fun. I went back to California and I was going to give it another shot with Robb Royer, and try to get another band going. I found that the market in California was real competitive and a lot different. We did some recordings and shopped them around a little bit, but it didn't meet with much success."

In fact, the duo did manage to put another band together, one they named The Circuit. Along with David Miner, filling in once again on bass, David Kemper on drums, and Ira Ingber on guitar, they performed a few shows around town and then spent some time in the studio cutting tracks such as "Be That Way" and "Midnight Lover." This was actually Robb's return to live performing, having maintained a lone studio presence since his departure from Bread fifteen years before, but, as James was unfortunately to note, it was such a competitive market during the 1980s in the music industry, even with the experience and fame they had both previously achieved, that the band went nowhere... fast, and the sessions remained incomplete. The same was to be said for a number of further collaborations with Robb from this period, including the Caribbean influence that ran through the songs "Shango" and "Throw The Bottle." Once more, both were to remain in the vaults, as was another composition, this time written and recorded with Ray Chafin, that became one of his most endearing ballads, the exquisite "Dance On The Moon," a song they pitched at the producers of an upcoming movie, *The Boy Who Could Fly*, but it remained unused.

"That title and lyric came from a poem in my book *Thoughts In Word Patterns*," recalls Chafin today when discussing the song. "This was a self-published book of poems I had collected over the years, and in 1990 actually went to print. The song itself was written in Jimmy's house in California and was recorded in Malibu. We took a mic outside to get the actual wave sounds."

A short while afterwards, James developed the ballad himself into a proposed 60-second commercial for the JetBlue Airways Corporation, editing it down and overdubbing a voiceover, with the intention of offering it to the airline for media use. Sadly, that concept also failed to meet its target audience, and the song once more returned to the archives. However, the main musical focus for James, having returned to the West Coast, was now directed towards a series of studio sessions that had initially commenced in Nashville, just 200 miles from his home in Memphis, a few weeks previously. Under the supervision of producer Reggie Fisher, and with studio assistance from T-Bone Burnett, this project had centered on a new working partnership with two fellow former "well-knowns": Randy Meisner, founding member of both Poco and The Eagles, and Billy Swan. With both Meisner and Swan living back in California, it made perfect sense for the trio to consolidate their talents during James's return visit. Together they went on to record an album's worth of new material in Fisher's own studio, using a vast array of established musicians and sidemen including Don Grusin, Richie Zito, Jerry Scheff, David Hungate, and Poco's pedal-steel maestro Rusty Young. In addition, also present in the studio at times was Robb, although his subsequent credit on the final sleeve notes was, in his words, "more of an honorary credit."

Robb: "They used me playing strings on one song, and I winged a couple of parts. I can't say I did a full out arrangement. I had introduced Jimmy to Reggie, who produced it, and that was my reward."

The chosen selection was heavily biased towards cover versions, including renditions of the Beatles' "I Feel Fine," The Drifters' "Save The Last Dance For Me" (a song that Meisner had already cut once before on his 1978 solo album), Rudy Clark's "If You Gotta Make A Fool of Somebody," along with exceptional versions of Sam Cooke's "Chain Gang," and Buddy Holly's "Learning The Game," the first of which suited Jimmy's expressive vocal range to a tee. Mixed in with a number of originals, composed by various participants in the project, and issued under the group name of Black Tie, the resulting release appeared on the small Bench Records label that same year. Titled *When The Night Falls*, after one of the newer compositions from T-Bone Burnette, the 14-strong collection never really made much of an impact within the industry, despite the depth of talent featured,

Black Tie live in 1986 (courtesy of Richard Walton/notlaw.com)

and the former high prominence of both Griffin and Meisner did little to sway the record-buying public. In truth, Bench Records was no more than a small independent label, without the financial budget to compete. Similar circumstances to those James had experienced with Shoe Productions just a few months before, and although the group did manage a number of shows to help publicize the record launch, the lack of promotional clout coming from the label itself saw it sadly slide unnoticed under the radar and sink swiftly. In total, James took the lead vocals on four of the featured tracks, two of which, "You're My Life" and "Oh My Lover," were brand new compositions from his own pen, and such was his initial commitment to the project that the trio undertook a number of successful live performances to aid the early promotion of the album. During the closing month of 1985, Black Tie appeared at both the Club Lingerie on Sunset Boulevard, and At Your Place, a similar but smaller venue, where, accompanied by another ex-Eagle, Bernie Leadon on guitar, they delivered an impeccable set, performing songs from the album alongside more publicly accessible hits such as Meisner's Eagles highpoint, "Take It To The Limit" and Billy Swan's 1974 best-selling "I Can Help."

"The vocal power of these artists is formidable," noted *Billboard* magazine in a brief overview of the concert, and three months later the band was still in action, playing to enthusiastic crowds across the country during a small nationwide promotional tour that took in New York City and Chicago. Although Bernie Leadon had by now been replaced in the line-up by former Beach Boy, South African guitarist Blondie Chaplin, and keyboard player George Michalski had also been added to the touring band. *Billboard* once again featured a write-up for a February, 1986 performance:

"Despite the lack of advance notice the club was almost full, and those who braved the weather saw a high velocity performance combining three of the industry's finest vocal talents. The band is scouting a major-label situation and, with its blend of country and rock roots, would certainly be a potential for Nashville's newly progressive record companies."

Unfortunately, despite the promise of the reviews, and the reception from the small club crowds, the band failed to get picked up by any major label and the trio folded shortly afterwards. Dissatisfied once again with the Los Angeles scene, and with further sessions for The Circuit also going nowhere (one additional recording, another new song entitled "Preacher On The Air," hails from this period), James packed his bags and returned to Tennessee. Although, having decided that Memphis no longer held the attraction for him as it had previously done, family bonds having broken down, he opted to up sticks from his hometown shortly afterwards and relocate to Nashville, the home of country music, during September of 1988. With a new family in tow, daughter Alexis having been born during the brief return to Memphis, it was in Nashville, this great, vibrant city, that James's music was to take a significant turn. He had always maintained a homegrown, country-styled honesty within his compositions, but it had usually been superseded in the final mix by the many other influences that surrounded him. The Deep South white-soul that he so loved, the driving Los Angeles rock, the slick AOR production, they had all prevailed to one degree or another, but now, surrounded by like-minded peers, with the angst-ridden days of old-style hillbilly music being replaced by an amalgamation of true country, rock, and pop, to a talented composer such as James, the new opportunities that opened up for him seemed endless. However, he wasn't the only one who was feeling the winds of change, and the pull to Nashville. One of his former band mates was also keen to explore the influences that this city had on offer.

Over the years Larry Knechtel had appeared on hundreds of recording sessions and television themes of varying description. From the highs of working with such established artists as Simon & Garfunkel, Phil Spector, and Brian Wilson, to the mundane in-and-out session work that gave us *The Munsters* TV theme and The Partridge Family's chart-topping hit "I Think I Love You." But during that productive period it had only really been his contributions to the music of Bread that allowed his own talents to flow, and his ideas to truly develop. Even then, he was restricted by the often-overwhelming control that the Gates and Griffin songwriting axis assumed over the band. Records had randomly appeared that gave brief glimpses of what Larry was truly capable of, from his 1966 *Boss Baroque* collection to his 1970s work with Patti Dahlstrom, but it was often assumed, and incorrectly so, that paid session men were simply that. Session men. Extremely talented individuals, but no more, no less. For the past few years, at home in his adopted state, he had maintained a relatively low profile, gigging locally, performing with fellow Washington-based musicians around the area, even forming another new band alongside his saxophone and bass-playing son Lonnie, former Bobby Fuller drummer Larry Thompson, and guitarist Ed Solem, coming together under the name of Blue Heron. But the prospects that Nashville had to offer were too tempting to pass by. Subsequently, in 1988, he too ventured east, moving away from his relaxed northerly lifestyle to the heartbeat of country music, intent on building up some studio contacts, working the sessions, but also developing his own musical identity.

Larry in Blue Heron (courtesy of Larry Thompson)

He quickly established himself among the Nashville studio fraternity, appearing on albums by Conway Twitty, Phil Keaggy, and Baillie & The Boys, along with a session for the 1990 John Denver album, *The Flower That Shattered The Stone*, where he performed alongside his old school friend Jim Horn, also working in the city at that time. As it had been in Los Angeles, Nashville demanded the very best musicians to play on the recording sessions around the city, and Larry had no problem integrating his talents among the top studio cats in town, despite his often laid-back, loose attitude.

As he recalled: "In the early days, there were no rock session players. In my three years with Duane Eddy, we played on his records, but by the early '60s a caste system had evolved. You didn't need to have a studio caliber player for the road, just someone good enough to copy the part on the record consistently, and he had all the time in the world to get it down and right. The studio guy did it on the spot. I spent six years in Nashville and there were maybe 30 or so studio guys and hundreds of road guys. No producer there would use a road musician on a recording unless the artist had a lot of clout, and the player was unusually good. It was fairly rigid, maybe unfair, but that's how it was. You had to pay your dues, be good, and lucky. I doubt if I would make it myself today, as the music in the music biz seems to be largely premeditated, very little spontaneity and microscopically examined, with no natural human 'looseness' allowed. I had a hard time in Nashville because of that. Hey, I am just a rock and roller..."[21]

But it was also during this period that he began to work on his own music, with the first of two Nashville-based solo albums appearing in 1989. *Mountain Moods*, a collection clearly inspired by his love of nature, particularly the mountains and streams that ran through his northern Washington ranch, was an impressive instrumental album, issued as a part of the Universal Master Series, via MCA records. Comprising eleven works, all composed by Larry himself, including two co-collaborations, the album was a far cry from the country music influences that he was now finding himself immersed in daily during paid session work. *Mountain Moods* was a gathering of new age, wistful melodies that drifted along, sequencing easily from track to track, with Larry's eloquent keyboards occasionally broken up by the graceful horns of Jim Horn and the intricate acoustic work of established session guitarist Larry Byrom. With production credits afforded to Jim Horn and Norbert Puttman, the latter a former Elvis Presley sideman and member of the legendary Muscle Shoals studio team, the sound was filled out by top Nashville players Jerry Kroon, Dave Pomeroy, and David Humphreys.

"I approached this album as a songwriter and arranger, not as a keyboardist," Larry stated on the accompanying sleeve notes, although during another later interview he suggested that this was not a trait he would continually follow. "I did not pursue writing per se at all. I made up musical stuff all the time but just didn't have the discipline to turn it into a song."[21]

Despite the brief sleeve notes offering no mention of his time as a member of Bread, the album was a dignified, if non-commercial, success, and encouraged him to issue a further collection the following year. For 1990's *Urban Gypsy*, this time appearing on the Capitol label, Larry undertook a series of cover versions, including The Doobie Brothers' "Taking It To The Street" and the perennial Burt Bacharach and Hal David collaboration, "Always Something There To Remind Me," mixed in with four of his own compositions. Perhaps of most interest among the covers were his renditions of two David Gates' songs, "Aubrey" and "Lorilee," interpreted in instrumental format. Although it is interesting to note that "Lorilee" was retitled "Laura Lee," perhaps causing some confusion among Bread fans familiar with the James Griffin recording of the same name. "Aubrey" was tackled with delicate precision, Larry's tinkling ivories rising above the synthesized accompaniment, while "Laura Lee," to be fair, sadly lacked some of the initial dynamics that his own organ arrangement had brought to the original. With support from Jim Horn and Dave Pomeroy once more, alongside guitarist Joe Khoury, bass player Michael Rhodes, and drummers Steve Turner and Eddie Bayers, and the occasional vocal contributions from Chris Eddy, son of Larry's good friend Duane, it was a confusing collection for the listener. At times one is led back into the mellow new age jazz feel with "Believe In Me" and the title track, both from Larry's own pen, then in comparison, one is also fed the funkier, harder edge of "Taking It To The Streets" or "Basically Bass," the latter again being a Knechtel composition.

"Cosmopolitan and nomadic, chic and comfortable" ran the liner notes, suggesting the album's diversity, but, in honesty, despite the classy production, it was never a release that was going to reach a mass audience, which was probably Larry's intention. He wasn't looking for solo success or individual fame. Satisfied only in recording an album that pleased himself, and one that reached up to his own high standards of professionalism, *Urban Gypsy* achieved just that – but little more.

The following year, while still in Nashville, he contributed the familiar piano accompaniment to the classic TV commercial for Chevrolet, *The Heartbeat Of America,* and continued with paid session work, one of which exemplified his loose approach to the strict regimes of the studio syndrome, resulting in his actually getting thrown out. With much amusement he later recalled: "I played on the album *Family Tradition* (for Hank Williams Jr.) which went well, and I was called for another album upon which I didn't think the songs were on the same level. But in the middle of the project we had to do a Christmas cut for an album featuring the country artists on Warner Brothers. One song for each artist. Hank chose 'Little Drummer Boy' and during the recording, when he sang 'rump a bump bum,' I broke out in an audible laugh and, of course, the tape stopped. Hank left the room, and the producer, Jimmy Bowen, called me into the back room and said, 'Hank's unhappy with you,' and immediately sent me back home. I also made the bass player laugh and he got fired too!"[21]

Despite his non-appearance on the eventual release of *Christmas Country Classics*, his reputation was still second to none, so it came as no surprise that, during 1991, he was contacted by one of England's most prominent songwriters of the past decade, and one of the most innovative, with a view to hiring him for a new Nashville-based project.

Declan MacManus, known by his stage name of Elvis Costello, had first recorded in the country capital back in 1979, and had then revisited the city on a number of occasions, the results of which had first appeared on his acclaimed 1981 album *Almost Blue*. Ten years later, with his reputation as one of the most significant artists to have arisen from, and survived, the English new wave explosion, Elvis returned to Nashville to cut his next album, *Mighty Like The Rose*. With Larry performing his familiar keyboard duties on the sessions, the record became a Top 5 hit in the U.K., while also reaching a respectable #55 placing on the *Billboard* charts. The result was that Larry became a core member of the Costello touring band for the next three years, traveling across America, England, and beyond, while also appearing on the 1995 album *Kojak Variety*, a Costello collection of cover versions recorded over a four-year period.

"His intensity killed me," Larry was to say. "I've never met a man who has more integrity." Two years later Elvis would request Larry's presence again when he appeared on the top-rated *David Letterman Show*, performing alongside gospel legends, The Fairfield Four. Who better to have in your corner for such a notable televised appearance?

Certainly, listening to the album today one can understand Larry's fascination with this relatively unknown quantity from across the pond. It was nothing like he had played on before. Just listen to "Hurry Down Doomsday" and see why. Costello had achieved some reasonable success in America, but was far from being the established voice that he was back home in his native U.K. Nevertheless, Larry's exquisite touch features throughout the album, from the *Pet Sounds*-esque "The Other Side Of Summer" to the closing off-beat "Couldn't Call It Unexpected #4" and it's easy to understand quite why Costello requested the talents of Knechtel, along with the other established studio aficionados such as Jim Keltner, Marc Ribot, Mitchell Froom, and James Burton. The album simply oozes class, while maintaining Costello's original approach to his songwriting.

Meanwhile, as Larry was revelling in this "new" music, James Griffin was also consolidating his position within the Nashville community. Almost immediately after his arrival in town, he hooked up again with one of his former Memphis songwriting partners who, not knowing that James had already moved there, had also made the three-hour journey across state. Rick Yancey had first met James back in 1981 by sheer chance when, while standing by a hot dog vendor at the annual "Memphis In May" festival, he noticed him casually walking through the crowds, enjoying the music, accompanied by Robb Royer.

"I went up to him, introduced myself, and asked him what he was doing here," says Rick, "and he says 'I'm thinking about retiring.' I said 'No. Retiring? You're crazy! I'll tell you what, I'm gonna make a prediction, I'm gonna sing with you. I'm one of the biggest fans you ever had. I know my voice and I know yours, and I'm one of the few singers in this city that can sing with you.' I swear it wasn't a week or two later, and I'm in The Daily Planet studio, and in walks Jimmy Griffin with another friend of mine named Paul Compton. From then on Jimmy and I were partners."

Yancey had previously achieved a modicum of success back in the early 1970s when, alongside his friends Richard Mainegra and Sherrill Parks, he had formed the band Cymarron, achieving a Top 20 hit with "Rings" in the process. Following the disbandment of that particular group, Rick had maintained a steady interest in the industry, but had achieved little success until his fortuitous introduction at the "Memphis In May" festival, and the subsequent meeting in the recording studio would guide him towards greater achievements. Following their re-introduction at Daily Planet, with retirement seemingly only a passing thought in his mind,

James, along with Rick and Paul Compton, had then linked up with the studio's sound engineer Andy Black, to form JARP, their own publishing company, but after a number of fruitful songwriting sessions the partnership had drifted apart once James had headed back out to California. For a few years Rick actually lost touch with his new friend while he continued with his own songwriting and recording, but on relocating to Nashville, during October 1988, he discovered that James had also arrived in town the month before.

"I don't recall how I found out he was up here, but almost immediately I introduced him to an old friend of mine," Rick continues. Richard Mainegra, who had been a member of Cymarron with him, had been living in Nashville for a number of years and was another wonderfully talented singer and songwriter, and there was an instant rapport between the three of them. One of their first compositions together was "Who's Gonna Know," a #51 hit on the Country Charts when recorded soon after by legendary performer Conway Twitty. "People then started liking our songs and our demos and we got a record deal..."

Artist and producer Josh Leo saw the trio, liked what he heard, and signed them to BNA Entertainment, a subsidiary of the larger BMG corporation where he worked for the A&R department. It was as simple as that. Not that James's former band was ever far from his mind either. During the late 1980s he had approached his erstwhile partner, David Gates, with a proposal for reforming Bread, a million-dollar offer reportedly having been put on the table. James certainly needed the additional financial input to his dwindling account, as did Mike and Larry, but David just wasn't interested. Perhaps the bitter court case had, in his mind, been one step too far to mend broken bridges. David himself was later to deny that any firm offer had been made. "Maybe if I had (heard of the offer) I wouldn't have turned it down!" he jokingly commented, referring to the amount suggested. "I think some promoter might have talked to James and said, 'If you guys would get back together and go out on the road, you'd make a lot of money.' I think that's what it was. I don't think it was an offer from a recording company."[13]

"He's comfortable up there playing cowboy," responded James in an interview at the time, referring to David's seemingly contented lifestyle on his Northern California cattle ranch. "He doesn't want to go out and be, as he puts it, a museum piece." Implying that he would be happy to work together with all his ex-partners again he continued sadly, "I don't think the feeling is mutual." Unfortunately so. Despite living and working in the same city, in a close-knit musical community, Larry had made no effort to reconnect with him, the wounds being still too deep to heal.

And yet the new music that James was helping to create was still finding an audience, for it was around this same period, the turn of the decade, that Black Tie reconvened, after a local disc jockey began to play their version of Buddy Holly's "Learning The Game," turning it into a small hit on the *Billboard* Country Charts. 1990 had seen the original album, now five years old, re-issued on compact disc, including newly re-recorded versions of both "Learning The Game" and "Chain Gang." With additional session time being undertaken in Nashville, overseen by original producer Reggie Fisher, listed among the revised credits for the re-issue was the name of Larry Knechtel. Maybe the close-knit Nashville community *had* eased old hurt. Maybe music speaks louder than words. It was a good sign...

A second single followed from the album, Billy Swan's "Jerry Lee," but in its original form it met with little acclaim, and although Black Tie would go on to do further work in the studio together, commencing sessions for a proposed second album the following year, it was a short-lived reunion. James was not as heavily involved this time around, although he did contribute a vocal to a rare Larry Knechtel composition entitled "They Don't Make 'Em Like They Used To" that was being considered for the project. Instead he preferred to concentrate on his new partnership with Rick Yancey and Richard Mainegra. Although *Black Tie Two* would eventually appear, many years later, as a short 3-song EP, there was little noticeable evidence of James's contributions to the chosen releases. And while the band did achieve further chart success during 1992 with the song "I'm Sure Of You," co-written by Billy Swan and new member Alan "Charlie" Rich Jr., the group folded for the second time shortly afterwards, only to reform a third time, without James, during 1994, but now billed simply as "Meisner, Swan & Rich." As for James's newest project, the partnership of Griffin, Yancey, and Mainegra was tied between a number of choices for a working band name, with the western influences of Winchester, Remington, and Blue Frontier included, although they initially opted to go out under the banner Dreamer.

Yancey recalls: "It was Dreamer originally, and then, in the process of the record company trying to get all of the legalities in place for naming the band, it came down to two or three different names. We were running around the country promoting our upcoming project and album, and I think we were in Cincinnati and we get a phone call that says, 'OK guys, you're The Remingtons.' Nobody could argue with that as a trademark!"

The debut single by the trio was issued via BNA towards the end of 1991. "A Long Time Ago," was written by Richard Mainegra and featured him on lead vocals, and the accompanying promotional video, featuring the three guitarists playing against the rocky backdrops of a mid-western landscape, was a wonderful introduction to the beautiful harmonies the new group had to offer. Clinical and precise, and yet delivered with such an accessible approach that was clearly intended for the mass country music market, it immediately went Top 10 on the U.S. Country Charts, starting a brief run of success that rightfully put James back in the media spotlight for the first time in over a decade.

Also working for BNA Entertainment at that time was Jim Della Croce, head of the label's Artist & Development department, and the founder of The Press Office, a successful PR company representing various artists and performers. "Jimmy was in a very productive phase of his career at that time," recalls Della Croce today,

The Remingtons (courtesy of Brandon Sinks)

"and when the band came in for a meeting, he and I became fast friends. I produced their videos and acted as their publicist, and we spent two or three years on the road promoting Remingtons records. Then, after I left BNA, The Remingtons became clients of mine at The Press Office…"

Further hits for James, Rick, and Richard were to follow, with "I Could Love You (With My Eyes Closed)" and "Two-Timin' Me," both achieving Top 40 status, and the trio worked hard on promoting their records, featuring heavily on numerous television and radio shows around the country. The debut album, *Blue Frontier* (also one of the early suggestions for the band name), recorded at the Nashville-based Reflections Studio, was issued in January 1992, and peaked at #55, a reasonable enough showing, and although James's songwriting contributions to the album were less than his new partners, with five co-credits to his name, his distinctive vocals still featured prominently, notably on "Takin' The Easy Way Out," "When Love At First Sight Goes Blind," and the highly infectious "Eternally Blue."

For a brief moment, The Remingtons were right at the forefront of new country music. The crossover appeal that they and bands such as Restless Heart, Diamond Rio, Sawyer Brown, and numerous others achieved, touched the very heart of American popular music, blending the varying country, pop, rock, and adult contemporary genres with ease. To the traditional country music buff, those with a seat in the Grand Ol' Opry, the crossover into pop music was often a step too far from their established traditions, but it revitalized the industry, putting country back on the map. It was a revolution, and with established country-pickers and purveyors of bluegrass such as Bernie Leadon, Gib Guilbeau, and Chris Hillman participating in sessions around the city, it was an industry that could only get bigger. James suddenly found himself right back in the heart of the action, and his music was once again reaching out to a vast audience. In addition to The Remingtons, he also found songwriting success during 1991 when his composition, "You Can Depend On Me," written with Randall Rogers, was recorded by the equally popular band Restless Heart, peaking at #3 on the *Billboard* Country Charts, and earning him a second BMI award.

"This was probably the most popular moment of country music history," believes Rick Yancey today, "and we were involved in it. We weren't all that country, but we covered a lot of ground, different types of music. We were different from all of the other country groups."

Once The Remingtons' debut album had proved to be a success, the band took to performing in concert, initially as a trio around the Nashville area. But, by adding extra musicians to the line-up, filling out the sound behind them, they soon headed out on the wider road, appearing at various shows across the eastern states. The set list naturally relied heavily on their recent hits, along with selections from the album although, to the delight of many audiences, James would often include a rendition of "Everything I Own," with his two partners adding an additional layer to the original two-part harmony that David Gates had initially adopted. James was undoubtedly proud of his past glories, enjoying the experience of revisiting such a classic song, although perhaps it came as a surprise to many of his colleagues when his next musical venture, a solo affair, resulted in the recording of a complete album of mostly David Gates compositions.

Without question, the motive for recording such a collection was money. Bread was still very much a marketable commodity, despite having not released any new product for almost fifteen years at that point, and James, in Rick Yancey's eyes, saw this as a perfect money spinner. "He was offered a deal to do those songs, and make some money. Guaranteed. I was there for it, but it was all Jimmy."

Working with fellow songwriter and co-producer Brandon Earl Sinks (the son of singer and guitarist Earl Sinks, who had briefly replaced Buddy Holly in The Crickets), James taped a number of versions of popular Bread songs over at Wolf's Studio on Nashville's Music Row, ranging from the obvious hits – "Make It With You," "Everything I Own," "If," "Baby I'm-A Want You," "Guitar Man," and "Lost Without Your Love" – to such lesser known singles and album cuts as "Make It By Yourself," "Dismal Day," "Hooked On You," and "Let Your Love Go," along with a couple of his own compositions including "Could I," a song originally featured on the band's debut release.

"We had Griffin and Larry Byrom on guitar, Roy Yeager from the Atlanta Rhythm Section on drums, Ronnie Godfrey on keyboard and strings, and Johnny Crocker on bass, along with Charlie Anderson, who was a guy that Jimmy knew. I didn't know him at the time but he was awesome," says Brandon today. "At first it was Jimmy and Mark Grey, and I was overseeing as an executive producer. But there was a disagreement with Mark and so he left on the first night, after which I took Mark's place as co-producer on it. We cut fifteen sides in three days... basic tracks. Then spent well over another three weeks with overdubs and vocals. Although the original budget was set for around $15,000, it wound up running us around $32,000..."

However, the tracks were never fully completed, and the final mixes remained unfinished. Yet, as Brandon himself was later to recall, "Jimmy had also included tracks with Gates, Larry, and Mike on them so we could use the name "Bread" after his deal with Elektra was up and he could use the name again. There was a copy made of the current mix-downs but they were stolen and put out without our permission."[27]

One of the songs intended for the album, incorporating his three former partners, and thus allowing use of the Bread name, was James's original recording of "That's All I Need." David, Larry, and Mike had all contributed to the song during the September 1974, session at the Elektra Studios and, although it had eventually surfaced on the 1977 European release, *James Griffin*, the latter version had been embellished with a guitar solo that was missing from the original take. It was James's intention to utilize the original mix for his new collection. As for choosing the remaining songs...

Sinks: "Well, we looked at a lot of the songs that were on the *Greatest Hits* pack from back then. But I remember us talking about it outside the studio steps one night, and I am pretty sure that this was a really hard and bittersweet time for Jimmy. Here was his chance to sort of take a shot at Gates by singing lead on all of the ones that Gates originally sang lead on, to show the world that he was very capable of doing the lead on the same ones that were always picked as singles. Whereas the ones that Jimmy wrote had more of a 'rock' feel to them. So it was a collective thing with us picking and choosing.

"(We were given) the right to use the Bread name and likeness, but we couldn't use it until Jimmy's restrictions under Elektra's agreement were up. It was all a mess because of that reason, and the tracks were never intended to be released in that way because the mixes were unfinished," he summarizes.

Unfortunately, due to the theft of the early mixes, a number of versions of the album did find a way on to the market, albeit illegally, issued at various stages under differing titles such as *Guitar Man, Let Your Love Go,* and *The Love Album*. With little or no mention anywhere of James Griffin on the front sleeves, these naturally led potential purchasers into believing they were, in fact, buying the original Bread recordings. However, one of the newly recorded tracks, "Could I," was not included among the theft, and remains unheard to this date.

Rick Yancey continues the tale: "In 1992 we (The Remingtons) were in England, we were doing an instore appearance at Tower Records and while we were there, I believe it was Marti, she was just looking around for things that were pertaining to Jimmy, and she found a whole display of that record! It wasn't supposed to be released. Nobody knew about it. Jimmy couldn't believe it, I remember him getting upset about it, because he said, 'What the hell's that doing here!' Someone had copied it and done a pirate version."

Following this "solo" excursion, and having reunited with his Remingtons band mates, James, Rick, and Richard returned to Reflections Studio in Nashville to start work on their second album. The band also assisted country starlet Lorrie Morgan on her 1992 *Watch Me* studio release, supplying backing vocals to the recordings, but even though a number of compositions by the three members had been readied for their own album sessions, there would be one major shake-up before the record was finally completed. Following an internal disagreement one night, Rick Yancey quit the band. Some of his guitar work had already been recorded for the tracks, but his vocals were noticeably absent once the final tapes ran to press.

"We had a management company that I thought was at the root of our disagreements, but it's difficult to talk about it without maligning someone..." says Rick tactfully, "but Jimmy and I never once had a cross word. We were always really good with each other."

To complete the vocal blend, James and Richard brought in Denny Henson, another talented singer and songwriter who had previously seen success as a member of the band Fool's Gold and who had hit the lower reaches of the charts with "Rain Oh Rain" back in 1976. Combining with James and Richard, Denny helped fill out the familiar three-part harmony that The Remingtons were becoming known for. But, despite their efforts supplying another sure-fire quality production, *Aim For The Heart*, again issued via BNA Entertainment, featuring five new James Griffin lead vocals, failed to match the success of its predecessor and the two songs issued as singles, "Nobody Loves You When You're Free" and "Wall Around Your Heart," surprisingly both featuring Denny on lead, barely touched the Country Chart listings. A televised appearance, broadcast on TNN's *On Stage* program, did little to help, despite the show, filmed before a live audience in Phoenix during February 1993, being sold out.

Not all of The Remingtons' recordings were to make it onto their albums, and a number of songs still remain in the vaults, including "It's A Cold Day In Hell" and "I Wonder If She Never Thinks Of Me," both co-written with Brandon Sinks, while "She's All I Got Goin' Now" only appeared as the flip-side to one of their singles. But the featured tracks that did appear on vinyl, certainly cannot be faulted for their production values, and the overall performances on this second album are equally as strong as those on the debut release, starting straight off with the opening track, the Griffin-led high energy "I'm Gonna Find A Way." However, this time around, there were also a few compositions from non-band members running throughout the ten chosen songs, with James turning in another stunning performance of his personal concert favorite, the ever popular David Gates composition "Everything I Own." Similar in arrangement to his recent solo version of the song, taped for the incomplete *James Griffin Sings Bread* album, this new cut prompted David Gates to say:

"It was interesting. I didn't feel they changed enough from the original to have a successful country record out of it. I don't know the exact motivation. Although James did a fine job on his vocal, I thought the arrangement and the production were too much like the original to stand out. A number of people have done that song and nobody has caught the emotion in it just yet. Somebody has got to catch it just right and will have a country hit single with it. They are going to have to put the emotion into it, they can't just sing it..."[9]

It is also worth noting that, of the music composed by "outsiders," hidden away on the second side of the disc, was a brand new song written by a good friend of James. One who, fairly soon, would also make the move to Nashville. "Lucky Boy," a tender ballad sung by James, featured the solo songwriting credit of Robb Royer.

Chapter Seventeen

Goin' Back To Tennessee

"It was Jimmy who picked me up at the airport," recalls Robb today, when reminiscing over his arrival in Nashville during 1994, "and I spent the first couple of months trying to get some stuff together, and then I heard Larry was in town, so I called him up."

Since leaving Bread almost twenty years earlier, Robb had maintained a fairly quiet public profile within the industry, plowing his own field, writing, developing, and composing. Naturally, his ongoing songwriting partnership with James had ensured that contacts with his former band were maintained, and the royalties had continued to flow in for him, his severance agreement guaranteeing that he wasn't drawn into the messy lawsuits that had followed the breakup of the band. He had even developed a working friendship with Larry, his subsequent replacement, following Bread's initial disbandment, and they had spent time writing and recording together during the late 1970s, principally with the group Bandit although, as previously noted, no evidence of such was forthcoming publicly. The remainder of the decade, and into the 1980s, had seen him develop work alongside various national television organizations, composing songs and music for established companies such as CBS and NBC, while still maintaining his desire for writing screenplays. Various film companies did actually take up the options on a number of his projects, including *King's Ransom*, *Club Fed*, *And Thurber Makes Three,* and *Locked Out*, with both Disney and Orion showing serious interest, but nothing was to come of these, although the Disney Channel did later offer airtime to one of his ventures, a *Live At Disneyland* segment that he had co-produced.

It was also during this phase of his career that he first came into contact with Mike Finnigan, an established Ohio-born session player and performer, who had previously worked alongside Jimi Hendrix, Etta James, Sam Moore, Crosby, Stills & Nash, and numerous other musical heavyweights. Acknowledged for his phenomenal keyboard playing, notably on Hendrix's *Electric Ladyland* album, Mike first came into Robb's musical circle when he was drafted in to replace Larry Knechtel in the outfit formerly known as Bandit. And while the prospect of replacing Knechtel was certainly no easy task, it was one that Finnigan was more than capable of undertaking, such was his musical resume and pedigree. Robb had initially been acting as producer for the band, and, while they had never actually achieved anything of significance, the principal group member, singer, and guitarist Chuck Cochran, was keen to continue working after Larry's departure, and subsequently restructured the line-up, renaming them "Tracks" and keeping David Miner on bass, but adding Finnigan on keys and vocals, Rick Jaeger on drums, and Harry Stinson on percussion and vocals. Robb maintained his contribution from behind the scenes.

"Robb was kind of the Svengali of the outfit," says Mike Finnigan. "He was a great songwriter, and he had a real sense of what works. We were trying out tunes of his and recording, and it was sort of a low-key attempt to make something happen, but we were more or less his vehicle."

Unfortunately, the new arrangement wasn't to last long, with Robb himself choosing to opt out, deciding instead to work with songwriter Roger Linn, with whom he would soon go on to co-write "Quittin' Time," a US Country Top 10 hit when recorded in later years by Mary Chapin Carpenter.

"'Quittin' Time' was a seminal moment in my life, to be a hit songwriter again after nineteen years, after the whole Bread, 'For All We Know,' Oscar whirlwind," Robb would go on to say.

"At that time, back in the early '80s, we were part of the cutting edge group in electronics; Iceberg, Roger Linn, Tom Oberheim, Dave Smith, Bob Moog. We had some electronics geeks visiting us from England so we took a trip to the wine country on Iceberg's bus, stopping at all the instrument manufacturers that were strung up and down the coast. At one point I heard Roger playing this riff on the way home, so I went back and asked him what it was. He said, 'I don't know' so we wrote it! That was back in 1982. T-Bone Burnette cut it first but it languished for eight years until Mary Chapin found it. I didn't even know it was out until I saw it on the charts! I was invited to Nashville to receive an award and then all kinds of co-writing opportunities opened up. Me moving there, and all that followed, was a result of 'Quittin' Time.'"

Nevertheless, despite the failure of Tracks, he and Mike had stayed in touch, with Finnigan often providing a voice in the studio with which Robb could record his demos. Then, in 1983, Robb agreed to take on board an assignment for the English rock band Queen, the renowned four-piece who had risen from the discarded glitter of English glam rock to become one of the world's premier stadium performers. The band's management had initially come to him, knowing of his involvement in both music and film, requesting he piece together some video footage from varying sources into a comprehensible project for them. Taking on the form of an extended promotional video, Robb pulled it all together, weaving a number of the band's distinctive compositions into one piece.

"I had sold a couple of projects at that point, and I was talking to Paramount, and I knew various people in the industry, so their management came to me and said, 'Can you do this film?' They dumped a whole load of footage in my lap, and I tried to do a long-form video that involved several of their songs. They liked it and I think it got made, but they were dogged with their new image at that point, and weren't that interested in the footage of the old days." During work on the project, Robb also accompanied the band on their 1983 European tour, and spent a short period living in England immediately afterwards. "They were an unbelievable band," he laughs.

Following his return to America, he continued writing and recording, still using Mike Finnigan as vocalist on his sessions, while also briefly reuniting with James Griffin in the sadly unsuccessful band, Circuit. However, it was with Mike's errant younger brother, Sean Finnigan, that Robb's next musical collaboration took place. Sean's background was notably in line with the traditional musical "outlaw." A talented composer and performer in his own right, he had literally been on the run himself after a series of misdemeanors against the law, the result being "time inside" for his crimes. With Sean now undertaking a series of counseling sessions and intent on rectifying his past misjudgments, Robb was clearly comfortable working with the youngest of the Finnigan brothers, having first met him back at the start of the decade. The duo had initially collaborated on a number of unsuccessful screenplays, including *Club Fed*, but now Robb and Sean chose to pool their musical resources to form another new band, one they called The Road Dogs. After adding drummer Michael J. Dohoney, bass player Gerald Johnson, and guitarist Drake Macy, the band started by playing a number of local gigs, and then taped a series of songs in the studio, including the Finnegan-Royer co-compositions "Run," "Modern Day Romeo," "Lonely River Rise," and "Pickup Truck," the latter containing a distinct "country" overtone, written in the wake of Robb's success with "Quittin' Time." With Robb on synthesizer and Sean supplying piano, the band was soon "discovered" by Ed Leffler, former tour manager for The Osmonds and Sweet, and currently to be found running the Van Halen empire. Leffler was reportedly extremely impressed with The Road Dogs having seen their stage act but, sadly for all involved, he couldn't maintain his enthusiasm due to failing health. Despite this setback, the band continued plugging away but seemingly to little avail, and by the turn of the decade they had each gone their separate ways – except, that is, for Robb and Sean. Instead, they pulled elder brother Mike into the fray, with Robb reverting to guitar, and The Finnigan Bros. band was conceived.

"That was Robb's idea," continues Mike. "I had demo'd several of his country tunes. It was kind of in that period when country made the transition from 'real' country music, like Merle Haggard and George Jones, into what it has become now, with a more pop sensibility. Robb was the driving force behind it. It was a project more focused on recording, and getting a record deal, than running around, y'know, doing gigs."

With recording sessions commencing at the Stagg Street Studios in the Van Nuys district of Los Angeles, and running over a lengthy period of almost two years, the trio worked doggedly on a series of new compositions. Mike: "It was something we would do when we could get together. We'd do a track here and there, maybe a couple of months later do some singin' on it. It wasn't like we were in there for two years. I was always working, doin' other things. To me, the best one of all of 'em was a song called 'All Heaven Broke Loose.' That was a great song. We cut a lot..."

With the vast majority of the songs being written by Robb, at least half being solo compositions, and the remainder comprising a selection of collaborations with writing partners Roger Linn, Ira Ingber, James Griffin, and the brothers themselves, the tracks impressively bridged the divide between the varying genres of country, gospel, blues, and rock. Sean also managed to bring one song of his own into the sessions, the gritty ballad "Last Night," which featured the distinct high harmonies and guitar work of James Griffin added to the mix. However, it was the addition of the Griffin-Royer composition "Let Me See The Light" that was to garner the most attention when, eventually, the songs were released. Originating from a co-composition between James and Robb, both writers had eventually finished work on it themselves after early attempts had stalled. James's version was to become "The Healing Has Begun," while Robb's approach featured an equally spiritual overtone.

"That was really interesting. That was done for the score of a film that was never completed," recalls Mike today. Dominated by the amazingly soulful vocal prowess of the elder brother, and recorded at a special studio session during March 1991, the song featured numerous luminaries from Mike's vast circle of musical acquaintances, all coming together under one roof, with the session also being videotaped. Viewed within the amassed crowd, the notable presence of Stephen Stills, Billy Preston, Bonnie Bramlett, Kim Carnes, Marilyn Martin, Ritchie Hayward, and legendary Chicago-bluesman Willie Dixon are all evident, along with both Robb and Sean, and the early gospel influences that James had grown up with, surrounded by his sister and extended family members, are all too clear in the initial structure of the song.

"The film was never completed, but Sean and Robb were involved and, I think, Sean just brought everybody in. That just happened to be the video for one of the tunes, intended for the score."

Also taped at these sessions was a new version of "Quittin' Time," featuring a duet between Mike and session vocalist Teresa James. However, the first Finnigan Brothers song to receive a public airing was another Sean-Robb contribution entitled "I've Fallen," issued on Robb's own Coyote Records label during the early months of the decade.

"That was a pretty good track," Mike adds. "Pretty clever. Robb took it into a kind of tongue-in-cheek love song deal. There was a commercial on television at the time, it showed this woman saying 'I've fallen…' and it was a play on that, because the commercial was all over the place in that period."

While it failed to garner any significant success, the accompanying video did manage a reasonable run on the televised Nashville network, TNN. And yet, despite their overall commitment to the sessions, and the genuine quality of such songs as "Boys," featuring some amazing guitar riffs from Robb, "Mornin' Came," "Feet Of Clay," and the wonderfully commercial possibilities of "My Apology," the remaining tracks were unfortunately shelved when, with a proposed deal with Curb Records on the table, the project was wound down. As Mike was to say later: "We had some killer songs and killer players and had the luxury of doing it slowly and thoughtfully. We came within a whisker of making a deal but when the label found out I was 47 years old, they panicked and backed out." It would take sixteen years for the album to finally see the light.

1991 would also see Robb reconnect with David Gates, again sounding out the idea of potentially reforming Bread in its original line-up but, as had James's similar suggestion a few years earlier, the proposal failed to develop, despite the two exchanging letters and ideas.

Robb: "David sent me his music at the time and I sent him some of mine, including 'Feet Of Clay,' (and) he was initially very interested but dropped the idea after meeting with Griffin and Knechtel in Nashville, a meeting I didn't know about. I got the usual 20-second call from David, simply saying 'changed my mind.'

Instead, Robb returned to work on yet another project, one that had originated almost two decades before, when he'd first made friends with composer Michael Iceberg, during the James Griffin *Breakin' Up Is Easy* sessions. Since the release of that album, the two musicians had remained in touch over the ensuing years, reuniting and composing together as time allowed (the unreleased "Fanfare" and "Robot Revolt" being two such examples), and by combining their love of classical music, most notably the works of Aaron Copeland and Johann Sebastian Bach, they had developed *Coplach*, a suitably labeled collaborative work that successfully intertwined Iceberg's instrumental abilities with Robb's visionary and arranging talents.

"We had written some songs together, and he was really the center of the whole electronic community of California," says Robb. "I was recording him one day doing this improv, and I was getting it on tape. I went through it, saying, 'What if we did this here, what if we did that there?' So I more arranged it than wrote it, but we made this really wonderful little classical piece."

It would be a work that Robb was to return to, on and off, over the coming years, finally completing the project during 2004 when an accompanying video, comprising surreal footage focusing on Mother Nature's beauty, season by season, was shot around Robb's Tennessee farm. Although the film was never intended for the market in a commercial sense, it was one of the first projects that was to bear the mark of Nashfilms, Robb's new media company and an extension of his Coyote Records label, based in the heart of Nashville. But, as of the early 1990s, all of this was still to come, despite the move to Nashville being imminent.

Over the past few years it had become clear that the new country movement establishing itself during that period was influencing much of Robb's composing.

Newer artists such as Dwight Yoakum, Hal Ketchum, and Mary Chapin Carpenter were revitalizing the industry, while the old guard of George Jones, Willie Nelson, Waylon Jennings, and the Cash-Carter alliance were still making inroads, continually stretching the boundaries for those that followed. James Griffin's current success with The Remingtons in Nashville, along with Robb's own songwriting achievement for Chapin Carpenter, naturally made the decision for him to relocate to the heart of country music an obvious choice, and in a role reversal of his former partner who went from Tennessee to California to find success, Robb took the return road along Route 66, moving out of his native California and settling down in Tennessee farmland during 1994. "Well, it *is* Music City, and here they were cutting my songs, while in L.A., it was like 'Robb who?' So I knew I belonged here," he would later comment.

As was James's custom for a get-together (no excuse needed), a huge "Welcome to Nashville" party was organized on Robb's behalf, held on the porch of Jim Della Croce's house, with attendees including Jim, Andy Taylor from Duran Duran, Dave Colwell and Robert Hart from Bad Company, Jim Horn, Henry Gross, Todd Cerney, and Billy Burnette. It was quite a night. Nevertheless, since he was met coming off the plane at Nashville International airport by his former partner, it now made sense that one of his first new musical undertakings since moving to the city would be beside James, but what made this next sequence of events all the more surprising was their decision to incorporate Larry Knechtel into the immediate set-up.

Once the euphoria of Robb's arrival in town had died down, and with his commitment to The Remingtons now having eased following the disappointing response to the band's second album (one final Remingtons recording, a rockabilly version of "Blue Christmas," later appeared on *Sounds Of The Season*, a 1993 BNA album), James's interest in reconnecting with Robb was undoubtedly foremost in his mind. But, since his falling out with his other former Bread band mates over the lawsuits, contact with David, Mike, or Larry had been minimal, despite both he and Larry working in the same musical circle. The fact that Larry had contributed to his Black Tie recordings was a sign that the thaw was gradually melting, but there had been no serious commitment to working together again until, that is, Robb moved to Nashville and unwittingly became the catalyst for a reunion.

"I worked with Jimmy immediately," says Robb of his initial arrival in Nashville, "and we met Todd Cerney, who we started working with. Together we wrote a song called 'Kyrie' which we wrote as a country pitch. When we wrote it, I was under a heavy Dave Loggins influence. Dave could write songs that were so natural and free flowing that there hardly seemed to be a form at all until you looked closely and saw the masterful construction. This was my shot at that kind of a song. I love that song. Then I rang Larry and we got together."

Todd Cerney was a young, successful, part of the Nashville music community, and a close friend of Jim Della Croce. Having himself been a Grammy nominee and an ASCAP award winner for his songwriting, his initial acceptance into this new collaboration certainly didn't faze the talented performer. On a musical level, Della Croce, like so many others, was keen to see Bread reform and had also approached David Gates with the idea of reforming the quartet, but, as with those before him, had also been knocked back. Still, it was his introduction of the youthful Cerney into the set-up that seemed to add that missing fourth ingredient.

Toast at 3rd & Lindsley (courtesy of Robb Royer)

In conversation with the author, shortly before his untimely death in March of 2011, Todd recollected his initial thoughts about working with Robb, James, and Larry:

"When I was in junior high school and I first heard Bread, I always thought Jimmy was the lead singer. He was always up front in the pictures and truth is he was the best singer and could sound just like David. Bread didn't really have any visual reference, they didn't tour much or do TV much so I didn't know the truth for years. At the same time I always wondered why David Gates needed to be in a band. Didn't he do everything by himself pretty much? It took being around these guys to really understand their contributions to David's songs."

Taken at face value, with three-fifths of Bread featured in the line-up, and now with Todd Cerney up front, this new working partnership initially took to calling themselves Toast (later names included both Radio Dixie and Bread Revisited), the name clearly a humorous take on their former band, although it was a name that didn't sit too comfortably with James. "Jimmy didn't like using 'Toast' for several reasons," continued Todd. "He didn't have quite the same sense of humor about it as Robb and Larry, and he also said someone had suggested that name to him years before so he worried about giving them credit."

Even so, it was under that name that the band began working up a set together, using local drummers Steve Turner and Martin Parker to fill out the sound and, while the band only went on to play a handful of dates around Nashville, appearing in clubs such as The Bluebird Café, Exit/In, The Boardwalk, and Café Milano, it was mainly a collection of newer songs that were performed before the audiences.

Cerney: "My idea was to have a three lead singer group à la The Band, with a blues base and hillbilly harmony and Robb's off the wall lyrics. We never found the other singer who could go along with the concept. The highlight of the live shows was usually the piano-mandolin instrumental duets that Larry and I had worked up, and Robb's song 'Feet Of Clay' (previously recorded with the Finnigan Brothers).

"We were asked to do some of David's songs for some of the shows, but Jimmy wouldn't hear of it except for 'Everything I Own.' He said that was his favorite of David's tunes. I had to work up 'Make It With You,' 'Baby I'm-A Want You,' and 'Guitar Man' for one gig and I think we only played one of them. I don't sound much like David Gates so that couldn't have been a very good plan. Out of spite we did work up a bluegrass medley that started with 'Deliverance,' and then morphed into 'Baby I'm-A Want You,' and then into 'If,' all at breakdown speed. It was pretty hilarious… at least to Larry and myself."

The band also cut an album's worth of material, provisionally titled *Radio Dixie*, mostly out of Todd Cerney's home studio, although James's interest in the project was not so involved as that of Royer, Knechtel, and Cerney, and he only actually appeared at a few of the recording sessions. Musically, the core of the band revolved around Larry on keyboards and bass, Robb on acoustic guitar and keys, with Todd filling in on both electric and acoustic guitars, mandolin, and bass, while also offering up the programming and engineering duties. Turner and Parker sat in on drums as and when required. James did, however, contribute to a number of the songs in his capacity as songwriter, with "Grenadine," "Slow Train," and "Radio Dixie" featuring the names of all four musicians listed as co-contributors.

Cerney confirmed this: "It was mostly Larry, Robb, and myself. Jimmy sang lead on 'Grenadine' and 'Slow Train' and was also a writer and sang harmony on 'Radio Dixie.' 'Slow Train' was the one we wrote at our first meeting. Larry had this great intro with the demodulation and we went from there. Larry on piano and bass, Robb on acoustic, me on mandolin and harmony and Jimmy on the lead vocal. Robb then brought in Larry Byrom to play slide and Steve Turner was the drummer. This was the one that got me excited because it was the right kind of vehicle for Jimmy's lead vocal with the Memphis thing. It was also perfect for my harmony because I could sing in a good range below him and I was hoping we'd do a lot more of this type of thing. Jimmy was so good at this style. I was in it mostly for the chance to play with Larry because he was the best and most compatible musician I had ever worked with. I've heard a lot of people say that about Larry. Most of the material we wrote together had roots in his heavy New Orleans piano player influences such as Huey 'Piano' Smith. Larry was interested in the project because it was one of the first times he got a chance to be involved with the songwriting process in a big way. I was playing mostly mandolin and ended up being the lead singer and front man as we went along because Jimmy's interest was slowly waning. Robb, of course, was instrumental in actually getting everybody in the same room at the same time to begin with."

Other songs taped during the sessions included "Cordellia," "Wrong Side Of Goodbye," "Feet Of Clay," "Larry The Piano Man," "Oolie's Cadillac," "Jethro's Doggett," "She Up And Let Me Down" (aka "Living On The Moon"), "Feliciana," and "Roadkill On The Highway Of Love," along with the wonderful Royer-Cerney- Knechtel composition "Magdalena."

Robb was later to comment: "I wrote the lyric (for 'Magdalena') as kind of a tribute to the generous spirit of my wife Madeleine. I imagined a story about a guy who is down on his luck, has taken a tremendous fall, possibly homeless, and is now obsessing on a girl he occasionally sees, who seems to embody everything that is positive and hopeful for him. The record is unfinished; we never got the guitars on. We have Todd's vocal and mandolin, my keyboard, and Larry's bass part but I had a really specific idea what the track should sound like and I guess I drove everybody nuts. I wanted a certain on-the-upbeat bass part that was completely foreign to Larry, but to his credit he hung in there and got it for me..."

One other song also hailing from that period was the Royer-Knechtel tune, "No More Smokin'," a number that gave Larry a rare appearance in the vocal booth.

"That was the first song Larry and I wrote when I got to Nashville," Robb continued. "It was a humorous take on his relationship with Vicki, written around '94. It was later cut by Toast, but we never finished it."

Unfortunately, the album never came to fruition, and the tracks remained in various vaults over the years. Todd was later to issue a number of them, including "Radio Dixie," on one of his own solo albums, the excellent *We'll Be Back*, but then, in 2011, a casual conversation between Robb and this author prompted a further dig into the Cerney archives, the result of which saw Robb revisit the tracks with the intention of a long-overdue release.

Despite the band originally remaining together for a reasonable period of time, playing and performing in one capacity or another, coming back together when the demand necessitated, it was always a loose aggregation, and never a committed "group" per se. The line-up would often splinter as they chose to work on separate, or individual projects, and on one such occasion a band consisting of James, Jim Della Croce, Terry Sylvester, Billy Kelly (formerly of The Bouys), Don Brewer, Rusty Russell, and Vince Melamed appeared together in Boston, performing at a charity benefit show, sponsored for the Boston Celtics basketball team. Yet the central focus for the union was always the gathering of Griffin, Royer, Knechtel, and Cerney. Unfortunately, it all fell apart once Larry decided that he wanted to return to his beloved Washington State, undertaking a self-imposed semi-retirement, simply resuming his part-time session duties.

"The last gig that Larry did with us was right before he left town. He was just ready to cut that tie and go back to his family and be more of a player-musician than a group-musician," says Robb, while the last word lies with Todd Cerney: "In the end I was glad to get away from it because the obvious Bread comparisons were going to come up. They were forbidden by lawsuit to use the name Bread or imply it but the clubs were always wanting to promote that aspect of it without knowing what we sounded like."

However, Larry's intended retirement was not to last too long as, once again, the Golden Goose was about to rear its head for one last time.

David Gates had been living a very quiet life for the past decade or so. Following on from the disappointment of his final Elektra album, *Falling In Love Again*, he had signed with the Arista label, releasing the brand new studio album *Take Me Now* during 1981. In the lead-up to the album he had gone on record during an interview with Tulsa journalist Ellis Widner, stating that, "I've been stockpiling ideas. I want to do a concept piece that may consist of four or five songs relating to one story. I'd also like to explore the jazz-rock side of music a bit more and work with more sophisticated chords and musical structures."

The resulting album was pretty much standard fare for David's followers, offering up little advance from the recognizable, well-worn, quality three-minute productions. And yet, it should be clearly stated, that this was by no means a complete throwaway on David's behalf. Simply put, it just wasn't any different from what his loyal followers were perhaps hoping for – a new album, with maybe a new sound. Nevertheless, some of the compositions were a considerable improvement on what had graced much of the preceding release, with the sentimental title track, the thoroughly enjoyable "Vanity," and the heavier "It's What You Say" being among the more successful inclusions. Certainly, the latter of these three was by far the most adventurous attempt at a serious rock number since Bread had initially disbanded back in the late spring of 1974, and the dueling of David's electric guitar and Larry Knechtel's keyboards is a delight to hear. In addition, just maybe some of those jazz overtones he had been talking about in interviews had actually come to the fore in the sessions after all, with the graceful swing-fusion that graced "Lady Valentine" containing some delightful horn arrangements. However, perhaps this idea went further than he was currently prepared for.

Discussing the release, this time with journalist Cathy Milam, David continued: "My contract with Elektra was up, and I had just built this new house with my own 24-track studio. I wanted to try doing my own recording there. Arista gave me the chance. Everything on the album is recorded there, except for the strings. I think it is a better sound. I listen to the old songs now, and think how much younger I sounded then, but I can still hit the falsetto notes. Plus, I sing out more. I'm not so timid about my voice."

A richly produced affair, with lush arrangements running throughout, the album was actually a critical success in hindsight, with seasoned performances from all participants. Although it's noticeable how the initial sessions revolved around a simple core of four musicians – David, Larry Knechtel on keyboards and bass, guitarist Hadley Hockensmith, and drummer Paul Leim – and other than the occasional contribution from an additional player (such as Mike Botts sitting in on "Vanity") it was taped very much in the style of Bread, a straightforward four-piece band.

Unfortunately, the lyrical aspect of David's work was still potentially his Achilles' heel, with some numbers suffering due to their lyrical absurdity. "Nineteen On The Richter Scale," a track benefiting from some refreshing Knechtel honky-tonk playing, is an obvious example. However, David's principal focus for the album was upon the title track, "Take Me Now," a gorgeous melodramatic number, notably superior in both sound and approach to the similarly-styled "Lost Without Your Love," but sadly, not so successful, peaking at #62. With this song alone, David had come up with one of his strongest ballads in a long, long time, but just maybe the industry had moved on one step too far for him. The disco theme of the previous album had been an unsettling experience for both artist and audience, but with this new release he had moved back to safer territory, yet had his fans followed back with him? Possibly not. The subsequent choice for a follow-up single did little to improve matters, with David opting to issue the album's strangest track, a seasonal composition entitled "Come Home For Christmas." It was a pretty enough piece, with David providing all the instrumentation himself, but it was certainly not one of the stronger cuts, and its inclusion seemingly made the album redundant for much of the year.

"I want to make the next big Christmas song," he had told Milam, "something that will last, like 'White Christmas.' You never hear really great Christmas songs anymore. That's why I wrote it…" Unfortunately, his faith in the song was sadly misplaced, despite a festive November 1981 release, and the single, and subsequently the album, faltered unceremoniously. It was not an auspicious start to his relationship with Arista. Additionally, sales were not helped by the seemingly little promotional work that he put into the release, with TV appearances few and far between. Certainly, two appearances on the TV show *Solid Gold*, hosted by Andy Gibb & Marilyn McCoo, one of which was performing "Goodbye Girl," went little way to aiding the dwindling retail figures. All the same, David still made himself available for press interviews, and in a further article by former *Rolling Stone* writer Rob Hoerburger, David suggested that his future plans might include branching out into Broadway music, or taking on more film themes although, commenting on his recent offering, he concluded:

"I don't think (the new songs) are dramatically different. I still really believe in melody and a good lyric that matches the melody as far as the emotion. I try not to repeat myself but I'd like to stay where I can write the best kind of music. My music is not slick, but it's well thought out and arranged.

"Perhaps it's less important to me now," he continued, "to have a big hit than it was ten years ago because I've had some major successes. But if you don't get a few pats on the back along the way you're going to say 'Why bother if nobody's listening?'"

And was anybody still listening? The album failed to chart on either side of the Atlantic and, despite his earlier thoughts regarding developing his career into musical theater and film, David instead withdrew to his Northern California ranch, appearing only sporadically over the coming years. He did make one guest appearance on an album track for fellow Arista recording artist Melissa Manchester, performing a duet on the enjoyable "Wish We Were Heroes," taken from her 1982 Top 20 *Hey Ricky* album, but such occurrences were sadly few and far between as the decade progressed.

In discussion with *NetMusic* in 1994, David would comment on his apparent withdrawal from the industry over this particular period. "I kept in touch. I listened a lot. I kept up my subscription to *Billboard*, watched MTV and *Video Hits One,* and stuff like that. I sort of backed off on the writing and performing part of it and I would jot down some ideas once in a while. But I really kind of got away from it. I had been at it so long that it was time for me to get on and do a few of those personal things I had wanted to do. And I just couldn't do everything at once, you know. So I decided to jump into this ranching full time and enjoy it, something I've always wanted to do."[9]

In a further interview, he revealed: "I figured that getting away from music might recharge me. I'd done it for so long I felt a layoff would be healthy, and I'd gone off to do this rancher-cowboy thing that I'd wanted to do since I was a kid. I did an awful lot of working with the livestock, baling hay, feeding cattle in the winter in the snow, all of those visions of the Old West you see! And, I have to tell you, the lifestyle, being close to nature, was just a fabulous experience. I wouldn't trade it for anything. I've got a two-story white frame house built in 1907 that looks like the Waltons' house. But after a while you begin to feel the hunger. You hear things on the radio and you think, 'I wonder if I could write something as good as that?'

"To begin writing songs again I'd need an outlet for them. I tried showing my songs to other artists but I kept running into situations where people would go, 'Well, why don't you go do it yourself?' After a while I ran into Jac Holzman who'd owned Elektra Records and signed Bread. I played him my songs and he liked them. He said, 'Why don't we try it again? We did pretty good the last time!'"

By the turn of the following decade, it had been nine years since David had last ventured into a recording agreement. Life on the ranch with Jo Rita and his youngest two children had been good for him, but clearly, as it had been with fellow landowner Larry Knechtel, the music still burned deep inside. Recent cover versions of his compositions had maintained his presence among the music charts around the world, with Julio Iglesias recording a version of "If' ("E Poi") on his best-selling 1984 album *1100 Bel Air Place*, while three years later English pop star Boy George took "Everything I Own" back to the very top of the charts in six different countries. In addition, a further 20-track compilation of Bread material, *Anthology*, had achieved platinum status upon its release by Elektra during 1985, and yet it would always be debatable as to whether David could once again conjure up the successes he had previously experienced. Nevertheless, the quality of his new music was unquestionable.

His first forays back into the scene came about during 1990 when he started demoing some of the recent ideas he'd been working on in his home studio. Then, in 1992, having heard country artist Billy Dean performing the CMA-winning song "Somewhere In My Broken Heart," he called up Dean's producer Jimmy Bowen, an old friend of his, to sound out if his new tunes would be deemed acceptable for the country music market. Impressed by what he heard, Bowen put David in touch with Billy, suggesting they collaborate. Meeting up in, of all places, Dean's home city of Nashville, the duo composed three songs that were to become the core of David's comeback release: "I Will Wait For You," "No Secrets In A Small Town," and "I Can't Find The Words To Say Goodbye." The two musicians also appeared on TNN's *American Music Shop* performing a rendition of "Guitar Man," among others.

"It took me a while to get the songwriting machine cranking again," said David at the time, now decked out with the obligatory Stetson hat. "But once I did they seemed to come along pretty good. Nashville seemed to be where it was happening, just as when I first left Oklahoma, Los Angeles was the place to be. I'd been following country and pop for a long time, and I felt some of the best songs were being written for the country market. My voice comes from a pop background, but a lot of my heart has gone over to country, so I'm kind of straddling."[9] [28]

Settling in Tennessee for the duration of the recording, David used some of the very best musicians the city had to offer, including Eddie Bayers, Jerry Douglas, Lee Roy Parnell, Michael Rhodes, and Brent Mason, and with experienced engineer Bill Schnee sitting alongside him in the control booth, they pulled together a fine collection of songs. Also in attendance for much of the time was Larry Knechtel, still resident in the city at that point and once again happy to fill in as David's right-hand man. For the first time, David also took to recording the work of an outside composer, with "Ordinary Man" being the work of David Martin, but the remainder of the recorded songs all bore the credit of David Gates, apart from the three co-compositions with Billy Dean, who also contributed some backing vocals to the sessions.

Meanwhile, friend and founder of Elektra Records, Jac Holzman, was about to play a pivotal role once more in David's career. Having recently taken up the post of label chairman for Discovery Records, a label distributed by Warner Music, Jac was now confident that, having listened to David's new songs, he could resurrect his career. Since arriving at the company, Jac had expanded the roster to incorporate a far wider spectrum than the early jazz releases the label had become famous for, and David Gates' new country-influenced recordings seemed an ideal addition. Subsequently, pen was put to paper and during 1993 David signed up as an official Discovery Records artist.

The resulting album was, simply put, an outstanding critical achievement and, for a man now in his sixth decade, it was a pleasure to hear him still rocking. Unlike some performers who, perhaps, should refrain from such upbeat deliberations, David produced a mix and variety of styles that belied his years, with the underlying sound of a country heartbeat thumping in time. And more importantly, he carried it off successfully – perhaps more so than he had ever done in his solo career before. *Love Is Always Seventeen* appeared in stores on September 6th, 1994, with the title track being shipped as a single in advance, but radio play was initially wary of the release, skeptical of David's past, with the MD of one of Nashville's top stations stating that "the problem that I would probably be dealing with is that he still has the old Bread baggage. I would see that as a minus."

"We're dealing with a pop icon here," Syd Birenbaum, Discovery's VP of Sales and Marketing was to state, "but at the same time we're dealing with someone who hasn't been in front of people on an ongoing or contemporary basis for years. David has an acknowledged and tangible base of interest at AC (adult contemporary) pop, but the audience for the musical values that he has always represented has shifted from pop in the '70s to country today." In other words, despite the overall appeal of the record, the audience that had given David so much success in the past was now scattered to the wind, the clouds, and the rain, and he was going to find it an uphill struggle to secure a comfortable niche from which he could once again find success. Clearly, the need was to break down such barriers, push the album forward, and promote it as a new product, a new beginning. But, with the confusing crossover between the AC stations and the country-dominated stations causing concerns, the initial reluctance among U.S. radio undoubtedly hindered the album's growth.

David himself was all too aware of the issues. "Well, I think that it's got the best collection of songs I've ever had. It's really excellent, I'm really pleased with it. We had a lot of good musicians there and Nashville helped me out. It's not reached the public yet in the numbers that I hoped it would. That is primarily because we can't get adequate radio play on the singles to make people aware that there is an album available. So it's fighting the battle. I think 'Love Is Always Seventeen' on that album is the second best song I've ever written, after 'If.' I love that song, (but) if it's not going to do a whole lot better, if this one doesn't get up and move, I probably won't stay with these people. I'll do something different, but I don't know what."[9]

Tough talking, but in truth David didn't really need the success anymore. Certainly not from a financial perspective. But, as with most musicians, it is the acceptance of all the hard work that becomes paramount, and if Discovery Records couldn't break what was, potentially, the finest solo work David had achieved to date, then what else could they do for him?

Kicking off with the bluesy-pop feel of "Avenue Of Love," the album progresses through the whimsical sentimentality of the title track, then shifts tempos and moods as it flows right down to the closing tribute to James Taylor, the delightful "Thankin' You Sweet Baby James." And yet, despite the class and sheen of the music, without the support of the radio station pushing the album release, it was a battle bound to be lost, and it clearly failed to find a home among the music-buying audience of America. Peaking at a disappointing #39 on *Billboard*'s Heatseekers chart, a list compiled for new and breaking albums, *Love Is Always Seventeen* failed completely to find a position in either the national Top 200 or the Country Chart. There was talk at one stage of a supporting tour to aid the poor sales, with a number of promoters reportedly keen to handle such an event, but, save for a lone date or two appearing as the support act for Judy Collins, nothing came of it.

> *"As a singer and songwriter of the '70s pop group Bread, Gates created a body of introspective love songs that was the mainstay of every high school prom playlist of the time. Although Gates did pursue a solo career after Bread disbanded, his current Love Is Always Seventeen album is his first solo project since the early '80s. In that decade and a half, the kind of melancholy ballads that Gates is famous for are now more at home in the country market, and Gates has taken that to heart right down to sporting a big black cowboy hat on stage.*
>
> *"Playing acoustic guitar and surrounded by a string quartet, "Yesterday" style, Gates offered a 45-minute retrospective of both old and new material linked by amusing anecdotes and chatter. The songs are oversentimental, to be sure, but they are very well crafted and quite tuneful. It is not an easy thing to come up with ditties so simple that they have an instant, irresistible appeal, but Gates has that gift."*
>
> —Dennis Polkow, *The Chicago Tribune*, August, 1995

As for a full tour, David remained skeptical: "There's a lot of demand for the old things," he said at the time. "It wouldn't be a nostalgia thing. It would consist of rhythm sections and orchestras. I've always wanted to do an orchestral tour, and there are a lot of these community symphonies we could use. There's a very good chance we'll do it next fall, where we'd mix the old hits with the new things." Such an opportunity would eventually arise, two years later, but circumstances would prove slightly different from what was envisaged at this stage...

One other solo composition was to see the light of day that year, with Billy Dean recording a new David Gates song entitled "Love & Bide" for his *Men'll Be Boys* album, issued on the Liberty Records label. Accompanied by Dean's own version of "I Can't Find The Words To Say Goodbye," one of the songs from their fruitful writing partnership, the album would actually go on to be the country singer's least successful release in his catalog, but it was one that would nevertheless put the name of David Gates back into the charts once more, something his own album had failed to do. In the meantime, for David himself, it was time to move on... again. But what would be that next move?

Back on the road (courtesy of Jonathan Boba)

Back on the road (courtesy of Susan Crowder)

Questioned by Bill Kornman for *NetMusic* in 1994 as to whether he would ever consider that lucrative reunion with his former colleagues in Bread he responded: "Never. I have no interest in that whatsoever. I don't have any desire to go back and rehash old ground like that. It would not be pleasant. There would not be any real reason to do it. (The music) can stay popular without us getting back together. I haven't really seen anyone get back together and really be successful and recapture the original spirit just yet. I've seen The Moody Blues, watched The Eagles, and it just is not the same when you are gone. You just can't pick up from where you left off..."[9]

Chapter Eighteen

Just Say When

Mike Botts, the only former Bread member not to have been drawn into regular work within the Nashville music scene, was still a busy man. Los Angeles-based studio sessions, television commercials, touring, all went towards maintaining steady employment, and fortunately for him, he was still very much in demand.

"Studio players are like the unsung heroes in a way. These guys come in and they're like fast-gun artists. Quick draw. They call them in and they do that number. Fortunately, for each guy in Bread, we worked for many years as studio players to keep the rent paid, until our salad days came along so to speak. That experience has probably affected all of us, professionally, more than anything I can think of. It gave me the edge to do the studio work for commercials, single recordings, demos, anything, just as a freelance. Through working as an independent, your own agent, your own manager, your own everything, you're going to have to get professional or hang it up."[31]

In an earlier interview Mike had laughingly made reference to the "tons and tons of commercial work" he had undertaken since the demise of Bread. "I'm sure that Americans across the country have been hearing me play on 'You asked for it, you got it, Toyota' and Chevy commercials."

One of his early 1990 collaborations resulted in the unlikeliest of partnerships, but one that would give him, and his former band, much credence during the coming years. During 1990 he first became associated with the decidedly yellow-hued, dysfunctional family hailing from the town of Springfield, somewhere deep within the United States. Known collectively as *The Simpsons*, this cartoon creation was widely accepted for being one of the "hippest" shows on TV, and initially Mike had supplied drums to the TV family's CD release *Simpsons Sings The Blues*, a gathering of spoof songs supposedly "performed" by the popular creation. This wasn't a wonderfully creative release by any stretch of the imagination, novelty status at best, but it was yet another astonishingly successful marketing ploy by the creators of the show, peaking with a *Billboard* Top 3 chart placing and achieving a double platinum award for sales. However, that wasn't to be the end of *The Simpsons* connection as, during the following years, Bread would be honored with a number of mentions within the TV series itself, courtesy of scriptwriter Donick Cary who had become good friends with Mike and Michele, having rented out their house during the financially "difficult" years. On two or three occasions during the series' lengthy run, Cary and his writing colleagues would "sneak in" humorous acknowledgments to Bread, while also occasionally using their music as a soundtrack to the comic capers of Bart, Homer, and company. At a more serious musical level, 1991 saw Mike link up with composer and multi-instrumentalist Dan Fogelberg, joining him on his North American tour, the results of which were to appear on the *Dan Fogelberg Live: Greetings From The West* album and video release.

"That was probably one of the most fun times Michael had, playing with Dan," says Mike's wife Michele. "But it was really funny. It was in 1991, and Michael got this call and he says, 'who's this guy Dan Fogelberg?' I said, 'Botts! You've never heard of Dan Fogelberg?' and he says, 'Not really.' I said, 'It's Bread, but with more diversity!' So he submitted a demo tape of his work and a day goes by and they call asking if he'd like to be Dan's new drummer. As I say, Dan's music was so diverse. One minute it was kick-ass rock'n'roll, then it was R&B, and then forty minutes into the show Dan would do some of his ballads, just him and the piano. Michael had a blast!"

Indeed, the subsequent video release from the tour would go on to show Mike at his prolific best, pounding the skins from behind the frontline, with Fogelberg noticeably introducing him to the cheering crowd as "one of Los Angeles' top session musicians," with no mention of his greatest claim to fame. Mike would also work with Dan on his next studio album, *River Of Souls* (1993). In between his times with the band, he would continue working the sessions (including further comic creations The Muppets and Alvin & The Chipmunks) while also developing his own material, either up in his small home studio or at Sound City Recorders, a popular recording complex owned by Mike's then-manager Joe Gottfried, from where Fleetwood Mac had based much of their early AOR success.

Then in 1996, following on from the issue of his collection of studio performances and samples (*The JBL Sessions*), he recorded and released *Double Platinum Drums*, a CD-Rom of yet more samples and loops distributed by ILIO Products, compiled in partnership with producers Anthony Harris and John Boylan. Michele: "Michael and Anthony had this idea to do the drum sounds, and they went to John Boylan because John had hired Michael for so many hits. 'Lookin' For Love' (a #1 smash for Johnny Lee), 'Harden My Heart' (Quarterflash), Mickey Gilley, Michael had so many hits with John, so they approached him as the producer. They used Sound City as Joe Gottfried would often let Michael book the studio for free to record some of his demos..."

Never intended for the mass market, this specialized release comprised numerous loops and patterns, expertly performed by Mike, spread over four discs and totaling up at nearly 2000 samples from which potential songwriters, musicians, and producers could select and work with. However, retailing at $300, adding Mike Botts to your home recording didn't come cheap. The partnership would also go on to create *Double Platinum Rock Piano* for the same market shortly afterwards.

While waiting for Dan Fogelberg to call him for the next tour, Mike instead received a call from a South African music entrepreneur named Selwyn Miller with a new proposition.

1995 had seen Robb Royer score another huge hit as a songwriter, consolidating his standing within the Nashville community. John Michael Montgomery had recorded Robb's co-composition, "Sold (The Grundy County Auction Incident)," written alongside Richard Fagan, and taken it right to the pinnacle of the *Billboard* Country Music charts. What with his songwriting status, and his involvement with a number of new projects, including the band Toast, Nashville looked like a very good place to be for Robb.

Meanwhile, James Griffin had also been maintaining his presence in the Tennessee studios, despite his waning interest in Toast, and had recently contributed to a number of noteworthy sessions. Firstly, in a journey that had gone full circle, he found himself offering vocal support to a forthcoming album for Paul Burlison, formerly the guitarist in The Rock & Roll Trio, fronted back in the late 1950s by Dorsey and Johnny Burnette. *Train Kept A-Rollin'*, when issued in 1997, would see James's name appear alongside other such notable contributors as Mavis Staples, Rick Danko, and Levon Helm, together with (following the deaths of both Dorsey and Johnny) Billy and Rocky Burnette, the next generation, both successful recording artists in their own right. The second session of note saw him adding his distinctive harmonies to the mix, this time for seasoned Nashville vocalist Bob Cheevers. With Larry Knechtel alongside him in the studio, and with a fleeting visit to the city by drummer Mike Botts, three-quarters of Bread were once more reunited to contribute to Cheevers' recording of "If This Old House Could Talk." It was yet another gathering of the diverse factions of the band, and yet it would take one further venture into the recording studios to trigger the final stage in reuniting Bread. This time it was a new series of recordings by popular soul singer Dobie Gray that set the ball rolling. James had known Dobie for over ten years by now, and they had become close friends since they first met while making the occasional appearance together at Ray Chafin's Horseshoe nightclub in Memphis.

"I introduced Dobie to Jimmy back in 1982," says Chafin today. "I had known him since 1965 when he recorded a song of mine called 'We The People,' and he lived in Nashville but he traveled to Memphis periodically. We became very close friends together from that point on. Although I wrote many songs with both Jimmy and Dobie, we never collaborated as a threesome, although Jimmy had joked to Dobie one day, 'Let's you and I do an album together, and we'll call it *Ebony & Ivory.*' I wish today I had run with those two doing that album."

Recently, James had been providing vocals to a number of Gray's songs and, at one stage, Dobie had introduced him to a business colleague who he'd worked with on tour in South Africa. This acquaintance, Selwyn Miller, ran his own established management and promotions company out of Los Angeles, and was currently to be found visiting Nashville on related matters. Upon meeting James, he commented that he'd love to get Bread back together to tour his native country where, as was often the case around the world, a recent *Best Of Bread* compilation album was to be found dipping in and out of the charts.

Selwyn recalls: "Jimmy said he'd love to get the group back together, but David didn't want to do it, but he'd give him another try. I told him that the (Best Of) album was #5 in the charts at that time, and climbing, but a number of months went by, and nothing. I kept calling Jimmy and he said, 'I've tried to reach David but I can't make any headway, but I'd be glad to give you his number.'"

For the next few months, Selwyn tried, without luck, to contact David, leaving a number of messages on his answer machine. Finally, while on a return journey to South Africa, Selwyn heard from the reticent Gates, asking him to make contact at his second home in Palm Desert, just outside of Palm Springs, upon his return Stateside. Needless to say, Selwyn immediately returned the call, excited at the prospect of finally talking with the retiring musician, and the two subsequently arranged to meet up in Los Angeles once Selwyn had made the long flight back to the West Coast.

"There was David and his wife Jo Rita, and we clicked immediately. David initially said, 'Selwyn, I don't really want to get together with the band. We haven't been together for seventeen years, but I'd like you to work with me.' But I said the first prize for me would be to definitely get the band back together because I think there's a market for them back in South Africa, and all over the world. He said he'd get back to me within a week..."

Despite all of the hard feelings that David held for his former band, he remained true to his word, and contacted Selwyn one week later, sending him a fax of his own personal arrangements stating what it would take to get him to reunite with his erstwhile partners. Quite what prompted David's eventual acceptance to reform Bread remains unclear. After all, it had only been a short while since he had refused such an offer from Jim Della Croce, but, just maybe, the continuing requests to reunite had finally sunk home. James had tried. Robb had tried. Jim had tried. He remains silent on specific detail but, as he realized, there was clearly a demand, and it was obviously an ideal launch pad from which to resurrect his solo career. Some even suggested that this was maybe his primary goal. He had recently completed a low key solo tour of his own, performing a number of shows around the southern states, but if Selwyn could now get all four members to agree to personal terms then, just maybe, a high profile Bread reunion could be given the green light. It all looked promising at the outset. One of David's other requests was that Selwyn himself was to manage the band, and spearhead the arrangements for a world tour, taking in countries around the globe that Bread, for one reason or another, hadn't managed to perform in during their earlier incarnations.

"I said to David that if I can get the other guys to agree, are you definitely going to go ahead with this? He replied, 'Selwyn, you have my word.' I then had individual meetings with Michael Botts in Los Angeles, and in Nashville with Jimmy Griffin and Larry Knechtel. After a series of lengthy meetings we came to an agreement and the next thing that happened was that on February 11th, 1996, at one of the function rooms at the Holiday Inn at Nashville airport, the four members of Bread – David, Jimmy, Larry, and Mike, along with myself – were together for the first time in seventeen years."

Needless to say, there was one notable absentee from the reunion. Was Robb Royer ever a serious consideration in the comeback? After all, he had been one of its founding members, and his recent partnership with both James and Larry had suggested he was more than happy to work alongside his former associates. In addition, had he not himself even suggested to David, five years before, that they consider resurrecting the group in its original form? But it was apparent, to both David and Selwyn, that it was the four group members who had seen the band achieve the dizzying success levels of their peak period, the *Baby I'm-A Want You* and *Guitar Man* years, that would be the focus of the reunion, and no additional invite was extended.

"I wasn't real happy about it," says Robb. "I knew what was going on, step by step, through Jimmy, but David had issued a manifesto to the other three guys, it went on and on for pages, and I figured that at one point David would get over this thing of whatever it was that I did."

Nevertheless, while it may appear that it had all been smooth sailing to date, with the various members putting aside any outstanding hostilities, bitterness, or disappointments for the sake of the reunion, all was not quite as it seemed. In order to get David to agree to participate, certain provisions would have to be accepted, one of which was that he was to receive 50 percent of all proceeds. Early on in the negotiations, James was offered a 25 percent cut and, although being co-owner of the band name and logo, he perhaps could have held out for parity with David but, with the latter's insistence on retaining the lion's share of the earnings before he would agree, James magnanimously accepted the offer without argument. After all, it promised to be a fairly lucrative outing. Larry, upon being told that his share would be just 12.5 percent, was also fairly swift in accepting the offer, although his reasoning for such a quick decision was undoubtedly still based around financial issues. That left just Mike to agree, and he was somewhat taken aback during his first meeting with Selwyn in finding that he, too, was only offered a 12.5 percent split, leaving David with the major share. Mike fully believed that, as a performing entity, the four individuals deserved equal shares. This was no longer about songwriting royalties, this was about *performing*. As a *group*.

Mike's wife, Michele, picks up the story: "When Michael went on that world tour, he told me that it was going to be really hard and I said, 'How so?' and he said, 'Because I have to put aside all of that bitterness of the last few years, and my feelings about David, but I have to do it for the benefit of the fans. Which means

Backstage (courtesy of Susan Crowder)

when I get on that stage it's neutral territory, and I have to give the best I can give, and when I'm off stage I have to be as congenial and loving with the other guys.'"

What had potentially most upset him was that, as the last to be approached, no one had pre-warned him of the offers already on the table. It would appear to some that Larry had accepted the deal put to him almost immediately, without thinking of his fellow band mates. And yet, when one considers the options, this was a four-piece band and to go out on tour, potentially without the rhythm section, one full half of the line-up, would have put a lot more weight on their justified claims for an equal share had they fully reunited but, sadly it seems, money talks, especially when one considers that David could just as easily pull the plug on the entire dollar-raking episode if his demands weren't met. So, by the time the offer had got around to Mike, it was, reluctantly, all he could do to accept. Especially when, with recollections of the *Lost Without Your Love* reunion, he was reminded that he could take it or leave it, and the result of his non-acceptance would be that the band would simply hire a drummer.

"I was at that meeting," recollects Michele, "and I just watched the color drain from Michael's face. He had no warning, and Larry had talked to him many times (about what was being proposed). The first thing Michael said was, 'Is Larry on board with this?' We never got a heads-up."

Despite the uncomfortable arrangements surrounding the percentage split, the legacy of the band came first, and the four members officially came together during early 1996 to plan the tour, with Selwyn Miller in charge of arrangements. Needless to say, once the reunion was announced to the media, officially named the "25th Anniversary Tour," despite its actually being the band's 27th year, the majority of the press focus fell upon David Gates as the front man, and the member that most people wanted to interview. This prominence was a deciding factor in the tour being labeled "David Gates & Bread," another of his provisions, and a fact that must have stuck in the throat of James Griffin, having spent so many years fighting for his rights within the band.

"It did bother Jimmy a great deal that David wanted top billing," recalls his wife Marti, "but he wasn't really surprised by his actions. He thought it was very unfair, especially to Michael and Larry. There was no negotiating the terms; that was the way it would be, or there would be no tour. Jimmy made up his mind to accept it, because he really felt the group still had a lot to offer, and hoped by doing the reunion tour that perhaps something more would come of it. He had a positive attitude about the tour and decided to take the high road even though he felt strongly that they should be billed as Bread, not 'David Gates & Bread.' But David would not do the tour unless he got his terms. Jimmy was happy about getting back out there and performing. He was always his happiest when he was using his God-given talent."

David, meanwhile, was clearly happy to offer a positive aspect on the forthcoming world tour, with everything balanced in his favor, regardless of his previous reluctance to participate. Commenting to journalist Alistair Armstrong, he said: "We're a little late getting to it. We always talked about doing it, and the timing is just perfect. There's still interest in the band, there's still interest in the music, we're available, we have a good manager who's able to put this together. It just seems like now's the time. If we're ever going to do it, we better get with it."

However, when talking with *Record Collector* magazine, he was a little more forthright about future plans. "I don't really consider this a Bread reunion, because it's missing two elements. First of all, we're not going to make any records. Secondly, we're doing very little touring in the USA, only a dozen or so shows. I don't want to crank up that big touring machine. The idea was to go back and do a world tour in those countries we never played first time around. We always wanted to tour places like Australia, South Africa, and New Zealand, and do more shows in Britain, but we never had the chance. So there's a specific purpose to this, a finite goal. We might make a live album, featuring the new songs we're playing on the tour. That's as far as it will go. Definitely."

A major focus during the tour, particularly in David's eyes, was to recreate the music as close to the original feel of the song as possible, as had always been the Bread rule. David was a perfectionist. People paid to hear the music they had grown up with, and expected it to be exactly as they remembered. There was no need to indulge themselves in "artistic licensing," something that perhaps the musical mind of Larry Knechtel was going to find hard to follow once more. Regardless of his loyalty to David throughout the years, he was still a musician's musician, and always liked to keep it fresh. While one cannot bring into question his professionalism or proficiency, he was ever the ivory-tinkler, rarely playing exactly the same notes night after night. He liked to entertain, and it had to remain interesting for such a musical mastermind. Acclaimed songwriter and producer Steve Barri, who worked with Larry on numerous occasions during the heyday of the 1960s studio scene, comments: "I don't think Larry would ever play the same piano solo twice, I don't think he would ever play the same thing twice through a song. It would always be different because he'd always want to change things, but whatever he'd do would always be very tasteful and would always work."[31]

Nevertheless, rigid structures aside, by adding two additional musicians to the stage band, Nashville players Scott Chambers and Randy Flowers on bass and lead guitar respectively, it allowed the musicians to offer a fuller, tighter six-man attack. They even used a ten-piece string section at every venue en route, often local orchestras, in order to add accompaniment to the ballads, reminiscent of their early 1970s shows.

"The string section was so passionate and emotional. It was unbelievable," states Selwyn Miller, with David agreeing, "It adds a lot of quality and dignity to the music. And strings are on the record, so any time I can get them, I like to have them."

With the first leg of the schedule taking in South Africa, New Zealand, and Australia, the band kicked off with three warm-up shows in the gambling capital of Atlantic City, New Jersey, starting on August 30th, 1996. Featuring a song selection that was, as expected, predominantly living out of the bell-bottomed 1970s, the six-man band expertly ran through the entire gamut of Bread hits, launching with the familiar opening chords of "Make It With You." With James sharing plenty of time in the spotlight, the group then ran through: "Look What You've Done," "It Don't Matter To Me," "Diary," "Love Is Always Seventeen," "Fancy Dancer," "Baby I'm-A Want You," "Been Too Long On The Road," "Sweet Surrender," "Didn't Even Know Her Name," "Too Much Love," "Aubrey," "Guitar Man," "Goodbye Girl," "Lost Without Your Love," "Mother Freedom," "Everything I Own," and "If." Although, to many present, the highlight of the entire evening was when James and Larry were positioned center stage, their partners left to view from the wings, and they performed a medley of their award-winning achievements, "Bridge Over Troubled Water" and "For All We Know." A resounding applause rang out across the auditoria each night as Larry deftly picked out the all too familiar notes, and James stepped up to the microphone and delivered the lines so eloquently sung by Art Garfunkel in previous years.

There was still time within the framework of the show to include some current material, with David delivering two new numbers, in addition to his wonderful nightly performance of "Love Is Always Seventeen." "Mirror Mirror" and "Love & Bide," the latter having been previously recorded by Billy Dean, were both strong compositions, and were received enthusiastically by audiences each night, ever eager to hang on to his every utterance. Mike, too, had the opportunity to plug his microphone in, delivering the fun-filled rocker "The Wait," one of the many songs he had recently been developing on his own, but it was often a brand new Griffin-Royer offering, the delightful "Say When," that would have the crowds baying for more. Performed during the "unplugged" portion of the show, with David and James sitting on stools, acoustic guitars in hand, the full Griffin vocal range was put on display during this number, equaling and often outplaying that of his front-stage partner. It was almost as if James was saying, "The billboards outside may be saying David Gates AND Bread, but listen to *this*..."

Drummer Mike Botts was to detail much of the ensuing tour on the band's own website, making regular postings around the globe as the band traveled from city to city, country to country, although his feelings towards the opening night summed up nicely the apprehension they were feeling as they stepped onto the stage together for the first time in many a year:

> *"It's really been pretty overwhelming. No matter how long you rehearse, you still never know what's going to happen in 'battle conditions.' Will everything go as you rehearsed? Will the pacing be right? How will the audience react? You just can't tell until opening night. And then if you add in the fact that we haven't toured together since '78, it was anybody's guess as to what was going to happen. After all, the last time we toured you could still buy records. Well, as it turns out, our opening night at the Tropicana in Atlantic City couldn't have been better. Obviously, everybody had some anxieties. You know, pre-show jitters, stage nerves and that included the audience. But once we got past the opening song, 'Make It With You,' it seemed like we went through the set seamlessly, like one fluid motion. It was amazing, as if we'd never stopped touring and it was just another show. Our musical minds and spirits blended together as if we'd never been apart. The string section was absolutely the cherry on top of the cake. They played flawlessly. And with their addition to the show, everything coming off the stage sounded like the original recordings. It was fabulous! It was obvious from the moment the curtain came up, that the audience were all 'BREADHEADS.' They couldn't possibly have been more supportive. It was really quite gratifying to feel that kind of fan support coming back across the footlights. I know it's been a while but believe me, we're definitely back..."*[29]

Tour manager Selwyn Miller, who accompanied the band on the road for the entire duration of the tour, reflects: "They came together initially for the money, but it was more than that. David was the decision maker on 90 percent of it, and Jimmy was quite accepting of everything. He was a perfect gentleman. There was no animosity whatsoever. The whole show was brilliantly put together, and David has this ability to communicate with an audience, almost like weaving a spell. They were guys who had fond memories of the good days and it was real refreshing for them to be back together. We all had a wonderful time."

Sound engineer Jeff Worrell concurs: "Their guitar tech, Buddy Webster, called me one day and asked if I would be interested in joining the tour. We had worked together on a few Fleetwood Mac tours and he thought I would be right for the position. (From the outset) I didn't sense any animosity. It felt like they all enjoyed being a part of the event. They were friendly to each other. However, they each had their own daily routines, which is common for many bands that have traveled so many years. David was *all* business, but that's how he is. I respected that. Jimmy was friendly and liked to work out in the hotel gym and I'll never forget the two of us side by side on the treadmills. Larry was very quiet, but one night at a group dinner he opened up. He began reminiscing about his time with Duane Eddy and Elvis. I can't remember the stories now, but he was himself, a living legend, on the forefront of so many of rock'n'roll's greatest moments. Mike always kept things light, telling jokes and stories. He kept everyone grounded. He became one of my best friends…"

Nine successful dates were performed in South Africa, before they headed off to New Zealand and Australia, where they were treated to an equally rapturous reception. The onstage camaraderie between the four musicians was evident. They clearly were enjoying themselves once more. Commenting on how smoothly and successfully the early shows had gone, David was to say: "The best analogy I have for you is that it's like riding a bicycle. Once you learn you don't forget. When we were in South Africa, people were singing 'Everything I Own' so loudly I could hardly hear myself. Attitudes are different in music today."

> *"It might have taken Bread the best part of 18 years to make it with us, but thank God for reunions. The years have done little to dent the appeal of their featherweight harmonies or sweetly-driven signature tunes. And despite the cynicism in the music press that greeted the announcement of their world reunion tour, the first of their four Auckland concerts was an executive massage for the emotions."*
> *—The New Zealand Herald*

A number of shows were recorded en route, including some from both the New Zealand and, later, the U.K. legs of the tour, with initial plans to include the possible release of a live album or DVD, a permanent memento from the outing. David also entered into discussions with Zomba Records, looking at recording a proposed show at the end of November, provisionally booked at London's Royal Albert Hall with the London Philharmonic Orchestra, but sadly, that wasn't to be, negotiations ending without an agreement between the various parties.

Jeff Worrell continues: "I knew this was very, very special. I'll never forget the audiences walking out of the theaters after the show. Most of them tear-eyed. Including me. I liked to record the shows, so one day, while traveling on the bus to the next show, I let David listen. He sat quietly with the headphones on for a while. Then he removed the headphones and said, 'My voice never sounded that good in the studio!'"

However, David Gates remained the purist, the stickler for detail, as both Selwyn Miller and Michele Botts experienced. "David Gates is the ultimate perfectionist, and if he considers anything less than perfect he would not authorize release. It's that simple," says Selwyn, while Michele adds, "When Michael came back from New Zealand and Australia we took a trip up north and he played the live recording in the car, and it's stunning. Absolutely stunning! And for David to deprive these Bread fans of the only live thing they ever did with an orchestra because it's not perfect? I once asked him if he thought the fans would really care? He said, 'I would care!'" The tapes remain in existence – but unheard by the legions of fans that remain faithful.

Following their return home after the Australian leg, the members took a six-month break before commencing the second stage of the tour, this time undertaking thirteen shows on home soil before the Far East and Great Britain brought the reunion officially to a close. James was pushing to have more say in the structure of the show by this second stage, hoping to add a few more of his songs to the performance, but David remained fairly resolute in that he wouldn't alter the set-up, and so the song selection remained consistent throughout. One new song that James was hoping to include was "I Remain," recently written as a solo composition and cut as a demo at a friend's house. With lyrics inspired by his friendship with Robb Royer, it stands as a lovely recording, even in demo format, with a soft piano accompaniment and double guitar line, and although both Royer and singer Dobie Gray had tried to add lyrics to it, neither had come up with a suitable approach.

James: "I wrote that about Robb a little bit. He and I were going to write that song about something else. I played him the track and he couldn't come up with a lyric. He and Dobie Gray were working on it, and nobody could come up with a lyric I liked, so I just finished it myself."[30] Sadly, due to David's unwavering control over the running order, the song never made a live appearance during the tour although, needless to say, the reception around the globe for the show was equally responsive for the second leg, with Selwyn Miller remembering: "Manila was incredible. These people couldn't even speak English but they knew every single word." For some reason, the proposed appearance at the Royal Albert Hall never materialized, and the final performance took place on November 9th, 1997, at the City Hall in Sheffield, England.

It comes as no surprise to note that yet another compilation album from Elektra, *David Gates & Bread – Essentials*, featuring twenty Bread classics along with four solo offerings from David, was propelled back up the U.K. charts in the wake of the tour, while a new 2-CD, 50-track collection, *Retrospective*, courtesy of Rhino Records in America, offered both fans and collectors the most definitive gathering of Bread recordings to date. Rhino was a label specializing in reissues, and one that had already released a number of the band's original albums onto compact disc. So it was a joy for many, to see the dedication put into the release, and highlights came not only with the extensive liner notes from Barry Alfonso, featuring interviews with David, James, Larry, and Robb, but with the actual track selection itself, mixing both hits and obscurities, group and solo, culminating in the previously unheard original 1970 demo from James of "For All We Know."

Upon their return home from overseas there were no immediate plans put into action. James, Larry, and Mike, still hoping for the reunion to develop further, drifted back to their respective families, initially unsure of the next move but, for David, it was clear to him from the outset what he wanted. During December 1997, he circulated a seasonal greeting to his bandmates: "Fun's over. Well is dry. Have a merry Christmas" it read. Yet no more than a month had passed since Bread had so successfully returned from England when David contacted Selwyn Miller.

"Everybody left the tour in happy spirits, but there was no set plan. About a month later, David came to me and said, 'Selwyn, I'd love you to continue managing me.'" The terminology clearly meant in the singular. Me, not us. He was no longer interested in going any further with Bread, and the future of the band was ultimately sealed once Larry wrote a letter to David, outlining his dissatisfaction over certain situations that continued to arise within the group. The details of the communication have never been disclosed, but those in the know claim it was not friendly. The line had been crossed and the bread bin was now firmly closed. After this, there was no going back.

In the immediate aftermath of the reunion, the pattern became a little convoluted as the various components of the band came back together, worked apart, started new projects. All without the presence of David Gates. For James, Larry, and Mike there were various ideas and partnerships running in tandem, simultaneously interacting with their separate careers. The concept that was Toast reared up once more, as did a renamed version, newly christened Radio Dixie. Then, for a fleeting moment, the possibility of a "Bread Revisited" tour was on the cards. Masterminded by Jim Della Croce, the idea was that James, Larry, and Mike would go back out on the road, making full use of the momentum built up by the recent world tour, performing all of the band's greatest hits, but this time with James center stage on lead vocals. David was clearly more interested in re-developing his solo career and had chosen to move on, but the remaining trio were keen to continue, and at one stage singer-songwriter Jim Photoglo was even mooted as a replacement, brought in to perform David's high harmonies. At Della Croce's expense a promotional brochure was pressed up, advertising their availability for bookings, suggesting that the audiences could "fall in love all over again to the music of James Griffin, Mike Botts, and Larry Knechtel of Bread."

> *"The quintessential evening of live '70s Pop-Rock performed by the Oscar and Grammy-winning artists who defined Adult Contemporary-Soft Rock! Packing 30 smash hits into one two-hour musical journey revisiting*

the songs you fell in love to. The music, romance, magic, and the '70s soundtrack to your life. Concerts, Casinos, Fairs, Festivals, Corporates, Symphony Dates. Bring your wife, husband, friend, lover or kids, but don't come alone!"

Songs listed on the color brochure were: "If," "Diary," "It Don't Matter To Me," "Let Your Love Go," "Everything I Own," "Baby I'm-A Want You," "Guitar Man," "Sweet Surrender," "Aubrey," and "Lost Without Your Love," along with "Bridge Over Troubled Water," "For All We Know," and "Rockin' Pneumonia & The Boogie Woogie Flu," the latter originally being a belting piano-driven New Orleans hit for Huey "Piano" Smith, but also a number that Larry had cut with Johnny Rivers back in the early '70s. Jim Della Croce, in conversation with the author, suggests that many of James's own compositions from the Bread era would also have been featured, making up the 30 potential songs, and a surviving compilation CD from Mike Botts' collection, highlighting his own interpretation of the proposed set list, indicates that "Take Comfort," "Look What You've Done," "Truckin'," and "She Knows" were indeed intended for the tour. But it was never to be. David Gates caught wind of the proposal and made his disapproval clear. They could tour as "James Griffin, Larry Knechtel and Mike Botts *formerly* of Bread," but could not suggest in any way, revisited or otherwise, that this was Bread. A familiar-sounding scenario, one feels, but one that drove James to adopt a simple *laissez-faire* attitude. Let it be.

Also shown on the brochure were the two supporting artists lined up for the proposed tour. James's longtime friend and occasional musical partner Terry Sylvester was now living on the westerly side of the Atlantic Ocean and had stayed in touch, occasionally sitting in with the circle of musicians that 'Bread Revisited' revolved around, and he was subsequently added to the schedule, bringing in a selection of his Hollies' hits. The second act to be included was another sharing a long history with Bread, having first supported them on their 1972 North American tour as one half of the duo England Dan & John Ford Coley. Now managed by Jim Della Croce as a solo performer, John Ford Coley was another comfortable addition, bringing along a wealth of popular songs such as "I'd Really Love To See You Tonight," "Love Is The Answer," "Nights Are Forever," and "We'll Never Have To Say Goodbye Again." With the tag-line of "both artists rejoin Bread Revisited for a finale," the tour promised to be an enjoyable affair, but, following on from David's voice of condemnation, and James's non-committal reaction, the initial momentum faded away. For a while they contemplated changing the name of the tour to "'70s Revisited," and actively began seeking bookings, but once it became increasingly difficult to tie everyone down and liaise with each other at the same time, the concept sadly was abandoned. Instead, following on from the 1998 charity performance in Boston, where both James and Terry performed three songs apiece chosen from their lengthy careers to date, the central focus began to fall upon James, Terry Sylvester, and John Ford Coley.

Jim Della Croce picks up the story: "Jimmy was very easy going, and if there was another opportunity to play music he was there. At that point, different opportunities came up and one of those was the Soft Rock Café. It was my idea, Terry Sylvester came up with the name and, again, it was at a party at my house. We started looking at the songs of The Hollies, Jimmy Griffin. We thought it would be great to combine all of these hits and put them into a package, and include Michael Botts and Knechtel. However, it became a little hard to get everyone together so Soft Rock Café became a three-piece."

The newly combined trio of Griffin, Sylvester, and Coley commenced their partnership with an hour-long TV Special on the TNN Network, appearing on *Prime Time Country* during late 1997. TNN was planning on changing its programming schedule and offered Jim Della Croce the opportunity to showcase the band for the full 60 minutes before the changes took that particular show off the air for the last time, and its subsequent success led to a promotional tour being booked. Performing before a live audience, the TV Special saw the trio perform a number of their most recognizable hits including "For All We Know," "I'd Really Love To See You Tonight," "He Ain't Heavy, He's My Brother," along with perennial Bread favorites such as "It Don't Matter To Me" and "Everything I Own," while also chatting amiably with the host, Gary Chapman. Then, starting off by selling the show in Las Vegas, the trio began successfully appearing at various corporate events and, while no studio recordings were ever to come to light, it would prove a popular live attraction over the coming years. Needless to say, the songs of Bread played a prominent role within the show each night and, despite James's previous reluctance to incorporate his former partner's songwriting contributions into his own set, he was always prepared to recognize the overall impact of a good song, and gradually the early hits of Bread began to infiltrate the set lists. In the words of Jim Della Croce: "Jimmy knew shit from Shinola…"

David Gates, meanwhile, was also still actively involving himself within the music scene. Since coming out of his self-imposed hibernation on his California ranch, and releasing his 1994 *Love Is Always Seventeen* album, followed by the reunion tour, he had rekindled his love of songwriting and of the music. Shortly after the band returned Stateside, David participated in a new recording of "Guitar Man," accompanying the successful Brazilian rock band Roupa Nova on their new interpretation of his composition. Recorded in Nashville, and eventually appearing under the title "De Ninguém" on the band's 1997 album *Através dos Tempos*, David contributed his share of the lead vocals in English, while the band performed in their native Portuguese language. He later appeared on a popular South American TV show alongside the group to help promote the record.

That same year he had also been approached to work on another new project; an offer to compose the theme for the forthcoming Commonwealth Games, scheduled to be held in Kuala Lumpur the following September. Malaysian-born songwriter Wah Idris had initially approached Paul McCartney and Andrew Lloyd Webber to see if they would be interested in collaborating on the project, but due to prior commitments, neither was available at that time. Having found that David Gates was accessible, Idris made contact with him, suggesting he fly to Los Angeles to discuss the proposal. However, as Malaysia was a scheduled port of call on the then-Bread reunion tour, David instead committed to meeting up on Idris's home soil, clearly interested in the high profile project.

"The first time I met Gates," recalled Idris, during an interview for *The Malaysian New Straits Times*, "I asked him, 'Are you *the* David Gates?' and he said, 'Well, there's no other unless you're looking for Bill Gates.'" The two songwriters then spent the following three hours composing, with Idris suggesting the ideas while David penned the lyrics. "All the while I'm thinking, 'Gee, I'm working with David Gates!'"

The result of the brief collaboration was the stirring ballad "Standing In The Eyes Of The World," ultimately recorded by David himself, with popular Malaysian singer Ella also releasing a version to coincide with the prestigious multi-national sporting event. Following on from this, David began a second collaboration with the popular country artist Billy Dean. Having successfully worked together on both Billy's and David's own albums a few years earlier, it was clearly a comfortable partnership, and when Billy turned his attention to recording a new album in 1998 he immediately thought of David, not only as a songwriter but as a co-producer and string arranger for the project. The resulting album, *Real Man*, featured four new co-songwriting credits, with the opening "Fall In Tennessee" and "I'm Not Needed Here Now" being two of the choice cuts from the release, while a third co-contribution, the enjoyable and lively "Innocent Bystander," reached #68 on the Country Charts when issued as a single. The duo even appeared on TV once more together, promoting their partnership, performing "Innocent Bystander," "Everything I Own," and "Make It With You," along with the title track of Dean's album, on *Prime Time Country* (still on the air at that stage). Yet, despite the focus of this joint project being based in the country music capital, shortly afterwards, in recognition of David's own musical contributions, his home state of Oklahoma bestowed on him an induction into the recently formed Oklahoma Music Hall Of Fame, alongside such previous greats as Merle Haggard, Woody Guthrie, and Patti Page.

David's activities weren't simply restricted to studio work though, and following the culmination of the Bread reunion, he was still keen to get his music out before a live audience. In 1999 he made a solo visit to Australia, accompanied by a 10-piece string section, performing a sixteen-song set that included old solo favorites "Soap (I Use The)" and "Clouds & Rain," coupled with newer songs such as "Thankin' You Sweet Baby James," "Mirror Mirror," and "Love & Bide," all featured among the obligatory hits. Then, over the subsequent years, he played a selection of shows around the Americas, both North and South, visiting Brazil, Argentina, Peru, and Chile, always pulling in an appreciative and loyal audience, keen to hear and see him as he performed songs from years gone by, telling stories and jokes, relating to the crowds on a personal level. Although the stage set-up was often on a more intimate scale, with just David and two accompanying musicians covering guitar, bass, and keys, void of any percussion or drums. This arrangement often left the more demanding of songs, the lengthy "Clouds & Rain" suite being the prime example, sounding a little shallow, but any audience concerns were soon cast aside once the opening guitar chords of "Everything I Own" and "If" rang out over the venues.

"After the Bread reunion tour, I began writing and stock-piling songs and doing 20 or 30 concerts in the U.S. each year. After one of the concerts, a year or so back, a woman came up to me and said, 'Where can I buy an album that's got everything on it that I heard tonight?' And I said, 'Well, ma'm, you can't,' and so the idea was born in my head to try to do an album that did have all of the best of everything I'd ever written, all the things that I do in concert."

This was David's explanation as to how the *David Gates Songbook: A Lifetime Of Music* came into being. A brand new 20-song, 2002 compilation album, issued in the U.K. by Zomba-Jive, gathering together ten of Bread's finest moments coupled with ten songs from David's own solo career, past and present, this was intended as the definitive collection of David's songwriting history. While 20 songs was never going to encompass the entire spectrum of all he had achieved, for the nostalgic music buyer, it was a near-perfect starting point. It ticked all of the boxes for those who wanted to relive the hits, and who wanted to discover just that little bit extra, and from David's perspective, it afforded him the opportunity to show that his newer compositions could still sit comfortably alongside the older hits.

"What I'm hoping," he continued, "is that the people who have known and enjoyed the old songs will latch on to these five new things and think, 'Hey, this guy's still writing, still doing the same thing,' and not forget about me."

The five brand new contributions included a studio version of "Mirror Mirror," the song he had first started performing during the 1996 reunion tour, along with two new ballads, "Find Me" and "I Can't Play The Songs," an infectious up tempo number titled "Mustang," and a reworked version of "Love Is Always Seventeen," featuring a new string arrangement. While this was the umpteenth collection to have graced the record racks or CD shelves across the globe, it proved the longevity of these great compositions by again gracing the higher echelons of the charts, achieving an impressive #11 slot in the British listings. To celebrate the success, a full U.K. tour was undertaken during 2003, followed by visits to Australia and New Zealand, selling out in cities across all three countries. One of the highlights was a return visit to the 5,000-seat Royal Albert Hall in central London, and during his U.K. visit he also performed on both national television and radio, appearing once again on the long-running *Top Of The Pops* TV show. Time, and absence, had certainly not diminished the popularity of the man, nor of his songs.

While David was enjoying the fruits of success once again, albeit mostly via a collection of music from his past, his former partners were still working equally hard, playing and singing the music that pumped through them. James continued to help out at numerous recording sessions around Nashville, happy to offer his vocal talents as support to a varying degree of artists in between his commitments to Soft Rock Café. Dobie Gray, Billy Burnette, TG Shepherd, Mickey Newbury, and Charlie Taylor all benefited from having James's vocals added to the mix during the late 1990s and into the 21st century, as did Micheal Smotherman on his Robb Royer-produced 2001 album, *Conjure Man*, but during this time he remained keen to push for another record deal of his own.

Perhaps most surprisingly however, it was to be drummer Mike Botts who was to claim bragging rights for the next solo album release from the original band members. And it was destined to be a mighty fine one at that.

Chapter Nineteen

(It's Such A) Shame

Over the preceding ten to fifteen years, Mike Botts had been slowly working on his own songs, gradually developing his skills as a songwriter, building up a catalog. Those who knew him well were fully aware of what a great singing voice he had, but he had never had the opportunity to step out from behind his drum kit, to take center stage to the extent that, perhaps, Don Henley or Levon Helm had managed. Even errant Beach Boys drummer Dennis Wilson had appeared from out of the shadows of his band during 1977 to issue the magnificent self-composed solo album *Pacific Ocean Blue*, but for Mike, his credibility and acclaim as one of Los Angeles' top session players and most in-demand touring drummers was seemingly enough to keep the four walls standing around him. He had seen one of his recent co-compositions appear on Andrew Gold's 1997 release, *Greetings From Planet Love*, but he had yet to make that move into the front position himself. To stand in front of the microphone, without the comforting support of his snare, tom-toms, and cymbal. However, as the years rolled by, and his catalog increased, he began to receive the encouragement of those around him.

"Michael had a great rock'n'roll voice, and he always had a folder with lyrics and ideas," recalls his wife Michele, "and, I think it was 1983 or 1984, that Dick Rosmini, who had initially made the call to Michael to arrange the session with Bill Medley (back in 1969), had heard 'Sailin' Shoes' and when he heard that he just said, 'Look, Botts, I have this studio at my house, and you need to start coming over here and laying some things down, and just find your voice, because you don't know who you are yet.'"

With the help of friends such as Rosmini and manager Joe Gotfried, who gave him free studio time at Sound City Studios, Mike began committing his songs to tape, and although it would take until the late 1990s before he actually began assembling the songs into some sort of reasonable project, the result of this would be his debut solo offering, the impressive *Adults Only*, issued in 2000. Later, on his own website, Mike stated: "I never started out with a solo CD in mind. It just seemed that singing and songwriting was the next natural step for me as an artist. Over a period of time, I began to find my own vocal style and began to collect a few good songs as well. I eventually went in to record some material to see if I could get a deal. Well, after a lot of frustrating meetings with record execs the project became dormant until (former Bread sound engineer) Jeff Worrell heard my recordings and urged me to finish the CD. So with the help of some outstanding musicians and Jeff's expertise at the mixing board, we finally completed *Adults Only*. It was soon after that Kent Hartman of *SonicOasis.com* heard the CD and expressed great interest in making it available on the internet."

Mike's vocal styling was definitely his own and, although in promoting the release he made reference to having been influenced by a number of great performers over the years (Little Richard, James Brown, Otis Redding, McCartney, Peter Gabriel, and, perhaps most notably upon listening to the final release, Sting), it remains clear that he *had* found his own individual voice. The tonal quality, and the rawness, often sounds remarkably akin to the former Police front man, especially with the arrangement on the song "Greed," but it was distinctly Mike. Nobody could deny him his individuality.

The final twelve songs that appeared on the album (a number of other compositions didn't make the final cut), all composed by Mike himself, varied in style and tempo, with the commercial rock appeal of "Squeeze," "El Dorado," and "The Wait" mixed in alongside the more demanding audio delights of "Avenue 63," "Old Man's Lament," and "Shame." It was with the latter composition, a gentle jazz shuffle interspersed with a searing guitar solo, that much of the attention fell, seeing that it was clearly based upon the sorry saga of his former band, with James Griffin in particular feeling the lyrical burden of his own former drug addictions. Needles, lawyers, and demons, friendships broken... it was not an easy listen, but maybe it was Mike's own way of laying the past to rest.

Michele: "When James heard the final release he called Mike up to say 'Wow!' he was impressed, but he had a comment about 'Shame.' He jokingly said that the lyric, 'an inflated ego and a deflated arm' should have said 'an inflated ego *caused* the deflated arm'... but he got it. He just said after hearing it he hoped that Michael would reconsider the lyric, 'no way left to make amends.'"

That particular song had been composed during the early 1990s, when the bridges had yet to be rebuilt, while others had their origins in even earlier periods. The soulful "Buns Of Doom" had been initially inspired during the days of touring with Linda Ronstadt, with Linda herself often using the term when the eyes of her all-male band were caught wandering towards the female form – *the jugs of madness, the buns of doom* – while "Avenue 63" came out of a visit Mike had made back home to see his mother and stepfather in Sacramento, and from where he had been inspired by the sad story in a newspaper of a nine-year-old boy who had been caught up among the gunfire of gang warfare. And that is one noticeable factor about the entire album. Lyrically, Mike was in a very mature place. Avoiding the clichéd pitfalls of the boy-meets-girl-love-story scenario he was later to remark, "A great set of lyrics can be timeless. But lyrically my work goes in a non-mainstream direction similar to artists like Tom Waits, Randy Newman, or Lyle Lovett."

Jeff Worrell, who worked on completing the album with Mike, recalls: "This project held a very, very deep meaning for Mike on many levels, and I understood that. That was my biggest contribution, I understood, and got him to finish. He had a lot of songs from a lot of years but he was having a hard time putting them all together. He thought that I might be the one who could help him finally gather it all together and shove it out the door. And that's what we did. Some of the songs were on analog tape, some in various digital formats, and some in his computer. I collected it all and put it in ProTools and away we went. We worked on a few overdubs here and there, I even played a guitar solo on 'Greed.' Mike was a great singer and lyricist. He was what I call a natural singer. He just opened up and sang. Beautiful tone. We worked hard but we never struggled. I didn't labor over pitch correcting and time correcting. He was old school. He played and sang the songs correctly from the start."

With studio support over the years coming from guitarists Chris Spedding, Dean Parks, Todd Sharp, Basil Fung, and Mike's old friend Andrew Gold; bass players Leland Sklar, Chris Colangelo, and Bob Glaub, George Clinton, Brad Cole, and Jai Winding on keyboards, plus supporting singers Brad Kipper, Brent Bourgeois, Paula Salvatori, and, on one occasion, wife Michele offering background vocals on "Murder," Mike had pulled together an astonishingly polished collection, and one that culminated in the long-overdue appearance of "Sailin' Shoes." To aid the launch of the release he taped a promotional video for the song "The Wait," a number he had been performing during Bread's reunion tour at David's request and one that, Michele believes, was simply the result of a "frustrating day." Waiting for this, waiting for that. Do the wait. Filled with family and friends, including Michele, the joy on Mike's face as he performs before the camera is apparent. He was loving it. This was his time.

The album title itself simply evolved from the fact that it was more adult oriented. There were no benign love songs, and the material dealt with things that the average sixteen-year-old wouldn't relate to. Adults only. In Mike's own mind, "it was an eye catcher" and he even produced a humorous 60-second promotional short entitled *The Peep Show* to publicize the album, cleverly playing on the title. Nevertheless, the SonicOasis label was only a small independent and it was never destined to reach a wide market, even if the fans of Bread, and of Mike as an individual, were only too keen to add it to their collection and shout about it. It was never going to be a commercial success, it was more of a personal success. "He told me he did it so that he could actually put something in his mother's hands," summarizes Michele.

Shortly after completing the album, Mike once again returned to the recording studios to undertake another new project. But this one was something extra special. Something very close to his heart. The Travelers were back in town. Mike had never lost contact with his former colleagues from the Travelers 3, and Joe LaManno had remained one of his closest friends, even if their diversifying work had kept them apart for months on end, while Charlie Oyama still remained loyal to Mike and Michele during both the good and bad times. The fourth member, Pete Apo, having returned to his native Hawaii, had also remained in close contact with the Botts' household, often staying over while in California.

"Our first trip to Hawaii had been with the Travelers 3," recalls Joe LaManno, "and on our first trip we got attached to Hawaiian culture as Charlie and Peter are native Hawaiians and we stayed with their families. We really saw Hawaii from the inside. Then one Christmas during the '90s, Charlie and Peter had got together and Peter was seeing that Charlie doesn't really have a lot of music in his life anymore. He said, 'Why don't we call Mike and Joe, and see if we can turn this around? We need to get you playing again.'"

So, shortly afterwards, the four members of the 1960s folk quartet reunited, adding songwriter, producer, and long-time friend Rick Cunha to the ranks. Another native Hawaiian, Rick had himself been a member of a 1960s folk band, co-founding the group Hearts & Flowers (before being replaced on their second album by future Eagle Bernie Leadon), and his skills as a multi-instrumentalist, in addition to his technical abilities (he had been sound engineer on Mike's *Adults Only* project) only added to the strength of the new line-up. Thus came about the formation of Na Kama Hele (meaning "The Travelers" in the native Hawaiian language). Charlie Oyama had always been proficient in a particular style of traditional guitar playing, a form known in Hawaii as "slack key," and the new five-piece chose to record a project in that vein, preserving the traditional form of Hawaiian song.

"So we got together at Rick's studio in his house (in Van Nuys, CA), talked about different kinds of songs, and just had a verbal contract about if anything sold what we'd do with the money, and off we went. We'd work on it whenever we could get together. Peter would block out a couple of weeks and come over from Hawaii. In typical Hawaiian style, we'd talk a lot, we'd laugh a lot, we'd eat a lot, and then once in a while we'd stop, make some music, and then we'd talk some more. We never wanted any of this to end," says Joe. If only all contracts were so easy. Na Kama Hele issued two albums over the next few years, *Ki Ho `Alu Journey* (2002) and *The One They Call Hawaii* (2004), and both remain highly infectious releases, complete with the gentle sounds of steel guitars and ukulele washing across the sun-kissed soundscape, and while Mike's contribution is far more in the background than his usual driving drumbeat, his smooth Hawaiian percussion adds an integral rhythm to the music. The five-man group only performed live once during their time together, at a small club in Southern California, but the entire project remains a cherished memory for all involved.

James Griffin's appetite for music was never ending. As one door closes, another opens. Soft Rock Café was still performing as the new century began, and would do so for another year or so, but James was always making music, regardless of whom he was with. The turn of the decade saw him perform with singer-songwriter Stephen Bishop, appearing in concert at the Wild Horse Saloon in Nashville, and then during December 2001, he performed a solo show at a benefit for the Ballet Memphis, helping out an old school friend. He had also remained close to Rick Yancey, after the latter had left The Remingtons, and it was only a matter of time before James and Rick would renew their working partnership. It was also around now that he struck up a friendship with Ronnie Guilbeau, son of the legendary country rock pioneer Gib Guilbeau, and a former member of both Palamino Road and a latter-day Flying Burrito Brothers line-up. As a talented singer and songwriter, Ronnie had also achieved chart success as the writer of Poco's 1989 comeback hit, "Call It Love."

Ronnie recalls: "The first time I met Jimmy was in Memphis in the mid-'80s. I was recording with Jack Holder, one of Jimmy's friends, and Jack brought him to the studio one night. We hung out a while. Then years later, Rick Yancey brought him to my studio in Nashville, and the three of us wrote and recorded about three or four songs over a period of time. Rick was always pushing for the three of us to work together. I always thought of it as something fun to do, didn't really see great commercial potential in it, but Jimmy really got behind it."

Eventually, this friendship would become the basis for yet another new group. Griffin, Yancey, and Guilbeau would continue to dip in and out of the studio together, initially on more of a friendship basis than taking it too seriously but, as Ronnie notes, James really began to see the trio's potential. They recorded some more tunes at Ronnie's house, including their own takes on both "Call It Love" and "Who's Gonna Know," the latter being the Griffin-Yancey-Mainegra collaboration that had been a hit for Conway Twitty. Before they knew it, an album's worth of material lay before them. James then sent the recordings to a friend at MCA Records, hoping for a deal, but the lead sadly went nowhere, much to his frustration, and it looked for a while as if the album would not get off the ground. Nevertheless, by 2003 the project was reaching a new level, and they started to play a few shows around town.

Guilbeau: "GYG (as we began to be known) did play around Nashville, as a three-piece acoustic band. We had a great time. We worked hard on our playing and singing, with three-part harmonies. We were always well received, and people came to see us, mainly because of Jimmy. There were a lot of Bread fans that came out."

One other acquaintance from the busy scene around Nashville was Drew Reid, an all-round musical figurehead – songwriter, performer, producer, promoter – who had relocated there from Florida during the early '90s. He, too, saw the trio perform, later recalling: "When I first saw GYG I sat six feet in front of them and for a while I could not tell who was singing what. That's how tight they were. Last cats I saw do that were Crosby, Stills & Nash."

He continued: "Rick asked me to manage GYG, but it was Jimmy's show, so Jimmy and I had to have lunch. We kicked around the general concept, I told him some of my ideas for pitching to independent labels, and Jimmy said, and this is a direct quote, 'Drew, I just want my boys to have a hit. I've had mine. Rick and Ronnie have worked so hard, I just want them to have a hit.' In his mind, that was a big part of the GYG project. I had nothing to do with the creative end. I recall GYG was rehearsing one afternoon, and I'm sitting in the next room, leafing through paperwork or something, and there was an abrupt stop. Jimmy says, 'What was that?'

"'Uh, we hit a bad note, Jimmy.'

"'We don't *do* bad notes!'

"It was impossible not to be caught up in Jimmy's energy. GYG would work their ass off in rehearsal for hours, and then take a breather. Believe me, a breather was all it was because Jimmy would be jumping up and saying, 'What are we doing now, boys? C'mon! Let's go!' and grab a guitar. So, starting in 2003, GYG was in business. We played the Bluebird, Douglas Corner, some places in Williamson County, more I can look up. I got them a showcase at that year's Country Radio Seminar, and was pitching the CD like crazy to mostly smaller, indie labels, but I was getting some feedback from the 'bigs' too..."

Sadly, and ultimately in tragic circumstances, the GYG project was never fully realized. When it finally appeared, via Reid's own distribution, during 2005, the ten-track collection of recordings showed just how much promise this particular act had to offer. Starting with Ronnie Guilbeau's acoustic-driven "All You Gotta Do," the distinctive three-part harmonies instantly shine, and, while it maybe lacked the polished sheen and finish of The Remingtons' big-production sessions, the overall "home-studio feel" of the resulting collection, along with the quality of the compositions, stand it up firmly against most projects doing the Nashville circuit at that period in time. James's own songwriting contributed to six of the featured tunes, and he handled three of the lead vocals himself, one of which, the truly delightful "Marbeja" (also known as "High On A Hill In Marbella"), was the result of his earlier writing sessions with Terry Sylvester.

"There was never a name for the GYG album," says Drew. "At one point I said to Jimmy, 'How about *Everything Is Important*?' He said, 'Oooh, I like that.' There were a few covers run off with a pen and ink drawing, with the title *Howlin' At The Moon*. That has been the title of several albums and books, and I pointed out it had little to do with the content. I wanted to call it *Marbeja*, but, again, I didn't do much of that sort of input, that was not my role."

During February 2004, James made a solo appearance at the Bluebird Café in Nashville, sitting in alongside Rusty Young, Walter Egan, and Bill Lloyd. The quartet each performed songs from their respective careers with James including Bread's "It Don't Matter to Me" and "Everything I Own," Black Tie's "Chain Gang," GYG's "Who's Gonna Know" and "Marbeja," and "Say When," a song he had previously debuted alongside Robb on the *Nashville Prime Talk* TV chat-show, hosted by former U.S. congressman Bill Boner, and then successfully performed during the 1996 Reunion Tour. In addition, he played a gorgeous new country ballad he had recently co-written with Royer entitled "All Of My Love, All Of My Life," plus his own rendition of "You Can Depend on Me," his hit composition for Restless Heart. Then, with a vacation in Hawaii in mind, he returned to GYG.

Drew Reid: "The last GYG gig was at the Bluebird on June 15th, 2004. Jimmy went on vacation, came back, and we had to cancel gigs because he was having trouble with his throat." Fate was now to play its part.

Larry Knechtel was once again living a quiet life up in Washington. With the Bread Reunion Tour now a distant memory, and the projected Bread Revisited project having fallen by the wayside, he had returned to the peaceful, rural life. He had sold his farm, downsizing to a smaller property in Naches, but was still to be found performing his music locally, around the bars and clubs. It mattered little to him that previous years had seen his talents grace multi-thousand-seat venues across the globe – Carnegie Hall, The Royal Albert Hall, The Monterey Pop Festival. He was now content playing the clubs around Bellingham and Blaine, often as a part of a local band. Before, it had been Silver Lake or Blue Heron, but now he was often to be found playing keyboards in line-ups such as the five-piece Everson Drive, more than likely with his son Lonnie in tow. Guitarist Erik Lloyd, who performed alongside Larry and Lonnie in Everson Drive (along with drummer Mike Gallagher and bass player Robert Hooff) recalls: "Everson Drive was basically all covers, but not run-of-the-mill ones for the most part. We just tried to do stuff you don't

Jimmy in concert (courtesy of Fran Hart)

hear every day. Over here there's a set list, stuff like 'Mustang Sally,' that just gets played to death so we tried not to do that, and having Larry and Lonnie we were pretty much able to do whatever we liked to…"

The band would perform versions of classic hits such as Free's "Alright Now," The Doobie Brothers' "Takin' It To The Streets," and the Beatles' "Dear Prudence" and "Lady Madonna," often supporting higher profile local acts, playing to indifferent crowds. Many of whom were blissfully unaware of the musical heritage of the graying keyboard player sat hunched before them.

"When I wasn't playing, I wasn't happy," Larry was to say to local journalist Kim Nowacki, who reported in *The Yakima Herald* that, despite his musical heritage, even finding local gigs around the area still didn't come easy. "They (the club owners) all wanted resumes and demo tapes," he said. "I don't have that stuff."

As Nowacki was to comment: "He could have just plunked down his Grammy. But Knechtel isn't like that. He's unassuming about his past and doesn't like to spend much time there. The box 'full of memorabilia crap' and his sixty gold albums are in storage collecting dust. He doesn't hang them up."

"It gets a little overbearing," he told her. "I like no notoriety. Some people get hooked on that, but nobody stays on top."

As well as paying gigs, he often sat in with visiting musicians, including his friend from Los Angeles, Johnny Rivers, who made a visit to the area during 2002. And he stayed in touch with both Mike Botts and James Griffin, but contact with David Gates was now minimal, if at all. His dissatisfaction over the reunion, and the subsequent correspondence between them, had all but diminished their working relationship. "I'm more interested in what I'm going to do next than what was in the past," he summarized to Nowacki. "I'll have time enough for that when I'm in a rest home."

It was during the early part of the decade that James Griffin had been building on his relationship with Paul Brazil, his natural father. Following a visit by James to Texas, where Paul and his family were now living, the two had begun to talk on a regular basis, content and accepting of their relationship. It was now a happy time for him. He was exercising daily, his marriage to Marti was joyful, and they had brought two young children, Alexis and Jacob, into the world.

Drew Reid: "One thing I learned from, and about, Jimmy. Always be up. Jimmy had a zeal for life, it was impossible not to feel charged up around him. I knew Jimmy when he didn't have a lot, and also when he had millions. There was no difference in his outlook or demeanor. As far as anyone knew, he was on top of the world, and that's the way he always looked and acted. The world was his oyster."

Over this particular period, early 2004, he continued to write, pairing off with Greek-born country songwriter Kostas Lazarides to compose "Take The Easy Way Out" and "You'll Never Leave My Heart." He worked with Robb on the composition "Share This Love" and with Nashville-based songwriter and producer Danny Borgers on "Built For Blue Jeans" (later used in the 2008 movie *Camille*) and then, most notably, followed this by reuniting with one of his earliest musical partners, Michael Z. Gordon, now a successful Hollywood producer, to compose the title song for a new version of the 1941 movie *The Devil & Daniel Webster*, retitled *Shortcut To Happiness*. That particular song, "Something Else Altogether," is truly a stunning composition, featuring a lead vocal by James, and yet was inexplicably axed from the finished production. It eventually turned up, albeit just as a brief snippet, during the Gordon-produced *A Killing On Brighton Beach*, issued in 2009. He also continued to undertake further session work, appearing with indie rocker Frank Black on his *Honeycombe* album, supporting country singer Edwin Lewis on his *Nashville Sessions* project, and then in June he accompanied Boston-born singer-songwriter Holly Cieri on a cover version of his own Academy Award-winning co-composition, "For All We Know."

"Although I'd achieved some success on the Adult Contemporary charts," recalls Holly today, "my radio promoter had said that now I'd had three songs of my own, I should probably do a cover. His advice was to go through my CD collection and see whatever was nice in the '70s. I got Carpenters, Bread, everything... and for some reason I've always loved Jimmy's voice."

With her focus on recording material in Nashville, she was taken aback to discover that James, who she believed still lived in Los Angeles, was currently residing in the city. Fortunately, her publicist also lived in Tennessee, and so, after a series of telephone conversations and emails, Holly flew down from Boston, and a meeting was arranged at Nashville's Sunset Grill.

"This was my first time in Nashville and I don't even know how the hell I got there, I was so nervous!" she laughs today. "But when I opened the door he was standing there, a big smile, such a gentleman. I told him what was going on and I even asked him as well if he'd be willing to sit down and write with me. He said, 'We can record one of my songs, and then we can get to writing', and he offered to help me with the whole CD! I couldn't believe it. He and I talked about a lot of songs, but Jimmy didn't care, he was easy. He said, 'Pick the one you want to do,' and we finally decided on 'For All We Know' and set the time to record it."

Ironically, the same day they had agreed to record "For All We Know," March 26th, 2004, the song's co-composer, Fred Karlin, passed away from a cancer-related illness.

The vocal session itself took place on June 7th, although Holly had already produced the actual tracks back home in Boston, following their initial meeting, using musicians she knew and trusted. James's only request had been that it have a slower, softer feel than that of the Carpenters' hit arrangement, to make it more of a heart-felt ballad, and that it be piano-based.

"I loved his voice so much. It was a beautiful instrument," she continues. "The recordings never captured it, you had to hear Jimmy live to hear the sheer soul, the tenderness and that beautiful clarion quality. I'm going, 'Oh my God, how can I possibly sing in front of this guy?' I don't even remember singing it – I was so nervous..."

Following the completion of this first track, they planned to work on some other songs together, with initial focus falling on "Once Again," another of James's recent compositions, and one that had, up to that moment, only been taped as a demo. After that the plan was to write fresh material. But it wasn't to be.

"He was an excellent singer and all-round musician and he wrote some beautiful music along with Robb Royer," says Holly. "All I ever saw was a sweet-minded gentleman, who had a huge heart for everybody. God bless him..."

Taking a break in between the various commitments, James flew to Hawaii for a family vacation, but it became apparent soon after that something was wrong.

"He went on vacation, and things changed," says his friend Jim Della Croce, still with sadness in his voice. "We were sequencing his songs, and I believe that Jimmy knew all along what was going on. He made comments to me that were foreshadowing. He would tell me, 'I'm not going to be around, so let's finish this record'. But there's a point where you take your friends seriously and you don't push them."

James continued to work, visiting the studios alongside Robb Royer and Jim Della Croce, who recalls one such instance with a rueful laugh. "I was also producing a record for an artist named Nate Barrett for Lyric Street Records, and Jimmy was in the studio visiting Dave Loggins who was singing backup. It came time for the harmony vocal but Dave refused to get up off of the couch as long as Jimmy Griffin was in the room! He said, 'I want to hear Jimmy sing.' Jimmy said, 'No, man, I didn't come in here to sing on this record,' but before the morning was out Jimmy sang the harmony vocals and Loggins never left the couch. He just sat back and savored the vocal!"

During the break in Hawaii, he had been suffering from a bout of laryngitis, and upon his return it was suggested that he refrain from vocal activities for three or four days. He called Holly to postpone their next scheduled session. Those three or four days stretched and he was subsequently referred to a specialist. Fears were confirmed. A tumor had been discovered, and James was diagnosed with lung cancer. Instead of recording sessions, he now faced chemotherapy.

His very last studio date was for a record that John Ford Coley and Vince Melamed were producing for one of Jim's clients, a new country singer named Lynn Bryant. James contributed vocals to two of the songs that ultimately appeared on Bryant's 2005 album *Woman Enough*: "I Want The Fairy Tale" and a version of the Todd Rundgren hit "Can We Still Be Friends," the latter of which was actually a duet between James and Lynn. Even with the disease, still undiscovered at that stage, now ravaging his body, James's vocals remained intact, with his range and phrasing sounding as strong as ever.

Nevertheless, shortly afterwards he was committed to hospital. It was a fight that wasn't to last for too long. He began to undergo the chemotherapy treatment and friends and family rallied round.

Jim Della Croce: "I was visiting with him in the hospital, and I was trying to get an understanding of what shape he was in and, as it became more and more apparent that things weren't improving, there were times I would say, 'Let's get Botts on the phone, let's talk to Knechtel.' And it depended on our discussions but at one point he said, 'Call Larry, call Michael,' and they had a great talk and made their peace. This was about true friendship. I would see him three times a day and we had these great heart-to-heart discussions, but it was getting to the point where it was harder for him to speak. I was hoping things would get better, but it was really hard on him and it was hard for him to leave Marti and the kids..."

Ronnie Guilbeau was another who took a call from James. "When he was in the hospital, he called. His voice was almost gone, just a whisper. He told me to finish a demo of a song we had written together. I told him that we couldn't do it without him, he was just going to have to get better. He kept saying, 'It's a hit, finish the recording.'" That song was called "Why Can't You Love Me Like That" and was the last new composition to bear the James Griffin name. With co-credit to Rick Yancey, Ronnie Guilbeau, and Drew Reid, both Ronnie and Drew would go on to record their own versions to honor James's wishes, and both versions featured the distinct harmony tones of James's longtime friend Rick Yancey.

I don't believe you're really asleep
And it's lonely over here where I'm at
I'm lying awake, I need you so much I ache
Why can't you love me like that
I live for you, I'd die for you too
I'm giving everything that I have
If you cry I can't breathe, if you're cut I bleed
Why can't you love me like that...

"Why Can't You Love Me Like That"
(Music & Lyrics by James Griffin, Rick Yancey, Ronnie Guilbeau, and Drew Reid)
Reproduced with permission

Michele Botts: "I was standing in the kitchen, I had just walked in and Michael was on the phone, and he was crying. And then I realized he was talking to Jimmy, and I heard him say, 'I just wanted to let you know I love you,' and then the last thing he said to him was, 'Save a place for me.'"

James Arthur Griffin died on January 11th, 2005. He was just 61 years of age. Only two days earlier, he had left hospital to return home, happy in the knowledge that he would spend his final days surrounded by his loved ones. His sister, Carol

Ann, held hands with Paul Brazil during the funeral service at the Christ Presbyterian Church in Nashville, comforting one another in their grief, while family members, fellow musicians and friends from all over Memphis and beyond gathered, all wishing to pay their final respects.

"The church was also a Christian Academy where Alex and Jacob attended school," says Marti Griffin today. "The day of Jimmy's service, which was held in the sanctuary, the administrators let school out for the day because so many of the faculty, staff, and students, wanted to attend his service. Some of his friends played live, acoustic guitars and piano, and sang a couple of his favorite songs. Those friends included Dobie Gray, Robb, Billy Burnette, Todd Cerney, and Jim Horn, and Jim Della Croce gave the eulogy. I don't know exactly how many people attended but the sanctuary was full and I was told there were a few hundred people there."

"Jimmy's passing has definitely left a vacuum in many people's lives," adds Ronnie Guilbeau, a thought with which many, many others concur. "I really miss him…"

"After the funeral we arranged a party in his memory," says Jim Della Croce. "Robb was as quiet as a mouse. Vince Melamed was there, Todd (Cerney) was there. Jim Horn… it seems like everybody in town was at the bar that night, and we couldn't make it stop so we ended up at Billy Burnette's house and we talked about Jimmy all night until the sun came up. It was the greatest party of all time."

After the service, Jimmy made one last journey back to his hometown. He was laid to rest in the Memorial Park Cemetery in Memphis, the city in which he had grown up.

Chapter Twenty

In The Afterglow

With the passing of James Griffin, the story of Bread ultimately reached its conclusion. There could be no more music from the collective, no more reunions, no more anything. To many, James Griffin was the soul of the band. David Gates may well have been the hit songwriter, the driving force, the face. To take nothing away from David, clearly without him there would have been no Bread. Period. He was the heart. But undoubtedly the soul lay within the music and the voice of James Griffin. The harmony, the quirky melody, the rock'n'roll.

Nevertheless, one can easily argue that without *any* of the band members – Griffin, Gates, Botts, Knechtel, or Royer – Bread would never have existed. And that is the charm of many collective gatherings. Without McCartney or Harrison, the Beatles would never have had the same beat. Without Bonham or Page, Led Zeppelin would never have rocked. Without any one of the Wilson brothers, the Beach Boys would never have surfed the crest of their own musical wave. Careers would still have developed, no one can say that John Lennon would never have made it on his own, but it took his partnership with Paul McCartney to make the Beatles work. Likewise, Brian Wilson, Robert Plant, *et al.*

David Gates would undoubtedly have found a musical niche *somewhere* to hang his multi-talented hats off, as would Mike Botts or Robb Royer, but it took the addition of James Griffin to make the original foursome gel in such a way that the audience related to them. The counterbalance was perfect. The same can be said for when Larry signed up. But with James now gone there was no turning back, just a catalog of wonderful music, achievements, and memories. Although, to be honest, such was the mixed feelings among band members that they probably would never have got back in the same room anyway. The reunion tour had been their farewell. The five young men who had come together in their twenties and thirties to create, experiment, and enjoy times were now long gone. Instead, there were now just four men, left aged and scarred by the memory of the taste that had gone sour. They had tried to sweeten it during the reunion, and for a while it had almost been pleasant, but it was now time to move on.

Drummer Mike Botts had returned to touring with Dan Fogelberg. Throughout the summer of 2003 the Fogelberg tour bus had rolled into 25 venues across the country, filling the auditoriums and thrilling fans. A couple of months later, the tour was followed by a specially taped performance with Dan and the band for the Chicago-based PBS music series, *Soundstage*. Yet once the Fogelberg obligation was complete, and Mike was back home in Los Angeles, he struck up the idea of another exciting project, one that was perhaps instigated in fun, but showed the great versatility his talents had to offer. Having been the subject of many interviews himself over the years, he chose to reverse the experience, and view things from the standpoint of the interviewer, undertaking five lengthy interviews for a proposed syndication of *Off-Mike* radio programs. His initial chosen subjects, all musical friends, were Andrew Gold, session bassist Leland Sklar, guitarist Nils Lofgren, singer, songwriter, and multi-instrumentalist Bill Champlin (then a member of rock monoliths Chicago)... and Larry Knechtel. Unfortunately, it would appear that only one of the interviews (Andrew Gold) was edited into a mix suitable for broadcast, and even that remains unheard over the airwaves. However, listening to the surviving tapes today underlines the sheer enthusiasm and exuberance that Mike was sharing with his friends. Talking to Andrew about the Ronstadt years, "Lonely Boy," Houdini, playing music, laughing and sharing with his friend, Mike was a natural, and it is a great shame that the remaining four shows lay unedited, with perhaps the most notable being the interview with Larry Knechtel which, reportedly, ran long enough to fill two complete shows!

Mike and Kent Hartman, who had assisted him with issuing the *Adults Only* release, had flown up to Washington to see Larry, and one can only imagine the subjects that the two friends discussed at such length during their time *Off-Mike*. Maybe, just one day, the tapes will see a release of sorts.

But fate is at times often cruel. The good guys in life sometimes have to face, for no understandable reason whatsoever, a world that has seemingly dealt them a harsh hand. Many have faced it before, many will face it again. And so it was that, in the spring of 2005, just twelve months after touring the country, full of vigor and energy, pounding his beloved drum kit with a love of life, Mike Botts now found himself facing up to an issue he could never have imagined. He was due to go back out on the road with Fogelberg, but had to pass. Only a few months had elapsed since he had been saying goodbye to James, whispering with an ironic fate, "Save a place for me," and he now found himself in a similar predicament. Colon cancer had taken hold of his body and before the year was out he, too, was to pass away. On December 9th, 2005, he lost the fight at the Providence St. Joseph Medical Center in Burbank, near to the home he shared with Michele, one day after his 61st birthday.

"He was a good friend and a good soul to all..." says his old friend Joe LaManno. "His relationship with Michele, he could never talk enough about that. Even through the bickering they used to do, sometimes we'd call them The Bickersons because they'd just be at each other, there was so much love there, and still is. I miss him all the time."

A memorial service took place shortly afterwards, with David and Jo Rita Gates driving up from their home near San Diego to be there, his wizened, thinning, and graying appearance forcing him to introduce himself to some of those also in attendance, fearful of not being recognized. "I wouldn't have missed it," David was to say to Michele. Now 65 years old, maybe the difficult times they had spent over the past few years had made it too hard for him to go back and rekindle the friendships once again. Once had almost been too much, but the fact that he made the two-hour journey north and arrived, unannounced, showed the respect that David held for his former band member. Respect and friendship can be poles apart, and they had all been through a great deal in the ensuing years. Although he had not personally spoken to James prior to his passing, that subject had never been brought up while James lay in the hospital, nor had he attended the church service. David had phoned Marti Griffin shortly afterwards, to offer his condolences. "He did call me right after Jimmy passed away," she recalls, "and he said some really wonderful things about him."

David now bided his own time at a leisurely pace. As the decade moved on, he developed a love for visiting the golf course on a regular basis, but had very little to do with the music industry and, although he still kept both guitar and piano in his home, he had little inclination to return to the studio full-time. He still talked wistfully of completing a series of classical works, but suggested that such a project would take time as he found it difficult to write. "It is a question of being reasonably original, and there is already several hundred years of stuff out there!" he commented at the time. The coming years would see his final few shows, including some intermittent performances in America, Asia, and Australia, along with a short visit to Mexico during 2006. In addition, there was a one-off recording session to revisit the Brazilian band Roupa Nova, taping a version of "Come Home For Christmas (Volte Nesse Natal)" for the band's 2007 seasonal release *Natal Todo Dia*, but this would do very little to reignite the spark. Nevertheless, despite his increasing distance from the industry, and regardless of the negativity that had flowed through his old band, David still held fond memories for much of the time they had spent together, most notably for the early days.

"I feel that James had the best harmony voice I ever heard, and he and I could sing so much alike you could not tell we were both singing lead simultaneously on many of the recordings, such as during the beginning of 'I Want You With Me.' Also, most of 'Mother Freedom' we are singing lead together in unison. He used to come out to my house in Hidden Hills, and we would sit in a couple of folding chairs on the veranda up at the barn, and harmonize for hours. Jo Rita would say, 'you guys are so good it's scary.'

"A few years before the reunion tour, he (James) actually made the two-day trip to travel from Tennessee to my ranch in California just to apologize for the grief he caused me, and we went to town and had a pie and coffee at Ruby's. My son Craig came out in the fields to find me, and said, 'James Griffin is here.' I didn't know he was coming, but appreciated the effort he made to come. He was always a very likeable person, and I know inside he had a good heart."[33]

Meanwhile, Larry Knechtel still had the music running through his veins. During 2004 he first came across the Yakima-born guitarist Wayman Chapman, an extremely talented player who had previously spent time in Los Angeles himself, touring with soul singer Oleta Adams. The two musicians formed a strong bond and began gigging locally together. As had been the case with the many other local bands Larry had been involved with, he simply maintained that desire to play. And a small town bar or grill was just fine by him. He cared not one hoot. The two musicians performed a variety of songs from across the years, with originals by Chapman sitting alongside the works of Miles Davis, Stevie Wonder, Otis Redding, and, of course, a certain Simon & Garfunkel song in their casual set lists.

"I got kind of known for it," he was to tell many of the listening audiences of that particular tune, "but I guess it's better than being known for nothing."

And yet, such was his disdain at the thought of retirement, he was more than happy to accept the offer of returning to the recording studios when the desire took him. In 2005 such a moment came along when producer Rick Rubin, the man who had masterminded the resurrection of Johnny Cash's career, alongside working with such diverse artists as the Red Hot Chili Peppers, Rage Against The Machine, Tom Petty, and New York rappers Run DMC, requested Larry's presence to play on the sessions for Neil Diamond's upcoming new album *12 Songs*. The record would go on to become one of Diamond's most acclaimed albums in recent years, debuting at #4 in the *Billboard* charts. Rubin then asked him to follow this and play keyboards on his next project, the upcoming release by the popular country trio The Dixie Chicks. *Taking The Long Way* would also go on to achieve phenomenal success, earning a multi-platinum sales status, numerous #1 positions around the world, and five Grammy Awards to boot, an occasion that saw Larry once again performing at the ceremony. He subsequently accompanied this lively and immensely successful trio on their next American tour.

Not that working with such a successful act once again took Larry away from his beloved rural homestead, for during 2005 he also assisted his friend Wayman Chapman in his local home studio, adding his scintillating touch to Wayman's own *Wine, Wayman & Song* album. "This," Chapman was to say at the time, referring to the upcoming series of local shows he and Larry were planning "is the start." To celebrate the release they played the local New Year's Eve party at the Selah Civic Center, just a twenty-minute drive from Larry's home.

Despite his seeming reluctance to step back into the bright beam of the spotlights, in 2007 he once again appeared alongside his former 1960s session associates, those infamously dubbed "The Wrecking Crew," when, as a team, they were honored and inducted into the Musicians' Hall of Fame in Nashville. Their roles as the uncredited, background team behind, literally, hundreds of hit recordings, had finally been acknowledged. A full-length feature documentary, highlighting their role and of their importance to the industry, was also put into production, as was a book detailing the same subject. It seemed as if Larry would simply keep on playing and playing. He started working on his own recordings once more and, with his son Lonnie alongside, they planned to release a new collection of instrumental compositions. They also started widening their musical scope together, exploring the boundaries of gospel-inflected jazz-fusion, and they occasionally performed locally as a duo, calling themselves The Elkays, a light-hearted reference to their initials. He also assisted another fellow Washington musician, Daniel Craig, with his excellent Quakers On Probation *Every Living Thing* album, as well as helping Dan's 16-year-old son (also named Daniel) with his debut release, an impressive folk-rock album credited to Dimestore Mystery entitled *Tea Leaves*. However, he also continued to take time to reflect on the finer things in life.

"Larry mostly enjoyed talking about his son and daughter, his wife, his grandkids, and his garden..." recalls Craig. "The music at that point was secondary to the important stuff. He got it right in that sense I think."

During 2009, Larry took a vacation to Italy with his beloved wife Vicki, and seemed in fine health. Upon his return, he played at a local Yakima music festival on August 13th, once again accompanying Wayman, but then, one week later, on August 20th, 2009, the music died. Larry was taken to the Yakima Valley Memorial Hospital where he unexpectedly succumbed to an undiagnosed heart condition. As sudden as that. He was 69. Two of his most recent compositions, "Kiddy Song" and "Goodbye For Now," were played at his memorial service.

It simply cannot be overstated how much of an impact Larry Knechtel's work had within the recording industry. For over 45 years he had appeared on the records and tapes of so many artists, adding his distinctive touch and musical flourishes. He graced the grooves of numerous bestselling singles, rode the airwaves of a thousand radio stations, filled the halls and amphitheaters with his presence. And all without a hint of grandeur. He may not have really been the guitar man, but to the many whose sessions he graced, he was the piano man...

Shortly after his passing, Larry's old friend, and the man who had helped him on his musical journey many years before, Duane Eddy, had this to say:

> *"Larry Knechtel was a rare and special man. He was like a brother to me. A friend, a co-writer and one of my favorite persons on the planet. I just wasn't ready for him to go yet... there were still a lot of things I wanted to do with him. I can still picture him striding into a room with his saddlebags slung over his shoulder, tossing them into a corner, and then sitting down at the piano and crossing his legs. That's the way he always played... with his legs crossed and looking kind of like Charles Bronson sitting at the piano, playing some of the most incredible music we've ever heard. I will miss him dearly."*
>
> —*Twangsville* (The Duane Eddy Fan Circle), 2009

The music that the five members of Bread created together remains timeless. It may always remain distinctly associated with that brief period of early 1970s soft rock, but today, over 40 years later, it still sounds fresh each time it appears on radios around the world. These stations may repeatedly play the wonderful hits that David Gates composed – "Make It With You," "Baby I'm-A Want You," "Everything I Own" – and the music of James Griffin and Robb Royer, or of Larry Knechtel and Mike Botts, may remain mostly ignored to the wider audience, but play it today and it still sounds compelling. Only time will tell if the long overdue re-assessment of the band's entire catalog will come to light. One can only hope it does, for, as this book has stated, there is product hidden within the grooves of the albums that has lain dormant for far too long. It was not just "three-minute throwaways." It was intelligent, well-constructed, well-crafted music. Effortlessly performed. Perfectly produced. As the years roll by there will undoubtedly be further compilation albums added to the Bread catalog and, regardless of David's comment back then, that they only recorded what was deemed suitable for release, there are still some unreleased recordings locked away in the vaults or in private storage. A rough cut of the incomplete *Baby I'm-A Want You*-era recording "Try" resides in Robb's own collection, as does "Together" (another pre-1973 composition), while "Before Long" and "Don't Give Up On Me Now" also exist. Additionally, James's "Your Love" and "It Doesn't Matter," both rumored to be further Bread outtakes, also sit on the shelves – but originate from which era? And there may well be others, although it now seems unlikely that, given the public's penchant for constantly wanting the familiar hits, these will ever appear publicly.

The five group members may have had their issues, with each other, with themselves, and some may have lost their way en route, diverting into territories that perhaps hindered their development for a period, but as a group, or as individual solo performers, or as studio sidemen, they all had something relevant to say. And as long as rock music continues to play an important part in the livelihood of millions then the music of David Gates, James Griffin, Robb Royer, Mike Botts, and Larry Knechtel should be heard. As a collective.

2006 saw the band immortalized within the Vocal Hall of Fame, a foundation dedicated to honoring the vocal contributions of many of rock'n'roll's great icons. A long overdue acknowledgment of sorts was finally received, but it went away as quickly as it had come. None of the band's surviving members, nor the families of those who had passed, attended the ceremony. In fact, during research it became apparent that none were even informed of the honor. Then again, Sharon, Pennsylvania, where the foundation and museum is based, is not a regular haunt along the tourist trail. Two years later Bread were also inducted into the Hit Parade Hall of Fame…

Today, Robb Royer keeps himself busy. Happily married for a third time, and with children and grandchildren around him, music still remains his life. With three of his former musical associates no longer here, and a fourth distancing himself from the industry, it is good to see his enthusiasm still intact, and he continuously adds to his growing songwriting portfolio. In 2003 he began expanding his Nashfilms business and a few years later Nashfilms Records was officially launched when a young 21-year-old from Wyoming, Karissa Hope la Cour, walked into Robb's office and performed three songs for him. "Well, there's no doubt you can sing," was Robb's reported response. Blessed with a deep, resonating vocal approach, with an ethereal "pop" quality and a talent for songwriting, the future looked promising for this rising star, and with the support of Robb's new company, built in the heart of Nashville's Music Row, her debut album, *Shades Of Green*, followed in 2008 to much acclaim.

"She's just the whole package… singer, songwriter, and quite a versatile character, who seems to subject herself to my orchestral schemes," Robb was to say at the time. Sadly, her career didn't take off as was hoped and, despite Robb's enthusiasm for his protégé, none of the major labels were interested in furthering her career.

Having established himself as a leading songwriter within the Nashville community, it was a pleasure to see his co-credits on a number of the featured songs, in addition to supplying keyboards and production. It clearly wasn't all business for him, and the joy and pleasure he still got from his music was evident to see, but the frustration at not being able to guide her beyond local success clearly niggled him.

"If I can't sell Karissa, then I am in the wrong business," he reflected recently. "I have great confidence in myself as a writer and producer, but I am obviously the worst manager in the world! I'm still in the studio finishing up some of the thirty or more songs Karissa and I cut together. I still don't even know if I will release an album or just market the songs. K is mercurial even for a female artist but it probably wouldn't improve my inability to get her noticed. I completely understand her frustration. Short of a *deus ex machina* I will finish these sides, put them in the hands of a plugger, and retire to the beach in St. Thomas with a joint and a Mai Tai."

He later added both Michael Smotherman, an established songwriter for Glen Campbell and Deanna Carter (amongst others), and his daughter, Kat Smo, to the Nashfilms Records roster, as well as finally issuing the long overdue collection by The Finnigan Bros. Then, in 2010, the company released an album that had been sitting in Robb's vaults, gathering dust, for over 30 years. Early rough mixes of the tapes had been circulating among collectors and fans for a vast number of these, and the status of the long-lost recordings had grown to almost mythical proportions among those in the know. Finally, Robb was made aware of the demand by a group of fans who visited him at his studio, a gathering known as 'The Breadheads'. He chose to fetch out the original masters of the album, re-mix them for a 21st century audience, and foist them upon the world. The work that he and his late songwriting partner, James Griffin, had conceived all of those years ago was finally to take off. *Cosmo & Robetta* were finally boarding for a distant and yet unpopulated planet.

It was time to fly away...

Epilogue

Forty-six years had passed since the young Jimmy Griffin had first headed out west, out of Memphis, destined for fame and fortune in the Golden State. In 2010 his home city finally acknowledged his musical contributions and honored his memory with a prestigious brass note on the Beale Street Walk of Fame. Coinciding with the announcement, and following the positive reception to *Cosmo & Robetta*, Jimmy's former partner Robb Royer once again delved deep into his own personal archives and also issued an impressive twelve-track collection via his Nashfilms Records label. Simply titled *Jimmy Griffin*, this set pulled together a wonderful gathering of previously unreleased Griffin-Royer collaborations.

During this same period, the Griffin Estate, in collaboration with a number of James's former musical friends, also set about compiling a number of previously unheard recordings from the 1980s Memphis sessions, intent on issuing them under the CD banner *Moon Over Memphis*. Sadly, the project didn't see fruition. This wasn't the first time such an idea had been mooted either. A number of years previously, shortly after James's untimely death, a similar collection (tentatively labeled *Break & Run*) had been prepared for release via a small independent label. Unfortunately, due to the questionable legitimacy of this release, prepared wholly without the consent of the Griffin Estate or the owners of the material, the collection never reached completion, but for now, finally, with the issue of *Jimmy Griffin*, the first signs that James's unheard musical legacy was perhaps beginning to reach an audience were evident.

On November 20th, 2010, James's sister Carol Ann sat happily nearby as his widow Marti, along with their two children Alexis and Jacob, Alexis's husband Travis (keeper of the Griffin Archives), and accompanied by Jamey and Katy, his two children from his earlier marriage to Kathy, each said a few words before a small but attentive gathering on Beale Street. It was a fitting honor to such a respected and talented musician. And long overdue. Sadly, a few short years later, Jamey was to tragically follow his father into the next life…

What lies ahead? Only time will tell. During 2013, as this very book was heading towards its first print run, Robb finally made the decision to fulfill that wish of a Mai Tai in St. Thomas, opting to sell up both of his Nashville homes, along with the Nashfilms business, and settle down to a new life along the coastline of the Virgin Islands, undertaking the lengthy task of writing his memoirs (the highly recommended *The View From Contessa*). The music still flowed, and his desire to record and produce was also still in evidence, but life for him was a little more...

relaxing. And as for the other slices of his former band? Well, with the support of the Griffin Estate, there is a strong possibility that more releases may follow in the near future. Maybe "Back In This Photograph," "Farmer God Bless You," "Dance On The Moon," "Song Rider Blues," or "Pieces Of Love" will see the light of day... or maybe David Gates, seemingly content in his retirement, now living outside of the Californian sunshine and into the rural surroundings of Larry's former home State of Washington, will finally relent and open up the doors to his own Bread archives. There is still so much material sitting in the vaults – so just maybe.

The Guitar Man (courtesy of Jonathan Robinson)

Selected Discography

U.S. Singles

1969 **Dismal Day / Any Way You Want Me** Elektra 45666 (Did not chart)

1969 **Could I / You Can't Measure The Cost** Elektra 45668 (Did not chart)

1970 **Make It With You / Why Do You Keep Me Waiting** Elektra 45686 (*Billboard* #1)

1970 **It Don't Matter To Me (single version) / Call On Me** Elektra 45701 (*Billboard* #10)

1971 **Let Your Love Go / Too Much Love** Elektra 45711 (*Billboard* #28)

1971 **If / Take Comfort** Elektra 45720 (*Billboard* #4)

1971 **Mother Freedom / Live In Your Love** Elektra 45740 (*Billboard* #37)

1971 **Baby I'm-A Want You / Truckin'** Elektra 45751 (*Billboard* #3)

1972 **Everything I Own / I Don't Love You** Elektra 45765 (*Billboard* #5)

1972 **Diary / Down On My Knees** Elektra 45784 (*Billboard* #15)

1972 **The Guitar Man / Just Like Yesterday** Elektra 45803 (*Billboard* #11)

1972 **Sweet Surrender / Make It By Yourself** Elektra 45818 (*Billboard* #5)

1973 **Aubrey / Didn't Even Know Her Name** Elektra 45832 (*Billboard* #15)

1976 **Lost Without Your Love / Change Of Heart** Elektra 45365 (*Billboard* #9)

1977 **Hooked On You / Our Lady Of Sorrow** Elektra 45389 (*Billboard* #60)

U.S. Albums

1969 **Bread** Elektra EKS-74044 (*Billboard* #127)

1970 **On The Waters** Elektra EKS-74076 (*Billboard* #12)

1971 **Manna** Elektra EKS-74086 (*Billboard* #21)

1971 **Bread (promotional release)** Elektra BRD-1 (Did not chart)

1972 **Baby I'm-A Want You** Elektra EKS-75015 (*Billboard* #3)

1972 **Guitar Man** Elektra EKS-75047 (*Billboard* #18)

1973 **2 Originals Of Bread** Elektra ELK-62014 (Did not chart)

1973 **The Best Of Bread** Elektra EKS-75056 (*Billboard* #2)

1974 **The Best Of Bread Vol. II** Elektra 7E-1005 (*Billboard* #32)

1976 **Lost Without Your Love** Elektra 7E-1094 (Billboard #26)

1982 **The Sound Of Bread** K-Tel PNU 9960 (Did not chart)

1985 **Anthology** Elektra 60414 (Did not chart. 2007 CD reissue reached #32)

1996 **Retrospective** Elektra/Rhino 73509 (Did not chart)

2002 **Make It With You & Other Hits** Flashback R2 78211 (Did not chart)

2005 **Hi-Five Volume One** Rhino 081227956066 (Did not chart)
2005 **Hi-Five Volume Two** Rhino 603497155965 (Did not chart)
2006 **The Definitive Collection** Elektra/Rhino R2 73388 (Did not chart)

U.K. Singles

Releases that did not achieve a chart position are not listed.
1970 Make It With You / Why Do You Keep Me Waiting Elektra 2101010 (*Music Week* #5)
1972 Baby I'm-A Want You / Truckin' Elektra K12033 (*Music Week* #14)
1972 Everything I Own / I Don't Love You Elektra K12041 (*Music Week* #32)
1972 The Guitar Man / Just Like Yesterday Elektra K12066 (*Music Week* #16)
1976 Lost Without Your Love / Change Of Heart Elektra K12241 (*Music Week* #27)

U.K. Albums

Releases that did not achieve a chart position are not listed.
1970 **On The Waters** Elektra K42050 (*Music Week* #34)
1972 **Baby I'm-A Want You** Elektra K42100 (*Music Week* #9)
1972 **The Best Of Bread** Elektra 42115 (*Music Week* #7)
1974 **The Best Of Bread Vol. II** Elektra 42161 (*Music Week* #48)
1977 **Lost Without Your Love** Elektra K52044 (*Music Week* #17)
1977 **The Sound Of Bread** Elektra 52062 (*Music Week* #1)
1987 **The Collection: The Very Best Of David Gates & Bread** Telstar TCD-2303 (*Music Week* #84)
1996 **Essentials** Warner/Jive CD 35408 (*Music Week* #9)

Other Releases Of Note

1977 **Hot Bread** Elektra 77001 (Australian issue)
1977 **Greatest Hits** Elektra FCPA 1031 (Japanese mail order issue)
1988 **The Very Best Of Bread** Pickwick CD PWKS518 (U.K. issue)
2007 **The Works: 3-CD Set** Warner 8122-79947-8 (U.K. issue)
2010 **The Original Albums: 5-CD Set** Rhino UK 8122798355 (U.K. issue)
2012 **The Very Best Of Bread** Rhino UK B0070CFQ4G (U.K. issue)

Editor's note: Elektra Records tended to issue worldwide 45rpm releases featuring many of the same songs that appeared on the original U.S. pressing. Occasionally, there was the odd exception – i.e. "Move Over" was issued in the U.K. instead of "Could I," and "Tecolote" appeared as a single in Germany – but the majority of singles releases were identical.

Notes and References

1. Interview with James Griffin, courtesy of the Breadfans Website
2. Quote from Bruce Johnston when questioned by the author, August 2009
3. Online interview with Michael Z. Gordon and the author, August 2009
4. Email conversation with David Kaufman and the author, August 2009
5. Online interview with Stephen Cohn and the author, August 2009
6. Interview with Stephen Cohn, courtesy of www.innerviewworld.com, 2008
7. Interview with Robb Royer, courtesy of www.penseyeview.com, 2009
8. Interview with James Griffin (origin unknown), courtesy of various internet sites
9. Interview with David Gates by Bill Kornman for NetMusic.com, 1994. Used with permission
10. Quote from Michael Z. Gordon when questioned by the author, September 2009
11. Interview with David Gates, *Discoveries* magazine, 1999
12. *Follow The Music* by Jac Holzman & Gavan Daws (see below)
13. Interview with David Gates, *Record Collector* 219, November 1997
14. Rhino Records sleevenotes. Interviews with Barry Alfonso
15. Interview with Armin Steiner by Maureen Droney, courtesy of MixOnline.com, 2001
16. Quote from Shadoe Stevens when questioned by the author, December 2009
17. Article by Bill DeMain, *Performing Songwriter*, 2003.
18. Emails between Bread members and Dean James Adshead. Reprinted with permission
19. Interview with David Gates, *Songwriter* magazine. May 1976
20. *Sounds* interview with David Gates, Penny Valentine, August 1973
21. Interview with Larry Knechtel by Dick Stewart, editor of *Lance Monthly*
22. "The Making of Pet Sounds" booklet, Capitol Records, 1996
23. Mike Botts "Off-Mike" radio show, courtesy of Michele Botts
24. *Linda Ronstadt: A Life In Music* by Peter Lewry (E-books 2009)
25. *Zig-Zag* magazine article, October 1970
26. Quote from Patti Dahlstrom: online letter to family and friends 2009, email to the author 2010
27. Emails between Brandon Sinks and David Crawt. Reprinted with permission
28. *Billboard* magazine article, 1994

29. "Mike Botts: From The Road – The Last Tour" courtesy of www.mikebotts.com, Reprinted with permission.
30. Interview with James Griffin by Fran Hart. Used with permission
31. Quote from the Robert W. Morgan "Radio Special Of The Week" promotional album
32. Interviews with Mike Botts & David Gates. Courtesy of Barry Scott of "The Lost 45's." www.lost45.com
33. Quote courtesy of the Marti Griffin collection
34. Quote from Frank Bez when questioned by the author, March 2012

Interviews with Carol Ann Jones (nee Griffin) and the author, November 2009 and May 2010
Interviews with Robb Royer and the author, September/October/November 2009 and January 2010 – plus subsequent emails and chats
Interviews with Kathy Lane and the author, January 2010 and May 2010
Interviews with Michele Botts and the author, January 2010 and April 2010
Interviews with Selwyn Miller and the author, January 2010 and June 2010
Interview with Ron Edgar and the author, April 2010
Interview with Phillip Rauls and the author, April 2010
Interview with Todd Smallwood and the author, May 2010
Interview with Rick Yancey and the author, May 2010
Interviews with Marti Griffin and the author, May 2010 and November 2011 – plus subsequent emails and chats
Interview with Mike Finnigan and the author, May 2010
Interview with Jim Della Croce and the author, May 2010
Interview with Erik Lloyd and the author, June 2010
Interview with Holly Cieri and the author, June 2010
Interview with Michele Shaw (Cochrane) and the author, January 2011

Additional Written References

The California Sound: The Musical Biography Of Gary Usher by Stephen J. McParland (CMusic Books, 2000)
Eleven Unsung Heroes Of Early Rock & Roll by Dick Stewart (Lance Monthly Press, 2010)
Follow The Music: The Life & High Times of Elektra Records by Jac Holzman & Gavan Daws (First Media Books, 2000)
Linda Ronstadt: A Life In Music by Peter Lewry (E-books, 2009)
Riot On Sunset Strip by Dominic Priore (Jawbone Press, 2007)
Simon & Garfunkel: The Definitive Biography by Victoria Kingston (Sidgwick & Jackson, 1996)
Waiting For The Sun by Barney Hoskyns (St. Martins Press, 1996)
The Wrecking Crew: The Inside Story by Kent Hartman (St. Martins Press, 2012)

Websites

www.bread.moonfruit.com
www.breadfans.com
www.jlindquist.net/bread
www.robbroyerpitchsheet.blogspot.com
www.jimmygriffinmusic.com
www.larryknechtel.com
www.mikebotts.com
www.drewreid.com
www.carlradle.com
www.kenbankphotography.com
www.wikipedia.org
www.bsnpubs.com/discog.html (Album Discographies)
www.globaldogproductions (45 Discographies)
www.repertoire.bmi.com (BMI)
www.researchvideo.com

Acknowledgments

Acknowledgments for input, emails and/or other sources:
Dean James Adshead, Maria Aguayo-Griffin-Potts, Barry Alfonso, Ken Bank, Frank Bez, Andy Black, Hal Blaine, Wim Boekhooven, Michele Botts (Dalcin), Klemen Breznikar, Ed Caraeff, Ray Chafin, Chris Charlesworth, Brian Chidester, Holly Cieri, Stephen Cohn, Paul Compton, Daniel Craig, David Crawt, Susan Crowder, Patti Dahlstrom, Michael Deasy, Jim Della Croce, Judy Donofrio, Robert Dunlap, Ron Edgar, Mike Finnigan, Rose Ann Fiorita, Reggie Fisher, Mary Ann Flannery, Lisa Jones Formica, Brian Gari, Sylvia M. Giustina, Michael Z. Gordon, Katy Griffin, Marti Griffin, Ronnie Guilbeau, Tim Hallinan, Fran Hart, Gordon Holland (and The Carl Radle Website), Michael Ivy, Carol Ann Jones, David Kaufman, Lonnie Knechtel, Joseph LaManno, Kathy Lane, Peter Lewry, John Lindquist, Erik Lloyd, Stephen McParland, Mark Meinhart, Primo Mendoza, Selwyn Miller, Charlie Oyama, Darryl Palagi, Dominic Priore, Phillip Rauls, Drew Reid, Travis Roman, Jessie Royer-Holmes, Robb Royer, Swain Schaefer, Tammy Glenn Shwartz, Barry Scott, Gene Sculatti, Michele Shaw (Cochrane), Brandon Earl Sinks, Todd Smallwood, Shadoe Stevens, Dick Stewart (with two 't's … LOL), Leonard Terry, Wayne Thomas, Larry Thompson, Jeff Worrell, Diana Yancey, Rick Yancey.

Posthumous acknowledgments also go to the following: Todd Cerney, Carol Parks (Carmichael), Andrew Gold, Sean Bonniwell, and James Ashley Griffin. Rest in peace...

Additional personal thanks go to:
Lisa F & John L: you guys started me off and helped me through it. Without you...
Marti & Michele: having your support on this project has meant so much. Thank you.
Robb: for putting up with my questioning for numerous hours and for patiently coming up with the answers, time and time again.
Jessie Royer-Holmes, Travis Roman & Joe LaManno: effort above and beyond the call of duty.
Judy Dee: for encouragement and assistance.
Carol Ann and Kathy: you didn't have to, but you did.
Jon Stebbins: for advice and inspiration.
Frank Bez: for allowing me use of the wonderful front cover photograph.
Alice D.: for support and enthusiasm.

Ken Bank: for the great inside pictures.
Steve Kirkham: for advice and assistance.
Mike Tetlow: for the endless hours of music sharing over the years.

SPECIAL THANKS go to Ken Bishton for his literary patience and skills, to Graeme Milton at Helter Skelter Publishing for his faith in the project, and to my big sister, Liz – for buying that *Best Of Bread* album in the first place, all those years ago.

Photographic Credits

All efforts were made to issue full photographic credits at the time of publication. However, if I have unknowingly missed out any then I would be happy to correct any missing information for future editions. Please contact the author.

About the Author

An avid biography reader himself, Malcolm C. Searles is Chelmsford-born through and through, his ancestry showing that the family line has continued living in the eastern English county of Essex for more than 500 years. Needless to say, his personal love of music, widely influenced by his elder sister's record collection back in the 1970s, stretches to far wider boundaries than the Suffolk border and his particular fondness for the American harmony and pop-culture has previously seen writing projects on The Beach Boys, The Monkees, and the Surf & Hot-Roddin' scene reach vast audiences on the internet... but this is his first venture into publishing, and hopefully won't be his last.

Happily married to Louise, with two ever-growing teenage boys, Sam and Matt, the security of family life has ensured that the endless hours, hunched over the Apple Mac, weren't in vain – even if the eyesight has begun to fail a little with age.